Fun with the Family™ Northern California

Praise for the *Fun with the Family*™ series

"Enables parents to turn family travel into an exploration."
—Alexandra Kennedy, Editor, *Family Fun*

"Bound to lead you and your kids to fun-filled days,
those times that help compose the
memories of childhood."
—Dorothy Jordon, *Family Travel Times*

Help Us Keep This Guide Up to Date

Every effort has been made by the author and editors to make this guide as accurate and useful as possible. However, many changes can occur after a guide is published—establishments close, phone numbers change, hiking trails are rerouted, facilities come under new management, etc.

We would love to hear from you concerning your experiences with this guide and how you feel it could be improved and be kept up to date. While we may not be able to respond to all comments and suggestions, we'll take them to heart, and we'll make certain to share them with the author. Please send your comments and suggestions to the following address:

The Globe Pequot Press
Reader Response/Editorial Department
P.O. Box 480
Guilford, CT 06437

Or you may e-mail us at: editorial@GlobePequot.com

Thanks for your input, and happy travels!

INSIDERS' GUIDE®

FUN WITH THE FAMILY™ SERIES

fun WITH the Family™

NORTHERN CALIFORNIA

HUNDREDS OF IDEAS FOR DAY TRIPS WITH THE KIDS

KAREN MISURACA

FIFTH EDITION

INSIDERS' GUIDE®

GUILFORD, CONNECTICUT
AN IMPRINT OF THE GLOBE PEQUOT PRESS

The prices, rates, and hours listed in this guidebook
were confirmed at press time. We recommend, however, that you
call establishments to obtain current information before traveling.

To buy books in quantity for corporate use
or incentives, call **(800) 962–0973, ext. 4551,**
or e-mail **premiums@GlobePequot.com**

INSIDERS' GUIDE®

Copyright © 1996, 1998, 2001, 2003, 2005 by Karen Misuraca

All rights reserved. No part of this book may be reproduced or transmitted in any form by any means, electronic or mechanical, including photocopying and recording, or by any information storage and retrieval system, except as may be expressly permitted by the 1976 Copyright Act or by the publisher. Requests for permission should be made in writing to The Globe Pequot Press, P.O. Box 480, Guilford, Connecticut 06437.

Insiders' Guide is a registered trademark of The Globe Pequot Press.
Fun with the Family is a trademark of The Globe Pequot Press.

Text design by Nancy Freeborn and Linda Loiewski
Maps by Rusty Nelson © The Globe Pequot Press
Spot photography throughout © Photodisc

ISSN 1540-305X
ISBN 0-7627-3441-8

Manufactured in the United States of America
Fifth Edition/First Printing

For Rachel, Wyatt, Melati, and Acacia,
my rising stars

NORTHERN CALIFORNIA

Contents

Introduction

Think of Northern California as a giant theme park, packed with everything that kids and parents like to do together on vacation. From ocean beaches to ski resorts, from cable cars to canoes, for outdoor fun and living history, it's hard to beat the top half of this state.

The problem is, how can a family decide where and how to spend precious vacation time together? *Fun with the Family Northern California* will help you choose destinations that are perfectly suited to the ages of your children and the activities your family enjoys.

This book is divided into twelve geographic regions. The major towns in each region are featured, together with information on nearby attractions, family-friendly restaurants, and places to stay that welcome and provide for children.

Does your family like water sports and camping? Consider spending a few days in California's Central Valley, at one of its many lakes and reservoirs, or on the inland Delta waterways, a paradise for families who love to fish, water-ski, houseboat, and camp out.

In the mountains of the Sierra Nevada, pitch a tent in a pine forest or settle into a rustic lakeside resort. Head for Redwood Country and park your RV beneath the tallest trees in the world, or hit the beach with your boogie boards in Santa Cruz.

Near the waterfront in San Francisco, your young scientists will enjoy one of the world's largest hands-on science museums. Shake hands with a robot at the Tech Museum of Innovation in San Jose, the birthplace of the personal computer.

Fancy accommodations can be hard on the family budget, so you'll find suggestions for comfortable, reasonably priced motels, inns, campgrounds, and hostels with amenities such as coin laundries, sofa beds, swimming pools, playgrounds, and games rooms; some offer supervised "kids' camps."

You'll find a strong focus on recreation, nature, and the environment. Many state parks and nature preserves are recommended as places to get close to wildlife and to see a tremendous variety of native flora and dramatic landscapes—images that stay with children for the rest of their lives. In the northernmost reaches of California, in the Shasta Cascade region and around Lassen Volcanic National Park, the trails and roads are lightly used, a key advantage if one of your vacation goals is to spend quiet time together in the wilderness.

Learning about the history of California is something that just happens in many of the towns and villages you will visit. In the perfectly preserved Gold Rush settlement of Columbia, shopkeepers and blacksmiths dress and work just as their forebears did a century ago, and you can still get a sarsaparilla and have your tintype taken. On the plaza in the Spanish mission town of San Juan Bautista, step into the stables to have a look at horse-drawn carriages and wagons from the 1860s, when a dozen coaches a day arrived with travelers from the East, bound for the boomtown of San Francisco.

Amusement parks, playgrounds, rest stops, and easy hiking trails are described in every region. On a driving trip with my children and their children, I like to have a few spots in mind where we can take a fresh-air break and the kids can let off steam.

Trip Planning and Resources

A new Web site features attractions in the rural areas of the state. Go to www.findyour selfincalifornia.com and look at "What's New" for the region in which you plan to travel. The site features everything from county fairs to railroad-oriented destinations, unusual museums, links to small towns, a calendar of events, and more.

Go to www.visitcwc.com to locate California Welcome Centers and roadside rest areas throughout the state. The centers are stocked with brochures, maps, and the latest information for travelers, and you can check your e-mail there, make hotel reservations, and enjoy the picnic grounds.

If wildlife is your family's passion, the Web site www.cawatchablewildlife.org offers excellent driving itineraries focusing on more than 200 places where you can get up close to birds, mammals, and other wildlife; animal- and bird-related festivals are described too.

California's state park system is the largest in the lower forty-eight states—with nearly 300 parks, more than 15,000 campsites, 280 miles of coastline, and more than 3,000 miles of trails—and it has the highest number of visitors of any state park system. An annual pass to the parks, which admits everyone in your vehicle, is $125. Apply online or by calling (800) 777–0369. For campsite reservations, call (800) 444–PARK (7275) or (916) 638–5883. Admission prices to some state parks and campgrounds, boat launch fees, and other park fees were raised by a few dollars each in 2004; check the Web site for current fee schedules (www.cal-parks.ca.gov).

The State of California's Web site for travelers, www.visitcalifornia.com, will keep you occupied for hours, browsing for theme parks, new attractions in each region, state and national parks, recreation and sports, driving tours, and much more. The free *California Visitor's Guide* is full of information about things to do, see, and enjoy throughout the state, and you get a large, pull-out map. You might also ask for the annual *California Celebrations* booklet, containing an extensive calendar of events, and another booklet, *The Best of California Driving Tours* (916–322–2881).

Lodging, Restaurant, and Attraction Rates

In the "Where to Eat" and "Where to Stay" sections, dollar signs indicate general price ranges. For meals, the prices are for individual dinner entrees. For lodging, the rates are for a double room, with no meals, unless otherwise indicated; rates for lodging may be higher during peak vacation seasons and holidays. Always inquire about family and group rates and package deals that may include amusement park tickets, ski area tickets, and tickets for concerts and other performing arts events. Visitor bureaus can steer you to lodging with family packages. Rates for attractions are a general guide to what you can expect to pay in admission fees. We note when attraction fees differ for adults and children, and we point out with the **free** icon when something is free.

Lodging

$	up to $79
$$	$80 to $110
$$$	$111 to $170
$$$$	$171 and up

Restaurants

$	entrees up to $10
$$	entrees $11 to $15
$$$	entrees $16 to $20
$$$$	entrees over $20

Attractions

$	less than $5
$$	$5 to $10
$$$	$11 to $20
$$$$	more than $20

Attractions Key

The following is a key to the icons found throughout the text.

SWIMMING		FOOD	
BOATING/BOAT TOUR		LODGING	
HISTORIC SITE		CAMPING	
HIKING/WALKING		MUSEUMS	
FISHING		PERFORMING ARTS	
BIKING		SPORTS/ATHLETICS	
AMUSEMENT PARK		PICNICKING	
HORSEBACK RIDING		PLAYGROUND	
SKIING/WINTER SPORTS		SHOPPING	
PARK		PLANTS/GARDENS/NATURE TRAILS	
ANIMAL VIEWING		FARMS	

Central Coast

Tracing the coastline south from San Francisco to Big Sur, Highway 1 is one of the most spectacular and diverse scenic highways in the world. Sandy beaches, rocky promontories, coves and harbors, dramatic mountain ranges, and farmlands create a rich geography. Along the way are a scattering of fishermen's villages and historic mission-era towns, the honky-tonk of a vintage seaside amusement boardwalk, the sophistication of European-style cafes, and state-of-the-art museums. Take time to stop frequently and make discoveries. Stroll on the beach; peer into tidepools; load up on veggies and fruit at a produce stand.

Whale watching and beachcombing attract weekenders to Half Moon Bay, the Pumpkin Capital of the World. South along the coast from here to Santa Cruz are a chain of redwood parks, dozens of tidepooly beaches, and tiny seacoast hamlets. At Año Nuevo State Reserve, thousands of elephant seals pose an unforgettable sight.

Fringed with 20 miles of wide sandy beaches, the classic beach towns of Santa Cruz and neighboring Capitola Village offer surfing, boating, seafood restaurants, and a boardwalk extravaganza of rides and games. Just inland from Highway 1, the Santa Cruz Mountains are crisscrossed by country roads meandering through ancient redwood groves and along the banks of the San Lorenzo River. Kids like the campgrounds and Roaring Camp, an 1880s logging settlement with a steam train.

Farther south the rich heritage of Spain is alive in the thick-walled adobes and colonial haciendas of Monterey. Museums and restored buildings from the days of the conquistadors are found on the "Path of History." The largest in the world, the Monterey Bay Aquarium is the most popular destination on the Central Coast.

The fairy-tale village of Carmel-by-the-Sea is chockablock with hundreds of shops. The glorious Carmel Mission and a jewel of a town beach are not to be missed. Carmel Valley is a good choice for a family vacation headquarters in the area, because of dependably warm, dry weather and less expensive lodgings.

Running 90 miles south from Carmel, Highway 1 threads along the Big Sur coast between high cliffs and river valleys above a coastline legendary for its wild beauty. A national forest and four state parks and rocky beaches are worth exploring here.

CENTRAL COAST

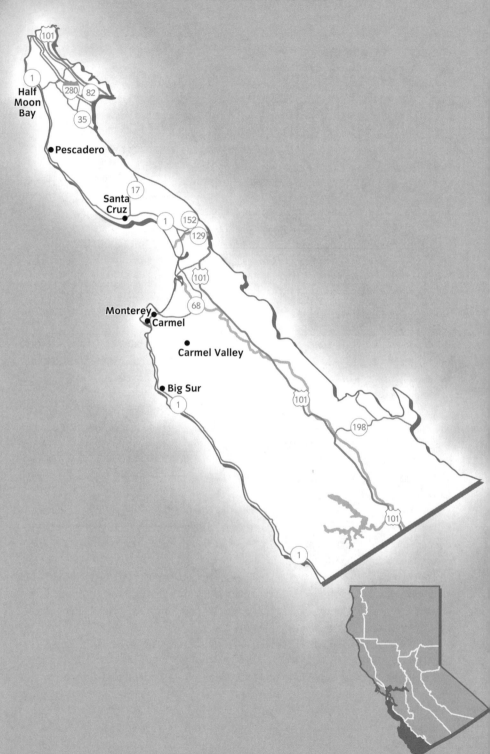

Half Moon Bay

Good weather, sea air, and lots of outdoor fun near the harbor town of Half Moon Bay lure weekenders from the Bay Area in great numbers. It's worth the drive for a day on a sandy beach or a walk in a silent redwood forest.

Besides commercial ocean fishing and tourism, the main activities in the area are flower and vegetable growing. Within huge greenhouses and in the fields around them, flowers such as carnations, roses, tulips, and iris are grown for shipment all over the world. You can buy plants and produce—and Christmas trees—at several places along the highway. Colorful flower markets take place on third Saturdays, May through September outside on Kelley Avenue, and November through April, inside at La Piazza, downtown.

A stroll through this small Victorian town turns up Western saloons, country stores, and hundred-year-old hotels and homes, many on the National Register of Historic Places. Trendy galleries and shops abound.

In October families come to the Art and Pumpkin Festival for pumpkin carving, pie eating, a haunted house, an exhibition of a 1,000-pound-plus winner of the Great Pumpkin Weigh-Off, and entertainment galore, plus 250 vendors (www.miramarevents.com). You can meet locals at the pancake breakfast and the Halloween costume competition. Come early to avoid the huge crowds.

Half Moonbay Nursery (all ages)

11691 San Mateo Road, 3 miles east of Half Moon Bay off Highway 92; (650) 726–5392.

Keep a sharp eye out for the turn into the nursery. This is a rambling, gorgeous kingdom of blooming garden and house plants, from orchids and ferns to thousands of geraniums, herbs, azaleas, camellias, climbing vines, hanging baskets, and seasonal bulbs—a veritable flower show. Wintertime, it's cozy in the main greenhouse by the wood stove.

Across the highway, Lemos Pumpkin Patch is popular with little kids, offering weekend pony rides and a play area.

Cunha's

448 Main Street, Half Moon Bay; (650) 726–4071.

A country store straight out of the Old West, with wooden floors, cowboy boots, hardware, and hardtack. They also have a scrumptious array of gourmet picnic foods. Look for the nice picnic-table area on the corner across from the store.

Pillar Point Harbor (all ages)

At Princeton, five minutes north of Half Moon Bay on Highway 1; (650) 726–4382.

Watch a fleet of more than 200 fishing boats and yachts go in and out of the marina, fish from the wharf, go shelling on the little beach west of the jetty, and hike or bike for miles. Tiny cafes, bars, and fish markets at the harbor are frequented by the locals. Whale-watching tours depart from the wharf. From December through April you are almost guaranteed to see California gray whales on their 4,000-mile migration from the Arctic to Baja. Surfers from around the world come to Maverick's off Pillar Point, where 30-foot waves breaking over a rocky reef up the ante; some say these are the biggest waves in the world. (Hang out with the Maverick surfers on the ocean-view deck at the Half Moon Bay Brewing Company here in Princeton.) Boat launch ramps, public restrooms, RV parking.

Pillar Point Marsh and Shoreline (all ages)

On Capistrano Road at Princeton (pass the Pillar Point Harbor, going left on Prospect Way; turn right onto Broadway, left onto Harvard to the end; go right on West Point, then 0.5 mile to the parking lot); (650) 728–3582.

A 0.5-mile easy walk, perfect for toddlers, where you will see great blue herons, snowy egrets, and red-winged blackbirds, as well as a variety of other sea- and shorebirds. Follow the trail to the breakwater and tidepools on the far side, and watch for sea lions on the offshore rocks. Restrooms, wheelchair access.

Half Moon Bay State Beach (all ages)

Just south of Half Moon Bay, west on Kelly Avenue; (650) 726–8820.

Buy a kite at Lunar Wind Inventions in town, and head for these 3 miles of adjacent sandy beaches. At Francis Beach, the most popular, are developed RV and tent campsites, cold showers, BBQs, picnic sites, and the ranger station. If the campground is full, try the nice Pelican Point RV Park on Miramontes Point Road (650–726–9100). Notice the skateboard park on the highway at Kelly Avenue.

Water temperature is chilly, even in summer, and the surf can be treacherous, so plan to dip your toes and play on the sand.

Coastside Trail (all ages)

From the coastal/west end of Poplar Avenue, 4.2 miles south of Pillar Point; (650) 726–8297.

A flat, easy, 5-mile paved biking and walking trail along the coastline—beautiful! There is a parking lot here, a picnic area, and a bridge to the southern coastal trail.

Fitzgerald Marine Reserve (all ages)

California Avenue off Highway 1, about ten minutes north of Half Moon Bay, in Moss Beach; (650) 728–3584.

A 0.5-mile easy trail loops through the tangled garden of an old estate, a spooky forest of Monterey cypress, and along a bluff above some of the richest tidepools on the Pacific Coast. At low tide a kaleidoscope of sponges, sea anemones, starfish, crabs, mollusks, and fish emerge. A California sea lion may be watching you, and you can see gray whales offshore December through April.

With a special fishing license, try your hand at rock fishing. For the best tidepooling call ahead to find out when the low tides are expected. Docent tours are available. Restrooms, picnic tables, interpretive center.

Where to Eat

Barbara's Fish Trap. 281 Capistrano Road at Pillar Point Harbor; (650) 728–7366. A fun, noisy, casual place full of families, overlooking the harbor. Oilcloth-covered tables and a covered patio with outdoor heaters. Try the daily fresh fish specials. $–$$

Cafe Classique. 107 Avenue Granada, Half Moon Bay; (650) 726–9775. At the north end of town near Pillar Point, a casual place that's been here forever, serving giant omelets, sourdough French toast and hotcakes for breakfast; steak hoagies and other unique sandwiches for lunch, homemade soup and desserts, with children's portions available. $

Half Moon Bay Coffee Company. 20A Stone Pine Road at the north end of Main Street, Half Moon Bay; (650) 726–3664. A casual place busy with locals and tourists digging into homemade pies and pastries, pancakes, burgers, sandwiches, and simple, hearty entrees. Breakfast, lunch, dinner. $

Ketch Joanne. Pillar Point Harbor, Princeton; (650) 728–3747. Big breakfasts, clam chowder, and fresh seafood in a booth by the potbelly stove. It's like a ship inside, with hatch covers, old photos, and paintings of sea creatures—and real seamen at the bar. Breakfast, lunch, and dinner. $–$$

Main Street Grill. 435 Main at Kelly, Half Moon Bay; (650) 726–5300. Cajun sausage, homemade waffles and muffins, grilled sandwiches, thick shakes, microbrewed beer, and a jukebox. Breakfast and lunch. $

Miramar Beach Restaurant. 131 Mirada Road, Half Moon Bay; (650) 726–9053. Formerly a circa-1918 Prohibition roadhouse, this joint jumps on the weekends with live music. Kids like watching the surfers off Miramar Beach. Fresh seafood and steaks, and a kid's menu. Lunch, dinner, and weekend brunch. $$–$$$

Where to Stay

Half Moon Bay Lodge. 2400 South Cabrillo Highway (Highway 1), south end of Half Moon Bay; (650) 726–9000 or (800) 368–2468; www.woodsidehotels.com. Eighty spacious rooms with small patios or balconies overlooking gardens; some fireplaces. Large swimming pool, enclosed oversize spa in a glass house, fitness center, sauna. Continental breakfast, and many extras, such as borrowable books, refrigerators, down pillows and comforters, beach blankets, cribs, and extra beds. Kids get kid-size robes, crayons and coloring books, and inflatable toys for the pool. Less than five minutes from here starts a coastal walking trail. $$$

Harbor View Inn. 51 Avenue Alhambra, El Granada; (650) 726–2329; www.harborview-inn.com. A Cape Cod–style motel near Pillar Point Harbor; large rooms with two queen beds, bay windows; cribs available. Walking distance to beaches, harbor, restaurants, walking trails. $$

For More Information

Half Moon Bay Coastside Chamber of Commerce. 520 Kelly Avenue, Half Moon Bay; (650) 726–8380; www.halfmoonbay chamber.org; e-mail: info@halfmoon baychamber.org.

Pescadero

South of Half Moon Bay along Highway 1 are a string of beautiful beaches, several wildlife preserves, and two tiny historic towns. The town of Pescadero is a block or so of clapboard buildings and steepled churches, circa 1850. Peek into a few antiques boutiques and stop at Arcangeli Grocery, where the irresistible aroma of warm artichoke and garlic-cheese bread wafts out the door; some of the twenty-four kinds of bread are "half-baked," to take home, stow in the freezer, and bake later.

Just south of here near Ano Nuevo State Reserve, the circa-1870, ten-stories-tall Pigeon Point Lighthouse is open for tours on weekends (650–879–2120). The Pigeon Point Hostel has inexpensive private and shared rooms, and marvelous views (www.norcal hostels.org).

Pescadero State Beach (all ages)
Fifteen miles south of Half Moon Bay, on Highway 1; (650) 879–0227.

Two miles of sheltered beach, with tidepools, huge dunes, and trails. The sea lions and the seagulls like it here, as do the fishermen who catch steelhead and salmon at spawning time in Pescadero Creek. Kids love investigating the big tidepools and sliding down the dunes. Restrooms, picnic tables, barbecues.

Just across the highway, Pescadero Marsh is 600 acres of uplands and wetlands, an important stop on the Pacific Flyway and a must for avid birders or for anyone who likes to walk on nature trails. Fall and spring are the best times to see thousands of birds nesting and feeding. An underpass provides safe access to and from the beach; no pets.

Duarte's Tavern
202 Stage Road, Pescadero; (650) 879–0464. $$.

Crowded on sunny weekends but worth the wait, Duarte's has for more than fifty years been a family restaurant serving cioppino, seafood specialties with a Portuguese accent, artichoke soup, deep-fried calamari, and olallieberry pie. Local ranchers belly up to the Old West–style bar. Daily breakfast, lunch, and dinner.

Costanoa Coastal Lodge and Camp (all ages)

P.O. Box 842, 2001 Rossi Road, Pescadero 94060; (650) 879–1100; www.costanoa.com. $–$$$$.

A new idea in upscale camping—luxury wood cabins, tent cabins, and lodge rooms, some with fireplaces, private decks, and down comforters; also, RV and tent sites. No kitchens; shared baths; mountain bike rentals. Complimentary light breakfast, spa and sauna, bikes to rent, well-stocked general store with gourmet and deli foods to take out or eat at picnic tables. Activities for kids include guided hikes on wilderness trails, and you can walk to Gazos Creek Beach, a sheltered curve of sand with shallow tidepools, driftwood, and interesting geological formations.

Phipps Country Store and Farm (all ages)

One mile east of Pescadero, 2700 Pescadero Creek Road; (650) 879–0787. Open daily from 10:00 A.M. to 6:00 P.M.

A combination produce market, farm, plant nursery, and menagerie of exotic birds and farm animals, just made for kids. Among the cacophony of sounds are parrots' squawks, green and orange canaries' songs, and peacocks' trumpetings. There are fancy chickens, big fat pigs, a variety of bunnies, and antique farm equipment. You can pick your own strawberries, raspberries, and olallieberries, and eat them at a picnic table in the middle of a flower-filled greenhouse. Restrooms.

Año Nuevo State Reserve (all ages)

Highway 1 at New Year's Creek Road, Pescadero; (650) 879–2025 or (800) 444–4445; www.anonuevo.org. Parking $; admission $; kids 3 and under are free.

On 1,200 acres of dunes and beaches, the largest groups of elephant seals in the world come to breed from December through April. A moderately strenuous, 3-mile round-trip walk through grassy dunes brings you to an unforgettable sight: dozens of two-ton animals lounging, arguing, maybe mating, cavorting in the sea, and wiggling around on the beach. As many as 2,500 seals spend their honeymoons here, and there's lots of other wildlife to see too. During the mating season it is necessary to reserve spaces in three-hour, guided interpretive tours (800–444–7275). At other times you can wander around on your own. The boardwalk enables wheelchair access. Affording great views of the coastline, the new 1.5-mile Whitehouse Ridge Trail connects Año Nuevo with Big Basin State Park.

Purisma Creek Redwoods Open Space Preserve (all ages)

Off Highway 1, 4.5 miles south of Half Moon Bay, west on Higgins-Purisma Road.

A beautiful path winds up Whittemore Gulch through redwoods along lovely fern grottos for a mile, then climbs out of the canyon into open foothills; take a short ramble or hike the whole way, 2.2 miles to Skyline Boulevard on the ridge.

Santa Cruz

The summer resort town of Santa Cruz is known for a 20-mile string of wide, sandy, warm-water beaches and an old-fashioned waterfront boardwalk with rides and concessions. Here at the top end of Monterey Bay, the climate is mild, and surf's up every month of the year.

The town is composed of hundreds of fanciful Victorian homes. The main street, Pacific Avenue—called the Pacific Garden Mall—is a pleasantly tree-shaded boulevard with outdoor cafes and dozens of shops. Musical performances and festivals take place on Pacific all summer long. In this artists' town, notice the many sidewalk sculptures, and watch for building-size murals on side streets.

From the Santa Cruz waterfront to Natural Bridges, a road winds above the ocean for several miles. Popular for walking and jogging, the West Cliff section runs north from Lighthouse Point.

In the Santa Cruz Mountains are ancient redwood groves, sunny riverbanks, quiet little resort towns, and a rollicking steam train.

Virtually every resident of Santa Cruz County lives within walking distance of a state park or beach. A water shuttle provides seagoing transport between Santa Cruz Harbor, Santa Cruz Wharf, and Capitola Wharf. A bus shuttle also runs to Big Basin State Park on weekends. You can stay overnight, hike back down on the 10-mile trail, or just shuttle back at the end of the day.

Santa Cruz Beach Boardwalk (all ages)

400 Beach Street, Santa Cruz; (831) 426–7433; www.beachboardwalk.com. Free admission; individual rides $; day pass $$$$.

The only beachside amusement park on the West Coast. The classic 1911 carousel and the Giant Dipper roller coaster are National Historic Landmarks. You'll need a whole afternoon for the thirty rides, an old-time arcade, shops, and restaurants. At Neptune's Kingdom on the indoor minigolf course, volcanoes erupt, pirates threaten, and cannons fire. If you hear screaming, it's probably coming from the $5 million roller coaster, the Hurricane. The Astro Canyon Virtual Coaster is not for sissies. Video arcade, pool tables, air hockey, laser tag, virtual reality, shooting gallery, and bowling are other attractions. New are the Cave Train, a prehistoric adventure ride; the Sea Serpent family roller coaster; and Space Race bumper cars.

Look for the Fun Spot skateboarding park across the street at the corner of Washington and Beach, with more than a dozen obstacles for intermediate to advanced skaters, including a 6-foot halfpipe, quarterpipes, and steel rails. Beginners can try the 3-foot halfpipe.

Surfin' Safari (all ages)

Surfers have been riding the waves in Santa Cruz since the early 1920s. Surfers and surf-kayakers from around the world congregate here for annual contests on the consistently big waves, and it's still one of the best places in the world to learn to surf—Monterey Bay provides a variety of facing beaches and types of breaks. The main beach at the board-walk, Cowell, is best for beginners, with a sheltered point break, long gentle waves, and a sandy bottom. The other top surfing beaches are Pleasure Point in Capitola and Steamers Lane, just north of the boardwalk; north a few miles, surfers also flock to Natural Bridges State Beach.

On Cowell Beach, Club Ed Surf School is the place for lessons and rentals of surf- and sailboards, kayaks, and more beach stuff (831–464–0177; www.club-ed.com). The other long-established, top-rated headquarters for lessons and surf camp is Richard Schmidt Surf School (831–423–0928; www.richardschmidt.com).

Above Steamers Lane in the Mark Abbott Memorial Lighthouse on West Cliff Drive, it's free to cruise through a hundred years of surfing history at the Surfing Museum; look for the Shark Attack surfboard.

Santa Cruz **Beaches**

- **Cowell Beach,** Beach Street, Santa Cruz; (831) 429–3747. The main Santa Cruz beach at the boardwalk and the pier. A popular piece of sand for sunning, swimming, and volleyball and free concerts. A special beachgoing wheelchair is available from the lifeguard. Restrooms.

- **Santa Cruz Yacht Harbor and Beach,** end of Fifth Avenue and East Cliff Drive, Santa Cruz; (831) 475–6161. Kayak and sail, sunbathe, and watch more than 1,200 boats go in and out of the harbor. RV parking, restrooms, restaurants, shops. Free water taxi.

- **Twin Lakes State Beach,** below East Cliff Drive at Seventh Avenue, Santa Cruz; (831) 429–2850. Where the windsurfers go. There are fire rings here, outdoor showers, restrooms, and a wild bird sanctuary at Schwan Lagoon and Schwan Lake. You can kayak and canoe on the lake.

- **Seacliff State Beach,** State Park Drive off Highway 1, Aptos; (831) 685–6444. Two miles of shoreline backed by steep sandstone cliffs. A 500-foot wooden pier and the wreck of a concrete ship are roosting spots for birds, and you can fish off the pier. There are a campground and a small visitor center where you can sign up for walking tours to see the fossilized remains of multimillion-year-old sea creatures lodged in the cliffsides. On the inland edge of the beach is a paved pathway frequented by joggers, parents with strollers, and skateboarders.

- **Rio Del Mar Beach,** just south of Capitola at Aptos; (831) 688–3241. A wide stretch of sand with a jetty and lifeguards. Shopping and restaurants are within walking distance.

Bookshop Santa Cruz (all ages)
Pacific and Front Streets, Santa Cruz; (831) 423–0900.

One of the largest bookstores in Northern California, a gathering place for locals and visitors. Throughout the store are benches, stools, and armchairs, comfortable spots to peruse the books and the huge variety of domestic and international magazines and newspapers. The children's books department is comfortable, and the store offers a cafe.

Pacific Edge Climbing Gym (all ages)
104 Bronson Street, Santa Cruz; (831) 454–9254; www.pacificedgeclimbinggym.com.
Day pass: adults \$\$\$; kids 11 and under \$.

At one of the largest indoor climbing gyms in the world, you can take an introductory class with two hours of instruction, equipment, and a pass for the day for about \$30, with discounts for more than one climber.

Forest of Nisene Marks State Park (all ages)
Aptos Creek Road, Aptos; (831) 763–7064.

A cool, green place to take a walk in the highlands inland of Santa Cruz. This densely forested, 10,000-acre wilderness on Aptos Creek is popular with runners, bikers, horseback riders, hikers, and picnickers. In elevations from 100 to 2,600 feet, unpaved roads and trails lead to a wide variety of mixed evergreen woods and creekside willows and ferns. Walk-in camping is permitted, as is horseback riding.

Capitola-by-the-Sea (all ages)
Three miles south of Santa Cruz, off Highway 1; (831) 475–6522; www.capitolachamber.com.

Located on the edge of a small, protected beach where Soquel Creek enters the sea, Capitola is a few short blocks of boutiques, art galleries, and beachwear shops—a quaint art colony that has welcomed vacationers since 1861.

Restaurants with outdoor patios are lined up on the waterfront. The shops and galleries are touristy but fun. Check out the charming Capitola Museum in a little red house (831–464–0322), rent a kayak for a paddle around the quiet cove (831–462–2208), amble along the river trail, take a blufftop walk at sunset on Grand Avenue.

Family **Hosteling**

Golden Gate Council Hosteling International information: www.norcal hostels.org. For a brochure describing all Northern California hostels, call (415) 863–1444 (fax: 415–863–3865). Hostels are not just for the young and footloose anymore. Many American hostels have private rooms and cabins for families and small groups. The advantages are cost (as low as $10 per person; a few dollars higher in big cities), location (nearby natural and cultural attractions that families want to see and explore), and the chance to meet travelers from all over the world.

You cook your own meals in a fully equipped common kitchen and socialize with other hostelers in a common living room. Clean beds are provided (bring your own linens/sleeping bags), as are laundry facilities and common bathrooms with showers. Some hostels ask you to do brief chores. On the coast of California are several hostels that are perfect for vacationing families. They are popular, so reserve well in advance.

- **Pigeon Point Lighthouse Hostel,** 210 Pigeon Point Road at Highway 1, Pescadero; (650) 879–0633. Four family houses, each with a fully equipped kitchen, clustered around one of the tallest lighthouses in the United States. An incredible location on a dazzling stretch of coastline, near state parks, tidepools, beaches, redwood forests, and the famous Año Nuevo State Reserve, where hundreds of elephant seals are a sight to behold.

- **Point Montara Lighthouse Hostel,** 25 miles south of San Francisco on Highway 1, P.O. Box 737, Montara 94037; (650) 728–7177. The 1875 Point Montara Fog Signal and Light Station became a hostel in 1980. Family rooms; fireplace in community room; great location near beaches, boat harbors, Half Moon Bay.

- **Hidden Villa Ranch Hostel,** 45 miles south of San Francisco and 15 miles north of San Jose, 26870 Moody Road, Los Altos Hills; (408) 949–8648. On a 1,600-acre ranch in the foothills of the Santa Cruz Mountains, the first hostel in California, established in 1937. Rustic, heated cabins, plus a fireplace and piano in the common room. This is a working farm with organic gardens. Nearby are hiking trails and parks.

- **Santa Cruz Hostel,** P.O. Box 1241, Santa Cruz 95060; (831) 423–8304. Newly renovated cottages close to downtown and the beach.

Natural Bridges State Beach (all ages)

A few minutes north of Santa Cruz, 2531 West Cliff Drive; (831) 425–4609. $$ to park.

Named for dramatic sandstone arches, this beautiful beach has tidepools rich with sea life. Guided tidepool tours are available. A short boardwalk from the beach parking lot leads through a eucalyptus forest to the California Monarch Butterfly Preserve. Depending on the time of year—early October through March is best—you'll see hundreds of thousands of butterflies hanging in the trees and moving about in great golden clouds. A 0.75-mile self-guided nature walk begins at the Monarch Trail and heads for Secret Lagoon, where blue herons, mallard ducks, and more freshwater and seagoing birds live.

Long Marine Laboratory and Aquarium (all ages)

100 Shaffer Road, Santa Cruz, near Natural Bridges; (831) 459–3800. $; kids 5 and under free.

A University of Santa Cruz research facility, open to the public. In addition to the aquarium are an 85-foot blue whale skeleton and "touch tanks" where kids can pick up sea animals. Docents take you behind the scenes where scientists do research.

Wilder Ranch State Park (all ages)

1401 Coast Road, 2 miles north of Santa Cruz; (831) 426–0505. $$ to park.

A 6,000-acre dairy ranch since the 1800s is now a leafy, meadowy park. Picnic in the apple orchard; see historic displays in the Victorian home and take a guided walk on weekends; or hike, horseback ride, or bike on your own on miles of trails. From here you can connect to the newly donated Gray Whale Ranch.

Davenport (all ages)

About 9 miles north up the coast from Santa Cruz on Highway 1.

The hamlet of Davenport makes a nice half-day trip from Santa Cruz. On the bluff, the Davenport Overlook is a perfect vantage point from which to see California gray whales on their annual trips to and from Mexico. The beach here is less crowded than others and a favorite of windsurfers. On the highway, the New Davenport Cash Store and Restaurant is definitely worth the drive for grilled chicken sandwiches, homemade soup, omelets with homemade chorizo, and big killer brownies in a wood-floored, sunny cafe; it's popular for weekend breakfast. The gift shop sells guidebooks, masses of jewelry, and a surprising array of African trinkets and crafts (www.swanton.com).

Nine miles north, at Waddell State Beach, while you explore the tidepools, watch the kitesurfers. It's the newest rage—windsurfing with a kite to lift the rider as high as 60 feet off the water.

Henry Cowell Redwoods State Park (all ages)
101 North Big Trees Park Road, Felton; (831) 335–4598. $$.

A rare opportunity to see first-growth redwoods in 1,800 acres of stream canyons, meadows, forests, and chaparral-covered ridges along the meandering San Lorenzo River and Eagle Creek. An observation deck overlooks the Monterey/Santa Cruz coastlines and the mountains. A lovely shaded picnic grove on the river has barbecues and water. Take the short, easy Redwood Grove Nature Trail to the Big Trees Grove.

The redwood-dotted campground in the park contains more than a hundred tent and RV sites, for vehicles up to 24 feet, with no hookups (831–438–2396).

Nearby is a photo op at the Felton Covered Bridge. Built in 1892, this is the tallest bridge of its kind in the country and one of the few left in the state.

Big Basin Redwoods State Park (all ages)
From Boulder Creek on Highway 9, go 9 miles west on Highway 236 to the park entrance; (831) 338–8861. Store, snack bar, shop, restrooms. Camping in RV and tent sites, walk-in sites, tent cabins, hike and bike sites. $ fee per vehicle.

California's first state park comprises 18,000 acres of 1,000-year-old redwood groves, fern canyons, waterfalls, and 80 miles of trails, a lush, green world for hiking, camping, picnicking, horseback riding, and mountain biking. The Sea Trail drops 11 miles from high mountain ridges through dense woodlands, past waterfalls and zowie sea and mountain views all the way down to Waddell State Beach.

The easiest and most popular trail, the Redwood Nature Trail opposite the headquarters, is a 0.6-mile loop, a tour of redwoods and Opal Creek. You'll see the Chimney Tree, the Mother of the Forest—329 feet tall—and the Father of the Forest, a really, *really* big-around redwood.

Roaring Camp and Big Trees Railroad (all ages)
Just south of Felton on Graham Hill Road in the Santa Cruz Mountains; (831) 335–4400; www.roaringcamp.com. $$–$$$; kids under 3 free.

Tops on kids' favorite places in the Santa Cruz Mountains, a re-creation of an 1880s logging town, complete with a covered bridge, a general store, and a wonderful narrow-gauge steam train to ride up through forests of giant redwoods to the summit of Bear Mountain on the steepest railroad grade in North America. A second route runs along the San Lorenzo River down to Santa Cruz beaches. A chuckwagon barbecue serves charcoal-broiled steak and chicken burgers in a forest glade, or you can have your own picnic on the mountain.

Annual events are eagerly awaited by kids who love Roaring Camp. In April 10,000 eggs are hidden at the Eggstraordinary Egg Hunt, and Civil War battles and camp life are reenacted at the largest encampment in the United States. The Jumpin' Frog Jamboree happens in July, as does a Harvest Fair in October, with 1880s crafts, scarecrow contest, pumpkin carving, and free pumpkins. Sunday melodramas are free.

Quail Hollow Ranch (all ages)
800 Quail Hollow Road, off Graham Hill Road, Ben Lomond; (831) 454–7900.

New in public domain, a meadowy former ranch with a historic house, a pond, a shady picnic area, and 5 or 6 miles of hiking trails. Take an easy, flat footpath, or trek up the 2.8-mile round-trip Sunset Trail to big views of the valley and explore the dwarf redwood forest.

Where to Eat

Crow's Nest. 2218 East Cliff Drive at the Santa Cruz Harbor; (831) 476–4560; www.crowsnest-santacruz.com. A casual, multilevel restaurant overlooking the busy harbor, with a heated, glassed-in deck. The food is not gourmet, but it's good, with plenty of fresh seafood and good choices for children. $–$$

El Palomar Restaurant Taco Bar. Pacific Garden Mall, Santa Cruz; (831) 425–7575. The best tacos in town, maybe in the world. Try the fresh seafood versions and the guacamole taco, while watching cable TV sports. $

Gayle's Bakery and Rosticceria. 504 Bay Avenue, on the corner of Bay and Capitola Avenues, Capitola; (831) 462–1200. The heated patio is comfortable summer and winter. Besides pies, cheesecake, and pastries, Gayle's is famous for breakfast and for homemade pasta, pizza, and spit-roasted meats. They will pack you a picnic lunch. $

Sea Food Mama's. 820 Bay Avenue, at the Crossroads Center, Capitola; (831) 476–5976. The menu is printed every day with a huge variety of what's fresh in seafood. This is a casual, fun place with a jukebox. $–$$

Tony and Alba's Pizza and Italian Food. 817 Soquel Avenue, Santa Cruz; (831) 425–8669. A favorite family place for wonderful brick oven pizza. Also in Capitola and Scotts Valley. $

Train Place Deli. 1820 Forty-first Avenue, Capitola; (831) 475–0150. On hundreds of feet of track, G-gauge toy trains trundle around the dining room, and right by your table, while families dig into big, homemade sandwiches, soups, and cookies, and more than a dozen varieties of subs from Italian meatball to chili dog. $–$$

Wharf House. 1400 Wharf Road at the end of the Capitola Wharf, Capitola; (831) 476–3534; www.wharfhouse.com. With bay and beach views; breakfast; burgers, sandwiches, clam chowder, and fish and chips for lunch; dinner; and weekend jazz brunch. Rooftop deck is open in the summertime. Ask about the family discount. $–$$

Zachary's. 849 Pacific Avenue, Santa Cruz; (831) 427–0646. Voted Best Breakfast in Santa Cruz, sourdough pancakes, scones, corn bread, and much more. Breakfast, lunch, brunch. $–$$

Where to Stay

Capitola Venetian Hotel. 1500 Wharf Road, Capitola; (800) 528–1234; www.capitolavenetian.com. Historical landmark on the beach, a 1920s Mediterranean pink stucco motel, unassuming eclectic/eccentric decor, kitchenettes, some fireplaces, no pets. Reasonable rates for families and groups. $–$$

Fern River Resort Motel. Near Roaring Camp, 5250 Highway 9, Felton; (408) 335–4412; www.fernriver.com. A nice, small, rustic resort with little red house-keeping cabins, some fireplaces, a private sandy river beach, and four acres of lawns, trees, and fern gardens. Fireplaces, kitchenettes, no pets. $–$$$

Santa Cruz KOA Kampground. 1186 San Andreas Road off Highway 1, Watsonville, just south of Santa Cruz; (800) 562–7701. A nicely kept, large facility near beaches, with tent and RV sites and air-conditioned log cabins, a pool, a store, bike rentals, minigolf, and a very lively atmosphere. $

Seascape Resort. 1 Seascape Resort Drive off San Andreas, Aptos, 9 miles south of Santa Cruz; (800) 929–7727 or (831) 688–6800; www.seascaperesort.com. Right at the beach, spacious, nautical-theme condos and villas for up to eight people, with ocean views, fireplaces, fully equipped kitchens, and small private balconies or patios. On-site are two ocean-view swimming pools, tennis courts, an excellent 18-hole golf course, a full-service spa, a fitness center, and shopping nearby. The beach stretches for miles in both directions.

Kid's Club in the summer offers supervised activities for ages five to ten—everything from water balloon tosses to nature hikes, tennis, sandcastles, pizza parties, and swimming; evenings are fun with videos and cookies and milk. Guests with children ages five and under get a free safety pack with electrical outlet plugs, nightlights, and tub faucet covers.

The sleek, Italian-contemporary restaurant and bar have ocean views from the terrace, which has outdoor heaters. A stunning aquarium and orchids lend elegance; the sophisticated food is wonderful; although it's pricey and a little formal for families, lunch on the terrace is doable. The nearby shopping center has cafes and a grocery.

A unique amenity at Seascape is "Fires-to-Go": A bellhop arrives with firewood and snacks for a beach bonfire and drives your family to the private beach, where he or she builds and lights the fire! $$$–$$$$

Tyrolean Inn and Cottages. 9600 Highway 9, Ben Lomond; (831) 336–5188. Seven simple cottages within walking distance to town and the river; fireplaces, kitchenettes, no pets. German/American restaurant on-site. $–$$

Villa Vista. 2–2800 East Cliff Drive, ten minutes from downtown Santa Cruz; (408) 866–2626; www.villavista.com. Two perfectly wonderful condo units; each contains three master bedrooms with baths, gourmet kitchen, sea-view patio, home entertainment center, laundry facilities. Great for several couples or a large family. $$$$

For More Information

Santa Cruz Visitors Bureau. 1211 Ocean Street, Santa Cruz; (831) 425–1234 or (800) 833–3494; www.santacruzca.org. Stop in at the Kids' Korner for free coloring books and sunglasses and at the iMAC computer for information on top kids' attractions.

Monterey

A Portuguese navigator sailed into Monterey Bay in the mid-1500s, and the Spanish landed here in 1602, beginning a 200-year occupation. A rich architectural heritage remains today. Gnarled old olive trees and courtyard gardens surround graceful tile-roofed adobes and haciendas built by the early conquistadors—the town looks like old Spain. A "Path of History" wanders between historic buildings and museums.

You're likely to spend much of your time on Monterey's waterfront on the edge of the miraculous Monterey Bay, on Fisherman's Wharf, at Cannery Row, and on the seaside walking trail. Seals, sea lions, and otters provide free entertainment offshore.

Most sights and amusements are within walking distance of downtown. Get a self-guided-tour map at the visitors bureau at 380 Alvarado Street (831–649–1770) and hop on and off the "WAVE" shuttle bus.

The annual Whalefest in January on Fisherman's Wharf is a multifaceted event that families love. Attractions include mural painting, whale watch cruises, free entertainment, and special exhibits and tours.

On Tuesdays in the late afternoons and early evenings all year, the Old Monterey Market Place downtown features nearly 150 vendors of prepared foods and produce, arts, crafts, and lots of music and free fun.

Monterey State Historic Park "Path of History" (all ages)

A district roughly from Fisherman's Wharf south to Pacific and Madison and east to Camino El Estero; (831) 649–7118; www.parks.ca.gov. Tickets for all forty Path of History buildings: adults $$, youth and children $; purchase them at all buildings open to the public.

In the oldest part of the city, historic buildings and museums are close together in a pleasant, gardeny network of streets. Plan on a leisurely half-day's exploration to do the complete 2-mile walk, with plenty of time for rest stops at little parks along the way.

Children particularly enjoy the Colton Hall Museum at Madison and Pacific, a century-old school on a grassy knoll, with little wooden desks and photos of the pupils from days gone by. Behind the school and around this part of town are small adobes, some of the first homes built in California. Every April, you can take a narrated tour of more than twenty-five adobes and see courtyard gardens inhabited by docents in period costumes.

The Cooper Store at Munras and Alvarado Streets sells antique toys, postcards, and souvenirs. Walk through the store to another museum and to gardens beneath a huge cypress tree.

Fisherman's Wharf and Wharf #2 (all ages)
Del Monte Avenue and Washington Street, Monterey; (831) 649–1770; www.monterey wharf.com.

Side by side stretching into Monterey Harbor, Wharf #2 is the home of the commercial fishing fleet and several seafood restaurants, while Fisherman's Wharf is a breezy board-walk, delightfully weather-worn and smelling of salt spray and caramel corn and crowded with cafes and souvenir shops, fish markets, galleries, and sightseeing and tour compa-nies. From here you can rent kayaks, go whale watching, and take a bike ride or a walk around the edge of the bay. One of the most fun things to do is to rent an overgrown bicy-cle, which is powered by two adults in back, with room for two little kids to ride in front.

Across from the entrance to Fisherman's Wharf, Custom House Plaza is the site of fes-tivals and special events, terraced lawns, fountains, and boccie courts.

Monterey Peninsula Recreational Trail (all ages)
The paved path from Cannery Row, past Fisherman's Wharf, to Asilomar State Beach is part of an 18-mile hiking and walking trail connecting the greenbelts and parks on the coast. Along the way are historic landmarks, drinking fountains, benches, picnic sites, restrooms, and bike racks. It's fun to dodge brown pelicans and watch sea lions barking to get your attention. Binoculars are great to have, for spying otters floating on their backs in the kelp beds offshore, knock-knocking on abalone shells; children are drawn to the friendly looking, inquisitive faces of the hairy little animals. Point Piños Lighthouse and Lovers' Point playground are two stops to make. Pets must be leashed, and skateboards are allowed only in designated areas.

Maritime Museum of Monterey (all ages)
5 Custom House Plaza, Monterey; (831) 373–2469. $; kids under 12 free.

Some 18,000 feet of exhibits focused on the Monterey Peninsula's long seagoing history. Priceless marine artifacts include the 16-foot-tall, 10,000-pound lens that once operated atop the Point Sur Lighthouse. When everyone in the family is ready for a twenty-minute rest, take in the historical film here—it's free.

Kayaking Monterey Bay (ages 8 and up)
Monterey Bay Kayaks (693 Del Monte Avenue, Monterey; 831–373– KELP) or Sea Kayak Monterey Bay (32 Cannery Row and 645 Cannery Row, Monterey; 831–647–0147). They also have bike, Rollerblade, and boat rentals.

Join the otters and sea lions in their watery living room by paddling around the bay. It's much easier than you might think. A child must be 4½ feet tall and weigh eighty pounds and can share a double kayak with a parent.

Monterey Bay Aquarium (all ages)

886 Cannery Row, Monterey; (831) 648–4888; www.montereybayaquarium.org. Tickets for adults, seniors, and youths $$$; kids under 13 $$; 3 and under are free. On weekends and holidays, arrive when the building opens, at 10:00 A.M. (9:30 A.M. in summer); otherwise, you may stand in a long line. Advance tickets are strongly recommended; purchase online at www.mbayaq.org, at BASS ticket outlets, or by phone at (510) 762–BASS.

In a cross between an old sardine cannery and a contemporary architectural masterpiece, more than 6,000 sea creatures reside in giant tanks. Their natural habitat is one of the most biodiverse marine environments in the world, the Monterey Bay, encompassing 4,000 nautical square miles of kelp forests and rocky reefs. You'll see an amazing variety of creatures in the 90-foot-long Monterey Bay Habitat—leopard sharks, brightly colored nudibranchs, anemones, eels, otters, dolphins, sharks, and hundreds more species. The three-story Kelp Forest is the world's tallest aquarium exhibit. Playful sea otters and bat rays have their own glassed-in homes.

When your feet wear out, sit down to watch live videos from an unmanned research submarine prowling Monterey Bay, as deep as 3,000 feet. From the aquarium's decks overlooking the harbor, you can peer down and watch otters and seals peering back at you.

Inside the building is an elegant restaurant (fresh seafood, pasta, appetizers, full bar service, and complimentary binoculars; reservations, 831–648–4870); an oyster bar; and a self-service cafe (pizza, pasta, Mexican food, clam chowder in a sourdough bowl, sandwiches, and salads), all with fabulous bay views.

In honor of its twentieth anniversary, the aquarium opened a thrilling new exhibit, Sharks: Myth and Mystery. A new entrance area makes admission easier and faster; newly developed Aquarium Adventures programs include overnight camp-ins in the aquarium, behind-the-scenes tours, kayaking and whale watching trips, and SCUBA, a basic version of scuba diving for kids.

The Outer Bay exhibit contains open ocean species such as 10-foot-tall, one-and-a-half-ton sunfish, huge stingrays, green sea turtles as big as dining room tables, vast schools of yellowfin tuna, and species of sharks too big for aquariums—until now. The Drifters gallery contains the largest scale jellies exhibit in the world. Otherworldly music and a dreamlike design for the jellies venue transfix viewers before the pulsing, drifting, rainbow-hued beings.

In the Splash Zone, young kids can stand inside a simulated penguin home, crawl into a "coral tunnel," touch sea creatures, enjoy entertainment, and play in a supervised area. There is even a play area for babies and toddlers.

Allow at least three hours for the aquarium; it can be crowded and sometimes overwhelming for little kids, so take breathers on the outdoor terrace, where salty breezes and the passing scene of watercraft will revive the spirits of even the crabbiest toddler.

Top Ten **Aquarium Zones for Kids**

- **Anchovies:** Thousands of them swim overhead at the Outer Bay.

- **Touch Pool:** Feel a sea cucumber, crabs, and more sea creatures.

- **Bat Ray Exhibit:** Touch one of the sea's strangest animals.

- **Wave Crash:** At the Shores exhibit, a (wet) surprise!

- **Otter Mealtime:** Watch hungry otters chow down at 10:30 A.M., 1:30, or 4:30 P.M.

- **Feed the Animals:** At 11:30 A.M. or 4:00 P.M. at the Kelp Forest, see a diver feed the fish.

- **Flippers, Flukes, and Fun:** Try on seal fins, test your skills, and catch whale food.

- **Bubble Windows:** Get a fish's-eye view at the Bay Habitats.

- **Kelp Lab:** Touch Kelp Forest creatures and view them under a microscope.

- **Splash Zone:** Dive into bright coral reefs; roam rocky shores; and visit eels, sharks, and penguins.

Asilomar Conference Center (all ages)

800 Asilomar Road, Pacific Grove; (888) 733–9005 or (831) 372–8016; www.asilomar center.com.

Unknown to most tourists, this secluded, rustic, historic resort hides in a pine and oak forest above beautiful Asilomar State Beach. Conference attendees sometimes fill up the place, but, when space is available, individuals and families rent rooms and suites here at very reasonable rates that include a bountiful, full breakfast buffet in a bright, pleasant dining room (dinner is available too). Rooms are clustered in small lodges that have a common living room and fireplace; blissfully, no TVs or phones, except in public areas. Some rooms have private patios, or balconies, and fireplaces.

Bikes are available, and you can take off right from here for the 17-Mile Drive, the aquarium and Fisherman's Wharf, and the 18-mile Monterey Peninsula Recreational Trail.

There is a heated pool, volleyball, a game room, and easy accessibility to the wonderful tidepools and the wide, sandy beach, which is unsuitable for swimming or wading. Sixty acres of dunes are traversed by a 1-mile-long boardwalk, and a trail leads to wildflowery clifftops and stunning sea views.

Dennis the Menace Playground (ages 1–10)
On Pearl Street next to the El Estero Ballpark, Monterey; (831) 646–3866.

For little kids who can use some respite from sightseeing, a unique park designed by Hank Ketcham, the cartoonist who created Dennis, with fantastic structures such as a steam locomotive, a giant swing ride, a roller slide, and a special play area for the handicapped.

The Invasion of the Butterflies

Millions of bright orange and black monarch butterflies escape winter cold and fly thousands of miles, returning to the same groves of eucalyptus, pine, and cypress on the California coast each year between October and March—a phenomenon occurring in a handful of places in the world. The city of Pacific Grove calls itself Butterfly Town USA and holds an annual children's parade to welcome the monarchs.

These are the most accessible places to see the unusual sight of the butterfly invasion:

- **Monarch Grove Sanctuary,** Ridge Road off Lighthouse Avenue, Pacific Grove; (831) 373–3304; www.pacificgrove.com. Self-guided or interpretive tours.

- **Butterfly Parade and Bazaar,** October, in downtown Pacific Grove; (831) 646–6540. Elementary school bands and children in butterfly costumes march to welcome the monarch's return to its winter home in Pacific Grove. A charming, beautiful hometown event.

- **Natural Bridges State Beach,** off West Cliff Drive, Santa Cruz; (831) 423–4609; www.santacruz stateparks.org. Boardwalk and wheelchair-accessible observation area. Self-guided or interpretive tours. In February a Migration Festival is held to welcome the butterflies.

- **Point Lobos State Reserve,** 3 miles south of Carmel, on Highway 1; (831) 624–4909; www.pt-lobos.parks.state.ca.us/. At the park entrance ask the ranger where to find the butterflies.

- **Butterfly Trees of Pismo Beach,** Pismo State Beach, 2 miles south of Pismo Beach, south of San Luis Obispo; (831) 489–1869. Guided tours offered.

Elkhorn Slough at Moss Landing (all ages)
Off Highway 1 between Santa Cruz and Monterey; (831) 633–2133.

A nice day-trip destination to view wetlands wildlife, Elkhorn Slough is home to thousands of sea- and shorebirds and animals. You can walk on 4 miles of easy trails in the mudflats and salt marshes and visit the Moss Landing Marine Laboratory, which is operated by nine California state universities (831–728–2822). A California record was set here for the most bird species seen in a day. You are likely to see herons, teal, plovers, golden eagles, terns, peregrine falcons, and dozens more wading and flying birds. Guided kayak and pontoon boat tours with natural history narration are the best ways to see wildlife. Try Slough Safari (831–633–5555), Venture Quest (831–427–2267), Kayak Connection (831–724–5692; www.kayakconnection.com), and Monterey Bay Kayaks (800–649–5357; www.kayakelkhornslough.com). Boat tours are scheduled to take advantage of the tides, and the guides know where to find leopard sharks, bat rays, seals, otters, and other creatures.

Here at Moss Landing, there is a block or so of old store buildings devoted to antiques and "junque" shops. In July a big antiques and flea market takes place. Have a seafood lunch at Phil's Fish Market and Eatery or yummy Mexican food at the Whole Enchilada.

The Farm (all ages)
Fifteen miles east of Monterey on Highway 68 off the Spreckels Road exit; (831) 455–2575; www.thefarm-salinasvalley.com. Free.

Showcasing the agricultural heartland of California, The Farm is a unique education center, demonstration farm, and produce stand. You can buy fresh, organic produce and take a farm tour where kids can do a little farm work, learn about tractors and other machines, and taste produce (tours are at 1:00 P.M. daily, $5.00 for ages twelve and older; $3.00 for ages two to eleven; free for two and under). Next to the produce stand are demonstration crops.

The oversize, outdoor art figures of farmers and farm workers offer great photo opportunities. Check on the Web site for harvest and holiday activities, lectures, and cooking demonstrations.

National Steinbeck Center (all ages)
1 Main Street, Salinas; (831) 796–3833; www.steinbeck.org. $$; free for children under 5.

Sometime during their schooling, most American youngsters read John Steinbeck's *East of Eden, Of Mice and Men,* and *The Grapes of Wrath.* If your family's trip to the Monterey area coincides with your child's interest in Steinbeck, make the 20-mile drive inland from Monterey. The museum is uniquely child-friendly, with interactive displays of the author's books and the time and place in which he lived. You can open a drawer to see his childhood treasures; feel the chill of an "ice packed" boxcar filled with lettuce; experience the smells and the sounds of "Doc" Rickett's science lab on Cannery Row; and learn of migrant life in the Salinas Valley. There are vintage photos, ongoing videos and movies, doors and windows that open into historic vignettes, and Steinbeck's charming camper truck in which he motored with his dog and wrote *Travels with Charley.* My granddaughter,

Melati, spent over an hour in the activities room, rearranging hundreds of magnetic words on a huge board and creating a quirky poem.

The cafe here is light and airy, with a sunny patio and reasonably priced snacks and lunches.

A few blocks away, Steinbeck's boyhood home is a beautifully restored, elaborately decorated Victorian loaded with memorabilia (132 Central Avenue; 831–424–2745). You can have lunch here, although it's a rather stuffy atmosphere for kids.

Where to Eat

Abalonetti's. 57 Fisherman's Wharf, Monterey; (831) 373–1851. A family-operated restaurant on the wharf for over forty years, with an outdoor deck and indoor cafe, and comfortable spots for watching the gulls fly. Enjoy the freshest seafood in town, plus pizza and pasta. $–$$

Bubba Gump Shrimp Company. 720 Cannery Row, Monterey; (831) 373–1884. Fresh shrimp in dozens of dishes, fresh fish, steak; informal and fun. Yes, this is *Gump* as in *Forrest Gump*. $$

The Fishwife. Near the Asilomar entrance to the 17-Mile Drive, 1996½ Sunset Drive, Pacific Grove; (831) 375–7107. A casual, popular, reasonably priced cafe with specialties such as Cajun blackened snapper, salmon alfredo, and Key lime pie. Reservations are essential; sunset views are legendary. Lunch, dinner, Sunday brunch. $$–$$$

Old Monterey Cafe. 489 Alvarado Street, Monterey; (831) 646–1021; www.cafe monterey.com. Voted Best Breakfast in the county. Try the buckwheat pancakes, huge omelets, and great salads and soups for lunch. $–$$

Pasta Mia. 481 Lighthouse Avenue, Pacific Grove; (831) 375–7709. Voted Best Italian Restaurant; homemade pasta, veal, grilled fish; country chic decor. $$

Where to Stay

Cypress Gardens Inn. 1150 Munras Avenue, Monterey; (831) 373–2761 or (877) 922–1150; www.cypressgardensinn .com. A gem on "motel row," completely renovated in 2001, with the largest hotel pool and Jacuzzi in the city. Rooms have king-size or two queen-size beds, private balconies or patios, refrigerators, and microwaves. Free continental breakfast, fitness equipment, laundry facilities. Walk to downtown Monterey. Ask about aquarium discounts. $$$–$$$$

Lighthouse Lodge. 1150 Lighthouse Avenue, Pacific Grove; (831) 858–1249 or (800) 858–1249. On the seaside at Point Piños, twenty-nine suites with ocean views, fireplaces, Jacuzzi tubs. Full breakfast, afternoon refreshments. Casual, with space to run and play; popular with families. $$–$$$

Lone Oak Lodge. 2221 North Fremont Street, Monterey; (831) 372–4924; www.loneoaklodge.com. A "best kept secret" for inexpensive family lodgings. Rooms, suites, kitchenettes, some fireplaces, sauna. $–$$

Marina Dunes Resort. 3295 Dunes Drive, Monterey; (877) 944–3863; www.marina dunes.com. Ranch-style bungalows rise from rolling sand dunes at the beach, just north of Monterey. Rooms and suites are luxurious with outdoor spa tubs, fireplaces, and private ocean-view balconies or patios, and gorgeous bathrooms. Two-bedroom suites are perfect for a small family; ask about aquarium packages. In the main lodge is a beauty and health spa and a workout facility. A.J. Spurs, an Old West–themed restaurant with cozy booths, serving hearty beef, chicken, and seafood dishes is nearby. One of the two swimming pools is designed especially for kids. For walking and biking, the 18-mile Monterey Peninsula Recreational Trail starts here. $$$–$$$$

Monterey Bay Inn. 242 Cannery Row, Monterey; (800) 424–6242 or (831) 373–6242; www.montereybayinn.com. A small, upscale seaside hotel; each room has a king-size bed and oversize double sofa bed, a refrigerator, game table, and a pair of binoculars to watch the sea from your private balcony! Continental breakfast on the sunny garden patio is free, and there is a private path to a small beach. $$$

Pajaro Dunes on Monterey Bay. 2661 Beach Road, Watsonville, between Monterey and Santa Cruz; (831) 722–4671 or (800) 564–1771; www.pajarodunes.com. Private beach community with rental homes, townhouses, and condos on 1.5 miles of private beach; nineteen tennis courts; no pets. $$$–$$$$

Bay Lodging Reservations. (831) 647–1107.

Monterey Getaway. (800) 555–WAVE; www.timetocoast.com.

Monterey Peninsula Reservations. (888) 655–3424; www.monterey-reservations.com.

For More Information

Monterey County Convention and Visitors Bureau. Camino El Estero at the foot of Franklin Street, between Fremont and Del Monte Avenues, P.O. Box 1770, Monterey 93942; (831) 649–1770; www.monterey info.org.

Monterey Peninsula Visitors and Convention Bureau. 380 Alvarado Street, Monterey; (831) 649–1770; www.monterey.com.

Carmel

A square-mile village of rustic country cottages and shingled beach houses, Carmel—the queen of quaint—nestles in an idyllic pine forest above a white-sand beach. Wandering the lanes off Ocean Avenue, the main street, you will see peaked-roofed doll's houses side by side with miniature castles and small summer cabins built in the 1920s and 1930s.

Shopping, shopping, shopping happens in hundreds of boutiques on Ocean Avenue and nearby streets, tucked into garden courtyards and in Carmel Plaza. Originally a Bohemian artists' and writers' colony, Carmel has more than seventy-five art and photography galleries.

There are kid-friendly shops, restaurants that welcome families, inland and coastal parks, beaches, and a fascinating California mission to explore.

Carmel is particularly dog-friendly. Dogs are allowed on leashes throughout the town and can run free on Carmel Beach. Some lodgings and even some restaurants make special accommodation for canine family members.

Mission San Carlos Borromeo Del Rio Carmel (all ages)
Rio Road, on the south side of town near the beach, Carmel; (831) 624–1271.
$; kids under 5 free.

The second mission founded by Father Junipero Serra, a glorious Spanish-Moorish cathedral surrounded by lovely gardens. Inside, the church is sienna, burnt umber, and gold, with soaring ceilings and star-shaped stained-glass windows. On a warm summer's day, walk beneath shady colonnades and sit beside a trickling fountain.

A warren of thick-walled rooms, restored from original mission buildings, holds a magnificent museum collection of Native American, religious, and early California artifacts. In September, the Carmel Mission Fiesta is a family affair.

On Rio Road across from the Mission (or at Mountain View and Crespi or Eleventh Street and Junipero), you can access Mission Trail Park, thirty-five acres of cypress and pine forest and native vegetation, with 5 miles of easy walking trails.

Carmel Beach (all ages)
At the bottom of Ocean Avenue, the main street of Carmel; (831) 624–3543.

Fine, soft, white granite and quartz sand makes this a popular place to watch the sun sink into the ocean. A kite-flying contest takes place here in May. A big annual event is the Sand Castle Contest in fall, when architects and amateurs vie for the biggest, best sand structure.

Carmel River State Beach (all ages)
Highway 1, just south of Carmel; (831) 624–4909.

Adjacent to Monastery Beach and the Carmel River Bird Sanctuary, frequented by a wide variety of waterfowl and shorebirds, a place to wander the dunes and pick up driftwood and shells, or make a 2-mile round-trip run or walk. Swimming is dangerous when the surf is up. You may see scuba divers getting ready to descend into the kelp forests of the Carmel Bay Ecological Reserve offshore. Restrooms, picnic sites.

Point Lobos State Reserve (all ages)
Four miles south of Carmel, on Highway 1; (831) 624–4909.

Named for the sea lions who lie about on offshore rocks, the rocky, forested point surrounded by a protected marine environment includes several miles of trails, pebbled beaches, and one of only two naturally occurring stands of Monterey cypress (the other is at Pebble Beach). Robert Louis Stevenson called it the "most beautiful meeting of land and sea on earth."

From 6 miles of coastline in the park, visitors often see whales, harbor seals, otters, scuba divers, and pelicans, gulls, and cormorants. In the meadows mule deer tiptoe through purple needlegrass and wild lilac. Point Lobos is completely protected: the land, the marine life on the beach and in the tidepools, and underwater. Not a thing may be removed or disturbed; dogs are not allowed; and visitors are required to stay on hiking trails or beaches. Kids particularly like Sea Lion Point, accessed by an easy half-hour walk to Headland Cove, where sea lions bark and you can see the otters. It will take a half-day to enjoy the sights of Point Lobos, and you are advised to come early on weekends. Guided interpretive walks are conducted by park rangers.

Shopping with Kids in Carmel

- **Carmel Doll Shop,** Court of the Golden Eagle; (831) 624–2607. A fairyland of antique European dolls, teddy bears, and Victorian gewgaws.

- **Come Fly a Kite,** Carmel Plaza, corner of Ocean Avenue and Mission; (831) 624–3422. A must-stop before the beach.

- **Cottage of Sweets,** Ocean Avenue between Monte Verde and Lincoln; (831) 624–5170; www.cottageofsweets.com. Thirty varieties of licorice. British sweets, homemade fudge, gummies, old-fashioned American "penny candy."

- **Toys in the Attic,** Carmel Plaza; (831) 622–9011. Collectibles, classic toys, Madame Alexander dolls, Steiff animals, Beanies, diecast cars, tin windup toys, stuffed animals and dolls, and mechanical banks.

- **Total Dog,** 26366 Carmel Rancho Lane across from the Barnyard; (831) 624–5553. Dog raincoats and boots, dog jewelry, books and toys, figurines, plush doggie beds and treats.

- **Gibson Gallery of Animation,** San Carlos and Seventh; (831) 624–9296. From Disney and other animation studios, a fabulous, changing collection of original animation cels and vintage cels. Provides a fascinating look at how animated movies are made.

- **Thinker Toys,** Seventh and San Carlos Streets; (831) 624–0441; www.thinkertoyscarmel.com. One of the world's greatest toy and game emporiums.

- **The Mischievous Rabbit,** Lincoln between Ocean and Seventh; (408) 624–6854. A warren of Peter Rabbit–inspired treasures—hand-painted baby clothing, rabbit videos and books, carrot surprises.

Where to Eat

Bruno's Market and Deli. Sixth and Junipero, Carmel; (831) 624–3821. Voted Best Grocery Store in the county. Wonderful gourmet sandwiches and salads, ready-made entrees, sushi, barbecued chicken and meats, beautiful produce. $

Caffe Napoli. Ocean between Dolores and Lincoln, Carmel; (831) 625–4033. Pizza, pasta, and bruschetta on checkered tablecloths. $

Carmel Mission Ranch. 26270 Dolores Street, Carmel; (831) 624–3824. Overlooking the Carmel River with views of Carmel Bay and Point Lobos, cowboys and cowgirls kick back and eat steak, local fresh fish, and California cuisine in casual surroundings. Plush, pricey rooms here are in charming former ranch buildings and can be great for family groups; some accommodations have several bedrooms, fireplaces, living rooms, and memorabilia from Clint Eastwood's movies (he owns the place). $$–$$$

General Store and Forge in the Forest. Corner of Fifth and Junipero, Carmel; (831) 624–2233. At an umbrella table under the oaks, on a heated patio, or inside by the fireplace, fresh fish, burgers, and salads are the best. $$–$$$

Katy's Place. Mission Street between Fifth and Sixth, Carmel; (831) 624– 0199. French toast with strawberries, nine kinds of eggs Benedict, and a million omelets. A locals' favorite, serving breakfast and lunch like grandma used to make. $–$$

Village Corner. Corner of Sixth and Dolores, Carmel; (831) 624–3588. Inside and on the sunny patio, sandwiches, salads, and lower prices than at most such places in Carmel. This is a locals' hangout.

I often lunched here with my mom, while she commiserated with her neighbors about how Carmel wasn't like it had been before the tour buses came to town. Breakfast, lunch, and dinner. $–$$

Where to Stay

Carmel River Inn. 2660 Oliver Road, Carmel; (831) 624–1575. On the south end of Carmel at the Carmel River bridge overlooking the river, with a swimming pool and simple rooms and cottages, all with private deck or patio. Some have fireplaces, two bedrooms, kitchenettes and refrigerators. The Trail's Head Cafe here serves breakfast, lunch, and dinner, specializing in fresh local seafood. $$$–$$$$

Carmel Village Inn. Ocean Avenue and Junipero Streets, Carmel; (831) 624–3864; www.carmelvillageinn.com. Lovely landscaped grounds with thirty-four rooms, some with two queen-size beds; microwaves, refrigerators, suites with kitchens and fireplaces; free continental breakfast. $$–$$$

Carmel Wayfarer Inn. Fourth and Mission Streets, Carmel; (831) 624–2711. Small rooms, some perfect for families, with fireplaces, kitchenettes, queen-size and twin beds. $$$–$$$$

For More Information

Carmel Visitor Center. San Carlos between Fifth and Sixth, P.O. Box 4444, Carmel 93921; (831) 624–2522; www.carmelcalifornia.com. Upstairs in the Eastwood Building, you can pick up a walking-tour map and brochures.

Carmel Valley

A few miles inland from Carmel, the Carmel River runs along between two small mountain ranges through horse farms and farmland. The tawny climate is warm and dry when fog blankets the coastline. Near tiny Carmel Valley Village, 11.5 miles from Highway 1, are a few small ranch resorts and not much else except horseback-riding and hiking trails, tennis courts, and swimming pools. Inexpensive lodgings, fewer people, and good weather make the valley a great headquarters for family trips to the Monterey and Carmel areas.

Shopping is one of the primary activities in the town of Carmel, but dragging young kids through quaint shops can quickly turn into a family disaster. One of the easiest and most fun places I've ever seen for shopping with kids is the Barnyard, at the entrance to Carmel Valley.

The Barnyard (all ages)
At the intersection of Highway 1 and Carmel Valley Road, 5 minutes south of Carmel; (408) 624–8886.

A rambling complex of shops and restaurants in contemporary barn buildings, this is a shopping place that children like. They can run around outside on terraces among a riot of blooming plants and flowers, or sit on a bench with a book or a game while parents browse. A horticulturist leads a guided tour of the voluminous gardens on Fridays. On selected Sunday afternoons in the summertime, live music and wine make this a place to linger. There are several casual restaurants in the Barnyard, including a crumpet cafe, an English pub, a Chinese place, and a pizzeria. The following are some of my family's favorite shops.

The delicate sounds of hundreds of wind chimes fills the air among the weather vanes, fountains, and fantastical plant "pictures" at **Succulent Gardens and Gifts** (831–624–0426). My granddaughters love **Avalon Beads** (831–624–4520), where they spend hours planning their jewelry projects. In the huge inventory are Japanese seed beads, precious and semiprecious stones, and Venetian glass beads. (The Web site, www.avalon beads.com, shows other Central Coast locations.)

The **Thunderbird Bookshop** (831–624–1803), with its large children's section, has been a beloved fixture in Carmel Valley for decades. **Sandcastles-by-the-Sea** (831–626–8361) features wooden toys, games, kits, costumes, musical instruments, and well-made, sturdy things that parents feel good about. **Twiggs** (831–622–9802) delights all ages with gnomes, trolls, raccoons, bunnies, twittering birds, and fantastical creatures.

Garland Ranch Regional Park (all ages) 🚶 👥 🚗 🔥

About 8.6 miles east of Highway 1, on Carmel Valley Road, Carmel Valley; (831) 659–4488.

The primary public venue for outdoor recreation in the valley, the park runs along the river and up onto the ridges in oak forests—5,000 acres of wilderness crisscrossed by trails. The most popular paths are the easy Lupine Loop, the Buckeye, and the Waterfall Trail to the mesa. In springtime wildflowers explode in great colorful clouds, water rushes over the falls, and lush grass surrounds the pond on the mesa. Up here views of the entire valley are mesmerizing.

Near the parking lot, picnic sites beside the river are pleasant on hot days. John Steinbeck wrote in *Cannery Row*, "The Carmel [River] crackles among round boulders, wanders lazily under sycamores, spills into pools, drops in against banks where crayfish live . . . frogs blink from its banks and the deep ferns grow beside it. It's everything a river should be."

Where to Eat

Baja Cantina. 7166 Carmel Valley Road, Valley Hills Center, Carmel Valley; (831) 625–2252. On a heated patio overlooking the valley or inside surrounded by funky auto memorabilia of the early 1900s, eat grilled and spit-roasted meats, fresh seafood, salads, and great enchiladas, tacos, and more California-style Mexican food. $$

Bon Appetit. 7 Delfino Place, Carmel Valley Village; (831) 659–3559. Sit outdoors under an umbrella, watch the passing scene of the village, and enjoy bouillabaisse, paella, mesquite-grilled fresh fish, gourmet pizzas, and a notable wine list. $$–$$$

Rio Grill. 101 Crossroads Boulevard, Carmel, in a shopping center near Highway 1 and Carmel Valley Road; (831) 625–5436. Santa Fe–style decor, butcher-paper-covered tables with crayons for the creative, and tons of awards, such as Best Restaurant in Monterey County, make this a top choice for Southwestern-style food. A woodburning grill and an oakwood smoker produce fresh fish, meat, and poultry specialties. $$–$$$

Where to Stay

Blue Sky Lodge. Carmel Valley Road at Flight Road, P.O. Box 233, Carmel Valley 93923; (831) 659–2256; www.blueskylodge .com. Large family units, living rooms and fireplaces, heated pool. Pets welcome. Walk to the village. $$–$$$

Riverside RV Park and Saddle Mountain RV Park. A mile off Carmel Valley Road on Schulte Road, Carmel Valley; (831) 624–9329. Tree-shaded RV sites, most with nice views of the valley. Large, attractive swimming-pool terrace, with picnic tables under oak trees. Day use is available for the pool and barbecues. $

Valley Lodge. 8 Ford Road, Carmel Valley; (800) 641–4646; www.valleylodge.com. Small, quiet, reasonably priced, with pretty patio rooms and suites with two queen-size beds; fireplace cottages with one or two bedrooms, living rooms, kitchens, Shaker furnishings, garden patios, or decks. Sixty-foot, heated swimming pool, sauna; dogs welcome. $$$–$$$$

For More Information

Carmel Valley Chamber of Commerce.
Oak Building, Carmel Valley Road, Carmel
Valley; (831) 659–4000.

Big Sur

Beginning just south of Carmel along Highway 1, Big Sur is a sparsely developed stretch of coastal wilderness that runs 90 miles south to San Simeon. High cliffs and river valleys are hemmed in by the rugged Santa Lucia Mountains on one side and a largely inaccessible seacoast on the other, with sheer 1,000-foot drops to beaches below. Offshore are natural arches and sea stacks, rocky remnants of ancient shores. The two-lane highway is crossed by nearly thirty bridges over wild canyons, deep valleys, and creeks that rush down mountains into ferocious ocean surf—a scenic drive but rather unrelentingly curvy for younger children if you drive more than a half-hour or so at a time. Fortunately, there are many stops to make for walks in forest parks, beach explorations, and lunches and snacks at a few—just a few—cafes.

Big Sur is a banana belt, with higher temperatures than Carmel and Monterey, receiving more rain but also more sunny days. In winter you'll often find clear, blue skies here when it's drippy just a few miles north. In several river and forest parks, including the Los Padres National Forest, are good campgrounds and walking and hiking trails.

Be aware there are only a handful of gas stations and grocery stores on the Big Sur highway, and prices are astronomical.

Point Sur Light Station (all ages)
**Nineteen miles south of Rio Road in Carmel on Highway 1; (831) 625–4419;
www.parks.ca.gov.**

A historic 1889 stone lighthouse, several buildings, and an interpretive center are open for guided tours, with reservations. The two- to three-hour tour includes a 0.5-mile walk with a 300-foot gradual climb to the lighthouse, located on a dramatic promontory over the sea. Wildflowers and whales are frequent rewards.

Andrew Molera State Park (all ages)
**Twenty-two miles south of Carmel, on Highway 1 (access not suitable for RVs); (831)
667–2315.**

The Big Sur River flows down from the Santa Lucias through 4,800-acre Molera State Park, falling into the sea at a long sandy beach. One of many hiking trails runs along the river through a eucalyptus grove, where monarch butterflies overwinter, to the river mouth, where you can see a variety of sea- and shorebirds. Besides ancient redwoods, you will encounter the Santa Lucia fir, found only here, and possibly the endangered peregrine falcon and bald eagles.

Reservations are not accepted for the walk-in tent campground in a meadow; the facility has picnic sites, a horseback-riding concession, biking trails, and restrooms. For trail maps and information, write in advance to the U.S. Forest Service, 406 South Mildred, King City 93930 (408–385–5434).

One of the most unforgettable ways to see Big Sur is on horseback. Molera Trail Rides offers daily two-hour rides in the park, each featuring a different perspective, such as the beach, redwood groves, mountain ridges, and sunset excursions (831–625–5486 or 800–942–5486).

Pfeiffer Big Sur State Park (all ages)
Twenty-six miles south of Carmel, on Highway 1; (831) 667–2171 or (831) 667–2315.

The most popular, easily accessible, and family-friendly park in the area, a place to hike, picnic, and fish on the Big Sur River. A system of short trails around the campground leads to giant redwoods, a waterfall, river boulders, and pools. A 1.8-mile creekside loop brings you to 60-foot Pfeiffer Falls in a fern canyon and to dazzling ridgetop views. Docent-led nature walks to Pfeiffer Beach are given in summer.

More than 200 developed, tree-shaded campsites offer fire rings, toilets, motel/cabins, a lodge, picnic areas, a restaurant, a gift shop, a Laundromat, restrooms, and showers. Next to the park at Big Sur Station, park rangers hand out trail maps and give advice on trail conditions.

Nepenthe
Twenty-nine miles south of Carmel, on Highway 1; (831) 667–2345. $$.

For decades a favorite destination for visitors in the Big Sur area, the restaurant features stone patios perched over the sea that offer a long and magical view of a spectacular shoreline. Try the ambrosia burger or the fresh fish, and plan to spend a leisurely lunchtime.

Julia Pfeiffer Burns State Park (all ages)
Thirty-seven miles south of Carmel, on Highway 1; (831) 667–2315.

A glowing jewel of forest and coastline on 3,600 acres of undeveloped wilderness. A 0.5-mile, easy trail along McWay Creek leads to a waterfall that plunges over an 80-foot cliff into the ocean. The Partington Creek Trail goes through a canyon and a 100-foot rock tunnel to Partington Cove Beach, where sea otters play in the kelp beds.

About halfway to San Simeon, Jade Cove is actually a string of coves, where Monterey jade is found at low tide and following storms.

On Highway 1 along the entire Big Sur coastline, deer and other wildlife frequently wander onto the road, especially at night, so it is best to drive slowly and enjoy the views, safely!

Where to Eat

Big Sur Bakery and Restaurant. Highway 1 near the post office in Big Sur; (831) 667–0520. In a garden setting with sweeping views of Big Sur Valley, breakfast, lunch, and dinner, pizza from a wood-fired oven; hearty, healthy comfort food and veggie specialties. Super-yummy baked goods. $–$$

Ripplewood Resort. Twenty-four miles south of Carmel on Highway 1, Big Sur Valley; (831) 667–2242. Good for breakfast, lunch, Mexican dinners. $–$$

Rocky Point. Ten miles south of Carmel on Highway 1; (831) 624–2933; www .rocky-point.com. Spectacular views of the coast from the dining room and the terrace make breakfast, lunch, and dinner memorable experiences. Try the enchiladas, the crab salad, or one of the fabulous steaks. $$

Where to Stay

Big Sur Lodge. Just inside the entrance to Pfeiffer Big Sur State Park, P.O. Box 190, Big Sur 93920; (831) 667–2171 or (800) 424–4787; www.bigsurlodge.com. Cozy, simple cottages in a forest; kitchens, fireplaces; lovely views; pool. The casual, family-oriented restaurant serves California cuisine, pasta, local seafood, and stuff kids like; the patio overlooks the Big Sur River—heavenly. $$–$$$

Deetjen's Big Sur Inn. Thirty-one miles south of Carmel, on Highway 1; (831) 667–2377. Quaint, rustic, Norwegian-style inn in a redwood grove, twenty simple cottages, fireplaces or woodburning stoves, down comforters. Each cottage has two or three separate guest rooms with shared bath (choose your unit carefully, as some can be noisy). The restaurant serves good American food. $$–$$$

River Inn. Pheneger Creek, Big Sur; (800) 328–2884. Eighteen queen rooms and family suites with balconies overlooking the river; simple, rustic accommodations. Restaurant and bar, swimming pool, general store; near state parks. $–$$

Riverside Campground and Cabins. Twenty-five miles south of Carmel, P.O. Box 3, Big Sur 93920; (831) 667–2414. Campsites, RV sites, communal bathhouse. $

Ventana Big Sur Campground. Thirty miles south of Carmel, on Highway 1; (831) 667–2331. A lovely private campground in a forty-acre redwood grove. $

For More Information

Big Sur Chamber of Commerce. P.O. Box 87, Big Sur 93920; (831) 667–2100; www.bigsurcalifornia.org.

Big Sur Reservations. (831) 667–2929. A variety of lodgings.

The Big Valley

California's rich agricultural heartland rolls for hundreds of miles between the Sierra Nevada Range and the Coastal Range. Freshened with many lakes and reservoirs, almost a dozen rivers, and 1,000 miles of inland Delta waterways, a string of verdant valleys—the Sacramento, the Santa Clara, and the San Joaquin—is paradise for families who love to fish, water-ski, houseboat, play outdoors, and camp.

The state capital and three good-size towns along the north–south valley route, Highway 99, are gateways to the central and southern Sierras, three national parks, and several national forests. And a tiny inland village, founded by the Spanish and the original Native American residents, is a side trip not to be missed.

Sacramento

The mighty Sacramento River—wide, cool, and green; fringed with overhanging trees; and loaded with fish—nourishes a valley that feeds the world. Astride the river the state capital, Sacramento, was a simple homesteader's fort that became a boomtown during the Gold Rush in the mid-1800s and was the western terminus for the Pony Express and the Transcontinental Railroad. The main historic and recreational attractions for families are the California State Capitol, Old Town Sacramento, the State Railroad Museum, and the river itself. Several excellent marinas, with outdoor restaurants and boat tie-ups, are found along the Garden Highway on the northern edge of the city. Thousands of magnificent old trees and glorious Victorian mansions line the downtown streets. Beautiful homes are found from Seventh to Sixteenth Streets, and from E to I Streets; don't miss the Heilbron home at 740 O Street and the Stanford home at 800 N Street.

Summer days average temperatures in the nineties, with many days topping hundred-degree temperatures, but this is a city of more than a million trees, as well as access to the water, so relief is never far away.

South from Sacramento along Highway 160, ramshackle fishing villages and small resorts are scattered on the banks of the river and throughout a vast delta. The tiny town of Locke is the state's only surviving rural Chinese community from the turn of the nineteenth century. Boats and ferries, sailboards, houseboats, and skiffs ply miles of meandering waterways.

THE BIG VALLEY

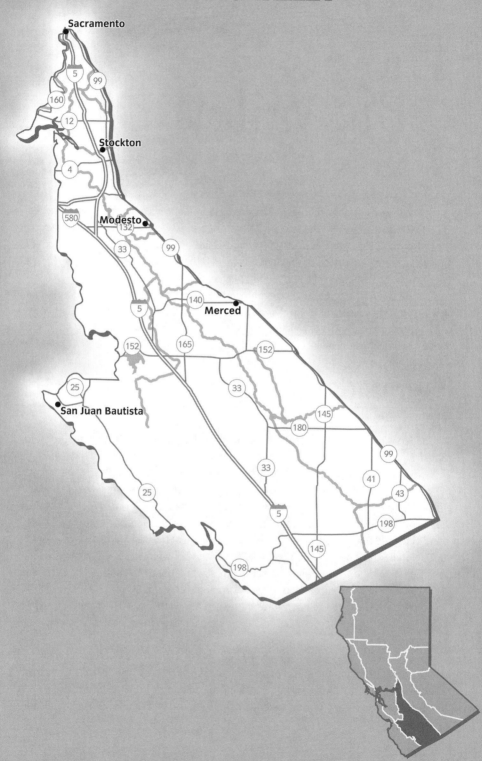

Sacramento

5 99

160

12

Stockton

4

580 Modesto 132

33 99

5 140 Merced

152 165 152

25 33

San Juan Bautista 145

180

99

33 41

43

25 5 198

145

198

California State Capitol (all ages)

Tenth Street and Capitol Mall, Sacramento; (916) 324–0333. Free.

The circa-1870, double-domed capitol is surrounded by forty acres of Capitol Park, a century-old botanical garden that explodes into pink and white clouds of camellias, azaleas, dogwood, and tulips every spring. You can take a guided tour of the gardens or stroll around on your own.

With toddlers and little kids, take a self-guided tour and let them meander up and down the marble hallways while you peek in at the museum displays. You'll see magnificent carved staircases, elaborate crystal chandeliers, marble parquet floors, and historic artwork. You might even be able to sit in on a legislative session. With children about eight years old and older, take the guided historic tour, where you'll hear stories of California's colorful politicos (call ahead to reserve).

Old Town Sacramento (all ages)

Between I Street, Capitol Mall, the Sacramento River, and Highway 5; (916) 264–7777 or (916) 442–7644; www.oldsacramento.com.

Early in the morning when the mist hangs low on the Sacramento River, footsteps echo on the boardwalks of Old Town, and you can imagine the rollicking port during the California Gold Rush, when as many as 800 sailing vessels tied up here at the docks. Reeling from months of sailing around the Horn, gold seekers raced down the gangplanks, bargained for provisions and livestock, then rode away in wagons and on horseback to seek their fortunes in the Sierra foothills. "Forty-niner" days are still alive in the restored wooden false-front saloons, firehouses, dining halls, and emporiums of Old Town Sacramento, a National Historical Monument.

Browsing the hundred boutique shops, more than twenty restaurants, and museums and historical sites will take a full day or two. Annual events in Old Town include the Festival de la Familia, with hundreds of vendors and free entertainment, such as Latin, Caribbean, and Native American music. At the Pacific Rim Festival, live entertainment includes the thrilling Japanese taiko drummers and martial arts demonstrations; kids can make art while parents browse for arts and crafts and try the exotic foods (www.pacificrimstreetfest.org). The Gold Rush Days festival over Labor Day weekend re-creates early days, with horse-drawn carriages, characters in period costumes, and living history events and performances.

From spring to fall, a bright yellow water taxi runs from the L Street landing to three marinas along the river, where you can stop and dine at waterfront restaurants. Make a reservation: tickets for adults $5.00, children under 42 inches tall $2.00; (916) 446–7704; www.riverotter.com.

Things to Do in **Old Town Sacramento**

- **Discovery Museum,** 101 I Street; (916) 264–7057; www.thediscovery.org. $; **free** for kids 3 and under. In a circa-1850 city hall, a huge gold nugget collection; a planetarium; hands-on science and technology exhibits; simulated space travel in the Challenger Learning Center. Nature trail and okay-to-touch animals in the Nature Center; history exhibits and more.

- **Towe Ford Museum,** 2200 Front Street; (916) 442–6802; www.toweauto museum.org. Adults $$; kids $. Crazy for cars? Visit this cache of more than 200 antique and classic cars and trucks, including every Ford car from 1903 to 1953. The kids can climb up behind the wheel of a Model T flatbed truck and other wheeled beauties.

- **Old Sacramento Schoolhouse,** 1200 Front Street; (916) 483–8818. **Free.** A replica of an 1884 one-room schoolhouse. Sit at a wooden desk with a slate and chalk; read the list of punishments for bad behavior (Telling Tales out of School, 8 lashes); ring the school bell; swing on swings in the schoolyard.

- **Rocky Mountain Chocolate Factory,** 1039 Second Street; (916) 448–8801. Hand-dipped ice-cream bars, caramel apples, chocolate-covered strawberries, and fresh, home-made candy. You could be in trouble here.

- **Southern Railroad Excursions,** Front Street at the railroad depot; (916) 446–6645; www.csrmf.org. Adults $$; ages 6 to 12 $; ages 5 and under are **free.** Weekends April through September, vintage steam-powered trains chug along on a forty-minute route beside the Sacramento River. Choose from enclosed coaches or open-air gondolas. The whistle blasts, the steam pours out, and the river breezes blow!

California State Railroad Museum (all ages)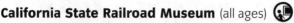

North side of Old Town Sacramento; (916) 445–7387 or (916) 445–6645; www.csrmf.org. Admission for adults $; ages 16 and under are **free.**

A 100,000-square-foot display of three dozen antique locomotives and railcars in pristine condition, the museum is a dream come true for kids fascinated by rail travel. You can hop aboard a real sleeping car that rocks back and forth and sounds as if it's rolling along.

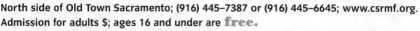

Retired conductors spin tales of the rails. One of the magnificent engines weighs a mere million pounds. On the second level a wonderful toy train runs through tiny towns and over bridges. A newly installed, gigantic, million-dollar collection of early twentieth-century toy trains is a dazzler. Children can climb around several cars indoors and outdoors and take a short train ride up and down the river. Next to the museum the Railroad Museum Gift Shop sells myriad toy trains, books, and railroad-related souvenirs. The annual California Railroad Festival is held here in June (916–445–7387).

Golfland/Sunsplash (ages 5–18)
1893 Taylor Road, 15 minutes south of Sacramento on Highway 80, Roseville; (916) 784–1273; http://roseville.golfland.com. $$$; adults over 55 $$; kids 2 or under $.

On a one-hundred-degree day (nearly every day in midsummer), stop here to cool off in the water slides and wave pool, plus two minigolf courses, a laser tag arena, and zillions of arcade games.

Jedediah Smith Memorial Bicycle Trail/American River Parkway (all ages)
A paved biking and walking path follows the river for 23 miles, from Old Town to Folsom Lake, in the foothills of Gold Country. Guided walks on the parkway are available through the Effie Yeaw Nature Center (916–489–4918). For a trail map contact the Parks Department (916–875–6961). Summer temperatures on the trail are often one hundred degrees or higher, with balmy evenings.

Sacramento Jazz Jubilee (all ages)
Old Sacramento and venues around the city; (916) 372–5277; www.sacjazz.com. $$$$.

Jazz fans assemble in droves on Memorial Day weekend to hear the top Dixieland bands in the world, as well as Latin jazz and big band music. This is definitely a family affair during the day—you will see kids kicking up their heels with moms, dads, and grandparents. On the free kids' stage on the grass at the north end of Old Sacramento, youngsters blow kazoos, crash around on drums, and have a ball. There is a Trainyard for Kids play area and a children's parade three mornings in a row! The main Jubilee Parade downtown is on Friday. Reserve lodgings well in advance.

Sacramento Zoo and Parks (all ages)
3930 West Lane Park Drive in William Land Park, Sacramento; (916) 264–5885. $$ for persons ages 13 and up and $ for kids ages 3 to 12.

Remodeled and expanded, with national recognition for the rare cat, primate, and bird collections, and the red panda exhibit.

Across the street from the zoo, Fairytale Town is heaven for the littlest angels, with play structures themed to Mother Goose, puppet shows, and more. Also here is Funderland, an amusement park with rides for kids of elementary school age. William Land Park is a large city park with playgrounds, picnic areas, and a duck pond.

Jelly Belly Candy Factory   (all ages)

Off Highway 80, take Highway 12/Rio Vista to 1 Jelly Belly Lane, Fairfield; (800) 953–5592; www.jellybelly.com. **Free.**

The most popular flavors of Jelly Bellies are buttered popcorn, very cherry, licorice, juicy pear, and watermelon. From a walkway above the factory floor, you can watch the jellies being made and get close-ups on TV monitors. Tours take forty minutes and are best on weekdays when the factory is in operation; come early in the day to avoid crowds. Other fun here is the jelly bean art gallery, free samples, lunch in the Jelly Belly Cafe (ever had a jelly bean–shaped burger?), espresso drinks at the Java Bar, and ice-cream cones.

The Great Outdoors Near Sacramento

- **Folsom Lake Recreation Area,** 25 miles east of Sacramento off Highway 50, between Folsom and Auburn; (800) 444–7275. Extending 15 miles up the canyon of the North Fork of the American River, an 18,000-acre lake that's great for camping, boating, swimming, hiking, and fishing. You can rent horses and bikes here for exploring more than 80 miles of trails. At the marina, reserve a campsite at one of the tent and RV camps, bike camps, or equestrian camps (916–988–0205). Windsurfing is popular, especially in April and May.

- **Brannan Island State Recreation Area,** Highway 160, 3 miles south of Rio Vista; (916) 777–7701. Another windsurfing paradise is Windy Cove, right in the middle of the Delta on the Sacramento River. Windy Cove was developed by local surfing fanatics and is one of the primo spots in the state. Hot summers are great for swimming, camping, and picnicking. Rangers lead canoe tours.

- **Grizzly Island,** take Highway 12 toward Rio Vista, go south on Grizzly Island Road at the Sunset Shopping Center, then proceed 9 miles to the wildlife preserve; (707) 425–3828. Entrance fee per car, $. You'll see river otters, turtles, tule elk, egrets, herons, coots, wigeons, grebes, and many more animals and birds in this 12,900-acre wildlife preserve in the Sacramento Delta. A relaxing place to take an outdoor break between Sacramento and the Bay Area, Grizzly Island is best in winter, when thousands of migratory waterfowl stop to feed and rest in the Suisun Marsh surrounding the island (avoid October through mid-January, which is duck-hunting season).

Western Railway Museum (all ages)

Ten miles east of Fairfield on Highway 12, Suisun; (707) 374–2978; www.wrm.org. Adults $$; kids 3 to 12 $; families $$$.

Ride on and explore more than one hundred historic cars: trolleys, streetcars, Pullmans, and steam locomotives. Exhibits trace railroad history, and there is a shop selling train-related books, toys, and souvenirs. Have a picnic here under the trees.

Where to Eat

Al the Wop's. On the blocklong main street of the Chinese town of Locke, near Walnut Grove; (916) 776–1800. Thousands of dollar bills are tacked to the ceiling, peanut butter and jelly sit on the tables, and the steak sandwiches and burgers are legendary in this atmospheric remnant of the little old town where Chinese fishermen lived. After lunch, take a peek into the Dai Loy Museum and the "junque" shop Locke Ness. $

Crawdads River Cantina. 1375 Garden Highway, Sacramento; (916) 929–2268. Try the Cajun popcorn (shrimp fried in beer batter) and watch the river roll by; children's menu, festive American food. $$

Fanny Ann's. 1023 Second Street, Old Town Sacramento; (916) 441–0505. Five floors of a crazily antiques-crammed restaurant and bar, a fun place to take the kids during the day; an adult crowd gathers at night. Play pinball and foosball while you wait for American comfort food, burgers, salads, and sandwiches. $–$$

Ford's Real Hamburgers. 1948 Sutterville Road, near William Land Park, Sacramento; (916) 452–6979. Big, wonderful, old-fashioned burgers from kiddie-sized to the Pounder. Also grilled chicken, turkey burgers, thick shakes. One order of fries is enough for a small army. $

Leatherby's Family Creamery. 2333 Arden Way, Sacramento; (916) 920–8382. An old-fashioned ice-cream parlor and cafe serving light lunches, dinners, and homemade ice cream. More than forty luscious flavors in huge sundaes, shakes, and other high-butterfat treats; plus burgers, sandwiches, and salads. $

Old Spaghetti Factory. 1910 J Street, Sacramento (also in Roseville and Rancho Cordova); (915) 443–2862. Sit in the trolley car or at a wooden table under the stained-glass chandeliers, in a bright, Old Town environment. The good, traditional Italian food is inexpensive, especially at lunch, and the children's menu features the simpler items that kids prefer. $

Sticky Fingers. 1027 Second Street, Old Town Sacramento; (916) 443–4075. On the second floor of a vintage building, dig into ribs, chicken, and seafood. A Dixieland combo often plays on the veranda. $$

Vic's. 3199 Riverside Boulevard, near Land Park, Sacramento; (916) 448–0892. For more than fifty years, homemade ice cream in a soda fountain diner with booths; thick shakes, egg creams. Try the turkey-salad special sandwich, a cheese dog, or egg-salad sandwich. $

Where to Stay

Best Western Sutter House. 1100 H Street, Sacramento; (916) 441–1314 or (800) 830–1314; www.thesutterhouse .com. Good value and convenient to downtown and Old Town Sacramento. Ask for a room on the pool courtyard. Simple rooms; continental breakfast included. $–$$

Radisson Hotel Sacramento. 500 Leisure Lane, Sacramento; (916) 922–2020 or (800) 333–3333. Five-minute drive from Old Town, a comfortable oasis, with swimming pools, parcourse, bike rentals, gardens around a small lake, and several restaurants. Each room or suite has a balcony or patio overlooking eighteen acres of gardens. $$

For More Information

Sacramento Convention and Visitors Bureau. 1303 J Street, Sacramento; (916) 264–7777; www.sacramentocvb.org.

Visitor Information Center. 1101 Second Street, Old Sacramento; (916) 442–7644.

California Division of Tourism. 801 K Street, Sacramento; (916) 322–2881, (800) 862–2543; www.gocalif.ca.gov. Information and brochures for travel statewide.

Stockton

The largest of the Delta towns, Stockton is a deepwater port anchoring hundreds of miles of inland waterways. If your family likes to fish and mess about in boats, the Stockton area has it all.

Fed by the Sacramento River, the San Joaquin, and five more rivers with origins in the snowpack of the Sierras, the Delta is one of the largest recreation areas in the country. Exploring this enormous labyrinth of sloughs, canals, and meandering rivers can be done on foot on a shady path; on slow, sweet days motoring about on a houseboat; or on water skis behind a speedboat. For the locations of launching ramps and marinas and to find out what's biting, call or stop in at a local sports equipment store.

In this town of 100,000 trees, enjoy a lovely historic district and a fairyland amusement park. The 10-block, downtown waterfront is undergoing dramatic development, including a cineplex and an amphitheater for concerts and events. Stroll the breezy promenade, enjoy the view, and let the kids loose in the nautical-theme playground and, on a hot day, in the fabulous fountain jets that erupt out of the courtyard. The Waterfront Warehouse houses cafes and delis; across the street, the Children's Museum is a fun, interactive destination for younger children (402 West Weber Avenue; 209–465–4386). A big annual family-oriented event is the Great Italian Street Painting Festival in May, when you can stroll the artfully decorated sidewalks. Kids can get into the act, too.

Just north of Stockton the last undammed river flowing from the Sierras through the Central Valley—the Consumnes—provides unparalleled wildlife viewing. The Nature Conservancy preserve on the river has easy trails through wetlands and forests rich with bird life.

Magnolia Historic District (all ages)

A rough rectangle between Flora Street and Harding Way, and El Dorado and California Streets. Get street maps from the Visitor's Bureau, 46 West Fremont Street, Stockton; (800) 350–1987; www.sanjoaquinhistory.com.

Take a short drive or an hour's stroll around Stockton's lovely old residential district to see homes from as early as 1860—extravagantly decorated Victorians, romantic Spanish Revival mansions, and Craftsman cottages, a rich architectural cache on tree-shaded streets.

Pixie Woods/Louis Park (ages 1–10)

Monte Diablo and Occidental Avenue, Stockton; (209) 937–8206; www.stocktongov .com/parks/pixie.htm. $.

Kids can ride a stagecoach and ponies in this fairyland-theme park built in the 1950s. Big shade trees and lawns make this a pleasant place for parents to linger while children enjoy the playground. Special shows are featured in the Toadstool Theater on Sundays. The park opens for the season in March. Kids to about ten years old will love riding the little train past Frontier Town, the carousel, and the steam paddlewheeler on the lagoon. Snacks and fast food available.

Micke Grove Park and Zoo (all ages)

Eight miles north of Stockton off Highway 99; take 8-Mile Road to 11793 North Micke Grove Road, Lodi; (209) 953–8840; www.mgzoo.com. Vehicle entry $; zoo $; kids 2 and under free.

A great place to spend an afternoon. The zoo houses a nice variety of wild animals, plus tropical birds and endangered species exhibit. You can picnic under the oaks, try out the playground equipment, go swimming in the public pool, or take a turn on the merry-go-round at the Funderwoods amusement park, which is designed for kids ages two to ten. A large museum complex in the park has historic exhibits and nearly one hundred tractors displayed outdoors. In the fall, maples and ginkgo trees are aflame in the Japanese Garden, a peaceful place with a waterfall and a stone pagoda.

Haggin Museum (all ages)

1201 North Pershing Avenue, Stockton; (209) 462–4116; www.hagginmuseum.org. $; children 9 and under free.

The history of Stockton represented in a variety of exhibits and the impressive collection of Native American baskets and artifacts distinguish this museum. Art from around the world includes paintings by famous nineteenth-century artists such as Albert Bierstadt. Look for the 1919 Caterpillar tractor—invented by the founder of Stockton—and a letter by Daniel Boone, a mummy, a great display of antique dolls, and "Willy the Jeep" from World War II.

Houseboating (all ages)

There is nothing like a houseboat for a real Huck Finn experience. From 28-footers to big, luxurious 50-footers, the boats are like floating apartments, furnished with every convenience for up to twelve people. You bring aboard bedding and food and pay for the gas, about three to five gallons an hour. No experience is necessary, and the boats move at a leisurely pace, about 10 miles an hour. For day trips try a "patio boat," a kind of small floating barge with a roof, seating areas, and not much more. They move a little faster and are fun for camping, picnicking, and fishing expeditions.

Kids especially like crawdad catching in the warm Delta waters, and some houseboat-rental companies will loan or rent you crawdad traps. May to December are the best months, and a fishing license is required. You bait the trap with dog food, drop it overboard on a line, and let it rest on the bottom overnight; you'll get anywhere from ten to fifty crawdads. Ask a Delta resident how to clean and cook them, and be sure to eat them with your fingers with a spicy dipping sauce.

Houseboat Rentals in Stockton

- **King Island Resort,** 11530 8-Mile Road; (209) 951–2188.
- **Paradise Point Marina,** 8095 Rio Blanco Road; (209) 952–1000.
- **Herman and Helen's Marina,** Venice Island Ferry; (209) 951–4634.

Tower Park Marina Resort (all ages)

14900 West Highway 12, at the Little Potato Slough drawbridge, Lodi; (209) 943–5656.

A large riverside resort with 400 RV sites, a guest marina, watercraft rentals, boat launching, a general store, picnic sites, and a beach. All tables face the water at the Terminus Tavern restaurant at Tower Park. An annual boat show in May, Deltafest, is held here; in addition to a huge show of boats in the water and ashore, live entertainment, fishing clinics, demonstrations, and food booths are part of the fun.

Houseboating Tips **for Families**

- **Plan ahead:** Make reservations several months in advance for high-season weekends. Just like motels and campgrounds, houseboats "sell out" quickly.

- **It's not cheap:** A boat sleeping six to ten people in the summer and on holiday weekends will cost $1,000 to $3,000 a week, plus gas, which runs $40 or more a day.

- **A good night's sleep:** If your group of friends and family fill up the houseboat and you plan to have children sleep on the floor, consider bringing sleeping bags and maybe a tent, for sleeping on the riverside.

- **Getting around:** Don't hesitate to bring with you or rent an outboard skiff to tow behind the houseboat. You'll be glad to have it for zipping to marinas for ice and groceries, for fishing quietly, and for getting away from what may be a noisy, lively life on the houseboat.

- **Save money on food:** Shop for groceries before you get to the houseboat marina. Food and drinks are expensive once you get there.

- **Upgrades:** Consider making this a truly primo family vacation by going for upgrades such as a water slide, air-conditioning, and an extra bathroom.

Oakwood Lake Waterpark and Camping Resort (all ages) 🏕️ 🎡 🌊
Located twenty minutes south of Stockton off Highway 99, at 874 East Woodward Avenue, Manteca; (209) 239–2500; www.oakwoodlake.com.

A huge park with more than thirty water slides, including an underground section, a river-rapids ride, the state's biggest activity pool, and the tallest, coolest speed slide. Plus, a sandy beach, a bungee-jumping tower, and shady picnic areas for hot summer days. Some 350 RV and tent campsites are well-maintained, with every amenity.

Consumnes River Preserve (all ages)

Twenty-six miles north of Stockton, take the Twin Cities Road exit off Highway 5; (916) 684–2816. Launch your own boat or take a guided kayak tour; (415) 456–8956.

Great numbers of migrating and resident ducks, geese, swans, and other waterfowl and land birds are found on this 5,400-acre preserve owned by the Nature Conservancy. Stop in at the interpretive center for self-guiding maps to the wetlands, riverside, and oak forest trails; on weekends you can take a guided tour. From spring through July the wildflowers are extraordinary. One-mile Lost Slough Trail has a boardwalk through marshy nesting grounds; Willow Slough Trail is an easy, 3-mile route meandering through beautiful cottonwoods along the river.

Where to Eat

Garlic Brothers. 6629 Embarcadero Drive, Village West Marina, Stockton; (209) 474–6585. Have refreshments on the deck above 14-Mile Slough, then go for the hearty meat, poultry, and seafood grilled on a wood fire or rotisserie. You can arrive by boat or car. $$

On Lock Sam. 333 South Sutter, Stockton; (209) 466–4561. For more than one hundred years, the Wong family has been serving Chinese food to the Stockton community—don't miss this one. $

San Felipe Grill. 4601 Pacific Avenue, Stockton; (209) 952–6261. A casual spot with super-duper traditional Mexican food. Try the gigantic burritos and the San Felipe tacos—plenty of napkins are in order. $

Ye Old Hoosier Inn. 1537 North Wilson Way, Stockton; (209) 463–0271. Families have been coming here since the 1930s. Casual and comfortable, with stained glass windows and antiques, the inn serves hearty fare, such as homemade sausage and buttermilk biscuits with cream gravy, chicken-fried steak, sandwiches, and burgers. Breakfast, lunch, and dinner. $–$$

Where to Stay

Marriott Residence Inn. 3240 West March Lane, Stockton; (209) 472–9800. Fairly new and extra nice; studios, one- and two-bedrooms; kitchens, fireplaces; pool, guest laundry, continental breakfast. $$

Snug Harbor. (916) 775–1455; www.snugharbor.net. Take the Rio Vista Bridge or the little auto ferries onto Ryer Island, home to Snug Harbor on Steamboat Slough, a quiet inlet where waterfront RV sites, simple, fully equipped cabins, and full marina facilities are popular with vacationing families and fishermen. This is a great headquarters for exploring the delta.

For More Information

Stockton Visitors Information. (290) 937–5089; www.stocktongov.com; www.visitstockton.org. Call or visit Web site to order a brochure.

Delta Rental Houseboat Hotline. For information and brochures call (209) 477–1840.

California Delta Chamber and Visitors Bureau. Tower Park Marina, 14900 West Highway 12, Lodi; (209) 367–9840; www.californiadelta.org.

Modesto

Within a short drive of the Sacramento Delta and the Sierras, Modesto—awarded the title of All-American City—is surrounded by vast fruit orchards and veggie fields: almonds, apricots, peaches, walnuts, and more. Spring is a glorious time in the Modesto area and throughout the Central Valley. Wildflowers—vibrant blue lupine, goldfields, poppies, mustard—cascade in great waves across the grasslands and in the riparian areas.

The town is a good jumping-off point for recreation on the Stanislaus River, where nine U.S. Army Corps of Engineers–maintained areas are located along 59 miles of the river; between Modesto and Knights Ferry are more than sixteen drive-in, boat-in, and walk-in campgrounds.

The movie *American Graffiti* was based on producer George Lucas's boyhood experiences in Modesto in the '50s and '60s, when cruising was a way of life. For a peek into the past, go to the A&W Root Beer drive-in at Fourteenth and G Streets, where carhops still cruise to your car on roller skates. Classic car shows are held in June.

McHenry Mansion (all ages)
Fifteenth and I Streets, Modesto; (209) 577–5344. Free.

In the heart of the lovely old home district and built in 1883, a spectacular, fully furnished and decorated Victorian Italianate mansion.

McHenry Museum (all ages)
Near the McHenry Mansion, 1402 I Street, Modesto; (209) 577–5366. Free.

In a 1912 library, displays from pioneer days through the middle-twentieth century. The grounds are shaded by magnificent oaks, elms, redwoods, palms, and magnolias.

West Bear Creek (all ages)
Off Highway 165, forty minutes south of Modesto; (209) 826–3508.

In the wintertime, until mid-March, a 2-mile auto tour of the West Bear wetlands is a peaceful experience. Half a million waterfowl rest here while migrating along the Pacific Flyway. White-tailed kites and harriers wheel above, while sandhill cranes, pelicans, and a variety of ducks and geese ply the ponds. This is a small segment of the vast San Luis National Wildlife Refuge.

Great Valley Museum of Natural History (all ages)
1100 Stoddard, Modesto Junior College, Modesto; (209) 575–6196. Family admission $.

Exhibits focus on the flora, fauna, and natural history of the Central Valley, with habitat dioramas; stuffed lions, tigers, and bears; Native American displays; and a native plant garden. Younger children like the interactive Discovery Room and the shop, which sells games, puzzles, toys, and educational books.

Free Tastes and Tours Near Modesto

- **Bloomingcamp Apple Ranch,** 10528 Highway 120, 2 miles east of Oakdale; (209) 847–1412. Stock up on dreamy apple pies and tarts, fresh-pressed cider, apples, jams, dried fruits and nuts, and fresh baked goods. This is a good place to make a rest stop, picnic by the duck pond, and enjoy the playground. The ranch is open daily from July through most of December.

- **Blue Diamond Growers Store,** 4800 Sisk Road, Salida, 5 miles northwest of Modesto on Highway 99; (209) 545–3222. See a film of a day in the life of an almond grower, watch almonds being processed, and taste the various seasoned nuts.

- **Hershey's Visitor Center,** 120 South Sierra Avenue, Oakdale; (209) 848–8126. Stop in for your chocolate infusion—the smell of freshly baked chocolate chip cookies will do the trick. All the varieties of Hershey's bars and candy specialties are here, plus gift baskets, Hershey souvenirs, and those killer cookies. Closed Sunday.

- **Hilmar Cheese Company,** 9001 North Lander Avenue, Hilmar, 18 miles south of Modesto off Highway 99; (209) 667–6076. Employing more than 500 people, this is the largest cheese producer, at one site, in the world. A wide variety of luscious cheeses is available to taste, and the cheese-making process can be viewed Monday through Saturday. In the Over the Moon Deli, try homemade fudge, cheese pie, a sandwich, or ice cream. Shop for packaged foods and collectibles, and take a walk under a waterfall to the picnic area.

- **Oakdale Cheese and Specialties,** 10040 Highway 120, Oakdale; (209) 848–3139. At this Gouda cheese factory and European bakery operated by a couple from the Netherlands, watch cheese-making through windows and on video, and tour the aging rooms. Besides yummy cheese and bakery items, locally grown fruits, vegetables, and nuts are on sale. Kids like the farm animal petting zoo and picnics under the trees by the ponds, which are inhabited by over a hundred koi fish.

Caswell Memorial State Park (all ages)

South Austin Road off Highway 99, Ripon; (209) 599–3810; www.parks.ca.gov. $.

Just north of Modesto along the Stanislaus River, this state park has the largest stand of oak riparian woodlands in the Central Valley and a lush understory of native plants and trees—a green and glorious place, winter through late spring (summers are super hot). The campground here is popular because of the swimming beaches and the fishing for bass, catfish, and crappie. Among a network of footpaths, the Riverlands Nature Trail is a three-quarter-mile route that accommodates wheelchairs and strollers. Near the sixty-four campsites are restrooms with showers. On summer weekends, park rangers put on campfire activities, guided walks, and Junior Ranger programs.

Knights Ferry Recreation Area (all ages)

On the Stanislaus River off Highway 108–12, Sonora Road, Knights Ferry; (209) 881–3517. A "Flow Fone" gives up-to-date information on water conditions (916–322–2327).

Stop in at the U.S. Army Corps of Engineers Information Center for information and maps on where to camp and fish on the Stan. Cast for big rainbow trout in the rapids, riffles, and deep pools between Goodwin Dam and Oakdale. Try for bass and catfish below Orange Blossom Bridge. Rabid river rafters put in above Knights Ferry for 4 miles of surging whitewater. Canoes and lighter-weight craft should stick to the river below Knights Ferry.

The 355-foot-long covered bridge is the longest west of the Mississippi, crossing the river near an old gristmill. Closed to vehicles, this is a scenic spot for photos. The park here has pretty picnic areas with barbecues. At the northeast end of the bridge, a hiking trail leads to sandy beaches and to swimming and fishing holes.

Sunshine River Adventures (ages 6 and up)

P.O. Box 1445, Oakdale 95361; (800) 829–7238; www.raftadventure.com. From $$$ per person; discounts for kids.

Guided whitewater-rafting trips on the Stanislaus, as well as canoe and raft rentals. An easy introduction to river rafting is the Knights Ferry to Orange Blossom Park Float, a self-guided, four- to five-hour trip popular with families (kids must be six or over). Bring a small ice chest, tennis shoes, a litter bag, bathing suits, and sunscreen. No pets. Return shuttle is provided. Rates include raft, paddles, life vests, and instructions.

My first river-rafting experience was on the Stan. The rafting company left my gear in the parking lot, so I lived in the same shorts, shirt, and bathing suit for three days. As soon as we hit the water, the world and my troubles disappeared. The water was cold and moving fast, rushing in my ears; the riverbanks rocky, leafy, sandy, and hot when we stopped for lunch. We saw waterfalls, river otters, snakes (harmless), an eagle, hawks, trout, wildflowers. We paddled hard; we held on tight through (what we thought were) scary rapids and over mountain-size boulders; we screamed and yelled and drank lots of water and beer; and food never tasted so good—fresh salads, bread baked in the coals, and barbecued steaks, all made on the beach by the boat people.

Lake Don Pedro (all ages)

31 Bonds Flat Road, La Grange; (209) 852–2396; www.donpedrolake.com.

At a low elevation northeast of Modesto, Don Pedro is a sprawling body of water with 160 miles of shoreline and several meandering arms. Summers are hot and dry, perfect for waterskiing, sailing, windsurfing, and using personal watercraft. Fishermen head to the northern, skinny arms of the lake, away from the noise and action, where fishing is good for bass, trout, salmon, crappie, bluegill, and catfish. You can lounge on a sandy beach by the swimming lagoon on the south shore, at Flemming Meadows. Two full-service marinas provide boat rentals, groceries, restaurants, gas stations, showers, and laundry facilities. Many of the 500 campsites have full RV hookups and are lakeside, enabling campers to moor their boats within view of their campsites.

Merced National Wildlife Refuge (all ages)

From Merced, 8 miles south on Highway 59, then 8 miles west on Sandy Mush Road; (209) 826–3508.

September through June huge flocks of lesser sandhill cranes, geese, herons, egrets, pheasants, pintails, teal, sandpipers, and many more stunningly beautiful migrating and overwintering birds and waterfowl flock here to the thousands of acres of grasslands and seasonally flooded wetlands. You can take a slow, 5.2-mile drive-through, stopping at pull-outs and the observation platform; there is an easy 0.6-mile walking trail. Call ahead, as the refuge is closed to visitors during hunting season.

Where to Eat

Modesto Stanislaus Firehouse Pub and Grille. 924 Fifteenth Street, near the McHenry Mansion, Modesto; (209) 575–3473. Home-style soup, sandwiches, burgers, ribs, pub food; 117 beers. $–$$

Olive Garden. 220 Plaza Parkway, Modesto; (209) 544–8057. How do you feed a car full of kids for not a lot of money? Platters of Italian food here are so big you can split them. $–$$

Outback Steakhouse Restaurant. 2045 West Briggsmore Avenue, Modesto; (209) 570–2410. Steaks, ribs and chicken barbecue, pasta, burgers and the famous Bloomin' Onion. Dinner only. $–$$

Where to Stay

Big Bear Park and RV Campground. Twelve miles east of Modesto, on Highway 132; (209) 874–1984. A water-ride and campground combo, with shaded lawns, a half-acre lake with swimming beaches, and fishing and swimming in the Tuolumne River. $

Holiday Inn of Modesto. 1612 Sisk Road (Briggsmore exit off Highway 99), Modesto; (209) 527–5074. An indoor and an outdoor pool, a playground, a wading pool, tennis courts, a coin laundry, and a coffee shop. Simple rooms; reasonable rates. $–$$

For More Information

Modesto Convention and Visitors Bureau. 1114 J Street, Modesto; (800) 266–4282; www.modestocvb.org.

Merced

Directly west of Yosemite, at the junction of Highways 99 and 140, the small town of Merced is within striking distance of a plethora of things that families like to do. A half-hour east of town are two beautiful, low-elevation recreation lakes, and a world-class museum of vintage aircraft that is well worth a stop.

More than a century old and designated as a Tree City USA, Merced has wide, shady streets with Victorian mansions and miles of bike trails connecting an open-space park system. If you are here on a Thursday night, May through September, plan to enjoy the live music, ethnic foods, craft booths, and children's activities at the farmers' market downtown.

From Merced you can take comfortable, reasonably priced public transportation into Yosemite National Park, departing several times daily (VIA, 800–842–5463; and YARTS, 877–98–YARTS).

Expected to open in 2005, the University of California Merced campus will bring new attractions and facilities, including a 750-acre vernal pool habitat preserve and other natural areas that will be threaded with walking and biking trails (209–724–4400; www.ucmerced.edu).

Lake Yosemite (all ages)
Five miles northeast of Merced, on North Lake Road; (209) 385–7426.

Within biking distance of town, a day-use park for picnicking, windsurfing, sailing, and fishing. Rent a rowboat! You're guaranteed to catch bass all year long. There are restrooms, a snack bar, and shady picnic grounds. Lifeguards are on duty on summer weekends.

Lakes Recreation Area (all ages)
In the Sierra foothills, 25 miles northeast of Merced off Highway 59; (209) 378–2521; www.lakemcclure.com.

Two meandering, warm bodies of water, Lake McClure and Lake McSwain form a sprawling, multifaceted recreation area popular with houseboaters, water-skiers, and campers year-round. Activities and public facilities cluster around five marinas, at elevations of 400 to 1,000 feet, in pine and oak woodland settings. Summers are quite dry and very warm; daytime temperatures reach into the nineties and the low hundreds, perfect for swimming and lying on sandy beaches. Six hundred campsites are available at the two lakes, many with shade and RV hookups. The cooler the season, the better the fishing in the lakes for the stocked fish: trout, king salmon, bass, crappie, catfish, and shad.

McClure has over 80 miles of shoreline and is abuzz in the summertime with fishing boats, waverunners, houseboats, patio boats, and ski boats, which are available to rent at the marinas. Swimming is primarily near the campgrounds. If you crave a quieter experience, with no waterskiing or houseboating allowed, the smaller Lake McSwain is your best bet. You can fish for trout here and enjoy the nice swimming beach.

Water Works! **Best Valley Water Parks**

- **Blackbeard's Family Fun Center,** 9 miles north of Fresno off Highway 99, on Chestnut Avenue; (209) 292–4554. Minigolf, water slides, bumper boats, games, and rides.

- **Waterworld USA,** 1600 Exposition Boulevard, at Cal Expo, Sacramento; (916) 924–0555. A huge wave pool, several slides, a tubing river, play venues, and a slide for kids ages three to six.

- **Oakwood Lake Waterpark and Camping Resort,** twenty minutes south of Stockton off Highway 99, at 874 East Woodward Avenue, Manteca; (209) 239–2500. Thirty water slides, a beach, bungee jumping, picnic areas, and a campground.

Applegate Park (ages 1–8)
1045 West Twenty-fifth Street between M and R Streets, Merced; (209) 385–6840. $.

Acres of green beneath shady umbrellas of trees, with a little zoo and summertime amusement rides for younger children. Open June through September.

Castle Air Museum (all ages)
Castle Air Force Base in Atwater, 6 miles north of Merced; (209) 723–2178; www.elite.net/castle-air. $; 8 and under are free.

One of the country's finest collections of World War II and Korean War aircraft, plus recent planes. It's quite impressive for children to stand beneath the wings of the black, batlike SR–71, B–29s, B–17s, big transports, helicopters, and more—a dramatic array. Indoors are the museum of wartime memorabilia, a gift shop, and a coffee shop. If would-be pilots are members of your family, try to be in Merced for the annual West Coast Antique Fly-In in June.

McConnell State Recreation Area (all ages)

Off Highway 99 at Delhi, between Turlock and Merced; (209) 394–7755.

Swim, fish, picnic, and camp at this delightful park beside the Merced River.

Where to Eat

Main Street Cinema Cafe. 460 West Main, Merced; (209) 725–1702. In a delightful courtyard, all-American comfort food, sandwiches and soups, homemade pastries, ice cream. Breakfast and lunch. $

Pacifica Grill. 1700 McHenry Avenue, McHenry Village, Modesto; (209) 526–9999. A bright, colorful cafe with an inventive south-of-the-border menu: ceviche tostadas; teriyaki chicken, veggie and fresh fish burritos; and simpler choices for kids. Everything is grilled, nothing fried. Try La Peninsula Caesar with green olives, pine nuts, avocado, and *Cotija* cheese. $–$$

Where to Stay

Ramada Inn. 2000 East Childs Avenue, Merced; (800) 2–RAMADA. Rooms with sitting areas and sofa beds, coffeemakers, microwaves, and refrigerators. Large pool, access to sports club and golf course, and adjacent to a very good restaurant, the Eagle's Nest, which has a good children's menu. $$–$$$

For More Information

Merced Convention and Visitors Bureau. 710 West Sixteenth Street, Merced; (209) 384–7092 or (800) 446–5353; www.yosemite-gateway.org. This is an official California Welcome Center with an extensive array of brochures, maps, and the latest information for traveling in the region and the entire state. You can check your e-mail here, make hotel reservations, and have a picnic.

San Juan Bautista

A Spanish village since the late 1700s, San Juan Bautista is a perfectly preserved, precious fragment of early California. In an agricultural setting in the Salinas Valley between the tawny Gabilan Mountains on the east and the coastal range of the Santa Lucias on the west, the town encompasses a large state historic park, one of the most beautiful of the California missions, and a few charming streets of antiques shops and Mexican restaurants shaded with pepper, mimosa, and black walnut trees. Everything is within a few short blocks. Among the charming shops in the tiny town, kids love the rocks and flashy minerals at Tops, which specializes in stones from around the world (5 Second Street; 831–623–4441). At Reyna's Gallerias and American Indian Museum, all ages enjoy the fascinating Native American clothing, artifacts, and crafts (311 Third Street; 831–623–2379).

Annual festivals and fairs focus on Native American entertainment and cultural events and on arts, crafts, antiques, and flea markets. In June, Early Days in San Juan Bautista is a celebration of early mission days, with carriage rides, period costumes, music, and dance.

One of the nicest characteristics of the mission complex is the proximity of the museum buildings to the large, grassy plaza. Children who can't bear to look at another artifact can run around outside on the lawn while parents soak up the history.

Mission San Juan Bautista (all ages)
Second and Mariposa Streets, San Juan Bautista; (831) 623–2127.

Founded in 1787, this is one of the largest and most impressive of all California mission churches, with three aisles and a glorious, 40-foot-high ceiling of grayed beams in traditional viga-lattia construction. Light floods the cathedral, making vibrant the rust and blue painted decoration, most of it created in 1816 by a Boston sailor who worked at the mission in exchange for room and board. Before and during the Sunday masses, local families mingle and chat near the giant entry doors and the soft singing voices of the congregation float out the door into the sunshine of the plaza.

Surrounding the cathedral are a series of open rooms housing a museum of early Indian, Spanish Colonial, and Victorian artifacts and one of the best collections of Mission furniture in the world. You will also see a small kitchen from which 1,200 people were fed from iron pots in an open fireplace.

The mission gardens are cool and lovely, with old cacti, aromatic lavender, and climbing roses. Behind the church, under ancient olive trees, are buried 4,300 Indians and early pioneers.

San Juan Bautista State Historic Park (all ages)
Midtown San Juan Bautista; (831) 623–4881.

Full of carriages and wagons today, the Plaza Stable was headquarters for seven stage lines in the 1860s, when as many as eleven coaches a day arrived, loaded with silver and gold miners, traders, and other travelers. Dusty travelers headed first to the Plaza Hotel to get a beer or something stronger in the bar and to book a room for the night. The owner of the hotel, Angelo Zanetta, built himself a magnificent house on the plaza, and the structure—the Zanetta House—now contains an outstanding collection of early California furnishings and personal items. The red-tile-roofed Castro House was owned by a family from the Donner Party who struck it rich in the Gold Rush. Behind the house is a glorious, 150-year-old pepper tree shading beautiful gardens.

Living History Day is held in the state park on the first Saturday of each month, from noon to 4:00 P.M. Here costumed residents demonstrate making tortillas, butter, and quilts and regale visitors with tales of the old days in San Juan.

Bonfante Gardens Theme Park (ages 1–12)

3050 Hecker Pass Highway/152 West, Gilroy; (408) 840–7100; www.bonfantegardens.com. Adults $$$$; ages 3 to 12 $$$.

This is one of the nicest and most beautiful family theme parks to open in many years, with forty old-fashioned rides and attractions, and hundreds of acres of gorgeous gardens and thousands of mature trees, from tropical plants in a giant greenhouse to trees grown into animal and other fanciful shapes, called the "circus trees." Among the charms are a 1927 carousel, a rock maze, a butterfly house, a monorail, the Quicksilver Mine Coaster, a swan ride, a miniature car ride, and some carnival games. My grandchildren's favorite rides are on the miniature antique roadsters; they "drive" Chevy Corvettes and Model Ts on a winding route through tunnels, forests, and gardens. Dining outlets are reasonably priced and offer barbecue, tacos, pasta, deep-fried artichokes, orange freezes, and more. Although teens will likely be bored, grade-schoolers, parents, and grandparents love Bonfante Gardens. This is a place to linger for the day to enjoy the birdlife, the flowers, the water features, and the lovely garden settings.

Pinnacles National Monument (all ages)

An hour south of San Juan Bautista, off Highway 25, Paicines; (831) 389–4485. $$ day-use fee.

Spires and crags rising dramatically out of the valley are what's left of an ancient volcano; the other half is 195 miles to the southeast, thanks to the San Andreas rift. All through winter and spring, and in fall after the rains have come, the 24,000-acre wilderness park attracts rock climbers, hikers, cave explorers, and picnickers. Short, easy paths make ferny creeks and mountain views easily accessible.

Spring is spectacular, with riots of wildflowers, which bloom here earlier than in most parts of the state. Winters are mild, fresh, and green. Midsummer can be extremely hot and dry, with temperatures in the hundreds. A nice private campground at the entrance to the park has a swimming pool (408–389–4462; www.pinncamp.com).

California Antique Aircraft Museum (all ages)

Six miles north of Gilroy in San Martin, at 12777 Murphy Avenue, across the street from the airport; (831) 683–2290.

On display are planes from 1928 to the 1950s, such as a Sopwith Pup, a Bowlus Albatross, and a Benson Gyrocopter.

Casa de Fruta (all ages)

Off Highway 101, 2 miles east of Highway 152/156 junction on Pacheco Pass Highway, Hollister; (408) 842–7282; www.casade fruta.com.

Antique farm machinery, shade trees, and fruit trees create a pleasant, country atmosphere at this farm-theme roadside stop.

Since 1908 when they planted a cherry orchard, the Zangers have produced luscious fruit in the Pacheco Valley. Today you can purchase a wide variety of picture-perfect, locally grown produce at their huge fruit stand. You and the kids can also ride a miniature locomotive; linger at the playground; have some homemade pie, candy, and ice cream at Casa de Sweets; see goats, ducks, rare white deer, llama, Longhorn steer, and a buffalo; and pan for gemstones and minerals—lots to do and see, and worth at least a couple of hours. Open twenty-four hours a day, the restaurant serves good American comfort food.

Events are scheduled on some weekends, including a Native American Pow-Wow, a Civil War reenactment, crafts fairs, and a pumpkin festival in October. You can stay here, too, in a nice RV park or the Peacock Inn motel (408–842–9316).

Where to Eat

Cutting Horse. 301 Third Street, San Juan Bautista; (831) 623–4549. Steak and hearty, traditional American fare is featured here in a comfortable and attractive establishment. $$

Dona Esther Restaurant. 25 Franklin Street, San Juan Bautista; (831) 623–2518. Real Mexican food in a warm, friendly atmosphere, with local art and photos decorating the walls. Inexpensive children's menu of simple dishes. Outdoor patio; live entertainment and all-you-can-eat buffet on weekends. $

Felipe's Restaurant and Bar. 313 Third Street, San Juan Bautista; (831) 623–2161. Where the locals go for Mexican and Salvadoran food, with live music on weekends. Salvadoran dishes are not complete without the zippy pickled cabbage, *curtido*. Try the specialties of the house: fried plantains and fried ice cream. $

Jardines de San Juan. 115 Third Street, San Juan Bautista; (831) 623–4466; www.jardinesrestaurant.com. A Mexican restaurant with a big, popular, Mission-style garden patio. Guitarists strum; breezes ruffle the fig and maple trees;

lunches and dinners are served at umbrella tables or indoors in cool, art-filled dining rooms. On the children's menu are mildly flavored burritos, quesadillas, and plain rice and beans with tortillas. Parents go for the fresh red snapper Veracruz and for *pollos borrachos*—chicken cooked in sherry, an old Puebla recipe. $$

Margot's Ice Cream Parlor. 211 Third Street, San Juan Bautista; (831) 623–9262. Icy delights, plus sandwiches and salads. $

Mission Cafe. 300 Third Street, San Juan Bautista; (831) 623–4521. Voted by the town as the best place for breakfast, and it's true! $

Where to Stay

Mission Farm RV Park. 400 San Juan–Hollister Road on the southeast corner of town, San Juan Bautista; (831) 623–4456. Old barns and a small store; tree-shaded sites surrounded by a walnut orchard. Sites for tents and RVs. $

San Juan Inn. 410 Alameda Street, San Juan Bautista; (831) 623–4380. Small motel with simple rooms, some with refrigerators and microwaves; swimming pool; gardens. $–$$

For More Information

San Juan Bautista Chamber of Commerce. 402A Third Street, San Juan Bautista; (831) 623–2454; www.sanjuan bautista.com. Stop here for the Historic Walking Tour map.

Gold Country

The foothills of the California Gold Country stretch more than 300 miles along the western slopes of the Sierra Nevadas, all the way to the southern gate of Yosemite National Park. Fed by snowy peaks, six major rivers carve dramatic, steep-sided canyons and rush down the valleys into the heart of the state.

Along the Yuba, American, Mokelumne, Stanislaus, Tuolumne, and Merced River corridors, dozens of boomtowns exploded in population when gold was discovered in the mid-1800s, only to be abandoned by the miners and adventure seekers when the lodes were exhausted a decade later.

Still looking much as they did more than a hundred years ago, small "forty-niner" Gold Rush towns on the "Golden Chain"—Highway 49—from Nevada City in the north to Jamestown in the south are both living museums and thriving towns of today. These communities that sprang up overnight for the miners and gold panners are carefully preserved, with wooden false-front stores and saloons, board sidewalks and gas lamps, and balconied Victorian hotels.

There is so much to see and do in Gold Country, and the area so vast, that your family may want to plan several trips, combining outdoor fun—such as rafting, fishing, and hiking—with sightseeing at historical sites.

Nevada City and Grass Valley

The sights of Nevada City and its adjacent sister city of Grass Valley, plus historic gold mines and outdoor pleasures on the banks of the Yuba and American Rivers, add up to busy vacation days in this area. Just a few miles to the east, 1.2 million acres of wilderness afford endless hiking, camping, fishing, and cross-country skiing opportunities.

The most completely original Gold Rush town in the state, Nevada City has more than a hundred Victorian mansions and western saloons and hotels clustered cozily together on a radiating wheel of tree-lined streets on small hills. At an elevation of about 2,840 feet, the whole place turns red and gold in fall, when thousands of maples, aspens, and oaks turn blazing bright.

There is much to discover today within the 8-block area surrounding Broad, the main street. As soon as you cross the bridge into town, take the first right to the visitor center

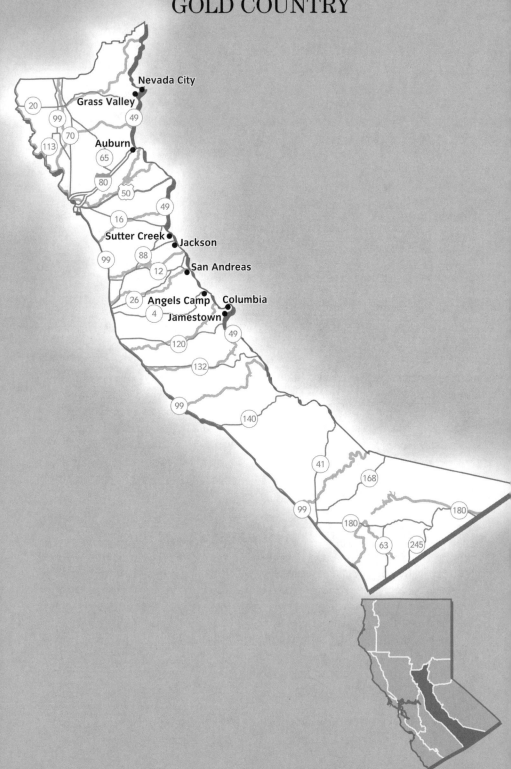

GOLD COUNTRY

for a walking-tour map. Step into the National Hotel at 211 Broad Street to take a look at the oldest continuously operating hotel west of the Rockies and see the elaborate long bar, shipped around the Horn more than a century ago.

Inhabited during the Gold Rush by thousands of English and Irish miners who worked five major gold mines in the area, Grass Valley is honeycombed with underground tunnels and shafts. On Mill and Main Streets remain dozens of buildings built in the mid-1800s when this was the richest mining town in the state. Antiques shops are clustered on Main Street and its side streets. At 212 West Main, the Holbrooke Hotel has been, since 1862, the grand old lady of Grass Valley. A glance in the hotel register turns up such famous guests as Presidents Cleveland and Garfield. Families take Sunday dinner and brunch in the dining room. A block off Main, take a stroll on Neal and Church Streets to see rows of magnificent Victorian mansions and churches.

Firehouse No. 1 Historical Society Museum (all ages) 🏛️ 🧑‍🦽

214 Main Street, Nevada City, next door to the visitor center; (530) 265–5468. Open daily 11:00 A.M. to 4:00 P.M. Free.

In a much-photographed building, circa 1860, with a bell tower and gingerbread trim, two floors of Gold Rush and Native American artifacts.

Gold Country Shops **that Kids Like**

- **Four Winds,** 310 Broad Street, Nevada City; (530) 265–9021. From an array of inexpensive folk art from Africa and South America, I stock up on small toys, dolls, and games that I save for those times in restaurants and on the road when little ones get restless.

- **Jewel in the Crown,** 109 West Main, Grass Valley; (530) 477–8697. Voted Best Toy Store in town, a great resource for educational and scientific crafts, books, games, puzzles, and toys for kids from toddler to teen.

- **Mountain Pastimes Fun and Games,** 320 Spring Street, Nevada City; (530) 265–6692. The shop is always full of people trying out the gizmos and the toys and games for all ages.

- **Swenson's Surplus,** 105 West Main, Grass Valley; (530) 273–7315. We regularly get lost in here browsing for camping, fishing, and gold mining equipment, fanny packs, water bottles, camo-clothing, winter boots, rain gear, auto gear—it's all here.

Grass Valley Museum (all ages)

Mt. St. Mary's Convent, 410 South Church Street, Grass Valley; (530) 272–4725. Free.

A restored school and orphanage exhibiting Gold Rush artifacts and domestic items. The fascinating cemetery on the grounds dates to 1852.

North Star Mining Museum (all ages)

On the south end of Mill Street, Grass Valley; (916) 273–4255. Free.

A delightful, shady spot for a picnic on the lawn beside an old powerhouse on Wolf Creek. Among the many pieces of antique equipment here are a working stamp mill and the largest Pelton wheel in the world, a waterwheel that produced power from the creek for the North Star Mine. A large collection of photos traces mining history, and there are hands-on demos for kids.

Deer Creek Miners Trail (all ages)

Broad Street, Nevada City; (530) 265–2692.

A short, easy walk along Deer Creek, with six stations that describe gold prospecting in the early days. Running through town, the creek once yielded a pound of gold a day.

Nevada County Traction Company (NCTC) (ages 1–12)

Behind the Northern Queen Inn, 400 Railroad Avenue, on the south end of Nevada City; (530) 265–0896. Adults $$; children $.

Take a one-and-a-half-hour ride in a forested area on a restored narrow-gauge train, while the conductor-owner, Al Flores, talks about local history. Part of the trip entails a short walk to see Maidu grinding holes and a fascinating Chinese cemetery; in October a pumpkin farm is part of the fun. The railroad is located on the grounds of the Northern Queen Inn, one of the best family motels in the area (see "Where to Stay" section).

Malakoff Diggins State Historic Park (all ages)

Twenty-seven miles northeast of Nevada City, on Highway 49; (530) 265–2740.

The largest hydraulic mine site in the world, a rather shocking and strangely beautiful remnant of gold mining in the 1800s, when giant water jets called monitors destroyed entire mountains. A mile of hillside here was washed away, the soil and rocks clogging rivers and streams until the practice was outlawed late in the century. Weird and colorful pinnacles, domes, spirals, and a milky lake remain, fringed with pines.

There are reconstructed buildings and hiking trails in the park, swimming

at Blair Lake, and a campground. Swimming and fishing holes on the South Yuba River and a 21-mile river corridor park are accessible near the Diggins. On weekends and holidays, rangers lead free gold-panning tours.

Empire Mine State Park (all ages)
Just south of Grass Valley off Highway 49, take the Empire Street exit; (530) 273–8522. $.

This is one of my favorite Gold Country parks, where big trees and lawns are a cool respite from hot summer days. At this beautiful mining estate, the largest, deepest, and richest hardrock gold mine in California operated for over a hundred years, producing $100 million in gold from 360 miles of underground channels, some 11,000 feet deep. On a one-hour ranger tour, see an extensive complex of buildings and equipment, including part of the main shaft. A visitor center recounts history in photos, exhibits, and films.

Sweeping lawns beneath 100-foot sugar pines surround the mine owner's home, Bourne Cottage, an outstanding example of a Willis Polk–designed English country manor with lovely gardens and a fountain pool. Also here are hiking and cycling trails and picnic areas. Come for the Miners' Picnic in June and enjoy the food, contests, gold panning, and entertainment.

Bridgeport Covered Bridge (all ages) ⓜ ⓧ ⊜ ⓖ
Pleasant Valley Road, southwest of Grass Valley near Penn Valley; (530) 432–3546.

On the Yuba River, one of only a dozen covered bridges still standing in the state. At 256 feet, it may be the longest single-span covered bridge in the world, with sugar pine shingles and massive, old-growth Douglas fir beams that are reminders of when buggies and mule teams clattered across the wooden floorboards. There are nice picnic spots, wading and swimming pools, and good kayaking. An easy footpath runs just over a mile, one-way, upstream. During much of the year, docents and rangers teach gold panning and conduct interpretive tours.

Pioneer Park (all ages)
Nimrod Street on the outskirts of Nevada City; (530) 265–2521.

Spend the afternoon under the trees here at the playground, picnicking; playing sand volleyball, horseshoes, and tennis; or swimming in the public pool (June through August). (In Grass Valley on Minnie Street, Condon Park has similar facilities, plus disc golf and walking trails; 530–274–4390.)

Teddy Bear Castle Museum (all ages) ⓜ
203 South Pine, Nevada City; (530) 265–5804; www.teddybearcastle.com.

Thousands of teddies, in elaborate costumes and in furry plainness, inhabit various decorated scenes in a charming, circa-1860 Victorian house. Open by appointment on weekends.

Lake Spaulding (all ages) ⚠ 👥 🏖 ⛺
Located 30 miles from Nevada City, on Highway 20; (916) 386–5164.

A glacier-carved bowl of granite, at 5,000 feet, the lake is surrounded by huge boulders and a forest. This is a great day-trip destination, with good fishing for trout, small lakeside beaches, and powerboating and sailing. A small, developed campground for tents and RVs is here too.

Three Easy Wilderness Hikes
Near Nevada City

- **Independence Trail,** 8 miles north of Nevada City on Highway 49, just before the arched Yuba River Bridge, watch carefully for the sign; (530) 477–4788. My favorite Gold Country trail, because it's easy for all ages and abilities, and you get into eye-popping scenery within a minute, on 7 miles of packed dirt paths and boardwalk that is wheelchair and stroller accessible. The trail meanders through forests and at times is dramatically suspended over the Yuba River Canyon. Along the way there are picnic platforms as well as ramps leading to fishing holes.

- **Sierra Discovery Trail,** from Highway 20 take Bowman Lake Road 0.6 mile to the parking lot; (530) 386–5164. A delightful loop along the Bear River, this 1-mile, easy trail is popular, for good reason. The partly paved, partly gravel, partly boardwalk path is accessible to wheelchairs and strollers as it winds through a pine and cedar forest. Meadows are awash with wildflowers, and a small waterfall rushes year-round. Watch for water ouzels at the waterfall—they are the only American songbirds that dive into the water.

- **Bullards Bar Trail,** north from Nevada City on Highway 49 to Marysville Road, turn left and follow signs to Dark Day Picnic Area; turn right for 0.5 mile; then take left fork to trailhead; (530) 288–3231. Along the edge of Bullards Bar Reservoir, a flat, scenic trail. Stop and take a swim, catch a fish, and enjoy a picnic under a giant ponderosa pine.

Scotts Flat Lake (all ages)

Twenty minutes from Grass Valley off Highway 20; (530) 265–5302.

A nice day trip for swimming, fishing, hiking, or waterskiing, or for camping at lakeside in the national forest. Two campgrounds have developed tent and RV sites, sandy beaches, a store, paddleboat rentals, a cafe, and picnic areas. Afternoons are perfect for windsurfing and there is a network of forest trails around the lake.

49er Family Fun Park (ages 5 and up)

314 Railroad Avenue, Grass Valley; (530) 272–4949. $–$$.

Rocket around in single or double go-karts. Putt around a Gold Rush–themed, 18-hole minigolf course. Swing away in a batting cage or play some of sixty arcade games.

Auburn State Recreation Area (all ages)

Access off Highway 49 at Auburn or from Auburn-Foresthill Road; (530) 885–4527 or (530) 367–2224; www.parks.ca.gov.

Along 40 miles of the North and Middle Forks of the American River, the state maintains trails, four campgrounds, and other development for wonderful hiking, swimming, boating, fishing, biking, horseback riding, motorcycle riding, and whitewater rafting. Boat-in campgrounds at Lake Clementine are popular with fishing and water-skiing families, with good swimming beaches at the campgrounds. For information about the designated Offroad Vehicle Area, call (530) 885–5821.

Nevada County Narrow Gauge Railroad and Transportation Museum (all ages)

From Highway 49 just south of Nevada City, take the Gold Flat Road exit to 5 Kidder Court, Nevada City; (530) 470–0902; www.ncngrrmuseum.org. Free.

A new attraction displaying narrow gauge railroad cars and massive engines built between the late 1800s and early 1900s—antique stock cars, boxcars, coaches, cabooses, and more. Open weekends in winter and daily in summer.

Where to Eat

Apple Fare. 307 Broad Street, Nevada City; (530) 265–5458. Where the locals go for breakfast and for pie. Try to get seats at the big round table and listen in on the gossip. $

Flower Garden Bakery. Next to Safeway on Neal Street, Grass Valley; (530) 477–2253. Yummy home-baked goodies, sandwiches, and salads made with healthy ingredients in a casual cafe and coffee-house. Inside the cafe is the Cyber Cafe, where you can play online while you eat lunch. The last time we were there, a fourteen-year-old computer genius was running the cyber-spot. $

Gourmet to Go. 110 York Street, Nevada City; (530) 265–5697. Homemade every-thing—sandwiches, salads, soups, desserts. If you don't have a picnic spot in mind, ask the deli staff. $

Marshall's Pasties. 203 Mill Street, Grass Valley; (530) 272–2844. Introduced by early settlers from Cornwall, England, who came to work in the mines, Cornish pasties are delicious, flaky, hand-size turnover pies in which savory fillings are baked, such as potato and vegetables, ham and cheese, and fruit combinations. In forty-niner days, each miner carried a three-tiered tin lunch pail every day. The bottom was filled with tea, the pasty was placed in the middle section, and a bun was on top. The miner lit a candle under his pail at the beginning of his shift and, by the time he ate, his meal was warm. Some of the best pasties in town are baked at Marshall's: broccoli and cheese, apple-figgy, sausage, and many more. (Another good place to get pasties in Grass Valley is **Mrs. Dubble-bee's** at 251 South Auburn Street; 916–272–7700). $

Posh Nosh. 318 Broad Street, Nevada City; (530) 265–6064. On a tree-shaded patio, sandwiches, pasta, salads, and homemade desserts are memorable. $

Tofanelli's. 302 West Main, Grass Valley; (530) 272–1468. Our favorite place to take our granddaughter who lives here, because we can sit on the patio while she runs around (and around). Hearty American menu with huge plates of food, breakfast burritos, raspberry chicken. Breakfast, lunch, dinner, and Sunday brunch. $

Where to Stay

Grass Valley Courtyard Suites. 210 North Auburn Street, Grass Valley; (530) 272–7696; www.gvcourtyardsuites.com. A block from Main Street, a lovely, unique property with a small heated pool and a laundry room. The suites have equipped kitchens, gas fireplaces, decks or balconies, dining rooms, sofa beds, and rollaways; some have two queen-size beds. Continental breakfast is included and dogs are welcome. $$$–$$$$

Northern Queen Inn. 400 Railroad Avenue, off Highway 49, Nevada City; (530) 265–5824; www.northernqueeninn.com. This is the best, and most popular, place for families to stay in the area. Motel rooms are simple and spacious; chalets on the creek have loft bedrooms and kitchens. Covered swimming pool; a very good, family-oriented restaurant with a deck over a waterfall; and narrow gauge train tours on the property. $$$

For More Information

Nevada City Chamber of Commerce. 132 Main Street, Nevada City; (530) 265–2692 or (800) 655–6569; www.nevadacitychamber.com. In the stone and brick Yuba Canal Building, built in 1850 on the banks of Deer Creek.

Sutter Creek

My favorite Gold Country town, Sutter Creek is surrounded by rolling pasturelands, vineyards, and orchards—a postcard-perfect settlement with white frame houses and picket fences, giving it a New England look. Clapboard houses with porches and balconies, coupled with steepled churches, look down from the hillsides over Main Street, which is riddled with antiques shops and quaint boutiques. Among the blizzard of shops, children like My Dolly's Department Store for dolls, teddies, Beanies, and Sanrio; and Lizzie Ann's Books and Gifts for children's books and collectibles. In the Gold Miner Candy Shoppe, barrels of penny candy (no longer costs a penny) line the aisles. A nice hotel here caters to families, and plenty of exploring can be done on country roads near town. Two miles north of here, Amador City is also an antiques center. The Saturday morning farmers' market is the place to meet locals.

Chatter Box Cafe (all ages)
29 Main Street, Sutter Creek; (209) 267–5935.

My favorite cafe in my favorite town, a walk back into the 1940s. It's an old-fashioned soda fountain, nostalgic with World War II posters, big band record covers, and a long counter where town regulars meet for burgers with homemade buns, grilled cheese sandwiches, world-class onion rings, and pies, floats, sodas, and thick shakes.

Knight's Foundry (all ages)
Eureka Street, Sutter Creek; (209) 267–0201. $.

The only water-powered foundry still operating in the world. Call ahead for a schedule of tours and pourings.

Daffodil Hill (all ages)
Thirteen miles east of Sutter Creek on Shake Ridge Road; (209) 296–7048. Free.

A lovely half-hour drive alongside a creek to see wildflowers and 300,000 daffodils and tulips bloom in a farmer's field, an entire hillside exploding with color, mid-March through early April. Picnic sites.

Sutter Gold Mine (ages 4 and up)

On Highway 49 between Sutter Creek and Amador City; (888) 818–7462; www.suttergold .com. Adults $$$; children 4 to 13 $$; under 4 free. Minimum age for underground tours is 4 years.

If your family really gets interested in gold mining and its history, this is the nicest, best-organized place to try gold panning and learn about the process. You ride in a cool "Boss Buggy" shuttle truck, go underground into a mine in your hard hats, and observe gold extraction and equipment.

St. George Hotel (all ages)

Near Daffodil Hill, in Volcano; (209) 296–4458. $–$$.

Lunch and dinner in a charming, rather eccentrically decorated dining room where the menu depends on the chef's whim of the day. In the little burg of Volcano, a clutch of historic buildings remain. Sit on the hotel veranda and imagine the village of 1,000 people when it was the center of a rich mining area that produced over $90 million in gold; some remnants are an old jail, a brewery, and "Old Abe," a Civil War cannon.

Indian Grinding Rock State Historic Park (all ages)

Pine Grove–Volcano Road, Pine Grove; (209) 296–7488. $ per car.

The only state park that is primarily a monument to Native American culture. More than 1,000 grinding holes used by Miwoks are gouged out of a vast limestone surface, and you will see many petroglyphs and replicas of bark dwellings. The museum displays beautiful baskets and artifacts. Once a month Miwok elders spend time at the park, telling stories and recounting tribal history to park visitors. Nature trails and a small campground with RV sites are here too.

Where to Eat

Bellotti Inn. 53 Main Street, Sutter Creek; (209) 267–5211. Bountiful, family-style Italian dinners in the oldest continuously running hotel and saloon in California, established in 1858. $

Caffe Via d'Oro. 36 Main Street, Sutter Creek; (209) 267–0535. A surprising Mediterranean influence emerges in unique pizzas and calzones, homemade pastas, polenta, and seasonal specials at a cafe owned by a former Chez Panisse partner. Parents like the exceptional wine list; kids are quite comfortable. $–$$

Susan's Place Wine Bar and Eatery. 15 Eureka Street, in the courtyard, Sutter Creek; (209) 267–0945. Under the arbor on the patio, cheese boards, salads, soups, and sandwiches. Lunch and dinner. $–$$

Sutter Creek Ice Cream. 51 Main Street, Sutter Creek; (209) 267–0543. Have a root beer float or a snack in this charming soda fountain out of the late 1800s, with creaky wooden floors and ragtime piano music. $

Where to Stay

Aparicio's Sutter Creek Hotel. 271 Hanford Street, Sutter Creek; (209) 267–9177.

Spacious rooms with two queen beds or two doubles, plus two-room suites. Contemporary Victorian-style architecture. $–$$

Historian Inn. 271 Hanford Street/Highway 49; Sutter Creek; (209) 267–9177; www.historianinn.com. Right in town, double queen-bed rooms and suites make this a good choice for families. $$

For More Information

Sutter Creek Visitor Center. 11-A Randolph Street, P.O. Box 600, Sutter Creek 95685; (800) 400–0305 or (209) 267–1344; www.suttercreek.org.

Amador County Chamber of Commerce. At junction of Highways 49 and 88, 125 Peak Street, Jackson; (800) 649–4988 or (209) 223–0350; www.cdepot.net/chamber.

Jackson

As you approach from above on Highway 49, Jackson looks like a toy town. Picturesque streets are lined with churches and balconied houses from the mid-1800s. In my opinion, the Amador County Museum here is the premier museum of everyday life in the early days of the Gold Country. A scattering of recreational lakes is located within a short drive. Nearly eighty shops and restaurants in historic buildings line the main street.

Every year, families congregate in Calaveras County for a number of events: Snyder's Pow Wow, a May weekend of arts, crafts, gems, minerals, food, and fun on a working cattle ranch (209–772–1265); Lumberjack Day, October, featuring a parade, logging competitions, music, and food (209–293–4324); and a Civil War Reenactment in September (209–728–1251).

Amador County Museum (all ages)
Above Main Street, 225 Church Street, Jackson; (209) 223–6386. Free.

In a neighborhood of churches and homes from the mid-1800s, one of the oldest houses in town shelters a huge collection of artifacts and antiques. On the hottest summer day, it's cool and quiet in the house. Hundreds of photos re-create the Gold Rush, and you'll find a fine collection of Indian baskets, women's and men's fashions, furniture, and many domestic items from throughout the era. Part of the thousands who worked the mines and built western railroads, the Chinese are featured in displays of clothing, musical instruments, and tools. A working scale model shows the Kennedy Mine, whose 5,000-foot shaft was one of the world's deepest. Bring a picnic and take a rest under the trees while the kids run around on the grass.

Winter Fun **Near Jackson**

Bear River Lake Resort, 42 miles east of Jackson, on Highway 8; (209) 295–4868. At 5,840 feet in the Eldorado National Forest are groomed and ungroomed trails for cross-country skiers around the lake. Several snow-play hills are perfect for sleds, saucers, and inner tubes, with rentals available. A 50-mile snowmobile road loops around the lake. A general store, a snack bar, and a small resort and campground are open all year.

Kennedy Gold Mine (all ages)

One mile north of Jackson off Highway 49; (209) 223–9542. Adults $$; ages 6 to 12 $; under 6 free.

One of the best places to learn about mining history through a film, equipment, and guided tours of the mine buildings. On the north end of Jackson, in a city park, are two of the original four giant wooden Kennedy Mine tailing wheels—58 feet in diameter—that were built in 1912 to remove more than 500 tons of mine tailings a day.

National Hotel (all ages)

2 Water Street, Jackson; (209) 223–0500.

Take a look at the lobby and public rooms of the most notorious of Gold Rush hostelries. With brass chandeliers and red velvet walls, it's still infused with a spirit of cowboy-style elegance. Across the street, the 1862 IOOF Hall once housed Wells Fargo offices, where more than $100 million in gold dust and bullion were weighed.

Mokelumne Hill (all ages)

Ten minutes south of Jackson, at the bottom of a canyon of the Mokelumne River.

The once lawless town of "Mok Hill" is a quiet ghost of its former rowdy self, now a village of winding streets shaded by magnificent old locust and oak trees. Have a cold drink on the veranda of the Hotel Leger at 8304 Main, or stay for a sumptuous Italian meal served family style—rosemary garlic chicken, calamari, polenta, and pasta at reasonable prices (209–286–1401). Across the street, take a peek into the Adams and Company Genuine Old West Saloon and Museum and Less.

Calaveras County Museum and Archives (all ages)

30 North Main, San Andreas; (209) 754–6513. Free.

A unique collection of Native American and mining artifacts, interesting old documents and papers, re-created miners' cabins and stores, and a Miwok teepee. The jail out back is where Black Bart, the famous stagecoach robber and poet, languished for a time.

Roaring Camp Mining Company (all ages)

Highway 88, P.O. Box 278, Pine Grove 95665; (209) 296–4100.

An old gold camp on the Mokelumne River, featuring prospectors' cabins, (modern) bath-houses, a wildlife museum, a trading post, and a snack bar. They drive you in for a four-hour tour, fishing, and swimming, and you can stay here in a simple cabin, which includes a free Saturday-night cookout.

River **Rafting**

Wilderness rafting on one of the big rivers of the Sierra Nevada can be the highlight of a childhood and a never-to-be-forgotten family memory. Be sure to connect with an experienced company that caters to families, choose your river and your time of year carefully, and start with a day trip. The water is high and rough in early spring, and it's cold; in the summertime, the water is warmer and the rapids calmer. The South Fork of the American River and the Merced River are the most popular choices for families with younger children and first-time rafters. The waters are warm, the rapids are exciting but not too scary, and there are plenty of quiet swimming holes.

- **Outdoor Adventure River Specialists (O.A.R.S.),** P.O. Box 67, Angels Camp 95222; (209) 736–4677; www.oars.com. Over thirty years in the business of guiding families on the river, with special parent-child trips and games and toys for kids ages four to thirteen, plus activities for teens.

- **Zephyr Whitewater Expeditions,** P.O. Box 510, Columbia 95310; (800) 431–3636; www.zrafting.com. Long-established rafting company on the American, Tuolumne, Merced, and Kings Rivers. You can camp at the company's private campground near Yosemite; bring a nanny to take care of younger kids in camp while you hit the river. Free wetsuits and paddle jackets, family rates.

Lakes, Fishing, **and Watersports**

- **New Melones Lake,** just south of Angels Camp, Highway 49; (209) 785–3300; www.newmelones.com. The result of the second largest earth-filled dam in the United States, more than 100 miles of tree-lined shore dotted with campgrounds and marinas, headquarters for fishing, sailing, waterskiing, and houseboating.

- **Pardee Lake,** 12 miles from Mokelumne Hill, off Highway 26; (209) 772–1472. Popular for trout, kokanee fishing, and sailing. Swimming, waterskiing, and Jet Skis are not allowed in the lake. Also there are a nice playground, a campground, and a swimming pool.

- **Lake Amador,** 9 miles from Jackson, off Highway 88; (209) 274–4739. Some 425 surface acres of warm water for fishing, sailing, and boating, plus a one-acre swimming pond with sandy beaches, as well as a coffee shop and playgrounds. At an elevation of 500 feet in the Sierra foothills, it can be very hot and dry in midsummer and early fall. Developed campground and RV sites.

- **Lake Camanche,** 15 miles southwest of Jackson, off Highway 88; (209) 772–1472. A big stretch of water, 33 miles around, created by a dam on the Mokelumne. You'll find it all here: large campgrounds, marinas, and cottage resorts; everything from riding stables, a dance pavilion, tennis courts, bike rentals, and water slides to Jet Skis.

Angels Camp (all ages)

At Highways 49 and 4; (800) 225–3764.

The site of the Jumping Frog Jubilee every May. Commemorating Mark Twain's famous story, "The Celebrated Jumping Frog of Calaveras County," the popular frog competition is open to all. You can even rent a frog and try your own version of the wild gyrations necessary to make the frogs win the jumping contests.

The setting for Brett Harte's famous story "The Luck of Roaring Camp," the town of Angels Camp is a complex of historic buildings, shops, hotels, and museums, enough to fill an afternoon. In a grassy, midtown park is equipment from five mines that pulled in more than $20 million in gold between 1886 and 1920. The **City of Angels Museum** at 753 Main (209–736–2181) displays pioneer and Gold Rush antiques and artifacts, carriages, mining and farm equipment, and a steam locomotive.

Where to Eat

Angels Creek Cafe. 1246 South Main Street, Angels Camp; (209) 736–2941. Stop in for local gossip and advice on the area at this popular breakfast spot. Dig into Sue's big omelets and platters of eggs and home fries with homemade biscuits. $

Cafe Max. 140 Main Street, Jackson; (209) 223–0174. Open early for Swiss pastries fresh out of the 1865 brick oven, and all day for sandwiches, salads, and desserts. $–$$

Piaggi's. 1262 South Main Street, Angels Camp; (209) 736–4862. Fresh pasta, cioppino, steaks, burgers. $–$$

Upstairs Restaurant. 164 Main Street, Jackson; (209) 223–3342. Upstairs is a "ferny," art-filled environment for a sophisticated California cuisine menu; downstairs the Streetside Bistro is perfect for sandwiches and pizza lunches. Both are casual enough for kids. $–$$

Where to Stay

Angels Inn Motel. 600 North Main Street, Angels Camp; (209) 736–4242. Nice motel rooms; and big family units with kitchens, dishwashers, refrigerators, and stoves, microwaves, books, king-size beds, two sofabeds, large living rooms, and two TVs. Small pool, laundry. $–$$

For More Information

Amador County Chamber of Commerce. At the junction of Highways 49 and 88, 125 Peak Street, Jackson; (800) 649–4988 or (209) 223–0350; www.amadorcountychamber.com.

Calaveras County Visitors Center. 1301 South Main Street, Angels Camp; (800) 225–3764 or (209) 736–0049; www.visit calaveras.org; e-mail: frogmail@calaveras .org.

Columbia

The most perfectly re-created Mother Lode settlement in the United States, Columbia is a state historic park where the 1850s are relived by costumed performers, by horse-drawn vehicles, and by sights and sounds of the past that make you feel as if you've fallen back in time. When gold was discovered here, the population exploded within a month from less than 100 to 6,000 people, and 150 saloons, gambling halls, and stores opened up. Many of the western false-front and two-story brick buildings with iron shutters remain, housing the shops, restaurants, and museums of today.

The town is absolutely captivating to children, who love the costumed storekeepers and wagon drivers, the innkeepers and blacksmiths, the street musicians and itinerant actors. Musicians and performers are encountered on the street corners and in the restaurants and theater. Horse-drawn stages clip-clop up and down the main street, which is free of auto traffic, while artisans demonstrate horseshoeing, woodcarving, and other vintage crafts. You can pan for gold in the creeks near town, take a horseback ride, and have a sarsaparilla at an old-fashioned ice-cream parlor.

Shops on **Main Street**

- **Dreamwest Trading Company.** Real gold nuggets and lots of interesting rocks, guidebooks, and history books.

- **Columbia Candy Kitchen.** Four generations of the same family make fresh taffy, brittles, fudge, and penny candy.

- **Cosmos Daguerrean.** Dress up the family in the forty-niner costumes provided and have your tintypes taken.

- **Village Pharmacy.** Rows of bottles of strange remedies, plus dentist's office exhibits with hand drills and anything-but-painless tools for the teeth.

- **Bearcloud Gallery.** American Indian art and curios.

- **Candle and Soap Works.** In an old feed store, freshly milled soaps in clove, chocolate, lavender, and more scents, as well as candle kits and homemade candles.

The town is crowded with visitors and hot during summer vacation, although pines and maples do shade the boardwalks. The mild months of spring and fall are the best times to visit. A lively schedule of festivals and special events is conducted all year in Columbia, from the Fireman's Muster in May to a "Glorious Fourth" celebration in July and the Fiddle and Banjo Contest in October.

William Cavalier Museum (all ages) 🏛 🔵
Main and State Streets, Columbia; (209) 532–0150. Free.

The Columbia experience is enriched by "talking buttons" outside several storefronts. Push the museum buttons to hear about the museum displays in the windows. Tread the creaky floorboards within to see photos of people who lived here during the Gold Rush, as well as to eye huge chunks of ore, quartz, and semiprecious stones. At the height of Columbia's fame as the Gem of the Southern Mines, $1.5 billion in gold was weighed on the Wells Fargo Express scales.

Columbia Grammar School (all ages) 🏛 🔵
On the north end of Main Street, Columbia.

In use from 1860 to 1937, with an endearing collection of antique desks, inkwells, books, and slates that children used in their schoolroom.

Columbia Stage (all ages)
Catch the stage on Main Street at the Wells Fargo Express, Columbia; (209) 588–0808. $–$$.

One of the greatest treats for younger children is a ride through town and into the woods and hills nearby.

Douglass Saloon (all ages)
Main Street, Columbia; (209) 533–2355.

Push open the swinging doors and step right into this classic western bar (children welcome) for a sarsaparilla and watch the street scene through the open shutters.

Coyote Creek at Natural Bridges (all ages)
Parrott's Ferry Road, near Columbia.

A short, easy walk on a streamside nature trail. You may see people swimming here and rafting through a colorful limestone cave—not as scary as it looks.

Columbia State Historic Park Walking Tours (all ages)
22708 Broadway, Columbia; (209) 532–4301; e-mail: tours@goldrush.com. Tickets $.

From the main museum, at 11:00 A.M. and 1:30 P.M. daily, forty-five-minute guided walking tours of Columbia, including historic structures unavailable to the public.

Where to Eat

Columbia House Restaurant. Main Street, Columbia; (209) 532–5134. Hearty American fare for breakfast, lunch, and dinner. $–$$

Goldstreet Bakery Cafe. 22690 South Gold Street, Columbia; (209) 532–5397. Just outside the state park, open early for breakfast and lunch. Owner Anne-Marie Holmes uses organic ingredients and local produce in healthy menu items like home-made soups, salads, and vegetarian dishes, inch-thick french toast, and fruit pastries. Breads are baked here and juices are fresh-squeezed. Sit outside under the trees. $

Lickskillet Cafe. 11256 State Street, Columbia; (209) 536–9599. American home-style cooking: rosemary roasted chicken with mashed potatoes and roasted garlic gravy, rib-eye steak, Cajun meat loaf, curried chicken—bring your appetites. In a historic cottage behind the museum, dine inside or on the porch; lunch and dinner served. $$

Where to Stay

Columbia Gem Motel. One mile from Columbia, 22131 Parrotts Ferry Road; (209) 532–4508. Simple cottages and motel rooms in a pine grove. $

Columbia Inn Motel. Adjacent to Columbia State Historic Park, 22646 Broadway Street, Columbia; (209) 533–0446; www.columbiainnmotel.com. Two-bedroom units, plus suites sleeping four; simple accommodations. Pool, restaurant, and picnic area. $

Marble Quarry RV Park. 11551 Yankee Hill Road, Columbia; (209) 532–9539; www.marblequarry.com. Wooded setting, pool, playground. $

Trails End RV Park. 21770 Parrotts Ferry Road, Columbia; (209) 533–2395. One of several RV parks near Columbia, offering shady sites, a store, and nightly campfire gatherings. $

For More Information

Columbia State Historic Park. Fourteen miles south of Angels Camp, off Highway 49, Columbia; (209) 532–0150.

Underground Adventures

If your family has never toured underground caverns, you'll be fascinated by how beautiful they are. On a hot summer day in Gold Country, it's totally cool to see fantastic crystalline formations; gigantic, multicolored mineral towers; and stalagmites and stalactites. Caverns are not particularly claustrophobic— believe me, I would know. Family members do need to be able to walk easily up and down stairs. Very small children should be carried in backpacks. Toddlers might be scared if/when the lights are turned off for a moment, which is sometimes done to show how dark the dark can be; ask about this possibility before you buy a ticket.

- **California Caverns,** 8 miles east of Highway 49 off Mountain Ranch Road, San Andreas; (209) 736–2708; www.caverntours.com. Open to the public since 1850. Eighty-minute tours wind through narrow passageways and limestone chambers 200 feet high.

- **Mercer Caverns,** 1 mile north of Murphys, at 1667 Sheep Ranch Road; (209) 728–2101; www.mercercaverns.com. $$. One-hour tour featuring magnificent mineral formations.

- **Moaning Cavern,** Parrots Ferry Road, 2 miles south of Vallecito; (209) 736–2708. Forty-five-minute tour, featuring a 100-foot spiral staircase. For the adventurous this cavern offers a three-hour, 180-foot descent by rope in the main chamber, with equipment supplied.

- **Black Chasm,** between Volcano and Pinegrove, off the Volcano-Pinegrove Road; (209) 736–2708; www.caverntours.com. Adults $$; ages 3 to 13 $. Descend steep and narrow stairways into a dreamlike world of wavering, dripping draperies of flowstone and glowing subterranean lakes, crystal formations, stalactites and stalagmites. It is a steady, damp sixty degrees year-round.

Jamestown

Boomed and busted several times in the past 150 years, Jamestown retains an anything-can-happen Wild West atmosphere, from the days when it was just a cluster of tents on a dusty road. When the gold began to rush, saloons and dance halls were erected, then hotels and homes. Antiques and curio shops line Main Street today, and almost as many saloons and restaurants. This is one town where children enjoy the shops as much as their parents do. Most of the restaurants in town are casual and reasonably priced for family groups.

You can pan for gold near Jamestown, stay in a vintage hotel, and take a ride on a steam train. If Jamestown looks familiar to you, it may be because the movie *Butch Cassidy and the Sundance Kid* was filmed here. As in most of the Gold Country, summer temperatures are in the nineties and higher. If you have any doubt about whether there is still gold in them thar hills, a sixty-pound slab of pure gold was discovered in the Jamestown Mine in 1993.

Visitors and residents get into the spirit of the Mother Lode by dressing in period costume for annual theme events such as Old West reenactments. You can purchase or rent beautiful Victorian and Western apparel at Dragoons (18231 Main Street; 209–984–1848). David and Deborah Wright will outfit you in cowboy boots and hats, fancy dresses and feathered hats, beaded purses, and fringed buckskin jackets and vests. The days of the desperadoes are re-created every September at the Jamestown Shoot 'Em Up, when bewhiskered cowboys and wild-eyed outlaws swagger up and down the sidewalks, their six-guns smokin'.

Railtown 1897 State Historic Park (all ages)
Fifth Avenue and Reservoir Road, Jamestown; (209) 984–3953; www.csrmf.org. Free.
Rides and tours: adults $$; children $; ages 5 and under are free.

Plan a half-day at this twenty-acre exhibit of vintage steam locomotives and passenger cars, a roundhouse, and a railroad shop. Take a one-hour train ride through the foothills or the two-hour Twilight Limited, a sort of sunset cruise with refreshments, entertainment, and a barbecue dinner at the end. Trains operate weekends, April through October, and there are special theme excursions on holidays. This is a great place for a picnic at tables or on the lawns under the aspens and maples, within sight and sound of the exciting action on the track—whistles, bells, steam, and smoke.

Costumed conductors and workers are railroad and train lovers, and they are loaded with great stories and information. You can take a guided or self-guided tour of the roundhouse to see one-hundred-ton locomotives and a blacksmith at his fiery task. Around the site are numerous photogenic artifacts from the many movies that were shot here, including *Dodge City, High Noon, Back to the Future III*, and *Wild Wild West*. In the train station shop is a huge collection of railroad- and train-related books and lots of fun things for kids, from games and toys to books and kits.

Gold Prospecting Expeditions (all ages)

18170 Main Street, Jamestown; (209) 984–4653 or (800) 596–0009; www.goldprospecting.com. **Panning on the sidewalk $; trips $$$$.**

When you see people panning for gold in a wooden trough on the main street, you're here. They will give you information about panning and prospecting day trips and about rafting trips on nearby creeks and rivers. One gold-bearing creek is less than five minutes away. They run a special one-day excursion to a re-created mining camp on Wood's Creek. You will get more gold on this trip than on others because of the use of a sluice box, and you can camp there too.

The Mossy Bog (ages 5 and up)

18145-8 Main Street, Jamestown; (209) 527–1845.

If your child loves fairies, gnomes, and elves, he or she will find this a magical place. Whimsical home and garden accessories and gifts are densely packed into this tiny shop, from frogs hiding under mushroom umbrellas to flying angels and colorful birdfeeders. Toddlers with busy fingers might get into trouble here as many of the collectibles are within their reach.

Where to Eat

Here's the Scoop. 18242 Main Street, Jamestown; (209) 984–4583. Incredible banana splits, shakes, and ice-cream concoctions, plus homemade desserts, sandwiches, salads, and espresso drinks. $

Historic National Hotel. 18183 Main Street, Jamestown; (209) 984–3446; www.national-hotel.com. In a shady garden courtyard, lunch, brunch and dinners are among the best in town; the wine list is a *Wine Spectator* award-winner. Kids may be uncomfortable in the elegant dining room, yet they will like sitting outdoors and digging into an Italian burger, potato skins with bacon and cheese, and cheese tortellini. Adults are partial to such sophisticated dishes as escargot, halibut with apricot glaze, steak sandwiches, and trout. A historic landmark built in 1895, the hotel is a beauty. $$

Lulu's Saloon and Grill. 18201 Main Street, Jamestown; (209) 984–3678. A ceiling full of vintage lamps and chandeliers creates a fun atmosphere in this former bank, built in 1916. $–$$

Michelangelo's. 18228 Main Street, Jamestown; (209) 984–4830. In an ultra-modern, Euro-cafe atmosphere, the best in town for pizza, nouvelle Italian food, pasta. The circa-1910 building served as the post office for decades. $–$$

The Smoke Cafe. 18191 Main Street, Jamestown; (209) 984–3733. Tex-Mex specialties, Southwest decor. Lunch and dinner. Built in 1927, the building is a good example of Pueblo revival architecture popular in the twenties. $–$$

The Willow Steakhouse. 18273 Main Street, Jamestown; (209) 984–3998. In a roadhouse built in 1862, dig into platters of steak of every description from filet mignon to pepper steak to London broil, plus hot and cold sandwiches. Ask about the ghosts. $–$$

For More Information

Tuolumne County Visitors Bureau. 55 West Stockton Street, P.O. Box 4020, Sonora 95370; (800) 446–1333; www.the greatunfenced.com. Among Gold Country souvenirs you can purchase from the Web site are gold nuggets, the book *California Desperadoes,* a Roy Rogers and Dale Evans T-shirt, and maps and guides to the area.

Jamestown Visitor's Information Center. 18239 Main Street, Jamestown; (209) 984–4616.

High Sierra South

Midway in the 400-mile wave of California's great Sierra Nevada Range, Yosemite National Park is a jewel box of granite monoliths sparkling with some of the highest waterfalls on the continent. Within the 1,070-square-mile park are snowy alpine peaks, subalpine forests, and meadowlands, all crisscrossed with hundreds of miles of hiking trails.

Add to this groves of giant sequoias—the largest living things on earth—and two mighty rivers, the Merced and the Tuolumne, plus historical museums, theaters, campgrounds, and lodges, and it's no wonder that more than three million tourists visit annually. Families return year after year to tent in sunny campgrounds along the Merced, to hike silent trails in the High Country, and to marvel again at El Capitan and Half Dome in Yosemite Valley. In fact, it's the most revisited national park in the country, as well as the oldest.

North of Yosemite, in a spectacular meadow at 7,200 feet, Bear Valley is surrounded by a panorama of snowcapped mountains. In summer families go mountain biking and hiking, play tennis, swim and float on the Stanislaus River, and camp and fish at eight nearby lakes. In winter a casual, reasonably priced ski resort brings families back to the valley.

A busy gateway to the south gate of Yosemite, the town of Oakhurst is a mecca for antiques lovers and for families on their way to Bass Lake and the Sierra National Forest. The small town offers family-friendly motels and restaurants, plus a few surprises. Within a few minutes' drive are a wonderful steam train, a magnificent sequoia grove, and a unique luxury resort that caters to families.

Bear Valley

Poised 7,200 feet high in Stanislaus National Forest, Bear Valley means good times on mountain lakes and quiet forest trails, along with laid-back Nordic and downhill skiing. Your family can spend several days here hiking the trails in Calaveras Big Trees State Park and camping and fishing on the Stanislaus River. Alpine lakes are sprinkled about nearby Ebbetts Pass and the Carson-Iceberg Wilderness area. Mountain biking and, on the river, canoeing and kayaking are popular summer sports. The midsummer Bear Valley Music

HIGH SIERRA SOUTH

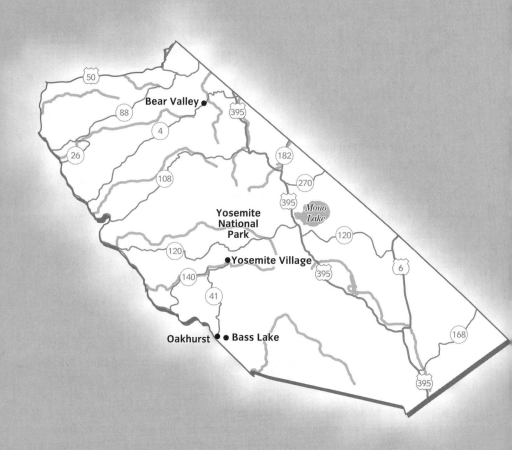

Bear Valley •

Yosemite
National
Park

• Yosemite Village

Mono
Lake

Oakhurst • • Bass Lake

50
88
4
395
26
182
108
270
395
120
120
6
140
395
41
168
395

Festival is a popular annual event that brings hundreds of visitors to hear big-name classi-cal, opera, and jazz performances outdoors in spectacular mountain meadow settings (800–458–1618).

Winter fun consists of skiing on one of the most extensive networks of cross-country trails in the nation, skiing downhill on Mount Reba, and skating on a frozen pond. Saturday nights around the ice rink are out of a storybook, with music, lights, and a bonfire.

With 450 inches of snow annually at Bear Valley, the white stuff can pile up. My chil-dren and I spent a weekend here learning to ski, and we literally climbed into and over 3 feet of snow to our cabin—which was fun . . . sort of. The next time I'll call ahead to be sure a path is cleared before we arrive. What I liked best about skiing with the kids here is that everything at the ski resort and within the village is close together and the atmos-phere definitely is family-oriented and reasonably priced.

Above Bear Valley on Highway 4, 8,730-foot-high Ebbetts Pass is the road to glory in spring, when heavy snowmelt rushes off in a million waterfalls and wildflowers run riot over the meadows and beneath aromatic forests of Jeffrey pine, incense cedar, white fir, oaks, and the massive sequoias.

Just past the state park on Highway 4, on the way to Bear Valley, stop at Dorrington, a tiny former stagecoach stop, where you can take a peek in the vintage saloon and have a Northern Italian dinner at the hotel. Ask for directions to the largest sugar pine in the world—32 feet around, 220 feet tall. Board's Crossing Road near Dorrington leads to sev-eral campgrounds on the Stanislaus River.

Snow **Play**

Around the valley and along Highway 4 above Bear Valley are several snow-play areas and cross-country ski trailheads, including U.S. For-est Service roads used by both skiers and snowmobilers. Besides the developed areas (listed below), watch for roadside play hills from Dorrington to Bear Valley.

- **Cottage Springs,** 8 miles east of Arnold, on Highway 4; (209) 795–1209. Tube hill and rentals; sledding hill for kids to age ten. There is also downhill skiing for beginners—a good, inexpensive place for younger kids to take lessons.

- **Bear Valley Sledding Hill,** Highway 4 in Bear Valley; (209) 753–2834. For kids four to ten, $$ including sled rental.

- **Lake Alpine Snow Park,** 2 miles west of Bear Valley, off High-way 4; (209) 795– 1381. Sledding hill with rentals. You must buy a parking permit at the ranger station on Highway 4, near at the Mount Reba Ski Area turnoff.

Bear Valley Village 🍴 🚌 🔒

Forty-five miles east of Angels Camp, on Highway 4; (209) 753–2327.

Two carved wooden grizzlies greet you at the entrance to the village, a small complex anchored by Bear Valley Lodge and the Village Center, where you'll find a general store, a coffee shop, a few galleries, and places to buy sports clothing and equipment (shop for groceries and essentials on the way up here in Arnold, 20 miles south, where prices are more reasonable). Surrounded by condos and houses that are rented by the day or the week, the village is the headquarters for the ski area and for renting summer sports equipment and boats. Most roads are not plowed in winter, giving the valley a picturesque, alpine look. Highway 4 stays open year-round to about 3 miles above Bear Valley Village.

Bear Valley Lodge 🍴 🚌

P.O. Box 5038, Bear Valley 95223; (209) 753–2327; www.bearvalleylodge.com. $$–$$$$.

Simple, spacious rooms in a five-story lodge, plus a pool, tennis courts, restaurants, and an inviting atrium lounge with a huge fireplace made of king-size boulders; European-style breakfast buffet. Among the accommodations are rooms with two twins and a double; rooms with two doubles; and nice suites with a queen and a sofa bed. In winter you can cross-country ski and access the lifts from the lodge. If you decide to stay more than a day or two, condominiums and cabin rentals in the village are the way to go (800–794–3866).

Calaveras Big Trees State Park (all ages) 🏕 👫 ⛺ 🎿

Four miles east of Arnold, on Highway 4; (209) 795–2334. Open all year.

In spring white-flecked branches of blooming mountain dogwood hover over your vehicle as you drive into the park on South Grove Road. Like red Christmas candles, snow plants burst up in flaming spikes through the last remnants of snow.

The really big trees, the sequoias, are here. One giant stands 320 feet high, and another measures 27 feet around. The biggest trees—1,300 of them—are found in the South Grove, 1 mile from the parking lot up the Big Trees Creek Trail. Short nature trails are accessible near the visitor center, and a network of trails leads to high ridgetops above the valley.

Winding through the park, the Stanislaus River has sandy, pebbly beaches for swimming and wading. Developed campsites are set up for RVs to 27 feet, and environmental campsites are available for backpackers.

The park is a popular cross-country ski area. A 1-mile loop near the main parking area and an outer 3-mile loop are groomed; snowmobiles are not allowed. At 4,800 elevation, snow is not always present, so it's best to call ahead for snow conditions.

Bear Valley Mountain Resort (all ages)

Highway 4 at Highway 207, P.O. Box 5038, Bear Valley 95223; (209) 753–2301; www.bear valley.com. All-day lift tickets: ages 13 and up $$$$; seniors and ages 7 to 12 $$$; kids under 6 free.

At this family-oriented ski mountain, the emphasis is on beginner and intermediate skiing. Special programs are set up for little kids ages four to eight (Skiing Bears), for nine- to twelve-year-olds (Bear Scouts), and for teens and adults. There is all-day "Bear Care" too. The Grizzly Snowboard Den is a boarder only rental and lesson center; snowboarders have a snazzy new terrain park. Among features of the recent multimillion dollar expansion are a new 300-foot Panda Carpet lift for beginner lessons, a huge dining deck overlooking the gigantic Mokelumne Canyon, and a new children's equipment rental center.

First-timers are VIPs, with free guided ski tours of the mountain on weekends. Lift ticket and rental prices are considerably cheaper here than at Lake Tahoe ski resorts. You can ski to Bear Valley Village on Lunch Run or Home Run or get to and from the village on the free shuttle.

The cross-country ski area has the largest track system in the central Sierras, 65 miles of groomed trails with warming huts and endless acres of unmarked meadows (209–753–2834; www.bearvalleyxc.com).

Ice skating is popular on a frozen lake. On weekend nights, lights, music, and a bonfire make skating fun to try and to watch. You can take lessons, too.

Bear Valley Adventure Company

Highway 4 and Bear Valley Road, Bear Valley; (209) 753–2834; www.bear-valley.org. Open all year. Rental and lesson prices vary.

In the summer families can rent kayaks, canoes, and mountain bikes here, and get fishing equipment and bait. You can rent a fishing pole for $5.00. This is a good place to get maps and advice about recreation in the area, including the *Bear Valley Mountain Bike Trail Guide*. Ask about the Morning Meadow Bike Tour, which meanders through a scenic private meadow, and the east bike trail to Lake Alpine. You can also arrange here for half-day kayaking lessons on Lake Alpine and for "Moonlight Paddles."

In the winter rent cross-country skiing, sledding, ice skating, and snowshoeing equipment.

Tamarack Pines Inn and Cross-Country Ski Center

18326 Highway 4, 2.5 miles west of Bear Valley, Tamarack-Bear Valley; (209) 753–2080; www.tamarackpinesinn.com. $$–$$$$; ask about ski packages.

Families return every year with their young children for the easily accessible Nordic skiing on 90 kilometers of groomed trails here, and they make this a summer headquarters for the myriad outdoor recreation activities nearby. The place is very child-oriented. The lodge rooms are simple and fresh, with small kitchens, and there is a complimentary continental breakfast. The common room for all guests has a fireplace, refrigerator and microwave oven, satellite TV, a VCR and video library, books, and a children's play area.

Some rooms have extra-long twins, sofa beds, and child's beds; no pets allowed. There is a little sledding hill, and sleds are available to use.

Lake Alpine ⚠️ 🚤 ⛺ 🎿
Two miles northeast of Bear Valley, off Highway 4; (209) 795–1381.

The closest lake to the village, Lake Alpine is popular for kayaking, canoeing, and sailing and is regularly stocked with rainbow trout. Hiking and equestrian trails lead to the Carson-Iceberg Wilderness and into the Mokelumne Wilderness. Situated around the lake are four campgrounds, a backpackers' camping area, and two swimming beaches, a restaurant, and a general store. At Lake Alpine Lodge you can rent a variety of boats, canoes, kayaks, and windsurfing boards. In the summertime this is a popular, crowded, sometimes noisy, yet idyllic mountain lake.

A snow-play area lies just south of the parking lot. Snowmobilers and cross-country skiers head from here into the backcountry on the road to Mosquito Lake.

Utica, Union, and Spicer Meadow Reservoirs ⚠️ 🚤 〜 ⛺
Four miles west of Bear Valley, off Highway 4; (209) 795–1381.

Quieter and less developed than the popular Lake Alpine and great for launching your own small boat and fishing for trout, bass, and catfish. No waterskiing, no Jet Skis—ah, heaven. A lyrical day trip can be had by renting lightweight kayaks and a car rack and spending the day paddling and picnicking and messing around on one of the reservoir lakes. Surrounded by dark forest and sun-warmed boulders, with plenty of shallow spots for wading, these glittering gems are easily accessible.

Another campground is available at Spicer; day-use facilities include picnic tables, barbecue grills, and restrooms. Boating here is restricted to a speed limit of 10 miles per hour.

Where to Eat

Creekside Dining Room. Bear Valley Lodge; (209) 753–2327. California cuisine and American comfort food are on the menu for dinner in the lodge dining room; light meals are also available in the Grizzly Lounge. $–$$

Headwaters Coffee House. In the Village Center, Bear Valley; (209) 753–2708. Yummy baked goods, ice cream, breakfast, and lunch; pizza, microbrews, and espresso drinks. Check your e-mail here. $

Lake Alpine Lodge. Two miles from Bear Valley off Highway 4; (209) 795–1382. By the stone fireplace or outdoors on the deck, chicken and mushroom fettuccine alfredo, prime rib, and steak for dinner; char-broiled sandwiches, soups, and salads for lunch; and hearty appetizers in the lounge. Children get the usual spaghetti and chicken nuggets on their menu, plus tri-tip steak and pasta primavera. $–$$

Where to Stay

Bear Valley Condominium and Cabin Rentals. Alpine Condo Management; (209) 753–2503. Bear Valley Condo Management; (209) 753–6201. Bear Valley Real Estate; (209) 753–2334. $$–$$$

Lake Alpine Lodge. Two miles from Bear Valley, off Highway 4; (209) 753–6358; www.lakealpinelodge.com. A family-oriented resort on the lake, offering house-keeping and tent cabins, a general store, a restaurant, boat and bike rentals, laundry facilities, and showers. $–$$$$

Tamarack Lodge at Bear Valley. Two miles west of Bear Valley Village; (209) 753–2080; www.tamarack-bearvalley.com. A unique complex with a variety of suites, chalets, and a cabin, all set up for large or small family groups. The atmosphere is casual, the mountain-theme decor fresh and unassuming. Some units have kitchens; some have microwaves and small refrigerators. Big advantages for families are the common room with fireplace, a separate kids' play area with TV and VCR, complimentary continental breakfast, and a sledding hill. $$–$$$$

U.S. Forest Service Campground Reservations. (209) 795–1381. $

For More Information

CalTrans Highway 4 Road Conditions. (209) 948–7858.

Calaveras Ranger District. 5314 Highway 4, Hathaway Pines; (209) 795–1391.

Yosemite National Park

Spring in Yosemite means wildflowers and waterfalls. The shining water curtains of Bridalveil, Nevada, Vernal, and Yosemite Falls are all visible from the valley floor. Within the spectacular view corridor of Yosemite Valley are Half Dome, El Capitan, Cathedral Spires, Royal Arches, and myriad more granite columns, domes, and pinnacles created by millions of years of glacial activity. Like the Grand Canyon, Yosemite Valley is one of those places that you and your children must see, at least once in your lifetime.

Campgrounds, lodges, and most of the public facilities—including grocery stores, theaters, and restaurants—are located in the eastern end of the valley. Sightseeing in the valley is best done on foot, on 12 miles of bike trails, and on free shuttle buses. Little kids can come along on a bike ride—at Yosemite Lodge or Curry Village, rent a bike with a trailer that fits one child (or two small toddlers or babies); helmets are free. You can also rent strollers and jogging strollers.

From spring through fall, the park service offers guided horseback rides in Yosemite Valley, Tuolumne Meadows, and Wawona; longer rides and wilderness pack trips are available, and you can rent horses or bring your own (209–372–8348). Rafting and tubing on the Merced River in Yosemite Valley are popular during the hot summer months, and that stretch of river is calm enough for first-timers and children. Rent a raft or bring your own nonmotorized flotation device; kids must weigh at least fifty pounds (209–372–8341). In what some claim is the world's premier rock climbing area, climbing lessons for all abilities are conducted in the valley and at Tuolumne Meadows, with equipment provided (209–372–8344).

When the snow flies in Yosemite, the number of visitors drops dramatically and activities center on Crane Flat, Badger Pass Ski Area, and Yosemite Valley. Rangers lead snowshoe walks and ski tours from several locations. With icicle-clad Half Dome looking on, skating is fun to try or to watch at the outdoor rink in Curry Village.

If you are nervous about driving on snowy roads, take a two-hour, narrated winter sightseeing tour of Yosemite Valley in a comfortable motor coach with large windows.

Plan your trip in advance by reading about the events, activities, and seminars offered throughout the year—download seasonal issues of *Yosemite Today* from the National Park Service at www.nps.gov/yose/index.htm. This is the free tabloid that is handed to you at the park entrance gates. You can also download the *Yosemite Guide,* which provides more general information and check out "Trip Planning" on the Web site for detailed information not shown in the publications. The park is open year-round, 365 days a year, twenty-four hours a day. Reservations are not required to enter the park; private vehicles are always welcome. The park entrance fee is $20 per vehicle and all occupants.

Summertime midday temperatures in the park, particularly in the valley, may top ninety degrees, and the sun is intense at this elevation, between 3,000 and 4,500 feet. Plan young children's strenuous activities for times other than between late morning and midafternoon. Have them carry a daypack loaded with water, sunglasses, a hat, sunscreen, and insect repellent.

Everyone Comes **to Yosemite**

One million people visit Yosemite in July and August, 80 percent of them remaining in the valley, which is just 1 percent of the park, where most of the public facilities and the best-known postcard views are found.

To avoid crowded campgrounds, high-season traffic, and people glut, opt to come in spring or fall. If summer is your only choice, come on weekdays and stick to the two quieter but no less attractive areas of the park, Wawona and Tuolumne. The southern section of the park, Wawona, is loaded with historic architecture, shady camping spots along a tributary of the Merced, and some of the tallest and oldest trees in the world.

You can get away from people and midsummer heat by heading for the Tuolumne High Country, to campgrounds, lakes, and cool, wildflower-bedecked Tuolumne Meadows at 8,600 feet.

Visitor Center (all ages)
Yosemite Village, shuttle stop 5; (209) 372–0299.

Come here for information and advice from park service rangers; make reservations for guided walks, hikes, classes, live theater, musical programs, and exhibits. Watch slide shows and films; browse dioramas, exhibits, and the excellent bookstore for guidebooks, posters, videos, maps, and great books for children. You will find a handy courtesy phone with which to make lodging reservations. The center is open daily 8:00 A.M. to 6:00 P.M. in summer, with more limited hours seasonally.

Ansel Adams Gallery and Photo Walks (all ages)
Yosemite Village, shuttle stops 5 and 9; (209) 372–4413; www.anseladams.com.

The works of the world-famous photographer of Yosemite, Ansel Adams, are on display and for sale here, along with fine-art prints, photos, calendars, posters, handcrafted home accessories, Indian-motif silver jewelry, great books for kids, and a terrific collection of fiction and nonfiction books, all in a serene, elegant atmosphere. Ask about the **free** photography walks that start here daily. (Check at Yosemite Lodge about the Sunrise Camera Walks held there.)

Happy Isles Nature Center (ages 5–12)
Shuttle stop 16; (209) 372–0287.

Films, puppet shows, exhibits, and wildlife programs designed for kids. Here and at Tuolumne Meadows, a Junior Ranger Program is conducted for eight- to twelve-year-olds. To earn a Junior Ranger patch, the children listen to interpretive talks on ecology, Native Americans, and wildlife and go on ranger-guided treks.

At the Happy Isles bookstore, consider purchasing an Explorer Pack, a daypack filled with a guidebook and activity suggestions. Each pack has a theme, such as Featuring Feathers, a bird identification kit, and Rocking in Yosemite, for rock and mineral discoveries. For children ages three to six, purchase the *Little Cub Handbook* here or online at www.yosemitestore.com. A fun teaching tool, the book is about matching animals with their homes, taking a hike, learning about bears, and more. When they have attended a ranger program and completed the book, kids receive a Little Cub button.

You can leave children at Happy Isles for **free** one-hour walks and talks on nature, birds, and forest lore. This area of the park is full of streams perfect for wading and scattered with mossy boulders. The open forest calls for a game of hide-and-seek. Happy Isles is the start of several trails, including the Mist Trail.

Art Activity Center (ages 10 and up)
Yosemite Village, shuttle stop 2; (209) 372–1442. Free.

Outdoor art classes are conducted in watercolor, sketching, and mixed media. Children over ten with long attention spans and genuine interest in art may participate; those under twelve must be accompanied by a parent or guardian. You will find here a small, well-stocked shop selling artists' materials and equipment, including top-quality watercolor paints and oils, brushes, paper, pens and pencils, and children's art kits. The store is open spring through fall.

Indian Village and Yosemite Museum (all ages)
Next to the Visitor Center; (209) 372–0282. Free.

Yosemite's native Miwok and Paiute hunter-gatherers from 1850 to the present are featured in photos; see priceless baskets, feather capes, and other artifacts. Local artisans demonstrate basket weaving, beadwork, and traditional games. Upstairs in the research library, which is open to all, wonderful nineteenth- and twentieth-century photos and books are worth a look.

Behind the museum in a pine and oak forest, a self-guided trail introduces the daily life, history, and language of the Southern Miwoks, in a reconstructed Miwok-Paiute village of 1872. Basketry, food preparation, and arts of the Ahwahneeche people are on display in the model village, and ranger talks and walks are offered frequently.

Ahwahnee Hotel
Shuttle stop 3; (559) 252–4848 or (209) 372–1488; www.yosemitepark.com. Room rates begin at about $357 for a double; packages are available.

A stunning masterpiece of art deco and California Craftsman architecture, the monumental Ahwahnee Hotel opened in 1927 and has been one of the icons of Yosemite Valley ever since, a must-see tourist attraction and a fabulous place to stay. Native American baskets and artifacts, historic photos and artworks, and Persian and American Indian rugs create a museum-like atmosphere. Notice the photos of cowboys and Indians in the Great Room.

Hung with baronial chandeliers, the 130-foot-long dining room is world-famous for its beauty and views through sky-high windows. A pianist plays for dinner, and on the menu are top-notch California cuisine and American comfort food. The dining room is elaborately decorated and glowing with candles and merriment every Christmas season, when the medieval-style Bracebridge Dinners are held.

The gift shop is loaded with pricey Yosemite-theme gifts and guidebooks, calendars, and postcards. You can purchase polo shirts, sweaters, purses, and Native American–inspired items such as kachina dolls, rawhide drums, handcrafted silver jewelry, pottery, and rugs. "Native Critters" are fanciful figures decorated with fur, feather, and leather, with price tags in the hundreds (209–372–1409).

There is a pool, and you can walk or bike from here, or take the shuttle, to all valley sites.

Each with a glorious view through big windows, guest rooms have been redecorated in mountain lodge style, with comfy sofas and chairs, original art, and nice, if small, bathrooms. Some are parlor rooms with separate sitting rooms. Cottages in a forest glade are spacious, with fireplaces. All accommodations are the same rate: Ask about midweek and off-season rates, and special event and ski packages. Among thoughtful amenities are honor libraries and morning hot drinks on each floor, newspapers at your door, refrigerators, and bathrobes.

The lobby bar has been redone in rich fabrics and warm colors, with booths in a cozy alcove, and historic photographs and art. Light meals are served in the bar and on the outdoor terrace.

High season and special events are booked months in advance; I like late fall, winter, and early spring, when we often have the public rooms to ourselves.

A Very Beary Place

Bears live in Yosemite and they love campers' food. A few precautions are essential or you may be awakened in the middle of the night by a furry creature eating your hamburger and marshmallows.

- Put every bit of food into the bear lockers provided, never in your car.

- Or, hoist your food by rope 10 feet or more up into a tree, and hang pots and pans from your food bag as an alarm.

- If bears arrive, make as much noise as possible and throw rocks.

- Before you set up in a campground or High Country hike-in site, ask a ranger about bears in the area.

- Take your children to the talk entitled "Thinking Like a Bear," held once a week at Happy Isles Nature Center.

Children's Corner in the LeConte Memorial Lodge (ages 3–12) 🧒📖🏛

Yosemite Valley at shuttle stop 12; (209) 372–4542; www.sierraclub.org/education/leconte.

In the charming, rustic Sierra Club museum in midvalley, a corner is set aside for kids to spend quiet time coloring, leafing through nature books, and playing with hand puppets, while their parents browse the library and displays. **Free** evening talks, slide shows, and programs are held on such topics as geology, history, Native Americans, flora, fauna, and the like. The lodge is open Wednesday through Sunday, May through September.

Top Ten Yosemite Sights **for Families**

Some families have only a day or two to spend in Yosemite. Here are my top sights to see, including the easiest trails in the valley. Shown in the visitor center, *One Day in Yosemite* is a short video offering advice to those with limited time.

- **Lower Yosemite Fall.** Walk a short path to the base of the third-highest waterfall in the world, dropping 2,425 feet in two mighty cataracts. The lower fall is the tallest waterfall in North America, crashing to the ground in an avalanche of vibrating sound and a refreshing, misty spray. Improvements underway are a stone amphitheater, benches, and a picnic area; a wheelchair-accessible trail; and restoration of habitat.

- **Mist Trail.** From Happy Isles it's 0.7 mile on a paved trail to Vernal Fall bridge for zowie views of the fall. With more time, continue on a half-mile steep trail to the top of the fall. A spectacular route, it may be strenuous and slippery for kids under seven or eight. Rewards are close-up views of the fall dropping over a 317-foot cliff and knockout vistas of peaks, domes, and water cascades.

- **Mirror Lake.** Take the popular, scenic, half-mile walk on a paved path to a small, glassy lake for fabulous views of Half Dome. The wildflowery trail around the lake takes a hour or so.

- **Bridalveil Fall.** Near the Highway 140/Highway 41 junction, a short, paved trail leads to the base of the fall, a miraculous, wispy sheet of water floating 620 feet to the valley floor. The fall flows year-round and is often decorated by rainbows. In the springtime, turn around for a view of Ribbon Fall, the highest single fall in the park, at 1,612 feet. The creek here is fun to play in on a hot day.

- **Glacier Point Road.** Bring cameras for the 32-mile drive past dazzling alpine scenery topped by stupendous views from Glacier Point, 3,200 feet above the valley, with peaks, domes, and massive cliffs in a dizzying array.

- **Happy Isles Nature Center.** Excellent source for kids' activities, exhibits, and tours.

- **Indian Village of Ahwahnee.** Wander the paths of a replica Miwok/Paiute village.

- **Pioneer Yosemite History Center.** On the banks of the Merced, a fascinating compound of nineteenth-century buildings with costumed docents, tours, wagon rides, and events.

- **Badger Pass.** Winter headquarters for snowboarding, downhill and cross-country skiing, snowshoeing, and tubing.

- **Mariposa Grove.** A magical world inhabited by the world's largest living things; walking trails and a tram ride to see the tallest trees in the world.

Valley Campgrounds Ⓐ
Call the National Park Reservation Service, (800) 436–PARK, for information.

Although they are crowded in the high season, and sometimes noisy with road traffic and RV generators, North, Upper, and Lower Pines Campgrounds are convenient to walking and biking throughout the valley and to most public facilities and trailheads. Many valley campers prefer North Pines, as it is a little more isolated than the others and is shaded by tall pines; sites near the river are the first to go, so make your reservations well in advance. For quieter, cooler places to camp, away from the valley, consider Bridalveil, Wawona, or Tuolumne Campgrounds. You can bring an RV up to 40 feet to some, not all, campgrounds. A fast way to check campsite availability year-round is on the Web site, www.yosemitesites.com.

Curry Village Ⓐ 🌀 ⊖ 🍴
On the eastern end of the valley; (209) 252–4848.

Sprinkled for 0.5 mile under cedars, oaks, and pines at the foot of Glacier Point, this spot is the coolest in the valley in the summertime, the coldest in the winter. Established in 1899, this is the camp that thousands of people remember from their childhoods. Expect lots of people, a lively atmosphere, and plenty to do within walking distance, perfect for families. Open spring to fall, and weekends and holidays in the winter.

Nice, motellike rooms with sleeping lofts start at about $100. Cabins with or without bath are $76–$88. Canvas tent cabins with a central bathhouse are $60–70; with wood floors, propane heaters, electricity but no outlets, and screened windows.

Curry Village is headquarters for outdoor recreation in the valley, including the Yosemite Mountaineering School and bicycle and river raft rentals in the summer. The Mountain Shop sells pricey outdoor, camping, and mountaineering equipment—

everything from backpacks, sleeping bags, parkas, footwear, ponchos, and tents, to guidebooks, maps, freeze-dried food, cooking utensils, and water filtration systems.

There are several food outlets, a gift shop and general store, a large swimming pool with lifeguards, and a post office. Almost daily, interpretive programs and entertainment are presented in the Curry Village Amphitheater. And the historic Lounge is a wonderful place to sit by the fire or on the porch, reading or making new friends; take a look at the vintage photos and artifacts around the room.

The outdoor skating rink here is a cozy place to be, with a warming hut, skate rentals, and hot drinks. You can rent one-speed bikes, a great way to get around the valley on 8 miles of bike paths in addition to the roads.

Glacier Point

Required sightseeing. Early morning or late afternoon is the best time for the 32-mile road trip to Glacier Point, to avoid gridlock and to see the dazzling array of granite monoliths when the light is most dramatic (early morning is when hang gliders sail off Half Dome).

From Glacier Point, a rock outcropping hanging out over the edge of the valley, you get a breathtaking bird's-eye view from 3,200 feet. Looking down into the chasm of the valley, your children will spot the river snaking far below and antlike cars crawling on the main roads. With the help of the plaques provided, it's fun to search for the landmarks. The Ahwahnee is easy to locate, at the foot of Royal Arches; Happy Isles is right below your feet; and Half Dome, with half its roundness chopped off as if by a tomahawk, seems to fill up half the sky to the east. Look for climbers making their ascent to the 7,000-foot summit of El Capitan, a startling vertical mass four times as large as the Rock of Gibraltar. The faint booming sound you hear in springtime is Nevada Fall, 2 miles away.

A relaxing way to get to Glacier Point is on a narrated bus tour that runs three times a day from the valley ($29.50 for adults, $16.50 for kids; 209–372–1240). You can also take the bus one-way up and walk all the way down to the valley, a 4.8-mile, three-and-a-half-hour hike for the superfit family.

Tuolumne Meadows

Overnight backpacking requires a wilderness permit, which is free and not necessary for day hikes. Trailheads have quotas that are occasionally "sold out" in the high season, so request permits online at www.nps.gov/yose/wilderness or by mail: Wilderness Office, P.O. Box 577, Yosemite 95389; (209) 372–0740. A hiker's bus from the valley will drop you off near Tioga Road trailheads.

An enormous open space at 8,600 feet, bordered by the snow-fed Tuolumne River and surrounded by peaks and glacier-polished domes. The boiling waters of two forks of the river come together here, then drop into the Grand Canyon of the Tuolumne. A hub for backpacking trails, the 2.5-mile-long meadow is the largest in the Sierras at the subalpine level. It may sparkle with frost or be awash in purple nightshade, golden monkey flowers, and riots of magenta lady's slipper orchids. A variety of ranger-guided walks begin here. The "Night Prowl," an after-dark caravan around the meadow, turns up great gray owls, spotted bats, and other nocturnal denizens of the High Sierras.

For good fishing and swimming, take the 1.5-mile one-way trek to Dog Lake, a little steep at first, but easy enough for kids age six and up.

At the Tuolumne Meadows Visitor Center, get information on where to picnic and take day hikes, and sign up here for guided walks and presentations (209–372–1240). Exhibits explain geology, alpine and subalpine ecology, bears and other wildlife, wildflowers, and human history.

Wawona Ⓐ Ⓧ Ⓣ ⊜

Southern section of the national park, 36 miles south of Yosemite Valley on Highway 41.

Families with small children love Wawona for the quiet, riverside campground; for the fun of the Mariposa Grove tram ride; and for the Pioneer Yosemite History Center, where costumed docents reenact nineteenth-century life. Beaches and swimming spots are easily accessible on the South Fork of the Merced River as it runs through Wawona.

Even toddlers can manage part of the 3-mile, flat loop trail around Wawona Meadow, and they like watching the herds of grazing deer (do not feed or touch them).

From Wawona take the Chilnaulna Fall Road 1.5 miles to a parking lot, then follow the trail to the lower cascade of Chilnaulna Fall, about 0.5 mile, uphill. For more spectacular falls crashing over massive boulders, hike another 4 miles on the trail.

Opened in 1917, the Wawona Golf Course is a 3,035-foot-long 9-holer on easy, rolling terrain bordered by towering cedars and pines; you can walk or take a cart, and clubs are available to rent. Horseback riding is offered at Wawona, and it is a perfect area for snowshoeing and Nordic skiing.

Wawona Hotel Ⓜ Ⓨ⎵ ⊖

Near the south gate of the park on Highway 41; (559) 252–4848, (209) 375–6556. $$–$$$; kids under 12 are free. Ski packages are available.

The oldest resort hotel in the state was built in 1870s, and she is in fabulous shape. Rooms in several beautiful, vintage buildings and cottages vary in size, and all have been redone in sumptuous fabrics, with armoires, new furnishings, and nice bathrooms with amenities. Some families return every summer to stay in their favorite rooms; some of the best choices are number 137 (three beds); Little White cottage (three adjoining rooms and private porch); and upstairs in the main building, connected rooms with shared baths. A small pool, sweeping lawns, a 9-hole golf course, wonderful walking trails, tennis, horseback riding, and swimming and fishing on the Merced River are nearby. Or you can just sink into a rocker on the covered porch. You don't need a car; just jump on one of the free shuttles to the valley and the Mariposa Grove, operating year-round.

The Victorian dining room, open for all meals, serves a cross between California cuisine and comfort food, with seasonal specials; don't miss the pine-nut pie and the summer barbecues. Every December the hotel is decorated in elaborate Victorian style with natural materials and vivid ribbons and fripperies. The lobby Christmas tree is lit at a special occasion calling for hot chocolate, cider, and cookies, while resident musician Tom Bopp leads guests in caroling.

Family Programs **in Yosemite**

Check the free tabloid *Yosemite Today* for more information.

- **Explore Yosemite Family Program,** Curry Village; (209) 372–1240. Offered two or three mornings a week in the summertime, a three-hour program introduces families to the natural and cultural world of Yosemite; topics are wildlife, geology, Ahwahneeche culture, and ecology; a couple of miles of easy walking are involved. Cost is $12 for the first child, $10 for each additional child, and two parents per child are free (at least one parent must accompany each family's kids).

- **Family Adventures in Yosemite Valley,** (209) 379–2321; www.yosemite.org. Just for families, a two-day expedition throughout the valley is sponsored by the Yosemite Association. Parents and kids scramble through rocks and caves, search for remnants of Indian villages,climb a dome, learn legends, wade in a lake, and more. Three to six miles of easy hiking are involved; cost is about $200.

- **Evening Programs.** Nightly talks and slide shows present the natural and cultural history of Yosemite. Learn about the secret life of bats, see Yosemite in the early 1900s through the eyes of a buffalo soldier, and view photography slide shows. Held at Curry Village, Yosemite Lodge, Lower Pines Campground, and Le Conte Memorial Lodge, the hour-long programs are free and require no preregistration.

- **Old-Fashioned Campfires.** June through September, families gather around blazing campfires in a gorgeous setting beneath tall pines and silvery granite cliffs. The program includes family-friendly interactive activities, songs, and stories; ranger talks about Yosemite history, ecology, and geology; and a marshmallow roast at the end. Campfires are limited to sixty-five people; purchase tickets at Yosemite Lodge or Curry Village; $20 per family. Outside the valley free campfire programs are offered in some campgrounds.

- **Ranger Walks and Talks.** See *Yosemite Today* for days and times. Stroll with a park ranger as he or she talks about geology, Yosemite history, wildflowers, or fauna in the park. The free talks are offered throughout the park, departing from campgrounds, popular attractions, and lodgings; reservations are not required. Walk along the Tuolumne River, learn about fire ecology, identify poisonous and edible plants, take a twilight trek to see nocturnal creatures, and find out about rivers and waterfalls.

- **Children's Storytime,** (209) 372–4413; www.anseladams.com. On Saturdays at 4:00 P.M. on the front porch of the Ansel Adams Gallery, a staff member reads from the great collection of children's books in the store.

- **Wee Wild Ones,** (209) 372–1240. For ages six and under, free forty-five-minute programs of stories, games, and fun surprises based on wildlife and geology. In summer they're in the outdoor amphitheaters at Yosemite Lodge and Curry Village; in other seasons, go to the Great Room of the Ahwahnee Hotel. A parent must accompany a child; preregistration is not required.

Pioneer Yosemite History Center

(all ages) 🏛 🚻
One-half mile from the Wawona Hotel.

A compound of circa-1880 buildings, offering antique horse-drawn vehicles, a covered bridge, a real live blacksmith, and stagecoach rides. Costumed docents reenact the period between 1890 and 1915, as blacksmiths, artisans, soldiers, and pioneer families. The walking tour is easy for all ages and abilities year-round, except during extreme snow conditions. For just a few dollars, you can ride a horse-drawn wagon in the summertime. About 200 yards upstream from the covered bridge are small swimming and wading pools in a river tributary, the warmest waters in the park. You can leave your vehicle on the side of the road and wade across to big, flat boulders warmed by the sun—one of my favorite places to picnic. A small grocery store and deli are located here.

Mariposa Grove 🏕 🚶 🚐 🍁

A five-minute drive east of the Pioneer Yosemite History Center, or take the free shuttle from the Wawona Store; (209) 375–1621. Tram tour tickets: adults $$, children $.

The largest of three sequoia groves in Yosemite. It's the home of the 209-foot, 300-ton Grizzly Giant, the Columbia (290 feet), and dozens more 2,000- to 3,000-year-old sequoias, the world's largest living things. One branch of the Grizzly Giant is more than 6 feet in diameter, and the cinnamon brown bark is 24 inches thick.

The narrated, open-air tram tour stops frequently for passengers to hop on and off to wander nature trails on the way to a vista point at 6,810 feet, overlooking the vast Wawona forest basin. Instead of taking the tram back to the parking lot, wander the 2.5-mile, easy downhill route on footpaths beneath the fragrant branches. In the cool stillness you'll hear only bustling chipmunks and the prattle of Stellar's jays; trillium and wild iris spring from carpets of moss and fern.

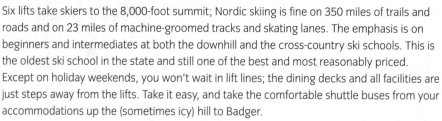

Gas **Up**

Gas is available in El Portal outside the Arch Rock entrance; at Crane Flat, 15 miles inside the Big Oak Flat entrance; at Wawona; and during the summer only at Tuolumne Meadows. No gas is available in Yosemite Valley.

Badger Pass Ski Area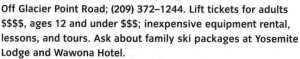
Off Glacier Point Road; (209) 372–1244. Lift tickets for adults $$$$, ages 12 and under $$$; inexpensive equipment rental, lessons, and tours. Ask about family ski packages at Yosemite Lodge and Wawona Hotel.

Six lifts take skiers to the 8,000-foot summit; Nordic skiing is fine on 350 miles of trails and roads and on 23 miles of machine-groomed tracks and skating lanes. The emphasis is on beginners and intermediates at both the downhill and the cross-country ski schools. This is the oldest ski school in the state and still one of the best and most reasonably priced. Except on holiday weekends, you won't wait in lift lines; the dining decks and all facilities are just steps away from the lifts. Take it easy, and take the comfortable shuttle buses from your accommodations up the (sometimes icy) hill to Badger.

Kids ages four to six like the Badger Pups program. For $26, little kids get a one-hour group lesson, equipment rental, and Turtle rope tow ticket; two-hour group lessons are $39.

Within the park are 90 miles of marked trails for Nordic skiing, with 40K of machine-groomed and skating lanes; no trail fees. You can rent "pulk" sleds, designed for pulling little kids behind you on the trail.

Winter Fun (all ages)

Most valley walking trails are open and relatively dry during the winter. Usually just a dusting of snow remains on the ground, so with boots you can get around on foot just fine. After a few days of dry weather, the Yosemite Falls trail is a great winter hike. Fit hikers carry their snowshoes up the John Muir Trail to Little Yosemite Valley and trek around, enjoying the incredible views. The low elevation of Wawona, about 4,000 feet, means that walking trails in that area of the park are usually quite accessible.

If you have never tried snowshoeing, it is easier than you think, with the new high-tech, streamlined, lightweight equipment. Daily, ranger-led, interpretive snowshoe walks at Badger Pass and at the Mariposa and Tuolumne Groves move at the pace of the slowest person. The cost is $3.00, including equipment. Tours take about two hours, and you can just show up. Wear warm clothes that can be peeled off and any kind of waterproof boots for this moderately strenuous trek. While snowshoes are provided, the sizes available are not recommended for children under ten years of age.

The end of the season is heralded by a big ski carnival at Badger Pass in April, the Yosemite Springfest, with races for all ages, a barbecue, a costume contest, and snow sculptures. At the Pioneer History Center, costumed docents recount early Yosemite winters, and there is caroling by candlelight and hot cider and cocoa in the old barn (209–742–6231).

Snow Play

- **Crane Flat** on Highway 120, developed snow-play hill and rentals; free to play.

- **Curry Village** toboggan hill, saucer rentals; free to play.

- **Goat Meadow** hill, 0.5 mile outside the South Gate/Highway 41 entrance to the park; free to play.

- **Badger Pass** has a new, 100-yard-long snow-tubing hill with a generous run-out and stopping berm at the bottom. Two-hour tubing sessions are scheduled for 9:00 A.M., 11:30 A.M., and 2:00 P.M. daily; $9.00 per person, including equipment. You are not permitted to use your own tubes or sliding devices, and a parent must accompany children ages ten and younger.

Where to Eat

Curry Village. East end of the valley; (209) 372–8333. The Dining Pavilion is a big, airy cafeteria with a nice, mountain atmosphere, serving good old American food buffet style at moderate prices; terrific chuckwagon barbecue in the summertime. At the **Hamburger Deck,** breakfast, lunch, and dinner to eat outdoors or take away, burgers, grilled sandwiches, salads, snacks; share the big orders of fries. At the **Pizza Patio,** good, fresh pizza and ice cream, for outdoors at an umbrella table with a meadow and forest view, or to take away. Sports fans huddle around the big screen TV. There is a taco stand, and the **Coffee Corner** is the place for fast takeout of espresso drinks, pastries, muffins, and Danish; yogurt, juices, hand-dipped ice cream, and prepackaged sandwiches and snacks. $–$$

Degnan's Deli, Cafe, and Pizza Loft. Yosemite Village, shuttle stop 10; (209) 372–8454. In the deli, custom-made and premade deli sandwiches, salads, snacks, espresso drinks, and other beverages to take out. The cafe serves gourmet sandwiches, homemade soups and pastries, soft-serve ice cream, burgers, and light meals. A central fireplace and valley views make the upstairs pizza and pasta place a cozy spot. $

Food Court at Yosemite Lodge. Shuttle stop 8; (209) 372–1274. A million-dollar renovation transformed the cafeteria of old into an attractive food court with fresh-looking green canvas awnings, decorative tiles, and a tree-shaded, enlarged patio with umbrella tables. Pass-through at food lines and check-out is faster than before; lodging guests can charge their purchases to their rooms. Separate venues offer fast snacks and prepacked lunches to go. Hot, made-to-order meals feature daily specials and healthy choices. At entree stations, you can order vegetarian and meat-based entrees and a daily rotating menu of ethnic foods. At the pasta station, specialty sauces range from traditional pesto, marinara, and bolognese, to roasted garlic, and sun-dried tomato pesto. The deli station offers cold salads, chef and shrimp salads, cheese and fruit plates, wrap sandwiches, and deli-style sandwiches. The grill station is popular for hamburgers, garden burgers, hot dogs, garlic fries, and chicken and fish sandwiches. At the bakery-dessert station are muffins, bagels, Danish, cakes, and pies; and at the hot breakfast station, it's bacon and sausage, eggs and pancakes, plus quiche, breakfast burritos and omelets, hot cereal, and fresh fruit. $

Mountain Room at Yosemite Lodge. Shuttle stop 8; (209) 372–1274. Blond wood paneling, low lights, and the killer view of Yosemite Falls make the Mountain Room a grand, if casual, dinner house. Mountain climbing is featured in photos, art, and a mural. Grilled and roasted meats are featured. This is one of the few places in the valley where outdoor dining is available. No reservations are accepted and the wait can be considerable—come early. Children are welcome in the Mountain Room Lounge, where a round fireplace is inviting. The casual lounge serves alcoholic beverages, light meals, sandwiches, salads, and snacks. Four TVs are tuned to sporting events, family-oriented sitcoms, and news. While parents enjoy views of Yosemite Falls, kids can get a s'mores kit

and a child-safe roasting stick to make their favorite treat in the fireplace. $–$$

Tuolumne Meadows Lodge and Grill. Highway 120 East, Tuolumne Meadows; (209) 372–4471. A restaurant in a tent in the High Country of the park, serving American comfort food for breakfast and dinner. Box lunches are available and beer and wine. Dig into Meadow Scramble in the morning, prime rib or veggie specialties for dinner. Next to the post office at the Grill, sit at the counter or take away sandwiches, snacks, hot breakfasts, lunches, and light dinners. In mid-summer when the Tuolumne food outlets are over-flowing with hungry campers, drive out of the park, east about 2 miles on Highway 120 to the Tioga Pass Resort, where you can get three meals a day of hearty American food and divine homemade pie. $–$$

Village Grill. Yosemite Village, shuttle stop 10. Pretty good fast food from a walk-up window: hamburgers, fries, onion rings, chicken strips, and the like. Eat at a table outdoors or take it away. $

White Wolf Lodge. Highway 120 between Tuolumne Meadows and Yosemite Valley; (209) 372–1316. A great old clapboard dining hall with a fireplace that serves hearty American breakfasts and dinners. You can buy sandwiches at the adjacent store. $–$$

Pets

Kennel facilities, (209) 372–1248. Pets are allowed in the national park if they are leashed at all times and never left unattended. No pets are allowed on trails, in the backcountry, or in lodgings.

Where to Stay

High Country Campgrounds at Yosemite. (800) 436–2725. Rustic tent cabins with wood stoves are at **Tuolumne Meadows Lodge** and the **Tuolumne Meadows Campground.** Tuoloumne Meadows is the largest campground in the park, with 325 sites; the most desirable are on the east side near the river. Campfire programs and special children's get-togethers with songs and stories are held most nights. Nearby are a grocery store, stables, and a restaurant serving substantial American fare. Tent cabins with wood stoves are in a picturesque setting near the river. **White Wolf Campground** is summertime-only headquarters for backcountry trails, with rustic tent cabins, a first-come campground, store, stables, and a lovely old clapboard dining hall.

Housekeeping Camp. Shuttle stop 12; (209) 252–4848. If you like to camp but do not enjoy sleeping in a tent or on the ground, this could be for you. Two hundred and sixty-six tent cabins sleeping up to six have concrete walls and floors and canvas roofs; each has a fire ring. A canvas curtain separates the sleeping and cooking/dining areas. With electricity but no phones or plumbing, the cabins are close together, with minimal privacy. Facilities include a central restroom and shower facilities (soap and towels are provided), a laundry, and a small grocery store. Bring your own linens or sleeping bags, cooking equipment, dishes, and food. $

The Redwoods. Chilnaulna Falls Road off Highway 41, Wawona, in the national park; (209) 375–6666; www.redwoodsin yosemite.com. Choose from more than one hundred privately owned cabins and houses to rent in a wooded setting near the river. Homes are varied sizes, all fully furnished and equipped. Make reservations months ahead for holidays; call early in the year for the December holidays. $$$–$$$$

Yosemite Lodge. Midvalley; (559) 253–5635. Four hundred eighty-four simple rooms, from traditional rooms with balconies to rustic cabins, with or without baths. The compound includes a cafeteria and restaurants; a post office; gift shops; a swimming pool; an outdoor theater; and a tour desk. Free nightly programs. $$–$$$

Yosemite National Park. National Park Reservation Service (campgrounds); (800) 436–PARK. Yosemite Reservation and

Information service (cabins, lodge/hotel rooms); (559) 253–5635; www.yosemitepark .com. For sites requiring reservations call three months to a year in advance to ensure your space. For campgrounds operating on a first-come, first-served basis, be sure to arrive early in the morning to avoid disappointment.

Yosemite View Lodge. 11159 Highway 140, El Portal; (800) 321–5261; www .yosemite-motels.com. Near the Arch Rock entrance to the park, a large, newly renovated motel with balconies or patios overlooking the roaring Merced River. Rooms are spacious and attractive, with rustic mountain lodge–style furnishings; some have equipped kitchenettes with microwaves, refrigerators, toasters, coffeemakers, and two-burner stoves; flatscreen TVs, fireplaces, separate seating areas with sofa beds, deep double whirlpool tubs, and double shower heads. Nicely decorated standard rooms are set up with two double beds. There is a small outdoor pool and a larger indoor pool; a pizza place and a small restaurant by the river serving breakfasts and dinners, with a cocktail lounge; a convenience store, gift shop, and the Gateway Mountain Center, where you can get information about the park and book guided tours. From here, take a bus into the valley for $16, including park entrance fee. $$$–$$$$

Yosemite West. Seven miles from Badger Pass, 30 minutes from Yosemite Valley; (209) 296–7364; www.yosemitewest.com. A wide variety of year-round vacation homes and condominiums in the Wawona area within the park. The Web site shows details and photos of everything from studios to luxury lodge homes sleeping ten people. Many of the homes and condos have sundecks with mountain or forest views; fireplaces or wood stoves; hot tubs or spas; and all have fully equipped kitchens. $$–$$$$

For More Information

Yosemite National Park. P.O. Box 577, Yosemite 95389; general information, (209) 372–1000; reservations for cabins and lodge/hotel rooms, (209) 252–4848; reservations for campgrounds, (800) 436–PARK; road and weather information, (209) 372–0200 or (209) 372–2009. Admission to the national park: $$$ per car. Weather changes rapidly in the Sierras; snow can fall as early as September, and storms can occur any month of the year. Before you leave home, call to check on weather, road, and trail conditions, and ask about the availability of campsites if you plan to camp without reservations.

Sierra National Forest Ranger District. (559) 297–0706.

Yosemite Web Sites

- **www.yosemitepark.com.** Book lodging and campgrounds on this site and get information on shopping, dining, and activities from Delaware North Parks & Resorts at Yosemite (DNC), the company that operates concessions, tours, and lodging in Yosemite.

- **http://reservations.nps.gov.** Camping reservations.

- **www.yosemite.org.** Yosemite Association, visitor information, bookstore, classes and seminars, weather, and live-camera views.

- **www.nps.gov/yose.** Official National Parks Association site.

- **www.yosemite.com.** Travelers' information, lodging, road conditions, and weather.

Y.A.R.T.S. (877) 98–YARTS; www.yosemite
.com/yarts. From Merced, Mariposa, and
Mammoth, big motorcoaches have reclin-
ing seats, large windows, bike racks, and
restrooms. The Highway 120 East route
from Mammoth may use multipassenger
vans; riders with children requiring car
seats or with bicycles should call ahead on
this route. YARTS connects with Amtrak
and Greyhound in Merced. Fares run
between $5.00 and $20.00 round-trip; kids
are discounted; with each adult passenger,
a child sixteen or younger rides **free.**

Amtrak. 800–USA–RAIL; www.amtrak
.com. Ask about off-season discounts and
special family fares for departures from
throughout the state to the park; you
arrive in Merced or Fresno, with free
connections to the park by bus.

Insiders' Guide to Yosemite. Globe
Pequot Press, www.globepequot.com. A
comprehensive, detailed guidebook to visiting Yosemite National Park, including
lodging and activities, recreation and
tours, a special Kidstuff chapter, hiking,
and backpacking; plus things to do and
places to stay and eat along the four gateway highways.

Sightseeing Tours and Activities

• **Delaware North Parks & Resorts at
Yosemite (DNC) Tour Desk.** Yosemite
Lodge; (209) 372–1240; www.yosemite
park.com. Experts lead walking tours,
as well as indoor and outdoor talks
focusing on flora, fauna, geology, and
history of the park. Bus and tram sightseeing tours operate in Yosemite Valley
and go to Glacier Point, Tuolumne
Meadows, Wawona, and the Mariposa
Grove. Children under age five generally ride free in the lap of an adult. For

information on tours and activities, see
Yosemite Today, the free tabloid available throughout the park and at park
entrance stations.

• **National Park Service Tour Desk.**
Visitor Center, Yosemite Village; (209)
372–0200; www.nps.gov/yose. Ranger-
led tours, hikes, films, and talks.

• **Tour and Activity Kiosks.** Yosemite
Lodge, Curry Village, Village Store, and
Valley Visitor Center; (209) 372–1240.
Wawona Information Station, Wawona
Hotel; (209) 375–1416.

Oakhurst

Between Yosemite and Kings Canyon National Park, the Lake Country of the Central Sierras remains relatively undiscovered by vacationers. Some 700 miles of trout streams, along with numerous lakes, reservoirs, and campgrounds, make this an area your family will want to explore.

Hit the **Trail**

- **Oakhurst River Parkway,** Oakhurst Community Park, Civic Circle, Oakhurst; (209) 683–7766. An oak-shaded 3-mile loop trail along the Fresno River and Oak Creek.

- **Lewis Creek National Recreation Trail,** 5 miles south of the southern Yosemite Gate, off Highway 41; (209) 683–4665. From the highway parking area, walk 0.25 mile south on the trail to Corlieu Falls, then 1.8 miles north to Red Rock Falls, through dogwood, azalea, and pines along Lewis Fork Creek. The creek is stocked with trout and is popular with anglers.

- **Shadow of the Giants Trail,** 10 miles north of Oakhurst on Highway 41, take Sky Ranch Road for 6 miles. A National Recreation Trail, an easy, 1 mile with interpretive signs along the banks of Nelder Creek, leading to a miraculous grove of over one hundred specimen sequoias and one of the largest trees in the world, the Bull Buck. Insiders know that this trail is less traveled and more beautiful than the Sequoia grove trails in Yosemite. The biggest and best trees are at the far end of the loop, so get there!

- **Way of the Mono Trail,** along Road 222 at Bass Lake, trailhead between the Forks Resort and the California Land Management Office. A nice, easy 0.5-mile walk to learn some American Indian history and see some great views of the lake.

- **Goat Mountain Trail,** trailheads at Spring Cove Campground and Fork Campground at Bass Lake; (209) 683–4665. Four strenuous miles one-way to the summit and the fire lookout, with nonstop views of the lake and the forested valleys along the way. Cut the distance and the degree of difficulty of this beautiful trail in half by starting at one campground, leaving a car at the other, and turning back where the two trails meet on the way up.

Fourteen miles from the southern Yosemite gate, Oakhurst is an antiques center and a busy stopover point for travelers on the way to the national park and the national forests. Just up the road at an elevation of 3,400 feet lies the popular recreation area of Bass Lake, with rustic resorts and campgrounds; marinas for sailing, fishing, and waterskiing boats; and endless hiking trails in the surrounding Sierra National Forest.

My favorite time of the year in the Central Sierras is after Labor Day. Traffic is light, and the weather has cooled from the high nineties of midsummer to the seventies. Nights are delightfully crisp, and color is beginning to show in the maples, dogwoods, and oaks.

The Talking Bear landmark in the center of Oakhurst, at Highway 41 and Road 426, is a great photo op. Around town, notice the elaborate chain-saw sculptures of bears, pine trees, eagles, and other flora and fauna. This does seem to be the chain-saw art capital of the Sierras.

Fresno Flats Historical Park (all ages)
One mile from Oakhurst, on Road 427; (559) 683–6570; www.fresnoflatsmuseum.org. Free.

A re-created western town from the region's early timber and ranching era. Old buildings have been moved here from all over the county—jails, schools, barns, wagons, buggies, and a furnished home. You can ramble around on your own anytime, or check in at the museum and gift shop to ask about guided tours. There are outdoor concerts on weekends, a playground, picnic tables, barbecues, and horseshoe pits, making this a busy hometown park.

Yosemite Mountain Sugar Pine Railroad (all ages)
Between Oakhurst and Yosemite, on Highway 41; (559) 683–7273; www.ymsprr.com. Most train rides $$–$$$; kids under 3 free.

A major destination for families with younger children. You might want to plan a couple of hours here riding the train, picnicking, and enjoying the beautiful forest. An eighty-four-ton vintage locomotive—the largest ever built for a narrow-gauge track—pulls open cars 4 miles through forestlands into Lewis Creek Canyon. It's exciting to climb aboard at the tiny station while steam rolls out from under the huge engine and black smoke belches into the sky. A conductor spins tales of when the railroad hauled timber out of the Sierras.

Watch out for masked horsemen, who are known to stop trains searching for passengers' loot. There is a gift and sandwich shop and the Thornberry Museum in a 140-year-old cabin. For a fun preview of the train whistles, bells, brakes, and other exciting noises, and to see a few photos of the trains, go to www.ymsprr.com/sightsnsounds.html.

From June through September a "Moonlight Special" evening train excursion ends with a steak barbecue and live music around a campfire ($$$$). Cross-country skiing is excellent throughout the Sugar Pine area.

Next door at the Narrow Gauge Inn, the Victorian era and the Old West come together in the restaurant and Bull Moose saloon—cozy in cool weather when logs burn in the big stone fireplaces (209–683–7720).

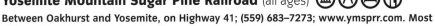

Oakhurst River Parkway
Oakhurst Community Park; (559) 683–4636.

An easy, 3-mile walking trail just off the main street of Oakhurst meanders past Fresno Flats Historical Park, the Fresno River, China Creek, and Oak Creek—the water flows in late winter, spring, and early summer. Stroll along the water and watch ducks, beavers, red-winged blackbirds, and other wild creatures; have a picnic or a barbecue in the small, grassy park.

Sierra Mono Museum (all ages)
Malum Ridge Road/Road 274 and Mammoth Pool Road/Road 225, North Fork; (209) 877–2115. $.

On display are Native American artifacts, basketry, and beadwork, as well as a grizzly bear, a mountain lion, elk, moose, antelope, wolves, and other wildlife. In August the Sierra Mono Indian Fair Days and Pow Wow are held here, featuring traditional dances, crafts, and games. Call ahead before driving up here, as sometimes the museum is closed. The Mono, Miwok, and Chuckchansi tribes call the southern Sierras their home, and many of them are artisans whose works are displayed and sold in shops and at fairs throughout the region.

The Forks Resort (all ages)
39150 Road 222, Bass Lake; (559) 642–3737; www.theforksresort.com. $$–$$$$.

Families return here year after year for their summer vacations in cabins on the southwest corner of the lake. Conveniently grouped together are a general store selling groceries and fishing and camping gear; a marina renting patio and fishing boats; and a casual, 1950s-style cafe serving three meals a day. The cabins are actually spacious houses in the trees, most with lake views. They are completely outfitted with everything you might need for a day or a week—just arrive with your clothes.

Bass Lake (all ages)
Fourteen miles from Oakhurst off Highway 41, on Road 222; (559) 683–4665.

The warm waters of this popular lake reach seventy-eight degrees in summer. Situated in the Sierra National Forest at 3,400 feet, the lake is good spring and fall fishing for trout, bass, catfish, and bluegill and in summer for partaking in water sports and camping. You can rent windsurfers and boats for canoeing, sailing, rowing, and waterskiing. At three main resort areas—Pines Village, Forks Resort, and Miller's Landing—are shops, groceries, gas, and rentals of all kinds.

At Pines Village you can take waterskiing lessons and hire a boat driver, or cruise the lake at your leisure in a party barge (800–585–9283; www.basslakeboatrentals.com). In the winter you can rent snowmobiles here too. Besides watercraft rentals Miller's Landing rents a few nice cabins (559–642–3633; www.millerslanding.com).

Where to Eat

Castillo's. 49271 Golden Oak Loop, Oakhurst; (559) 683–8000. Terrific tacos and homemade Mexican food. It's a cantina, too—try the blackberry margaritas. $

Ducey's on the Lake. Pines Village, Bass Lake; (559) 642–3131. Overlooking the lake, the dining room looks like a cross between a yacht and a hunting lodge, with great old photos on the walls. Ask for a comfy booth. The dinner menu includes steaks, lamb, and prime rib of pork; plus crab cakes, lobster, and more fresh seafood. On the sunny deck at lunchtime, have grilled chicken, salads, burgers, fresh fish, or pasta. Traditional American breakfasts, eggs Benedict, French toast, and omelets. Friday evenings from late May through late August, enjoy live jazz outdoors and fireworks. $$

Meadows Ranch Cafe. 5023 Highway 140, Mariposa; (209) 966–2065. On the way to Yosemite, a great place to stop for breakfast, lunch, or dinner. Very family oriented, with a huge menu of comfort food from steak to chili, pasta, burgers, gourmet pizza, barbecue, and luscious desserts; plus a large kids' menu. $–$$

The Pines Resort. Pines Village, Bass Lake; (559) 642–3121. Good barbecue and American food; indoor/outdoor casual dining. $$

Sierra Meadows Ranch Golf Course. 6516 Opah Drive, just west of Oakhurst off Highway 41, Oakhurst; (559) 642–1343; www.sierrameadows.com. A pleasant place to be on a sunny Sunday for the breakfast buffet, from 9:00 A.M. to 2:00 P.M. Call ahead to get a table on the deck, overlooking the golf course. Prices are reasonable for a big brunch. $$

Tenaya Lodge. 1122 Highway 41, Fish Camp; (800) 635–5807. The Sierra Restaurant offers an upscale casual atmosphere, fresh fish, local produce, Italian cuisine, a fireplace, and mountain views. The Parkside Restaurant is a casual coffee shop, serving sandwiches, salads, and deli takeout. Breakfast, lunch, and dinner are offered at both restaurants. $$

Three Sisters. 40291 Junction Drive, Oakhurst; (559) 642–2253; www.three sisterscafe.com. In a bright, colorful, casual atmosphere, exotic and fabulous food. For breakfast the San Francisco–style Joe's Special, chicken quesadillas, banananut French toast, eggs Benedict with crab, exotic omelets, and traditional breakfast fare. On the extensive lunch menu may be asparagus, shrimp, and brie crepes; seafood cioppino; Thai chicken salad; and sandwiches. Gourmet dinners include Oysters Rocksisters, chicken cacciatore, veal stew, spicy Asian entrees—the list goes on. Definitely make reservations. $$$–$$$$

Where to Stay

The Pines Resort. Right on Bass Lake, P.O. Box 109, Bass Lake 93604; (800) 350–7463; www.basslake.com. Rustic condos and chalets at the lake and luxury suites; restaurant; tennis, swimming pool, sauna, hot tub; boat rentals. $$–$$$

Tenaya Lodge. 1122 Highway 41, Fish Camp; (800) 635–5807; www.tenaya lodge.com. A destination resort overlooking forested mountains and valleys, five minutes from the southern gate of Yosemite National Park. The two-story atrium lobby and the restaurants have a casual yet luxurious feel and are decorated with Indian artifacts and Western-style furnishings. In the spacious, elegant rooms are many amenities: ironing boards, coffeemakers, Nintendo; some have two double beds and a sitting area with sofa bed. Recreational facilities include a full-service spa and fitness center, saunas, indoor and outdoor pools, a playground, and a snow-play area. Tours from the hotel get you into the park and to the Badger Pass ski area.

Kids check in at their own station at the front desk and pick up an activity pack. Camp Tenaya day camp is popular with five- to twelve-year-olds who like volleyball, Ping-Pong, swimming, games, movies, music, crafts, and nature hikes. Campers get personal attention and special meals, and there are evening programs, too. Babysitting can be arranged for toddlers.

You can hike right from the lodge through pine forests and along streamsides. Bikes are available at the hotel, and you can walk to a stable for guided horse-back rides. Cross-country ski out the door and rent equipment here too, to ski on your own or take a guided tour.

Barbecue evenings start with a horse-drawn wagon ride to the cookout, with campfire singing and marshmallow roasting with cowpokes. $$$–$$$$

U.S. Forest Service (USFS) Campground Information and Reservations. The forest service operates many campgrounds, seasonally, near Yosemite in the Inyo, Sierra, Stanislaus, and Toiyabe National Forests. Many are on a first-come, first-served basis; in some campgrounds, at least half the sites may be reserved (877–444–6777; www.reserveusa.com, www.fs.fed.us). The USFS Summerdale Campground at Fish Camp has a nice, streamside location. Off Highway 41 near Fish Camp, the tiny, tents-only Summit Campground is 6 miles down a gravel road near good fishing on Big Creek.

Yosemite Gateway Inn. 40530 Highway 41, Oakhurst; (800) 545–5462 or (559) 683–2378. Motel and family units in a park-like setting, with oak trees, some kitchens, indoor and outdoor pools, restaurant, barbecue area, playground, laundry, and mountain views. Some two-bedroom family units. $$–$$$

For More Information

Yosemite Sierra Visitors Bureau. 40637 Highway 41, Oakhurst; (559) 683–4636; www.go2yosemite.net.

Bass Lake Chamber of Commerce. P.O. Box 126, Bass Lake 93604; (559) 642–3676; www.basslake.com.

South Bay and East Bay Towns

The cities and the countryside surrounding San Francisco are easily accessible and packed with opportunities for family adventures—from ridgetop hikes in the East Bay hills to science museums, ethnic festivals, and a wild water park.

Hop a fast underground train to Berkeley for a day on a university campus, or shop in the outlet stores, and later take a hike in a ridgetop forest. Ride the ferry to Oakland for a seafood dinner in Jack London Square and to an art museum that kids like. Spend the day in San Jose at high-tech play-and-learn centers; you will need another whole day to play at Paramount's Great America theme park, and yet another to explore a mystery house and a cool museum of mummies and Egyptian tombs.

Highway 280 is the fastest route south to San Jose. Take Highway 80 across the Bay Bridge to Oakland and Berkeley, or a ferry or BART across the bay.

Berkeley

Just a skip and a jump across the bay from San Francisco, Berkeley is the home of one of the largest and most beautiful university campuses in the western United States, the University of California at Berkeley. Attractions here for visiting families are museums, educational buildings, walking paths, and shady glades on the campus itself; ethnic restaurants on the surrounding streets; and recreation in Tilden Regional Park in the verdant hills above the city. You might also enjoy the reasonably priced accommodations and the factory outlet stores.

At the base of a range of forest-covered hills overlooking San Francisco Bay, the small city is laid out on either side of University Avenue, which stretches from a lively marina to the campus.

University of California (all ages)

101 University Hall, at Oxford Street and University Avenue, Berkeley; (510) 642–5215. Free tours.

Budding scientists in your family will find a plethora of fascinating museums, as well as the world-famous Lawrence Hall of Science, on the campus. Student-led campus tours are

SOUTH BAY AND EAST BAY TOWNS

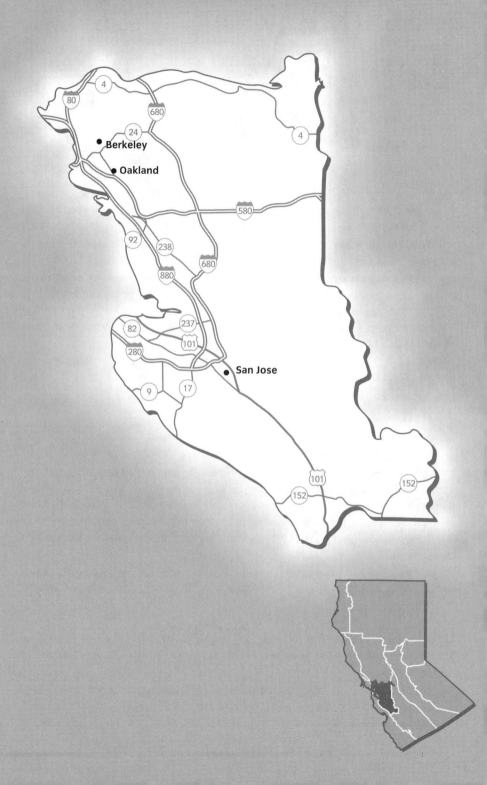

offered daily, and you can get maps for a self-guided tour at the visitor center. Maps are also posted at the campus entrance, or you can get one by mail by sending a self-addressed, stamped envelope to 2200 University Information Center, 2200 University Avenue, Berkeley, CA 94720. Call ahead for tour reservations.

Highlights of **the UC Campus**

- **Sather Tower,** central campus, visible from Sather Gate on Bancroft; (510) 642–5215. A campus landmark built in 1914 as a replica of St. Mark's campanile in Venice. Take a heart-stopping ride to the top for 360-degree views of the Bay Area. The last elevator of the day leaves at 3:00 P.M.; on Sunday, at 1:30 P.M. $.

- **Lawrence Hall of Science,** Centennial Drive near Grizzly Peak Boulevard; (510) 642–5132. Get involved in interactive displays of lasers, computers, medicine, dinosaurs, and outer space; pretend to be a doctor, an archaeologist, and an astronaut. Planetarium shows and physics and biology labs are here too. The littlest kids like "OK-to-touch" frogs, tarantulas, rabbits, and other animals. Call for a schedule of special weekend events. Adults and students $$; ages 3 to 4 $.

- **Valley Life Sciences Building/Museum of Paleontology,** (510) 642–1821. A huge collection of fossils are laid out in the hallways, and a triceratops skull awaits in the library. A two-story-high *Tyrannosaurus rex* presides in the atrium, while a pterosaur flies overhead. Cool! **Free.**

- **Phoebe Hearst Museum of Anthropology,** Kroeber Hall on Bancroft at College Avenue; (510) 643–7648. California Native Americans are featured, plus ancient artifacts from all over the world. Adults and students $; ages 12 and under **free**; everyone **free** on Thursday.

- **International House,** 2299 Piedmont Avenue; (510) 642–9460. A chance to have a meal in the company of students from all over the world. Good, basic international cuisine is served from a buffet in a unique Spanish/Moorish–style restaurant, indoors or on the garden patio. $.

I went to school here and now find the campus a little more crowded with buildings and students yet still a great place to spend an afternoon, wandering the garden pathways and having a picnic beneath one of the century-old redwoods or oak trees. The oldest of the UC campuses, established in 1868, this one has a fascinating variety of architectural styles. Delicatessens and casual cafes are clustered on the streets near each campus entrance.

Fourth Street **Shops and Cafes**

To reach the restaurant and factory outlet ghetto on Fourth and surrounding streets, take the University Avenue exit off Highway 80, then the first left turn; then turn left again onto Fourth Street.

- **Bette's Oceanview Diner,** 1807 Fourth Street; (510) 644–3230. My family's favorite restaurant in the East Bay, and a favorite with the people who stand in line to get in. This all-American, circa-1940 cafe with booths and a counter opens at 6:30 A.M. and goes full blast all day long, through dinner; take away as well as eat in. The epitome of comfort food. $.

- **Royal Robbins,** 841 Gilman Street off Fourth; (510) 527–1961. Top-quality outdoor recreation equipment and clothing, at a discount. My husband has Royal Robbins shorts that's he's worn every summer for twenty years. Really!

- **HearthSong Toys,** 1810 Fourth Street; (510) 849–3956. Toys that run on imagination instead of batteries. Games, audiotapes, books, and toys from all over the world.

- **Earthsake,** 1805 Fourth Street; (510) 559–8440. Interesting eco stuff, including toys, games, and books.

- **REI,** 1338 San Pablo Avenue, near Fourth Street; (510) 527–4140. Top-of-the-line camping and outdoor recreational equipment, clothing, bikes, a climbing wall, boots, running gear, guidebooks, and ski stuff.

- **Discovery Channel Store,** 740 Hearst Avenue off Fourth Street; (510) 841–1279. Emphasis on nature, history, science, and travel, through a wide variety of electronic toys and games; travel accessories; books; DVDs of Discovery Channel, Travel Channel, and Animal Planet programs; and clothing. Teens love it.

- **Sweet Potatoes,** 1716 Fourth Street; (510) 527–5852. Fabulous bright cotton duds for babies and toddlers.

UC Botanical Garden (all ages)

Strawberry Canyon on Centennial Drive above Memorial Stadium, Berkeley; (510) 643–2755. $; free on Thursday.

Wander through the redwoods, the old roses, and the Chinese medicinal herb garden in one of the world's leading collections of flora; bring a picnic.

Berkeley Pier/Cesar Chavez Park (all ages)

West end of University Avenue, west of Highway 80, Berkeley Marina; (510) 644–8623.

Extending 3,000 feet out into the bay, the pier is a good place to stroll, take photos of the skyline, and watch freighter traffic. Many people fish for perch and flounder, and you may see sharks and stingrays caught too. The dependably breezy waterfront park is the site of the annual Berkeley Kite Festival in July, when amateur and professional kite flyers compete. There is a 1.7-mile loop of paved walking trail, a playground, and room to roam.

Tilden Regional Park (all ages)

In the hills above Berkeley, accessed from Spruce Street, from Centennial Drive, and from Grizzly Peak; (510) 525–2233; www.ebparks.org.

A vast, green open space for hikers, bikers, and picnickers. Little kids like Little Farm, where they can pet and feed animals and birds, as well as ride ponies and a 1911 carousel. Lifeguards are on duty for swimming at the sandy beach, spring through fall, at Lake Anza. Take a ride on a miniature steam train through the redwoods and a tunnel. An easy 1-mile walk through woods and meadows circles Jewel Lake, leading to a marshy pond where frogs and ducks hold court.

Where to Eat

Fatapple's Restaurant and Bakery. 1346 Martin Luther King, Jr. Way, Berkeley; (510) 526–2260. Wildly popular with families, for burgers, chili, potpies, pork barbeque sandwiches; in-house bakery makes great pies, cakes, and cookies. All at reasonable prices; takeout, too. $–$$

Long Life Vegi House. University Avenue at Shattuck Avenue, Berkeley; (510) 845–6072. Rub elbows with the locals who like good, inexpensive Chinese, vegetarian, and seafood specialties. Try the mu-shu veggies. $

Mondo Gelato. 2106 Shattuck Avenue, Berkeley; (510) 883–1568; www.mondo gelato.com. An artisan gelato maker in Italy invents the more than fifty flavors of gelato, showcased elegantly in a Nuevo-Italo gelateria. Choose from exotics like Nutella, Ferrero Rocher, honeymelon, pear, and pistachio, or traditional flavors such as strawberry, milk and dark chocolate, and lemon. North American ice cream is made with a high percentage of air and about 16 to 20 percent fat; the high fat content creates a creamier texture, while somewhat masking true flavors. Gelato has less air, only 2 to 8 percent fat, and is frozen at a lower temperature, resulting in intense flavor. $

Pizza Rustica Cafe and Tapas Bar. 5422 College Avenue, Berkeley; (510) 654–1601. Some say this is the best pizza in town. $

Where to Stay

Claremont Resort Hotel. Ashby and Domingo Avenues, Berkeley; (510) 843–3000. The only resort in the East Bay, a classic Victorian-style hotel within elaborate gardens and grounds, along with a major tennis complex and a complete spa. Olympic-size pool, lap pool, children's wading area, playground, parcourse, restaurants, and babysitting service. $$$–$$$$

Radisson Hotel Berkeley Marina. 200 Marina Boulevard on the waterfront, Berkeley; (510) 548–7920 or (800) 243–0625. Glistening from a multimillion-dollar renovation, a big hotel conveniently located to the entire Bay Area. Each room has a balcony or patio. Two indoor pools, fitness center, guest laundry, free shuttle to BART, restaurant. $$–$$$

For More Information

Berkeley Convention and Visitors Bureau. 2015 Center Street, ½ block west of the downtown Berkeley BART station, Berkeley; (510) 549–7040 or (800) 847–4823; recorded information on events and more: (510) 549–8710; www.visitberkeley .com.

Oakland

The main family attractions in the port city of Oakland are Jack London Square and Lake Merritt. You can get here by ferry and on BART.

Lake Merritt and Children's Fairyland (ages 1–8)
Grand Avenue and Bellevue Street, Oakland; (510) 425–2259; www.fairyland.org. $$; kids 1 and under **free.**

For younger children, a three-dimensional nursery-rhyme playground, a merry-go-round, a puppet theater, train rides, and farm animals. A 3-mile paved path runs around the lake, and you can rent paddleboats, rowboats, and canoes. Glide on the lake in an authentic gondola built by hand in Venice, complete with serenading gondolier (510–663–6603). On the lakeshore the **Camron-Stanford House** is a beautifully restored museum of the Victorian period. You can take a guided tour on Wednesday and Sunday afternoons (1418 Lakeside Drive; 510–444–1876; www.cshouse.org). The cost is $5.00 for adults; $3.00 for ages twelve to eighteen; kids eleven and under are **free.**

Jack London Square

Broadway at Embarcadero, Oakland; (510) 814–6000; www.jacklondonsquare.com.

Named for the notorious and prolific adventure story author Jack London, who was a roustabout in Oakland early in the twentieth century, the waterfront is a hodgepodge of old and new seafood restaurants and cafes, souvenir shops, a few historic sites, toy stores, bargain bookstores, and Cost Plus. The Sunday farmers' market is great fun, and so is the monthly antiques fair and the weekend artisan fairs. There is a waterfront walking path, a movieplex, and inexpensive hotels within easy reach of the Oakland airport. Ferries ply the bay between here and downtown San Francisco, Pier 39, Fisherman's Wharf, and Angel Island. On Friday afternoons the ferry becomes a pleasure cruiser, complete with music. The Jack London Water Taxi, a kind of covered barge, will take you on a cruise in the Oakland Estuary from the square to Alameda (next to Chevy's restaurant) for $5.00 a person (510–839–7572; www. jacklondonwatertaxi.com).

The California Canoe and Kayak company is based here, too, where you can rent boats to paddle the estuary (510–893–7833). And, stop in at Timeout for Fun and Games, a small, friendly store chock-full of toys and games (510–444–4FUN; www.timeoutforfun .com). At Whales and Things, kids get lost in the aisles of fun and educational things related to wildlife, art, science, and ethnicity, from whale dolls to stickers, books, videos, toys, games, and cards (510–763–0585). A gigantic Barnes & Noble is open late and has a cafe with tables in a shady grove of trees. You can join a free, city-sponsored, guided Jack London History Walk (510–627–1670), or guide yourselves, following the bronze "wolf tracks" to trace the history of the square.

USS *Potomac* (all ages)

540 Water Street at Jack London Square, Oakland; (510) 627–1215; www.usspotomac.org. Adults $$; ages 6 to 12 $; under 6 are free.

FDR's "Floating White House" is a sweet reminder of a beloved president who escaped humid Washington summers and the pressures of World War II and the Depression by cruising on this yacht, which has been beautifully restored. While browsing the artifacts of that tumultuous era, you can imagine FDR playing poker with his buddies and poring over his stamp collection. Elvis was another famous owner.

Chabot Space and Science Center (ages 4 and up)

10000 Skyline Boulevard, Oakland; (510) 336–7300; www.chabotspace.org. $$, with separate admission to theater and planetarium.

Plan most of a day for the huge, new educational center with the largest public telescope in the U.S.; the most advanced planetarium in the world; and an IMAX theater showing fabulous films of outer space, the ocean floor, volcanoes, and more. Explore planetary landscapes, meteorites, the sun and the solar system, build a telescope, see a lunar lander. The amazing telescopes are free for viewing on Friday and Saturday nights. Be an astronaut or an engineer on a simulated space mission at the Challenger Learning Center. Take a break on six acres of nature trails and at the Celestial Cafe, an indoor/outdoor cafe serving simple, hearty American food, and slurpees! Back home, kids can interact with the center online at the Virtual Science Center.

Ebony Museum of Arts and Store (all ages)

1034 Fourteenth Street, Oakland; (510) 763–0141. Museum free.

From Africa, everything is handcrafted and everything is fabulous: baskets, sculpture, art, jewelry, masks, clothing, and crafts.

Rockridge (all ages)

From the beginning of College Avenue at Broadway, up College to the Oakland/Berkeley border.

Spend an afternoon strolling, noshing, and shopping in a charming, leafy neighborhood that seems lost in the early twentieth century. Shop the fresh produce, fruit, cheese, and bakery vendors at the pleasant, open-air Market Hall; peruse the spectacular tile murals at the BART station; buy outdoor- and nature-oriented books and gifts at Sierra Club Books. Grab burgers at Rocky's, a Chicago-style pizza at Zachary's, satay at Sabuy Sabuy Thai, toys and games at Rockridge Kids, and a treat at Buttercup Bakery.

Oakland Museum (all ages)

1000 Oak Street at Tenth Street, Oakland; (888) 625–6873; www.museumca.org. $$; kids 6 and under free.

Not just another boring museum, this one is a playful construction of three tiers topped by a four-acre roof garden of outdoor sculpture and a koi pond. The open layout makes this a child-friendly, comfortable place to see contemporary and vintage California art. Stop at the video stations to watch Native American demos and interviews with artists. A cafe serves sandwiches, salads, and yummy desserts.

Western Aerospace Museum (all ages)

8260 Boeing Street, North Field, Oakland International Airport; (510) 638–7100; www .westernaerospacemuseum.org. Adults $$; children $; 6 and under are free.

Among the fabulous aircraft in a lofty hangar are a giant flying boat used in the movie *Raiders of the Lost Ark*; a Lock-heed Electra similar to the one flown by Amelia Earhart; an A-6 fighter; bombers, and a couple of dozen others. Artifacts, memo-rabilia, and photos trace the history of aviation.

Where to Eat

Il Pescatore. 57 Jack London Square, Oakland; (510) 465–2188. Overlooking the Oakland Estuary, a pleasant place for fresh seafood and Italian-American food. $–$$

Ratto's. Corner of Ninth and Washington Streets, Oakland; (510) 832–6503. Founded in 1897, a turn-of-the-century-style grocery store filled with wooden bins, barrels, and jars offering products in bulk and prepared foods. Browse the fantastical assortment of gourmet deli items, homemade pastas and soups, imported foodstuffs, cheeses, oils, and spices; then order sandwiches to eat at outdoor tables or take away. $

Red Tractor Cafe. 5634 College Avenue across from Market Hall in the Rockridge district; (510) 595–3500. Down-home comfort food, from macaroni and cheese to sumptuous meat loaf and garlic mashed potatoes, barbecued chicken, and chicken-fried steak and gravy. Kids get crayons and Big Bird plates. Lunch, dinner, weekend brunch. $

Where to Stay

Best Western Inn at the Square. 233 Broadway at Jack London Square, Oakland; (510) 452–4565; www.innatthesquare .com. In a perfect location for exploring the East Bay and saving money on a San Francisco visit, this motel has a heated outdoor pool, a fitness room and sauna, and a garden courtyard, and offers complimentary continental breakfast. The Buttercup is a pretty good coffee shop-style restaurant; try the banana cream pie. You can walk to the ferry and BART. $$–$$$

Executive Inn and Suites. 1755 Embarcadero, Oakland; (800) 346–6331, (510) 536–6633; www.executiveinnoakland.com. A sheltered swimming pool with a view of the Oakland Estuary; private balconies; complimentary, expanded continental breakfast; a fitness room; guest laundry; and interactive TV systems with digital movies, music, Nintendo, and free Internet access make this a good choice for families. Add to that the free shuttle to Oakland International Airport, Jack London Square, Alameda, the San Francisco ferry, BART, and Amtrak. A typical, 500-square-foot suite has a sitting area, refrigerator, microwave, and two queen-size beds. Smaller, more basic rooms have two queens. $$–$$$$.

For More Information

Oakland Convention and Visitors Bureau. 474 Fourteenth Street, Oakland; (510) 839–9000; www.oaklandcvb.com.

San Jose

Families visiting in the Bay Area may have heard of Paramount's Great America theme park, but many are unaware that several other fantastic family-oriented attractions are located in the South Bay. Your big and little cyber-nerds will spend their time in three dazzling technology museums: the Tech, the Intel, and the Children's Museum.

In San Jose's trendy arts and dining hub, SoFA (South First Street), it's fun to explore sidewalk cafes, galleries, and bookstores. At the Fairmont Hotel's Fountain Restaurant, monumental ice-cream concoctions are served at tables under a grove of palm trees; on hot days in the public plaza across the street, kids splash and play in an assemblage of 4-foot-tall water spouts.

A refurbished "Old Town" district downtown, San Pedro Square is a dining mecca with delightful new shade trees, landscaping, and sidewalk cafes. "Tuckered out" tourists rest on the lawns and benches of Plaza de Cesar Chavez, and kids run up and down on 3 miles of landscaped paths and parks in Guadalupe River Park. Look for the carousel and a visitor center in the south end of the park at Arena Green.

Adding to San Jose's value as a family destination are a water park, the urban oasis of Kelley Park, an eerie mystery mansion, and one of the premier Egyptian museums in the world.

Annual events that families like best are the Japanese Obon Festival in July, the Cinco de Mayo parade and festival in May, and Hoi Tet—the Vietnamese New Year celebration in February. The wildly colorful International Folklórico Festival is held in May at the Mexican Heritage Plaza, a lively headquarters for Hispanic music, art, and performing arts events all year (www.mhcviva.org).

In December an incredible "Christmas in the Park" at Plaza de Cesar Chavez features 400 decorated trees and an animated village and Nutcracker display; a block away, an outdoor ice skating rink is set up from late November through mid-January.

Children's Discovery Museum of San Jose (ages 3–12)
180 Woz Way, San Jose; (408) 298–5437; www.cdm.org. $$.

In a bright purple building, the largest hands-on science facility in the West is loaded with educational and fun activities for children through grade school age: Drive a fire truck, make tortillas, climb on a movable jungle gym, invent thingamajigs, crawl through tunnels, play on computers, conduct an orchestra, walk through an ambulance, get your face painted.

Light spills in through two-story glass walls onto indoor city streetscapes complete with traffic lights. The museum shop sells great toys, games, and puzzles, and there is a cafe. Get here early (the facility opens at 10:00 A.M.) to avoid crowds and noise, pick up a map to the 150 exhibits, and let the kids go. Snacks and light meals in the Kids' Cafe; picnic area nearby.

The Tech Museum of Innovation (ages 5 and up)
201 South Market Street, San Jose; (408) 294–TECH; www.thetech.org. $$; kids under 3 are admitted free.

Silicon Valley is the birthplace of the personal computer and world headquarters for technology-oriented businesses. It's no wonder that their dazzling mango-colored edifice of learning and tech fun is state of the art. More than one hundred exhibits are mostly interactive, including experimenting with the virtual bobsled simulator, piloting a real robot on the ocean floor, floating in a jet pack like the astronauts, designing a roller coaster, making your own movie, and much more—an IMAX theater, a Robot Zoo, computer games, demos of high-tech inventions, and a cafe. For the techie in your family, this could be an all-day affair.

San Jose **Area Parks**

- **Guadalupe River Park and Gardens,** west of Highway 87, with attractions around Springs Street and Taylor, the Alameda and Delmas, and Woz Way—see map on Web site; (408) 277–5904; www.grpg.org. A 3-mile-long park along the Guadalupe River. More than 3,700 varieties of roses, playground of net structures with adjacent, shaded picnic area; carousel, toddlers' play lot near a refreshment kiosk and restrooms. Visitor center is on the north side of Santa Clara Street at the river, in the pocket park of Arena Green across from the San Jose Arena. A good place to start the river walk is at the Children's Discovery Museum on Woz Way.

- **Kelley Park,** 1300 Senter Road; (408) 277–3000. Happy Hollow Zoo, a miniature train ride, the Historical Museum, an outdoor complex of Victorian buildings, a trolley barn and firehouse with old engines, all laid out on beautiful Coyote Creek. Younger children love the merry-go-round, the carousel, and the petting zoo.

- **Lake Cunningham Regional Park,** Capitol Expressway and Tully Road; (408) 277–4319. Adjacent to Raging Waters, picnic areas, windsurfing, bike paths, marina with pedal boat rentals, and fishing.

- **Los Gatos Creek Trail,** above Los Gatos at Lexington Reservoir; (415) 691–1200. For biking, walking, skating, 9 miles of trail along a riparian corridor.

- **Castle Rock State Park,** 15000 Skyline Boulevard, Los Gatos; (408) 867–2952. More than 3,000 acres of semiwilderness with big views, waterfalls, forests, meadows, hiking and horse trails, picnic areas.

Intel Museum (ages 7 and up)
Take the Montague Expressway exit off Highway 101 to 2200 Mission College Boulevard, Santa Clara; (408) 765–0503; www.intel.com/go/museum. **Free.**

Learn about the life and times of the microprocessor chip through exhibits and demos that make tech science comprehensible to all of us. You can also find out about clean rooms, transistors, and memory technology, and try out the hands-on computer-based learning lab. The gift shop is great fun, with techie souvenirs, clothing, and semiconductor jewelry.

Winchester Mystery House (ages 6 and up)
525 South Winchester Boulevard, San Jose; (408) 247–2000; www. winchestermystery house.com. Ages 13 and up $$$; ages 6 to 12 $$; under 6 are **free.**

In a Victorian mansion with 160 rooms, doors open into blank walls, stairways lead nowhere, and ghosts and spirits are afoot in a strange and spooky atmosphere. Also here is a large collection of antique Tiffany glass windows. The house tour is guided, but you can wander the vast, glorious gardens on your own. Come at Halloween for entertainment and flashlight tours.

Rosicrucian Egyptian Museum (all ages)
1342 Naglee Avenue, San Jose; (408) 238–9900. $$; kids 5 and under **free.**

Do you love your mummy? Sphinxes, temples, chariots, statues from ancient Thebes, gods of the Nile, a pharaoh's tomb, and delightfully scary, shrouded mummies are a few of the artifacts and reproductions here. A large collection of fascinating stuff, the largest Egyptian museum in the West. Kids love it. Little ones can run around in the gardens.

Raging Waters (ages 5 and up)
233 South White Road, San Jose; (408) 238–9900; www.rwsplash.com. Anyone 48 inches or taller $$$$; seniors and those shorter than 48 inches $$$; kids 2 and under **free.**

A fourteen-acre water park with more than thirty exciting slides. The little ones have their own wading pools and minislides; big kids take off in the Barracuda Bluster! Adjacent to the water park, Lake Cunningham Regional Park offers picnic areas, windsurfing, bike paths, fishing, and a marina with pedal boat, canoe, and sailboat rentals.

Paramount's Great America (all ages)
Great America Parkway, Santa Clara; (408) 988–1776; www.pgathrills.com. Adults and ages 3 and up $$$$; children under 3 or under 48 inches tall go **free.**

Plan one long day here for fifty rides, coasters, and spectacular, Broadway-style shows; movies and TV are the theme. This is the only theme park in the state with a water park— Boomerang Bay has thirty water slides, lagoons, rushing rivers, and surfable waves (in the Tazmanian Tornado, you slide through a completely dark, 300-foot cavern and rocket out into a funnel that tosses your raft around). Toddlers like Kookaburra Bay, a quiet, shallow pool with waterfalls. The big thrills are the roller coasters—including Top Gun, a suspended jet coaster; the Vortex, a rare stand-up coaster; the Drop Zone Stunt Tower; Invertigo; and more scary machines. For smaller kids and less brave adults, there are many easy, fun rides, too, like Rugrats Runaway Reptar and Psycho Mouse. The fancy double-decker carousel is the tallest in the western states and may be the tallest in the world. One admission price gets you on all the rides and into live and filmed extravaganzas. At the Days of Thunder motion simulator, strap yourselves in and get ready to scream around a stock car racetrack. Take the littlest kids to the audience participation Flintstones show and to Rugrats. See IMAX movies, live ice shows, and rock bands. Fort Fun and the Smurf Woods are filled with rides and entertainment for toddlers.

Stanford Linear Accelerator Center (ages 11 and up)

2575 Sand Hill Road, Menlo Park; (650) 926–2204; www.slac.stanford.edu. Call ahead to book the free, two-hour tour of the accelerator, the Gallery (offering an incredible photo-op of the 2-mile tunnel), the Collider, and more.

On the Stanford University campus, the Klystron Gallery is the longest building in the world, housing 2 miles of cutting-edge scientific machines and devices. If you have children who are mad scientists and interested in subatomic collisions, synchroton radiation, antimatter, quarks, and leptons, they will love this place (you may not know what these words mean, but your children probably do).

Santana Row (all ages)

400 South Winchester Boulevard, San Jose; (408) 551–4643; www.santanarow.com.

A unique, European-style covered arcade of upscale shops and cafes makes this a nice stop for a couple of hours. Between the sidewalks, a wide, tree-shaded park is filled with fountains and water features, gardens, and sixteen chess tables with pieces provided. Sit in an outdoor cafe, browse the Sunday farmers' market, catch an outdoor movie or live music in the summertime, or check your e-mail with the wireless access available.

Where to Eat

A.P. Stump's. 163 West Santa Clara at San Pedro, San Jose; (408) 292–9928. A short walk from the Tech Museum, "new American" cuisine at lunch and dinner; salads and sandwiches to go next door at A.P.S. Express, for picnicking in Cesar Chavez Plaza. $$

Las Brasas. 763 East Julian Street, San Jose; (408) 971–9639. One of the best *taquerias* in a town that knows tacos. Go for outside service on balmy summer weekend nights, and don't miss the melt-in-your-mouth spicy beef, *suadero*. $

Old Spaghetti Factory House. 51 North San Pedro Avenue, San Jose; (408) 288–7488. Good, traditional Italian food, fun, casual surroundings. $–$$

Sam's Bar-B-Que. 1110 South Bascom Avenue, San Jose; (408) 297–9151. Beloved by the locals and serving barbecued brisket, ribs, chicken, and burgers. A model train entertains the youngsters. $

Where to Stay

Hyatt San Jose. 1740 North First Street, San Jose; (800) 233–1234. A big hotel, with an airport shuttle, a pool and garden courtyard, a fitness center, a parcourse, an on-site jogging path, some refrigerators, and a coffee shop and pool cafe. Tennis nearby; hotel is near main San Jose attractions. $$–$$$$

For More Information

San Jose Convention and Visitors Bureau. 333 West San Carlos Street, Suite 1000, San Jose; (408) 295–9600 or (888) SAN–JOSE (recorded events: 408–295–2265); www.sanjose.org. Ask about travel packages that include lodgings and admission to local attractions and events, and about 50-percent-off weekend hotel discounts.

Valley Transportation Authority (VTA). (408) 321–2300; www.vta.org. Light-rail service in San Jose, Santa Clara, and throughout Silicon Valley, and historic trolleys downtown.

Bay Area Rapid Transit (BART). (510) 441–2278. High-speed trains between major cities in the Bay Area, including Santa Clara.

San Francisco

I n America's favorite vacation city, a massive, magical complex for children seems to float among the skyscrapers surrounding it. Around the urban park called Yerba Buena Gardens are the Rooftop play and learning garden; the Zeum, a tech-based visual, performing, and media arts center for ages eight to eighteen; an ice skating rink; a bowling center; and a historic carousel in a glass house. Looming above all this, Sony's Metreon is a three-story, blockbuster family entertainment center.

The Embarcadero from Fisherman's Wharf to China Basin has been transformed into a dazzling waterfront esplanade, with a wide sidewalk for jogging, biking, walking, and baby "strollering." Tall palms, historical plaques, Victorian-style benches and lamp stands, cobblestones, antique trolley cars, restaurants, and a Major League baseball park are all part of the shiny and new bayside sweep.

Old favorite attractions are the cable cars, Alcatraz, Golden Gate Park, and Chinatown. More than 200 parks and playgrounds are places to let off steam and have a picnic. Kids love the outdoor recreation and amusements on Marina Green and Fisherman's Wharf, while parents like the romantic Victorian neighborhoods, the museums, and the choice of over 3,500 restaurants—more per capita than any other American city. A visit to San Francisco is not complete without a ferry ride around the bay and a walk across the Golden Gate Bridge!

Only locals know of the more than 300 hidden stairways that wind up and down the hills, through forest glades and lush gardens. With a little investigation your family will discover the stairways and other hidden treasures, such as mysterious Chinese temples smoky with incense, a museum of antique nickelodeon games, and a students' cafe with knockout views and yummy, inexpensive food.

Walking is the best way to explore the ethnic districts of North Beach, the Hispanic Mission District, and Chinatown, as well as the neighborhoods inhabited by the "Painted Ladies," as the city's thousands of early twentieth-century mansions are called.

Local mariners share the bay with visitors on sightseeing sails, whale-watching cruises, and deep-sea fishing expeditions. Whale-boaters row, kayakers paddle, and flotillas of windsurfers flit like butterflies.

SAN FRANCISCO

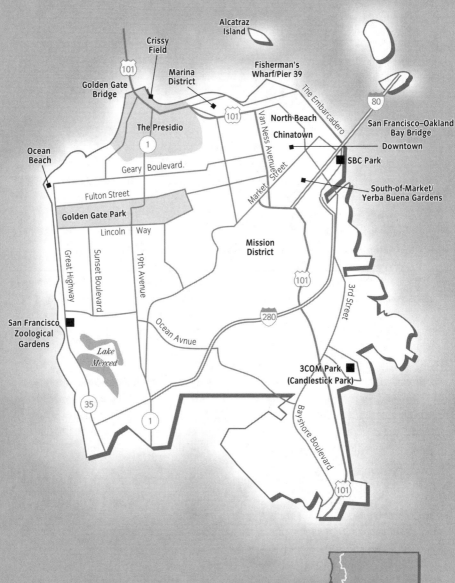

- Alcatraz Island
- Crissy Field
- Marina District
- Fisherman's Wharf/Pier 39
- Golden Gate Bridge
- The Embarcadero
- 101
- The Presidio
- 1
- North Beach
- Chinatown
- Van Ness Avenue
- Market Street
- San Francisco–Oakland Bay Bridge
- Downtown
- SBC Park
- Ocean Beach
- Geary Boulevard.
- Fulton Street
- South-of-Market/ Yerba Buena Gardens
- Golden Gate Park
- Lincoln Way
- Mission District
- Great Highway
- Sunset Boulevard
- 19th Avenue
- Ocean Avnue
- 101
- 280
- 3rd Street
- San Francisco Zoological Gardens
- Lake Merced
- 3COM Park (Candlestick Park)
- 35
- 1
- Bayshore Boulevard
- 101
- 80

Parking is scarce and expensive, and streets are congested throughout the city, so preplanning and lots of walking is advised, with the occasional use of a taxi to get from one district to another. Bay Area Rapid Transit (BART), the clean, safe, and on-time subway and commuter rail system, connects the city with the East and South Bays and the San Francisco International Airport, commonly referred to as SFO. "Muni," the streetcar and bus system, is neither clean, safe, nor on time; the refurbished vintage streetcars running along the Embarcadero and Market Street are the exceptions. Bicycles are more popular than ever, with all garages and ferries required to have bike parking.

Bring light jackets for the city's mild but changeable marine climate. Summer mornings and evenings can be chilly, due to foggy fingers blowing in through the Golden Gate, the city's natural air conditioner. Fall and spring are the best seasons to visit, when days are sparkling clear and warm and the summer crowds are gone.

Marina District

Marina Green (all ages)
Along Marina Boulevard between Scott and Webster.

A vast greensward on the edge of the bay and a yacht harbor, the most popular place in town for jogging, walking, and kite flying. You can get picnic goodies at the Safeway across the street.

The Exploratorium (ages 3–16)
3601 Lyon Street in the Palace of Fine Arts; (415) 397–5673; www.exploratorium.edu.
Adults and children ages 5 to 17 $$; 4 and under are free; Tactile Dome $14 all ages.

Called the best science museum in the world, the Exploratorium is housed in the Palace of Fine Arts, a fanciful Greco-Romanesque remnant from the Panama-Pacific Exposition of 1915. Here kids and adults are encouraged to play with and explore more than 650 exhibits. It's fun to bend lights, step into a giant kaleidoscope, fly without leaving the ground, touch a tornado, make bubbles 3 feet across, and create on computers. The Playsquare has climbing structures and role-playing venues for toddlers, as well as a place for infants to play with mirrors and experimental toys. Reservations are necessary for the Tactile Dome, a labyrinthine, pitch-black, crawl-through experience of a lifetime! (Call 415–561–0362.) Special exhibitions have featured animation, digital technology, TV editing; the biology and stimuli of memory with live nerve cells; and body imaging and the physics of sight.

When you're all reeling from cerebral stimulation, grab a snack in the indoor cafe or a hot dog at the outside food cart, take a walk around the lake, and relax on the lawns. On weekends you'll see wedding parties in full regalia, having their photos taken in the elegant pink rotunda of the Palace of Fine Arts.

Fort Mason (all ages)

On the east end of the Marina yacht harbor at Bay and Franklin Streets; (415) 441–3400; www.fortmason.org.

A sea-breezy complex of former military buildings on the waterfront, where cultural events are held on weekends. There are small museums and frequent weekend festivals; parking is free for up to four to twelve hours, depending on the parking spot location. The Children's Art Center in Building C offers drop-in and extended art workshops such as clay, printing, and painting for children twenty-seven months to ten years (415–771–0292; www.childrensartscenter.org).

Every year the San Francisco Blues Festival (415–826–6837) is held on the lawns above Fort Mason. There are easy-to-find public restrooms in each of the Fort Mason buildings.

Cooks and Company is a terrific take-out counter for sandwiches, soups, and scrumptious desserts; picnic tables just outside, or take the five-minute walk to the Marina Green.

Crissy Field (all ages)

Old Mason Street off Marina Boulevard, at the east end of the Marina; (415) 561–7690; www.crissyfield.org.

Restored to its original duney state, this is a nice place to walk, take photos of the Golden Gate Bridge, sit on a narrow beach, fly a kite, bird-watch in the wetlands, Rollerblade or stroll on a 1.3-mile trail, and enjoy watching boating and windsurfing activity offshore. Stop in at the Gulf of the Farallones Marine Sanctuary visitor center to see photos and exhibits of sea creatures, including great white sharks, and touch marine animals in a simulated tidepool. The Warming Hut Cafe and Bookstore is a cozy spot where you can stop for drinks, light meals, and snacks (415–561–3040). You can walk from here to Fort Point, and on the Golden Gate Promenade, all the way around the Embarcadero to Pacific Bell Park and beyond.

Golden Gate Promenade/Embarcadero (all ages)

Along the North and East Waterfronts, from Fort Point under the Golden Gate Bridge to Pac Bell Park at China Basin, about 5 miles.

A wide sidewalk perfect for in-line skates, baby strollers, and your feet. Cruise along through Crissy Field, past the small craft harbor and the Marina to Aquatic Park, Ghirardelli Square and the Cannery, past Fisherman's Wharf to Pier 39. Continue along the commercial piers to the Ferry Building and Justin Herman Plaza, beyond the Oakland Bay Bridge and the outdoor cafes of South Beach, to SBC Park, enjoying the fishing piers, benches, historic markers, restaurants, and rest stops along the way. Take the F Line trolley back from Market Street to Fisherman's Wharf.

Where to Go **in San Francisco**

The most popular family attractions are located in these districts of the city.

Marina District In the shadow of the Golden Gate Bridge, bordered by San Francisco Bay, Van Ness Avenue, Pacific Avenue, and the Presidio.

- Marina Green
- The Exploratorium
- Fort Mason
- The Presidio
- Fort Point
- Golden Gate Promenade

Waterfront From the Marina east to the Embarcadero.

- Hyde Street Pier and Maritime National Historical Park
- Fisherman's Wharf
- Maritime Museum
- Aquarium by the Bay
- Pier 39
- Alcatraz
- Bay Ferries

North Beach The old Italian district, bordered roughly by Broadway, Mason, Kearny, Lombard, and Telegraph Hill.

- Washington Square
- Coit Tower
- Italian restaurants
- North Beach Museum

Golden Gate Park/Ocean Beach

- Japanese Tea Garden
- Stowe Lake
- Land's End
- Conservatory of Flowers
- Outdoor Recreation
- Beach Chalet
- San Francisco Zoo

Downtown/South-of-Market

- Yerba Buena Gardens
- MOMA, the San Francisco Museum of Modern Art
- Zeum/Rooftop
- Cable cars
- Sony's Metreon

Chinatown

- Chinese Historical Society Museum
- Chinese restaurants and shops

More San Francisco Other attractions well worth a stop if time permits.

- Mission Dolores
- 49-Mile Scenic Drive
- China Beach
- Mission Cliffs

City Tours for Families

- **City Guides Tours,** Main Library, 100 Larkin Street at Grove, Civic Center; (415) 557–4266; www.sfcityguides.org. You can just show up for a wide variety of free guided and narrated walking tours of the city. Some of the choices are Chinatown, Victorian landmarks, Japantown, earthquake and fire history, ghosts, Golden Gate Bridge, Gold Rush history, Mission murals, Telegraph Hill, and many more. Go to the Web site for complete information; most walks are one to two hours.

- **Fire Engine Tour,** Beach Street at Columbus Avenue; (415) 333–7077; www.fireenginetours.com. $$$–$$$$. Outfitted in firefighters' jackets, twelve passengers at a time climb aboard a beautiful 1955 red fire engine for a seventy-five-minute city tour and ride across the Golden Gate Bridge into Sausalito. The lively husband and wife owner/operators keep up a steady narration of sights and history and lead the group in rousing songs. My grandkids absolutely loved it. If you have any doubts, show up at Beach and Columbus seventy-five minutes after 1:00 P.M. and watch the laughing customers return from their ride.

- **Wok Wiz Tours,** (415) 981–8989, (650) 355–9657; www.wokwiz.com. $$$$. The ultimate expert on Chinatown, high-energy Shirley Fong-Torres conducts fabulous, fun tours. Choose from I Can't Believe I Ate My Way Through Chinatown; Ciao Chow!, a two-hour walk highlighting Italian and Asian history; general Chinatown tours, and more. The advantage to touring with Shirley is that she knows everyone in Chinatown and arranges special visits to secret shops and great restaurants. Check out the Web site for Shirley's restaurant reviews, recipes, and more fun stuff.

- **Do-It-Yourself Walking Tours,** (415) 346–2000; www.sfhistory .org. Stop in the San Francisco Convention and Visitors Bureau (see "For More Information" at the end of this chapter) or at the Museum of the City of San Francisco at Pier 45 for maps of great walking routes around the city. A popular trek is the Barbary Coast Trail, a 3.8-mile walk marked with bronze medallions and arrows set in the sidewalk. The trail connects twenty sites from the city's rollicking history, from the Spanish to the Gold Rush, the 1906 earthquake, and more. You can also print out the map and descriptions from the Web site.

The Presidio of San Francisco (all ages)

Near the Golden Gate, bordered by Baker Beach, the bay, Lyon Street, and West Pacific Avenue; (415) 561–5300; www.presidiotrust.gov. Maps and information at the Presidio Museum, corner of Lincoln Boulevard and Funston Avenue; (415) 561–4331. Free admission.

These 1,480 acres of wooded highlands, beaches, and vintage buildings were used by the military for more than 200 years, from the Spanish and Mexican armies to the U.S. Army, from Civil War times to the 1990s. Now part of the National Park System, this magnificent park is threaded by quiet roads and paths for walking and bike riding. You can easily spend a day here, starting with a ranger-led tour or a self-guided expedition of the museums and architectural relics, from seventeenth-century bronze Spanish cannons to Civil War barracks, pre-earthquake Victorians, adobe walls built by the Spanish conquistadors, and picturesque rows of Queen Anne–style officers' homes. Call for tour reservations: (415) 556–0865. Easy two-hour walks focus on history, architecture, nature, or historical personalities.

Secluded trails wind through cypress, pine, and eucalyptus forests. Picnic tables are found in sunny meadows, hidden in lush rhododendron groves, or perched on breezy headlands with sea views. A meandering creek and a spring-fed pond are habitats for hundreds of birds.

On the west side of the Presidio, Baker Beach is unsafe for swimming but great for sunning and shore fishing, and there are World War II bunkers to explore. Smaller, more sheltered beaches and a waterfront promenade are found at Crissy Field beside the bay—also part of the Presidio.

Fort Point National Historic Site (all ages)

Under the Golden Gate Bridge adjacent to the Presidio, take Long Avenue to Marine Drive; (415) 556–1693. Free.

A Civil War–era fort where costumed docents show you around a gunpowder storehouse, barracks, jail cells, and a museum of military artifacts. Little boys really go for the swords, guns, and cannons.

Take photos here of the bridge with waves crashing and sailboarders in the bay. You can fish along the seawall. A beach at the foot of the cliffs on the west side of Fort Point is sometimes enjoyed by nude sun worshippers.

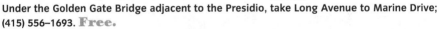

Waterfront

Wax Museum (all ages)

145 Jefferson Street; (800) 439–4305 or (415) 202–0400; www.waxmuseum.com. Adults and children ages 12 and up $$$; ages 4 to 11 $$; children under 4 free.

It's downright spooky to see Princess Diana, George Burns, and King Tut in the (waxed) flesh. From their posts in 100,000 square feet of elaborate, movielike settings, nearly 300 celebrities and historical figures look you right in the eye: Caruso, Castro, Chaplin, Cinderella, even Bruce Willis. This is a fun but pricey experience, a genuine Fisherman's Wharf tourist trap. The Rainforest Cafe has a beautiful, huge aquarium, live birds, and a three-story indoor waterfall. If you decide to go for it, come at opening time, 9:00 A.M. weekends, 10:00 A.M. weekdays, to avoid the crowds.

Hyde Street Pier and Maritime National Historical Park (all ages)

Hyde and Jefferson Streets at Pier 45, Fisherman's Wharf; (415) 556–3002; www.maritime.org. Admission to the museum building is free. Admission to Hyde Street Pier: adults $$; ages 12 to 17 $; under 12 are free with an adult. A family ticket admits two adults and up to four children under 18, $$$.

The only floating national park, anchorage for the world's largest collection of historic ships. Dozens of antique vessels are open to explore and clamber on, from tiny fishing boats to steam tugs, a houseboat, an 1895 lumber schooner—with 100-foot beams in its hold—and an ornate 1886 square-rigger. Vintage autos line the decks of the *Eureka,* an 1890 ferry. Knot tying, sail raising, and sea-chantey singing take place on weekends. Annual events include the Haunted Halloween Ship, storytelling, engine room tours, birding tours on the pier, navigation, and more. Every Saturday rangers give free presentations, especially for kids: scrimshaw, signal flags, stories, ship models, and knot tying.

Fisherman's Wharf

On the waterfront, from Aquatic Park to about Powell Street; www.fishermanswharf.org.

The bawdy, brawny Barbary Coast of a century ago is now a warren of seafood restaurants, shopping complexes, commercial fishing wharves, museums, tourist traps, and one of the great waterfront promenades in the world.

National Maritime Museum (all ages)

900 Beach Street, foot of Polk, Fisherman's Wharf; (415) 561–7100; www.maritime.org. Free.

A glorious and historic art deco building resembling a cruise ship, awash with ship models, figureheads, maritime paintings, photos, and artifacts. Watch ships in the bay through the telescope on the "bridge," and translate Morse code in the World War II–era radio room. The USS *Pampanito,* a World War II submarine, is docked at Pier 45 (a short walk east). Self-guided submarine tour: adults $$; ages six to twelve $; ages five and under are free.

The Cannery

2801 Leavenworth, at the foot of Columbus overlooking the bay; (415) 771–3112; www.thecannery.com.

The largest peach cannery in the world at the turn of the twentieth century, this three-story brick complex now holds dozens of smart shops and restaurants, with an olive-tree-shaded patio for free entertainment and dining. The cable car turnaround is ½ block away.

Pier 39

One of the most popular tourist attractions in the country, Pier 39, at the Embarcadero at Beach Street, is a carnival of entertainment, shopping, restaurants, and places to enjoy the outdoors. The long pier juts out into the bay on the northernmost point of the city, making for glorious sea views from many of the more than 110 shops. Prices are high, but there are plenty of gadgets and souvenirs in the $5.00-and-under range. Each shop focuses narrowly on some catchy type of merchandise, such as puppets, movie memorabilia at Hollywood USA, souvenirs at the National Park Store and the Cable Car Store, zillions of magnets at Magnetron, the Marine Mammal Store, and Russka Babushka Dolls. The atmosphere is clean and commercial in a Disneyesque way. It is the best shopping center in town for kids because there is plenty of free entertainment—musicians and performers outdoors, sea lions, a carousel, plus a big games arcade. Sea-view cafes and snack carts serve fresh seafood and ethnic specialties, and they are expensive. Check out the Web site at www.pier39.com.

- **Aquarium of the Bay,** (415) 623–5300; www.aquariumofthebay.com. Adults $$$; ages 3 to 11 $$; two adults and two children $$$$. On moving walkways, travel through two crystal-clear 150-foot tunnels, surrounded by 700,000 gallons of San Francisco Bay seawater, and through exhibits of thousands of marine animals, from bat rays to hundreds of schooling fish and deep-sea predators to rare angel sharks and giant octopus. Touch leopard sharks and other tidepool animals in the "touch pools." Shop for seagoing gifts.

- **K-Dock.** Herds of 600 or so cavorting sea lions put on a daily show, barking, cavorting, and showing off on the docks at the end of the pier. The males can be 7 feet long and weigh 1,000 pounds.

- **Riptide Arcade.** More than one hundred video games in the Cyber Station games arcade. Kiddie rides and some video games are just for ages three to twelve.

- **Turbo-Ride,** adults and children ages 5 to 12 $$. A wild big-screen trip in hydraulic seats to see jolting, tilting, rocking multimedia extravaganzas such as 3-D Dino Island; Deep Sea, the Ride in 2-D; and Comet Impact.

- **Eagle Cafe,** (415) 433–3689. At a seventy-six-year-old landmark moved to the pier, start the day with eggs, country fries, and big buttermilk pancakes taken family-style at long wooden tables.

…s (ages 3 and up)
436–0633; www.bicyclerental.com.

…t or guided bike tour of the city, or go on the 9-mile, easy, guided ride …ate Bridge to Sausalito, with a ferry ride back, including helmet, sight-seeing stops, …ticket, and snacks, for about $35.

Musée Mécanique (ages 3-12)

Pier 45 at Taylor Street; (415) 346–2000; www.museemecanique.com. Free admission.

In a high, airy pier building, next to the docked USS *Pampanito* submarine, an eighty-three-year-old museum of coin-operated arcade games and curiosities. With handfuls of quarters, have fun making them go: fortune-tellers, dioramas, stereoscopes, strength testers, dancing puppets, road racers, and player pianos are among the 180 vintage machines. The bad news: A few modern arcade games have been added at the back of the building. The good news: Displays of the Museum of the City of San Francisco are here, and you can walk right out onto the breezy dock of the bay.

Alcatraz (all ages)

Pier 41; (415) 705–5555; www.blueandgoldfleet.com. Fee for self-guided or guided tours: adults $$$; ages 5 to 11 $$; ages 4 and under free.

Site of the notorious federal penitentiary that once housed Al Capone and Machine Gun Kelly, the island in the middle of the bay is a top tourist attraction. The Alcatraz experience takes about three hours and includes a ferry ride, a walk in the sea breezy outdoors, narrated or self-guided tours of the echoing, empty cell blocks and other historic buildings, and stunning views of the Bay Area. An electric tram trundles people and wheelchairs up the steep hill. Tours often sell out in summer; make reservations in advance.

The Alcatraz Kidz Tours, September through November some evenings, have such titles as I Spy; Pirates, Rebels, and Spies; Slime and Spine; and the Flashlight Tour. With special guides, kids become Alcatraz inspectors, hear tales of pirates, and explore secret areas.

The Island Hop is a popular five-hour tour combining visits to Alcatraz and Angel Island State Park. Included are ferry rides, admission fees, an audio tour of Alcatraz, and a motorized, open-air tram tour of Angel Island. Lunches and snacks are available to purchase on Angel Island, or you can bring a picnic. On clear days—almost every day in the spring and fall—the islands and the ferries offer unequaled views of the city skyline and much of the Bay Area, including five of the region's eight bay bridges.

Red and White Fleet Golden Gate Bay Cruise (all ages)
Pier 43½, Fisherman's Wharf; (800) 229–2784; www.redandwhite.com. Tickets for adults and kids ages 12 to 18 $$$; kids ages 5 to 11 $$.

If you have time for just one quick boat trip, this is the one: a one-hour sail under the bridge and around the bay past Angel Island and Alcatraz, including personal audiotape with historical overview, in your choice of six languages. From Pier 43½ or from the Ferry Building, Red and White also offers ferry tours to the aircraft carrier, USS *Hornet,* in Alameda.

North Beach

Between Telegraph Hill and Russian Hill near the waterfront.

In the heart of Italian North Beach beneath the towers of the Romanesque master-piece Church of Saints Peter and Paul, Washington Square is an outdoor meeting hall and social center, where Chinese practice tai chi, Italian grandpas sit on park benches, and artists set up their easels. Surrounding streets are crowded with family-style Italian restaurants, pizza joints, bakeries, and more than a dozen espresso cafes. Picturesque against the murals of Cafe Roma and Cafe Viva, people from all over the world sip cappuccinos. At Caffé Verdi and Cafe Puccini, you'll hear opera, and at Cafe Italia the click of pinball and pool. The tiny Bohemian Cigar Store, famous for foccacia sandwiches, is a good place to pick up picnic goodies (415–362–0536). Just up the street, the fragrance in Molinari's Delicatessen is of dozens of kinds of Italian cheeses and salamis (415–421–2337).

A main tourist attraction in North Beach is Coit Tower on top of Telegraph Hill overlooking the entire north Bay Area (415–362–0808). The 210-foot tall art deco tower is decorated with l930s murals of early California. Take the bus up to the tower, then return to North Beach by way of the woody Filbert Street steps past mansions, pre-earthquake cottages, and gardens. Sit quietly on a bench and you may see raccoons or a small red fox.

Tucked away on the mezzanine of a bank, the tiny **North Beach Museum** exhibits fascinating old photos and a few artifacts that make the early days of the city come alive (415–989–2220, **free** admission).

Golden Gate Park/Ocean Beach

In the 1,017-acre garden that is one of the world's greatest metropolitan parks, you can row on a lake, ride a horse, play tennis, take long walks, browse in museums, or just laze on the lawns. Historically located in the park, the California Academy of Sciences, which includes Steinhart Aquarium, is temporarily housed at 875 Howard Street. In 2008 the expansive new facilities will open in Golden Gate Park. See the Web site www.calacademy.com. The academy is the country's only combined aquarium, planetarium, and natural history museum.

My kids, grown up now, still love having tea and cookies in the Japanese teahouse when the cherry trees bloom in early spring. The Japanese Tea Garden is a fairy tale of a place, with a moon bridge, a brightly painted pagoda, a brooding bronze statue of Buddha, and lily ponds swimming with koi fish. Glorious maples blaze in autumn, and clouds of rhododendrons and azaleas burst into flower in spring.

On a huge network of walking and biking trails, you will pass people playing boccie and tennis, tossing horseshoes, fly casting, and playing checkers and chess in the checkers pavilion. For pot stickers to pizza, make a quick side trip to a clutch of restaurants at Ninth Avenue and Irving Street.

On Sunday afternoons the main park road is closed to vehicles, and impromptu Rollerblading and skateboarding happen; I mean, they really happen—fantastic free entertainment. As in any large urban park, it's advisable to stay together, leave before dark, and avoid isolated areas. Guided walking tours are offered free on weekends; call ahead for times and location (415–263–0991). Maps of the park are available at McLaren Lodge, at Stanyan and Fell, weekdays. On weekends, when parking is hard to find, hop on and off the free shuttle bus that runs between McLaren Lodge and Ocean Beach, stopping throughout the park at major attractions along the way. You can park at the nearby UCSF parking garage (at Parnassos and Fifth Avenue) and shuttle into the park from there.

Best **Playgrounds**

- **Golden Gate Park Children's Playground,** Bowling Green Drive between John F. Kennedy and Martin Luther King Drives, Golden Gate Park; (415) 753–5210. Climbing equipment, slide, swings, sandboxes, circa-1912 carousel with sixty-two vintage animals. Restrooms.

- **Chinese Recreation Center,** Washington and Mason Streets, Chinatown; (415) 292–2017. The usual playground equipment, an ethnic mix of kids. Restrooms.

- **North Beach Playground,** Lombard and Mason Streets; (415) 274–0201. Olympic-size pool with special hours for kids, a big playground, and an excellent children's library. Restrooms.

- **Huntington Park Playground,** at California and Taylor Streets on Nob Hill. A grassy spot with play equipment and a pink marble fountain that is a replica of a famous fountain in Italy.

Conservatory of Flowers (all ages)

JFK Drive, Golden Gate Park; (415) 666–7001; www.conservatoryofflowers.org. $; under 4 **free.**

Shipped around Cape Horn from England in the 1870s, this monumental glass greenhouse encloses a steamy, dreamy jungle of trees, exotic plants, and flowers in a sort of Victorian biosphere. Leaves as big as Hummers, lily ponds, Tarzan vines, gorgeous orchids, and blooming flowers are among the sights. The butterfly enclosure captivated my grandkids, who played for more than an hour with the bright creatures, which perched on their hands and shoulders. Outside are flower beds and vast lawns for running and picnicking. Except on weekends, you can usually park on the street nearby.

Beach Chalet (all ages)

1000 Great Highway; (415) 386–8439; www.beachchalet.com. $–$$$.

In a terra-cotta-tiled 1925 masterpiece of Willis Polk architecture overlooking Ocean Beach, this museum and park visitor center is on the ground floor. The museum contains Depression-era murals, mosaics and wood carvings, a model of Golden Gate Park, and historic exhibits. There is also a shop selling San Francisco logo souvenirs, guidebooks, old street signs, and city memorabilia. Upstairs is a great place for a sunny Sunday brunch or lunch; it's rather noisy, so squirmy kids attract little notice. The bistro and brewery menu is robust, featuring sausage sandwiches, beer-battered prawns, macho onion rings, grilled fish, and Cajun/Creole specialties, with some plain choices that kids like. Try the "sand castle" chocolate truffle cake. The museum is **free** and makes a convenient restroom stop at the beach. Daily lunch and dinner $$.

Land's End Trail (all ages)

Take Geary Boulevard west to the Cliff House Restaurant, where the trail begins; (415) 556–0560.

An easy, 2.5-mile walk, with views of the Golden Gate, the Marin Headlands, and the shore, plus seabirds and marine mammals for company. There are benches along the way.

San Francisco Zoo (all ages)

Three miles south of the Cliff House Restaurant, Sloat Boulevard at Forty-fifth Avenue; (415) 753–7083. Ages 12 and older $$; ages 3 to 11 $; kids under 2 are **free.**

The zoo shelters many rare and endangered animals, such as black rhinos, snow leopards, condors, elephants, and Prince Charles—a rare white Bengal tiger. In the world's largest naturalistic gorilla exhibit resides a family of lowland gorillas, including an adult male silverback and adorable youngsters. The feeding of the African lions and the highly endangered Sumatran and Siberian tigers takes place at 2:00 P.M., a big hit with all ages. A walk through the magical aviary of Rainbow Landing is an intimate encounter with some of the most colorful birds in the world—rainbow lorikeets. Kids can feed them nectar from their hands, then take home a photograph of themselves with these beautiful Australian birds. A sweet home for the North American river otters has climbing logs, pools, and waterfalls.

Little ones like the circa-1920 carousel and the Children's Zoo, where they can feed, pet, and play with barnyard animals.

Downtown/South-of-Market

Moma, The San Francisco Museum of Modern Art (ages 4 and up) 🔣

At Yerba Buena Gardens, 151 Third Street; (415) 357–4000; www.sfmoma.org. $$$ for adults; $$ for students with ID; and free for children 12 and under who are accompanied by an adult. Tickets are half price on Thursday, 6:00 to 9:00 P.M. Free admission on the first Thursday of each month.

Like a striped spacecraft about to lift off, a dazzling brick and glass temple to the arts designed by world-famous Swiss architect Mario Botta. Step inside to see the gigantic, upslanting skylight pouring light into the atrium. A whirl of gallery floors flow one into another, showing the works of Matisse, Kline, Warhol, and countless more contemporary masters. A glitzy cafe and an upscale shop with truly fabulous children's educational and artistic toys and games complete the MOMA experience. When popular exhibitions are in residence, avoid standing in line by coming a few minutes before the museum opens at 11:00 A.M. (10:00 A.M. during the summer). At Family Sundays, introduce your child to modern art at hands-on workshops in a light-filled workroom, with docent-led gallery activities, live music, and performers, often related to the current special exhibition.

Metreon Sony Entertainment Center (all ages) 🎵 🍴 🛍️

101 Fourth Street at Yerba Buena Gardens; (415) 369–6000; www.metreon.com.

A four-story silvery dazzler of a family entertainment complex, Metreon houses a 3-D IMAX theater and fourteen more movie screens, several restaurants, shops, and a children's world of interactive play. Browse, if you dare, in Sony Style, among the high-tech games and gadgets, and in PlayStation, the first and only completely hands-on game store. Digital Solutions is a marvel of entertainment and technology, featuring Sony Music, ImageStation, Screenblast, Everquest, and Sony Eco. The Bandai Shop sells the hottest Gundam series toys, action figures, model kits, and DVDs. The Games Workshop is the world's largest tabletop gaming store. You could leave teenagers here for hours.

At Portal One are surreal games and interactive experiences, such as karaoke for your feet at Dance Dance Revolution; HyperBowl virtual bowling; Quaternia, a capture-the-flag game in a strange feudal world and the Extreme Sports Adventure Room. Lots of places to spend money, lots to see that is free. A wide variety of restaurants includes A Taste of San Francisco—designed to be a street of city neighborhoods—sushi at Sanraku, Mexican food at Luna Azul, pasta and pizza at Firewood Cafe, Asian food at Long Life Noodle and Jook Joint, sweets at Just Desserts. A destination in itself, the glass lobby offers a panoramic view of the high-rise skyline. The Maurice Sendak–designed Where the Wild Things Are is larger than life, with a maze, a bubbling cauldron, and a 17-foot-high puppet.

Yerba Buena **Gardens**

An art and culture ghetto and urban park South-of-Market, Yerba Buena Gardens was built atop the underground Moscone Convention Center, bordered by Third, Folsom, Fourth, and Howard Streets. A greensward surrounded by astonishing contemporary architecture, museums, and theaters, Esplanade Park is a place to sit at an outdoor cafe, lounge on the lawns, and enjoy the larger-than-life sculpture flanked by a 60-foot-wide, torrential sheet of water that creates a misty grotto for trees and a butterfly garden.

- **The Rooftop** (ages 2 to 8); (415) 522–9860. Free. An outdoor amphitheater where frequent performances are held for young audiences. A lawn bowl, robot sculptures, and fabulous playground with rubberized surfaces are also here.

- **Yerba Buena Bowling Center** (ages 6 and up); (415) 777–3727. $$–$$$. Twelve lanes of high-tech bowling with newfangled "bumpers" that pop up on either side of your lane, the better to corral the ball. Upstairs, Mo's makes its famous smoky grilled burgers, thick shakes, sandwiches, and salads, with incredible views of the gardens and the surrounding cityscape.

- **Yerba Buena Ice Skating Center** (ages 2 and up); (415) 777–3727; www.skatebowl.com. Adults $$; ages 12 and under $. Surrounded by windows with stunning views of the city, this 100-foot-long, NHL-regulation-size rink flashes with plenty of action—ice dancers, hockey players, and figure skaters of all ages and abilities. It's free to watch. You can rent skates and get in on public sessions every afternoon. The Kristi Yamaguchi Holiday Ice Rink is open outdoors at Embarcadero Center from mid-November through December, with rentals available. Just before Thanksgiving a free ice show and lighting ceremony takes place (www.embarcaderocenter.com).

- **Zeum** (ages 8 to 18); (415) 777–2800; www.zeum.org. Adults and ages 4 to 18 $$. Leonardo da Vinci meets R2-D2 at this pumpkin- and mauve-colored visual, performing, and media arts center. Peer docents help kids get involved in multimedia production, animation, Web page design, and all kinds of tech-based art and drama. Your children can simply observe and enjoy the exhibitions and performances or jump right into interactive play and learning, from virtual reality games to high-tech puppeteering, making a video, making music, sculpting, or participating in backstage theater production. The average visit is about three hours.

Cable Cars (all ages)
Call (415) 673–6864 for information. $.

National Historic Landmarks, the famous cable cars of San Francisco are fun, rain or shine. You get fresh air, great photo ops, and roller-coaster rides up and down the steep hills. To avoid standing in line, very early in the day during the week is the best time to hop on and off the Powell–Hyde, Powell–Mason, and California Street lines, each ending at a "turn-around." From the Powell–Hyde turnaround on Market Street, walk 2 blocks up to Union Square for an exciting ride on one of the St. Francis Hotel's thirty-two-story glass elevators, an eye- and ear-popping, 1,000-feet-per-minute flight with dizzying views at the top.

SBC Park
Between King, Second and Third Streets, and China Basin; (415) 972–2400, (800) 544–2687; www.sfgiants.com.

No other stadium in the world has these views—the San Francisco Bay, the Bay Bridge, and the city skyline. Some right-field home run balls actually end up with the fishes. Kids love the Coca-Cola Fan Lot, an interactive play area with slides, a mini-ballpark, autograph rubbings, and the world's largest baseball glove and Coke bottle. Along the waterfront from right to center field, you can line up at portholes to watch games at no charge. As few parking spots are available on this South-of-Market site, ferries drop people off right at the park. CalTrain arrives from South Bay cities a block away, and BART is nearby. In the city's tradition of the best food on the planet, the food vendors in the stadium sell everything from cappuccinos to gourmet burritos, cheesecake to chili. Take the Insiders' Tour to learn about how the unique new ballpark was built and see the areas that only the players and staff see, including the dugout, clubhouse, field, batting cages, the press box, and more (415–972–1800; tickets are $$ adults, $ ages twelve and under; ask about the doubleheader tour including a bay cruise).

Asian Art Museum (all ages)
200 Larkin Street at Civic Center; (415) 581–3500; www.asianart.org. $$; ages 11 and under are free.

A spectacular new cultural attraction in a stunningly redesigned building, this is one of the largest museums in the western world devoted exclusively to Asian art. Kids will find fascinating the huge East Indian stone sculptures, intricately carved Chinese jades, Cambodian buddhas, Japanese kimonos, arms and armor, puppets, and daggers from Indonesia. Daily from noon to 4:00 p.m., AsiaAlive is a free interactive program for all ages, with art demonstrations, videos, and hands-on activities. A Family Festival takes place in May, and you can come for free art workshops on first Saturdays. On Sundays and first Saturdays, storytellers keep kids mesmerized with Asian myths and fairytales. Within the museum, Cafe Asia is a serene indoor/outdoor environment for enjoying Asian-style snacks: bento boxes, rice bowls, noodles, sushi, salads, and sweets.

The Mexican Museum (all ages)
Fort Mason Center, Building D; (415) 202–9700; www.mexicanmuseum.org. Adults $$; children $; kids under 10 are free.

Even kids who hate museums will like the vibrant colors and whimsical shapes of the pre-Hispanic and contemporary Mexican, Chicano, and Latino art and rotating exhibits, which are presented with exciting creativity. You will find the shop full of papier-mâché animals, books, toys and games, masks, Day of the Dead figures, folk-art dolls, and fabulous ornaments at Christmastime. In late 2006 a spectacular, new, deep-orange-colored Mexican Museum will open across the street from Yerba Buena Center.

Chinatown

Chinatown begins at the ornate Chinese Gate at Bush and Grant. It comprises twenty-four square blocks, including most of Grant Avenue and the streets and alleys off Grant.

Stand on Grant Avenue and look in both directions at the blizzard of neon signs, pagoda roofs, and dragon-bedecked lampposts, all in the colors of China—blood red, gold, and bright green. Flying from the rooftops of the more elaborate buildings are banners and flags heralding the family and benevolent associations that unite Chinese people with a common heritage. At one of these, the Chinese Six Companies building at 843 Stockton, the steps between the green dogs are a good place for a family photo.

Do You Know About **the Golden Gate Bridge?**

- **Length:** 1.7 miles
- **Height of roadway above water:** 220 feet
- **Height of towers above water:** 746 feet
- **Color:** International orange
- **Toll in 1937:** 50 cents
- **Toll in 2004:** $5.00 southbound
- **Cables:** The two great cables on which the bridge is suspended contain 80,000 miles of steel wire, enough to encircle the equator three times
- **Best photo:** North side of the bridge from the Marin Headlands (take the Alexander Street exit)

The best time to explore Chinatown is in the early morning, when chattering house-wives flock around produce stands and little kids walk to school with their grannies. As handcarts clatter along, heaped with winter melons and crates of live chickens, you'll hear nary a word of English. In Portsmouth Square rows of people move in silent unison, practicing their daily tai chi exercise.

The larger souvenir stores and Asian antiques emporiums are on Grant, while the small shops are found in the forty-one narrow alleys crisscrossing the main street. As you prowl the alleys, watch out for laundry dripping from balconies overhead.

On Washington Street look through the open doorways of the fragrant shops and watch herbalists concoct potions and medicines by scooping fungi, roots, spices, and herbs into paper packets.

A meal in a Chinatown restaurant is a must, from an elegant dining room to a hole-in-the-wall noodle shop or a dim sum emporium. Most of us are familiar with Cantonese-style food—chow mein, sweet-and-sour dishes, fried rice—and you can get that all over Chinatown, but it's fun to try "hot pots" and noodle dishes from northern China or hot-and-spicy Szechwan-style cuisine. In dim sum teahouses, steamed dumplings and stuffed buns and turnovers are rolled by on carts.

Reflecting the large Asian and Pacific Islander population, a "New Chinatown" has emerged in the Richmond district along Clement Street from Arguello Boulevard to 25th Avenue. Here you can shop for the same roasted ducks, ginseng, mangoes, and star fruit as in Chinatown, and browse for old records, flowers, and books. The many family-owned restaurants are multicultural, from Chinese and Japanese to Thai, Persian, French, and Burmese cuisine. You may hear some of twenty-five different languages while hanging out with teens at Java Source Coffee Shop or stopping in at Green Apple Books and Vinh Khang Herbs and Ginsengs. Sweet Delite sells popular coconut- and taro-flavored tea shakes with tapioca balls at the bottom, which customers slurp up with a fat straw.

Chinatown Kite Shop (all ages)
717 Grant Street; (415) 391–8217.

At one of the world's great kite shops, there are Asian fighting kites; multilevel, dual-control stunt kites; dragon kites; windsocks; and even plain diamond-shaped paper kites you put together yourself. The nicest ones are made of fabric, and they make dramatic decorative pieces for the home, especially in a child's room. The best place in town to fly kites is on the Marina Green, where you have plenty of room to roam and the chance to see some fabulous, big kites in the air on weekends.

Great Wall Ginseng and Herbs
821 Pacific Avenue; (415) 397–2040.

This is the archetype of the colorful, fragrant, crowded Chinatown shops where herbalists concoct potions and medicines by scooping fungi, roots, spices, and herbs into paper packets—quite an exotic environment. They don't mind if you watch and ask questions.

Golden Gate Fortune Cookies Company
56 Ross Alley; (415) 781–3956.

Workers sit at machines from the 1920s, twisting fortunes into hot cookies as they come off the press. You are welcome to step in and sample the goodies.

Ten Ren Tea Company
949 Grant Avenue; (415) 362–0656.

Wide open to the street, welcoming you for free samples of steaming green, jasmine, or black teas. More than fifty varieties of special teas, priced up to $60 a pound, are scooped from big canisters. When tea samples are poured for you, tap your fingers or knuckles on the table to show thanks.

Chinese Culture Center (all ages)
Holiday Inn, 750 Kearny Street; (415) 986–1822; www.c-c-c.org. **Free.**

In the lobby of the hotel is a small, impressive museum of antique Chinese pottery and musical instruments, beautiful ancient statuary, and the gold-adorned costume of an empress. An annual holiday bazaar is held in December, when reasonably priced Chinese ceramics, toys, gifts, and home accessories are on sale.

Chinese Historical Society of America (all ages)
965 Clay Street; (415) 391–1188; www.chsa.org. $; **free** for 5 and under; **free** to all on the first Thursday of each month.

In the wonderful Julia Morgan–designed, former YMCA building, displays of clothing, slippers of nineteenth-century Chinese pioneers, a colorful 1888 Buddhist altar, antique swords, photos, parade dragons, opium pipes, a fishing sampan, and other artifacts tracing the history of Chinese immigration in America from the early 1880s to today. The gift shop here is a good place for inexpensive souvenir shopping.

Chinese New Year (all ages)
January and February; (415) 391–2000.

The most spectacular of annual festivals in the city, starting with the New Year Flower Fair in late January, on Grant and Pacific Streets: plants, flowers, produce, traditional dance, music, art, and cultural displays. A mid-February weekend is the big deal, with a Chinatown Community Fair—kite and lantern making, arts demos, folk dance, puppet shows—and the big nighttime New Year Parade. With kids and grandkids in tow, my family prowls the parade route for a prime spot where the smaller children can see, and we wait breathlessly to hear the first blast of the firecrackers. Up the street come the glowing lanterns, crashing cymbals, marching bands, booming drum troupes, and famous dragons—roaring, fire-breathing, twisting, leaping, and sparkling red, gold, and green, accompanied by costumed attendants holding long strings of popping fire-crackers. When the parade is over, having cleverly made dinner reservations in advance, we then have a big Chinese dinner, usually at Brandy Ho's (217 Columbus; 415–362–6268).

More San Francisco

Mission Dolores (all ages)
Dolores Street at Sixteenth, in the Mission District; (415) 621–8203. $.

The beating heart of the city's Hispanic community, the mission is the oldest and one of the most beautiful structures in the city; it was founded in 1776, five days before the signing of the Declaration of Independence. Within the thick adobe walls a miraculous painted ceiling glows in early Native American designs. Next door the larger church was built in 1918. In a tiny cemetery lie thousands of the Mexican, Spanish, Indian, and Irish builders of America's favorite city by the bay.

Mission Cliffs Rock Climbing Center (ages 4 and up)
2295 Harrison Street; (415) 550–0515; www.mission-cliffs.com. Day pass $$–$$$.

No, Virginia, there are no mountains in San Francisco, but you can learn to climb on 16,000 square feet of cavernous indoor terrain. Rock climbing is a happening sport in California, and this state-of-the-art climbing gym in the Mission District is a fascinating place to visit, even if your family doesn't have the desire to hang upside down from great heights. There is a large "bouldering" area, short top-roping routes for beginners, longer routes for experts, and lead-climbing routes as long as 55 feet for those who are Half Dome– and Everest-bound. The gym is membership based, with day passes available to the public. There are free weights, exercise machines, locker rooms, showers, and saunas. A lively schedule of classes, clinics and world-class competitions goes on, with programs for kids, too.

Coyote Point Museum (ages 3–12)
Five miles south of the airport, take Poplar Avenue exit, 1651 Coyote Point Drive, San Mateo; (650) 342–7755; www.coyoteptmuseum.org. $.

Save a half day for exploring the many attractions here and for a bayshore walk and maybe a picnic at the beach. New is a walk-through aviary where you can ramble around a pond, waterfall, and gardens to get up close to native birds. Designed especially for kids are extensive science and wildlife exhibits and live animal venues. River otters are fed daily at 12:15 P.M.; foxes at 11:30 A.M. There are picnic tables under the trees, a playground, walking trails, and beach access.

San Francisco International Airport (all ages)

Thirteen miles south of San Francisco near the junction of Highways 101 and 380; (650) 821–6700; www.flysfo.com/guide_nonflash/airportinfo/Kids.htm.

On the departures/ticketing level of terminal 1, three beautiful aquariums are mesmerizing. In boarding area F, terminal 3, you can rent DVD players and movies for use at the airport, during a flight, or for your entire vacation. Near gate 87A, boarding area F, terminal 3, is the Kids' Spot for interactive exploration with exhibits from the Exploratorium plus a crawling apparatus, a plasma wall, and other fun stuff. In terminals 1 and 3, special nursery rooms are set up for babies and toddlers who need a change.

About forty exhibitions at a time are on view throughout the airport, focusing on culture, art, history, and science. You might see Halloween costumes, Indonesian puppets, or American flags. Check the schedule and locations at www.sfoarts.org. In the international terminal is the Aviation Museum, showing vintage planes and exhibits of space travel (650–821–9909).

Don't settle for junk food. Restaurants at SFO are among the most sophisticated and varied of any airport in the world, from Il Fornaio Caffe del Mondo to Jamba Juice, Just Desserts, the North Beach Deli, and Harbor Village Kitchen, a quick-serve version of one of the city's top Chinese restaurants. The Discovery Channel Store, Kids City, and Shift N' Gears are a few of kids' favorite shops among dozens of upscale retailers in the airport.

Where to Eat

Bill's Place. 2315 Clement Street; (415) 221–5262. Zillions of celebrity-named burgers, thick malteds, fabulous fries, and rubbing elbows with the locals at vinyl-topped stools at the counter. New owners have freshened up the place, retaining the favorite menu items and adding a wider choice of comfort foods. Try the hot vanilla shake. $

David's Deli. 474 Geary, near Union Square; (415) 771–0431. Kids like to sit at the counter for gigantic deli sandwiches, hot pastrami to die for, New York–style cheesecake, and huge slices of pie. $

Hard Rock Cafe. Pier 39; (415) 956–2013. Noisy and fun, a 1950s dream of hot cars and hot music and the place to meet young people and families from all over the world. Fabulous memorabilia displays feature the gamut of rock stars, from the Grateful Dead to Jimi Hendrix, The Who, and Ringo Starr. Validated parking. $–$$

Kate's Kitchen. 471 Haight Street; (415) 626–3984. Let out your belts, belly up to the blue-and-white-checked tablecloths, and tuck into big chunks of French toast, biscuits and sausage gravy, piles of bacon and cheddar cornmeal pancakes, and gigantic scrambled egg concoctions. Tops on the lunch menu are meat loaf sandwiches, homemade chicken soup, and incredible pie. Now, walk the 15 blocks to Golden Gate Park. Breakfast and lunch daily. $

La Taqueria. 2889 Mission Street; (415) 285–7117. Whimsical murals create a festive backdrop for fresh-fruit sodas, smoky *carne asada, carnitas* (slow-cooked pork), grilled chicken, and steak tacos and burritos. The neon sign says, THE BEST TACOS IN THE WHOLE WORLD. It could be true. You can sit on a bench inside or outside to eat, or take away. $

Lichee Garden. 1416 Powell Street; (415) 397–2290. Squeeze around a table in the bright, crowded dining room for great dim sum, crispy fried chicken, and lots of veggie dishes—good service, good food for lunch and dinner. $–$$

Mel's Drive-In. 2165 Lombard Street, 3355 Geary Boulevard, 1050 Van Ness Avenue, and 801 Mission Street; (415) 921–3039; www.melsdrive-in.com. No longer a real drive-in, Mel's is *American Graffiti* revisited. Jukeboxes are stationed at every booth, burgers come in a car box, shakes are thick, and crayons, balloons, homemade apple pie, and banana splits are abundant. Open just about all hours of the day and night. $–$$

R and G Lounge. 631 Kearny Street; (415) 982–7877. Don't bother to open the huge menu, just ask what fresh seafood specialties are being prepared today. From the province of Canton, the dishes are primarily seafood—wonderful whole steamed fish, crispy fried catfish, salt-and-pepper-roasted Dungeness crab, and savory claypot casseroles that may be anise-scented oxtails or spicy chicken. As in most Chinese restaurants, the dining room is plain and brightly lit; group tables are upstairs, which is nicer. Lunch and dinner. $–$$

Sears Fine Foods. 439 Powell Street, at Union Square; (415) 986–1160. For years and years, breakfasts of sourdough French toast and tiny Swedish pancakes for tiny tots, plus all-American favorites for breakfast and lunch. $

St. Francis Fountain and Candy Store. 2801 Twenty-fourth Street; (415) 826–4200. Since 1918, the city's best sodas and root beer floats, egg creams, homemade ice cream, grilled cheese sandwiches, BLTs, and burgers. $

Swan Oyster Depot. 1517 Polk Street; (415) 673–1101. Since 1912 just a counter with twenty stools and the best clam chowder, cracked crab, and other fresh seafood in town. Breakfast and lunch. $

Where to Stay

Argent Hotel. 50 Third Street; (415) 974–6400; www.argenthotel.com. A large, elegant, Art Deco–style hotel in the SOMA/Yerba Buena district; guestrooms and suites have floor-to-ceiling views of the city and the bay; sitting areas, work stations, overstuffed lounge chairs and ottomans; and a state-of-the-art health club. Unique here is the Kid's Koncierge, who gives kids a kit filled with toys, coloring books, and booklet of city activities and discount coupons, and counsels parents on family attractions. Kids' specials are on the menu at on-site Jester's Restaurant, with a things-to-do booklet and crayons at the table, plus old-favorites chicken fingers, peanut butter and jelly sandwiches, and more. Ask about family packages that include free parking, passes to family-oriented attractions, coupons for ice skate and bowling rentals, and discount restaurant coupons. $$$$

Argonaut Hotel. 495 Jefferson Street at Fisherman's Wharf; (800) 790–1415 or (415) 563–0800; www.argonauthotel.com. Brand new, a boutique hotel on the waterfront. Kids can step up to the steamer trunk front desk and choose a welcoming gift from the treasure chest. Families like the rooms set up for four; fresh nautical decor and bay views; flat-screen TVs, DVD/CD players, Nintendo, Internet access; fitness center; dogs are welcome. Some rooms have original brick walls, a separate parlor and bedroom, spa tubs,

and brass telescopes; "tall" rooms with extra-long beds. The Neptune's Adventure package includes a double queen room, full breakfast for four, cable car passes, gift for kids, Pier 39 discounts, and more. With Starbucks next door, Hyde Street Pier across the street, and the National Historical Maritime Park just out the door, you can't beat this location. $$$

Hotel del Sol. 3100 Webster Street; (877) 433–5765; www.hoteldelsol.com. Looking just like a California beach town motor lodge from the 1950s, the two-story Del Sol is Day-Glo yellow, bright orange, royal blue, and flaming red inside and out, with fabulous striped canvas drapes to pull across the carports. With low rates, a small swimming pool, free parking, a sauna, even hammocks, and an unbeatably convenient location near the Marina and Union Street shopping, this is a rare find in this city. Smallish rooms and spacious suites. $$$–$$$$

Hotel Metropolis. 25 Mason Street; (800) 553–1900 or (415) 202–8787; www.hotel metropolis.com. In a mid-downtown landmark a block from the cable car, one- and two- bedroom suites have refrigerators, Nintendo, and more amenities for families. A special just-for-kids room has bunk beds, Sponge Bob pillowcases, toys and a chalk board, kid-size furniture, and rubber ducky decor in the bathroom. Bringing Fido? Ask for a pet-friendly room which includes gifts of a squeaky toy, biscuits, treats, and a bath brush. The Family Plan includes Cokes, a disposable camera, postcards, discount coupons, and more. Fitness facility and library too. $$$

Motel Row. On Lombard Street, between Baker Street and Van Ness. Several inexpensive and medium-priced motels are located on Lombard Street within walking distance of the waterfront, restaurants, and public transportation. Reasonable choices are the Buena Vista Motor Inn (800–835–4980), the Lombard Motor Inn (800–835–3639), and the Cow Hollow Motor Inn, which has big family suites with kitchens (415–921–5800). All have free parking and connecting rooms. $$–$$$

Ocean Park Motel. 2690 Forty-sixth Avenue; (415) 566–7020; www.oceanpark motel.citysearch.com. Unusual in this city, very family-oriented rooms with equipped kitchens, some with separate bedrooms and up to three queen-size beds, private entrances, free parking. Playground, hot tub, nice gardens, dogs allowed. Two blocks to Ocean Beach and bike/walking path, 1 block to the zoo; public transportation at the front door. $$$

San Francisco Hotel Reservations. (888) 782–9673 or (415) 974–4499; www.sf visitor.org. Two hundred and twenty hotels and inns are described by location, type, price range, services, neighborhood, comfort level, and quality ratings, with availability up to twelve months in advance and photos.

San Francisco International Hostel. Bay and Franklin, above Fort Mason; (415) 771–7277; www.norcalhostels.org. For families on a strict budget or for those looking for a unique experience, two- and three-bunk private rooms (bring sleeping bags) and a communal kitchen; brief chores are required. The location above Fort Mason is unbeatable. $ per person; also family rates. For a brochure describing all Northern California hostels, call (415) 863–1444 (fax 415–863–3865).

Seal Rock Inn. 545 Point Lobos Avenue; (415) 752–8090. At the beach near the Cliff House Restaurant, simple units with an ocean view, some with fireplaces, kitchenettes. $–$$

For More Information

San Francisco Convention and Visitors Bureau. 900 Market Street, corner of Powell, P.O. Box 429097, San Francisco 94142–9097; (415) 391–2000; www .sfvisitor.org.

California Welcome Center. Pier 39, Marina Plaza, 2nd Level, Building P; (415) 956–3493; www.visitcwc.com. Get traveler's information, brochures, and maps for the entire state. Check your e-mail, make hotel reservations, and ask for advice.

Bay Area Rapid Transit (BART). (650) 992–2278 or (510) 465–BART; www.bart .gov. Subway and rail connecting San Francisco with Colma, Daly City, and the East and South Bay, including Oakland Airport, and SFO. Ticket prices start at $1.10; ages four and under ride **free.** Call for schedules, discounts, stations.

Passport. (415) 673–MUNI; www.sfmuni .com. Purchase at visitor centers and the cable car terminals at Fisherman's Wharf and Ghirardelli Square. Prices are: one-day $9.00, three-day $15.00, and seven-day $20.00 for unlimited travel on citywide Muni buses, cable cars, trolleys, and streetcars. Regular Muni adult fares are $1.25 and 35 cents for seniors and youth to age seventeen, ages four and under **free.** Exact change is necessary.

Streetcars. One of the nicest ways to ride about the city is on the colorful, historic streetcars. Beginning at Embarcadero Station, five streetcar lines (J-Church, K-Ingleside, L-Taraval, M-Ocean View, and N-Judah) take you along Market Street to various stops west and southwest in the city, including Ocean Beach. The F-line extension runs from SBC Park to the Ferry Building and around the Embarcadero to Fisherman's Wharf every ten minutes, stopping frequently.

CityPass. Purchase at visitor center and at the major attractions on the pass. (888) 330–5028; buy online, www.citypass.net. Prices: adults $36; ages five to seventeen $28; younger kids are **free** at most of the venues. If you plan to visit these attrac-

tions, you will save at least 50 percent on SFMOMA, Blue and Gold Bay Cruise, Exploratorium, Palace of the Legion of Honor, California Academy of Sciences, Muni transportation, and cable cars.

Preferred Travel Card. (888) 346–3467; www.sfvisitor.org. The Convention and Visitors Bureau joins annually with VISA to offer an extensive program of discounts on tours, cruises, and transportation; "priority entry" into major attractions; two-for-one tickets; complimentary items at restaurants; retail store gifts and discounts; savings at hotels; and more. Check out the benefits on the Web site. It's **free** to join.

Bay Trail Maps. (510) 464–7900; www .baytrail.org. Explore the entire San Francisco Bay shoreline with the help of a set of six maps that trace 230 miles of trails for walking, biking, and wildlife watching; each route is described in detail. The set costs $15.

Ferries. One of the least expensive and most fun ways to get around the bay is by ferry, from Vallejo, Marin County, and the East Bay to Pier 41 or to the Ferry Building on the Embarcadero. Schedules for seven ferry operators can be found at www .transitinfo.org.

Golden Gate
North: Marin County

Streaming out of the city like the tide under the Golden Gate Bridge, day-trippers escape into Marin County. Within an hour's drive are Pacific beaches, shady roads for bike rides, and footpaths beneath ancient redwood giants.

The profile of 2,600-foot Mount Tamalpais, the "Sleeping Maiden," lures mountain bikers and hikers into the canyons, forests, and meadows of Mount Tamalpais State Park. Scenic two-lane Panoramic Highway runs steeply over the mountain and down to Stinson Beach.

For freeway-free getaways take a ferry from San Francisco's Embarcadero to Tiburon or Sausalito for a day in the sun when the city is socked in with fog. With shops, restaurants, and waterfront promenades, the two Mediterranean-style villages overlook San Francisco Bay and the quiet inlet of Richardson Bay.

Miraculous double peninsulas that point jaggedly into the Pacific, Point Reyes National Seashore is one of the greatest coastal wilderness preserves in the world. The tiny towns of Inverness and Point Reyes Station are headquarters for provisions, meals, and lodgings near the national seashore. If your family craves oysters, head for Tomales Bay.

Inverness/Point Reyes

Inverness (all ages) 🍴 🚲 🔺 🏃
Highway 1 on the west shore of Tomales Bay; (415) 663–9232; www.pointreyes.org.

A vacation village since the late 1880s, Inverness, population 1,000, is a day-tripper's rest stop and a community of country cottages in the dark forest of Inverness Ridge, overlooking Tomales Bay. Keep your eyes open for cafes, a small marina, and eye-popping scenery.

From February through early summer, the meadows and marine terraces are blanketed with California poppies, dark blue lupine, pale baby blue-eyes, Indian paintbrush, and some wildflowers existing only here. The summit of Mount Wittenberg, at 1,407 feet, is reachable in an afternoon's climb.

A string of beaches and protected bays, hilltop and meadow trails, and an astonishing variety and abundance of birds and wildlife make the area a magnificent resource for families who love the outdoors. Often cool and foggy in summer, the weather is dependably clear and warm in spring and fall, and midwinter days can be surprisingly mild.

GOLDEN GATE NORTH: MARIN COUNTY

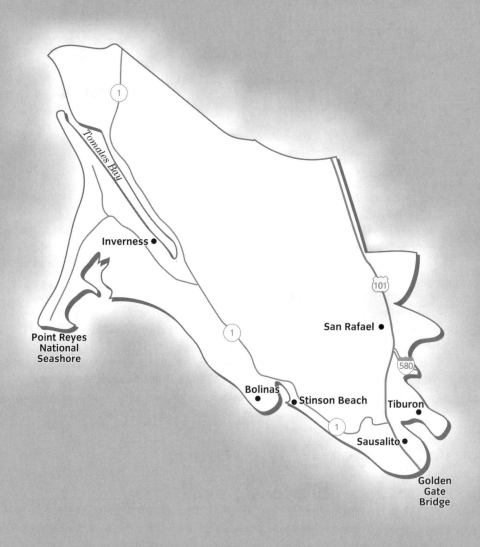

Tomales Bay

1

Inverness ●

Point Reyes
National
Seashore

101

San Rafael ●

580

Bolinas
●

● Stinson Beach

Tiburon
●

1

Sausalito ●

Golden
Gate
Bridge

Tomales Bay State Park (all ages)

Adjacent to Point Reyes National Seashore, 8 miles north of Inverness on Pierce Point Road, Inverness; (415) 669–1140.

Thirteen miles long, a mile wide, and shallow, Tomales Bay is a quiet finger of water surrounded by acres of mudflats and salt and freshwater marshes. Commercial oyster farms line the eastern shore. More then one hundred species of resident and migrating waterbirds are the reason you'll see anorak-clad, binocular-braced birdwatchers at pullouts on Highway 1 along the shore. Four beaches, hiking trails, and picnic areas. Heart's Desire Beach is a wind-protected, easily accessible beach, great for swimming, sailboarding, kayaking, and clam digging; picnic tables and 6 miles of easy-to-moderate trails.

Hog Island Oyster Company

20215 Highway 1, between Point Reyes Station and Tomales; (415) 663–9218.

Shucking knives, waterfront picnic tables, and barbecue kettles are provided—and the best oysters in the world! This is not a restaurant, so bring your own picnic to have with the oysters.

Tomales Point Hike (ages 6 and up)

About 2.5 miles past Inverness, turn right onto Pierce Point Road, following signs to McClure's Beach, and continue 9 miles to white ranch buildings and the parking lot; (415) 663–1092.

A breathtaking route on the bluffs above the Pacific, windswept moors that remind some visitors of Scotland. Wildflowers float in the meadows, whales spout December through February, and a herd of 500 tule elk live in the grassy fields of Pierce Ranch, a historic and photogenic dairy ranch. Stroll around the buildings to discover interpretive signs. The entire loop is 6 miles round-trip.

Point Reyes National Seashore (all ages)

Bear Valley Road, Highway 1 and Sir Francis Drake Boulevard, Point Reyes; (415) 464–5100; www.nps.gov/pore.

When the English explorer Sir Francis Drake sailed his *Golden Hind* into the great curve of Drake's Bay in 1579, he knew this was a bit of earth like no other. Part of the national seashore, the bay remains largely as it was 400 years ago—fringed with sandy beaches and tidepools alive with anemones and crabs, sometimes even rays and leopard sharks. North from the point—Point Reyes, where the lighthouse stands—are miles of beaches accessible from Sir Francis Drake Boulevard. Exposed to the full force of storms and pounding surf, these beaches are unsafe for swimming or surfing. The headlands, tidepools, sea stacks, lagoons, wave-carved caves, and rocky promontories are alive with birds—endangered brown pelicans, cormorants, surf scooters, sandpipers, grebes, terns—and sea life such as giant anemones, sea palms, urchins, fish, and even the occasional great white shark offshore of Tomales Point.

At the visitor center are exhibits, guidebooks, trail maps, and daily postings of whale sightings. Rangers are on hand to orient you to the diverse ecosystem and the many destinations within the huge park.

Short, easy walks near the visitor center include Kule Loklo Trail to Miwok Village, where an ancient Indian site has been re-created. On the Earthquake Trail are photos of the effects of the 1906 earthquake and signs explaining earth movement; the entire peninsula was once located some 250 miles to the south!

The Coastal Native American Summer Big Time takes place here in July, with demonstrations of crafts, skills, music, and dancing. October brings the Acorn Festival, a celebration of Miwok Indian history.

The weather can be foggy and windy on any day of the year, so warm jackets are advisable.

Bear Valley Trail (all ages)
Point Reyes National Seashore; (415) 663–1092.

The 4.4-mile trail to the Arch Rock overlook at the beach is the most popular and the easiest trail. The route wanders through forest tunnels, along creeks, and through meadows, ending on a bluff 50 feet above the sea. The last 2 miles are downhill. Bikes are allowed on all except the last 0.75 mile, where a bike rack is provided. From Arch Rock, you have several choices of return routes. Restrooms are located midway.

Limantour Beach and Limantour Estero Reserve (all ages)
Within Point Reyes National Seashore, at the end of Limantour Road; (415) 663–1092.

Just a few steps from the parking lot, this long stretch of windswept sand is good for surf fishing and sunbathing. Look for the Muddy Hollow Trail for a short birdwatching walk. Birdwatching is popular in the 500-acre Drake's Estero, a large intertidal lagoon with a giant tidepool.

Point Reyes Lighthouse (all ages)
Within Point Reyes National Seashore, at the end of Sir Francis Drake Boulevard; (415) 669–1534. Free.

Until the lighthouse was built, in 1875, many shipwrecks occurred off the Point Reyes Headlands. The lighthouse is reachable by 308 steps leading downhill from a high bluff, and it can be a windy, windy spot. During whale-watching season, December through March, a shuttle bus operates between the lighthouse and the beach. Some 20,000 California gray whales travel the Pacific coastline south to breed in Mexico, returning a few months later with their babies to the Arctic.

Kayaking Marin

If you haven't been in a kayak since years ago when they were heavy and awkward, you have no idea how easy and safe they are these days. When they say, "for all ages," it's really true. I started kayaking when I became a granny in my forties, and I have a friend who started designing, selling, and paddling kayaks in her seventies.

Kayaking companies will teach you the basics, outfit you, and suggest short or long paddling routes. Besides single "open deck" and sea kayaks, these proprietors rent junior-size kayaks, doubles, and triples. Even first-timers can learn in a few minutes with the free instruction offered by the kayak companies; kids will feel secure riding with a parent or older sibling. Call ahead to reserve the boats.

- **Blue Waters Kayaking,** next to Barnabys by the Bay, 12938 Sir Francis Drake Boulevard, Inverness; (415) 669–2600; www.bwkayak.com.

- **Tamal Saka Tomales Bay Kayaking,** Marshall Boat Works, 8 miles north of Point Reyes Station; (415) 663–1743; www.tamalsaka.com.

- **Open Water Rowing,** 85 Liberty Ship Way, Sausalito; (415) 332–1091; www.owrc.com.

- **Sea Trek Ocean Kayaking Center,** Schoonmaker Point, Liberty Ship Way, Sausalito; (415) 488–1000; www.seatrekkayak.com.

Point Reyes Station (all ages)
Highway 1 and Sir Francis Drake Boulevard.

Many century-old buildings remain on the short main street of a picturesque railroad town founded in the 1800s. The train depot is now the post office, the Fire Engine House, a community center. Dairy ranches and commercial oyster companies fuel the rural economy.

Toby's Feed Barn
Point Reyes Station; (415) 663–1223.

Hay, feed, souvenirs, T-shirts, and cool stuff crafted by local artists.

Into the Blue (all ages)
In the Livery Stable, corner of Third and B Streets, Point Reyes Station; (415) 663–1147.

On the way to the beach, kites and wind toys galore.

Tomales Bay Foods
Fourth and B Streets, Point Reyes Station; (415) 663–9335. $$.

Owned by a graduate of Chez Panisse, the birthplace of California cuisine. An airy emporium of luscious take-out foods, hot and cold, plus organic produce, homemade ice cream, flowers, and more from local farms, ranches, and wineries.

Five Brooks Ranch (all ages)
P.O. Box 99, Olema 94950; (415) 663–1570; www.fivebrooks.com. Guided trail rides $$$$; pony rides $$$.

Guided horseback rides in glorious Point Reyes for buckaroos and buckarettes, from a one-hour slow trail ride to longer treks up the Inverness Ridge and incredible beach rides. The littlest riders like the hand-led pony ride around Five Brooks Pond.

Where to Eat

Barnaby's By the Bay. At the Golden Hinde Inn, 1 mile north of Inverness; (415) 669–1114. A glassed-in dining room and decks overlooking a marina on Tomales Bay; the only waterside restaurant in the area. Clam chowder, deep-fried calamari with cornmeal crust, fresh fish, and barbecued oysters, chicken, and ribs from the apple-wood smoker. $–$$

Drakes Beach Cafe. At the visitor center at Drakes Beach off Sir Francis Drake Boulevard, Point Reyes National Seashore; (415) 669–1297. A tiny, cozy cafe at the water's edge, with outdoor tables and a telescope for whale watching. Hearty, simple American food, breakfast all day, and fresh oysters. $

Olema Farm House Restaurant. 10005 Highway 1, Olema; (415) 663–1264. Once an 1845 stagecoach stop, a farmhouse decked out with beautiful old bottles, Elvis memorabilia, and antiques. The heated garden patio is the place to be. Fish and chips, clam chowder, meat loaf, prime rib, roast chicken, oyster stew, Philly cheese steak; lunch and dinner, with breakfast on weekends. $–$$$

Station House Cafe. Main Street, Point Reyes Station; (415) 663–1515. Eclectic American cuisine in a lively bistro atmosphere, specializing in oysters, mussels, and more local seafood. Live music on weekends. When accompanied by our toddler grandkids, we ask for a table in or near the garden patio. Reservations, definitely. Breakfast, lunch, and dinner. $$

Where to Stay

Golden Hinde Inn. 12938 Sir Francis Drake Boulevard, Inverness; (415) 669–1389; www.goldenhindeinn.com. A fresh-looking, white-painted, unassuming motel right at the marina on Tomales Bay, with a small swimming pool and fishing pier. Two-room suites have queen beds and sofa beds, microwaves, refrigerators, and fireplaces. Suite #5 has a king bed, a sofa bed, kitchen, and dining area. Some rooms have kitchenettes, two doubles or queen and sofa bed, and fireplaces. $$–$$$

Olema Ranch Campground. 10155 Highway 1, Olema; (800) 655–2267 or (415) 663–8001; www.olemaranch.com. Thirty-two acres of shade trees and grassy meadows with 150 tent and 80 RV sites and cabins, showers, and laundry facilities. They've thought of everything: mountain bike rentals, kayak tours, volleyball, a U.S. post office, ice-cream socials, storytelling around a bonfire, and buffet breakfast Sunday morning. Dogs okay. $

Point Reyes Hostel. From Bear Valley Road, go about 6 miles on Limantour Road, P.O. Box 247, Point Reyes Station 94956; (415) 663–8811. A ranch house and bunkhouse, with spacious kitchen, outdoor barbecue, and common rooms with wood-burning stoves. A family room is available by reservation. $

Point Reyes Lodging. P.O. Box 878, Point Reyes 94956; (800) 539–1872 or (415) 663–1872; www.ptreyes.com. Check online for information, availability, and links to a long list of cottages, suites, and inns in the area.

Point Reyes Seashore Lodge. 10021 Highway 1, Olema; (415) 663–9000; www.pointreyesseashore.com. One of the few B&Bs appropriate for families, a luxurious country estate in an idyllic garden setting with sweeping lawns, large trees, and a creek. The best rooms for families have tiny, private patios; some have fireplaces and double Jacuzzis. The complimentary breakfast is generous. The super-comfy Casa Olema cottage has a kitchen, a living room, a spa, and a loft bedroom, and sleeps up to six; the rate, for Marin, is reasonable, at $295 for four people. The Creekside Cottage sleeps four, and some other rooms have queen/twin combinations or two doubles. A large library of guidebooks and restaurant menus is a big help. The staff will arrange bike, kayak, and horse rentals for you. $$$–$$$$

For More Information

West Marin Chamber of Commerce. P.O. Box 1045, Point Reyes Station 94956; (415) 663–9232; www.pointreyes.org.

Weather Information for Point Reyes National Seashore. (415) 663–1092.

Sausalito/Tiburon

Tumbling down steep, forested hillsides to the edge of San Francisco Bay as if it were on the Mediterranean, the small tourist town of Sausalito makes a great day-trip destination. Running along the edge of Richardson Bay, the main street, Bridgeway, is chockablock with galleries and upscale shops, seafood restaurants, and yacht harbors, all sharing postcard views of San Francisco.

At midtown is the ferry dock from San Francisco and Tiburon. A little farther north on Bridgeway, you can wander around the houseboat docks—look for the floating Taj Mahal—and stop in at the Arques School of Wooden Boatbuilding, between noon and 1:00 P.M. most days, to watch the intricate woodworking, casting, and bronzing activities (call first, 415–331–7134). Back toward town, at the end of Liberty Ship Way near the marina, Schoonmaker Beach is an artificially created patch of sand shaded by date palms. Boat owners and kayakers like the Waterfront Cafe for light lunches and early dinners on the deck.

A community of 400-plus houseboats, permanently located at the north end of Bridgeway, is a phenomenon in itself and fun to see. In this part of town you can take kayaking and windsurfing lessons on Richardson Bay.

On the opposite side of Richardson Bay from Sausalito, Tiburon is another hamlet of vintage mansions, with outdoor restaurants overlooking the San Francisco skyline and Raccoon Strait. You can get here via ferry from Pier 41 in San Francisco, as well as by car. On opening day of yachting season in April, decorated pleasure craft sail and motor back and forth while families engage in springlike behavior on the grassy shoreline, such as flying kites and playing boom boxes.

Bay Model (all ages)

2100 Bridgeway, Sausalito; (415) 332–3870. Free.

From the ferry dock a pleasant, twenty-minute walk or bike ride north brings you to the one-and-a-half acre, hydraulic, working scale model of San Francisco Bay and the adjacent Sacramento River Delta. The natural and cultural histories of the bay are traced in exhibits of wetlands, wildlife, shipwrecks, antique equipment, videos, and video games—kids love it.

Marin Headlands (all ages)

Take the Alexander Avenue exit off Highway 1, the first exit north of the Golden Gate Bridge; (415) 331–1540; www.nps.gov/goga.

Part of the Golden Gate National Recreation Area, wild open spaces with miraculous views. Hiking trails above the Golden Gate are breezy and bracing, and kids like to climb around in the remnants of World War II fortifications. Stop at the visitor center at Field and Bunker Streets for maps to myriad hiking, biking, and equestrian trails and beaches. Besides the Marin Mammal Center (listed below), the main attractions are Rodeo Beach, Rodeo Lagoon, Muir Beach, and the Point Bonita Lighthouse. The lighthouse is perched on a bit of rock at the entrance to the Golden Gate, with incredible views and a (slightly) swaying footbridge over crashing waves; walk down and back on your own and get the history from the ranger in the tiny visitor center, or opt for the guided walk, which takes (it seems) forever. Precipitous clifftop trails near here are not for little kids.

Marine Mammal Center (all ages)

Marin Headlands, Sausalito; (415) 289–SEAL. Free; donations accepted.

A must-see for families fascinated by the largest denizens of the sea, the center serves as a hospital for orphaned, sick, and injured seals, sea lions, dolphins, otters, and whales. Many of the patients are endangered or threatened species, and you can watch them being fed, treated, and comforted. The twin goals of the center are (1) to ready the animals to return to their watery habitat, and (2) to create public understanding of and appreciation for our fellow creatures. During some months, there are few animals on view; call ahead. The gift shop has a nice array of kids' books and guidebooks and some exhibits.

Bay Area Discovery Museum (ages 1–10)

Fort Baker, 557 McReynolds Road, Sausalito, at the south end of Sausalito near the Golden Gate Bridge; (415) 487–4398; www.baykidsmuseum.org. $$; free for kids under 1; children must be accompanied by an adult.

An extensive renovation and expansion brings more fun and education to kids. In a complex of historic buildings by the bay near the north end of the Golden Gate Bridge, the museum comprises a Media Clubhouse with games, art, music, animation, video projects, and more on the latest multimedia equipment; a science lab; a maze of illusions with optical tricks; and a fishing boat to climb aboard. Crawl through an underwater tunnel; make ceramics, crafts, and art projects; touch sea animals; develop photos; drop in on a workshop; or ride a carousel. The newly enlarged Tot Spot offers indoor/outdoor, hands-on fun for toddlers including a walk-under waterfall. Lookout Cove is a new outdoor exploration area with a rocky shore, sea cave, and tidal pools. Little architects build and design highrise construction.

Multicultural shows are put on in the new theater, from acrobats to plays and musical presentations. The museum store sells science projects and imaginative toys and books, and the cafe serves reasonably priced sandwiches, soups, and salads. You can take a short walk by the bay and have a picnic on the lawn; don't forget jackets, as it can be windy and cool.

Richardson Bay Audubon Center and Wildlife Sanctuary (all ages)

At the north end of the Tiburon Bike Path, 376 Greenwood Beach Road, Tiburon; (415) 388–2524; www.egret.org. Free.

In this lovely wetlands preserve, thousands of waterfowl and birds and harbor seals show up in the wintertime. There is a self-guided nature trail and a bookstore adjacent to Lyford House, a lemon-yellow landmark Victorian open to the public.

Nature Conservancy Ring Mountain Preserve (all ages)
3152 Paradise Drive, Tiburon; (415) 435–6465.

In the hills on the north end of Tiburon, a 377-acre ridge top offers walking trails and wonderful views of the Bay Area. It's less than 1 mile to the summit on an easy trail edged with knee-high native grasses dotted with wildflowers in the spring.

Angel Island State Park (all ages)
Accessible via a short ferry ride from Tiburon, and from Pier 41 in San Francisco; (415) 435–3522 or (415) 897–0715; www.angelisland.com. Tram tours: adults $$$; ages 6 to 12 $$; under 5 free.

There are miles of hiking trails and mountain biking roads on this breezy island, plus gull's-eye views of three bridges and the skylines of the Bay Area. Among the historical sites are an ancient Miwok hunting ground, a cattle ranch, and a U.S. prisoner-of-war camp. The easy way to learn some history and get some fresh air is to take the narrated tour in an open-air tram.

Mountain bikes are available to rent, and you can take sea kayaking tours conducted around the island with historical and ecological interpretation. Have an espresso and a light lunch on the deck of the cafe, or bring a picnic and sit on the lawn to watch sailboats and freighters gliding by. Environmental campsites (800–444–7275). No dogs, skateboards, or in-line skates are allowed.

China Camp State Park (all ages)
North San Pedro Road on the east side of Tiburon; (415) 456–0766.

Along San Pablo Bay, here is a hidden jewel of Bay Area parks, where the protected beach is often warm when fog chills the rest of Marin. Windsurfing is a big deal from May through October. Walk-in campsites are in lovely meadows about 1 mile from parking. Trails along the ridge have views of the north Bay Area, and there is a small museum and remnants of a late 1800s Chinese immigrants' shrimp fishing village. Leashed dogs are allowed.

Tiburon Peninsula Historical Trail (all ages)
Just off Highway 101, from Blackie's Pasture on Tiburon Boulevard to Tiburon; (415) 435–5490.

A beautiful, 2-mile, paved path for biking, Rollerblading, and strolling along Richardson's Bay, with lawns for picnicking and kite-flying and benches for resting.

Where to Eat

Harbor Grill. 305 Harbor Drive at Clipper Yacht Harbor, Sausalito; (415) 331–5355. In a light-filled boathouse sort of place, checked tablecloths and a casual atmosphere, burgers, pasta, calamitously good clam chowder, crab cakes, and American comfort food, all at reasonable prices, indoors or out. $

Houlihan's. 660 Bridgeway Avenue, Sausalito; (415) 332–8512. Casual atmosphere with water view; seafood, pasta; lunch and dinner. $$–$$$

Kitti's Place. 3001 Bridgeway, Sausalito; (415) 331–0390. In a homey atmosphere, comfort food extraordinaire, from homemade soup to Asian-inspired salads and entrees, and great sandwiches (try the portobello). Breakfast, lunch, and early dinner. $–$$

Sam's Anchor Cafe. 27 Main Street, Tiburon; (415) 435–4527. One of the all-time best places in the Bay Area to sit on a sunny deck, contemplate the San Francisco skyline, and watch sailboats float by. Tuck into clam chowder, cracked crab, and fresh fish while the kids check out the seagulls and the boats. Bored older children can window-shop on Main Street, while you figure out how you can move to Tiburon. $–$$$

Seven Seas. 682 Bridgeway, Sausalito; (415) 332–1304. The best in town for breakfast, indoors or on the patio. Lunch and dinner too. $–$$

Where to Stay

Corte Madera Inn. 1815 Redwood Highway, Corte Madera, five minutes north of Tiburon on Highway 101; (800) 777–9670; www.bestwestern.com. One of the best choices in the North Bay for families, an attractive, comfortable motel arranged around gardens and lawns, with swimming and wading pools, a laundry, playground, putting green, and an excellent coffee shop. Continental breakfast is free, and so is the shuttle to the San Francisco ferry. Walk across the street to a large shopping center and around the corner to a world-class bookstore. Can't beat it! $$$

For More Information

Sausalito Chamber of Commerce Visitors Center. 29 Caledonia Street, Sausalito; (415) 331–7262; www.sausalito.org.

Tiburon Peninsula Chamber of Commerce. 96 Main Street, Tiburon; (415) 435–5633; www.tiburon.citysearch.com.

Marin County Visitors Bureau. 1013 Larkspur Landing Circle, Larkspur; (415) 925–2060; www.visitmarin.org.

Stinson Beach/Bolinas

A unique tropical undercurrent keeps the waters off Stinson Beach surprisingly warm year-round. Below the western slopes of Mount Tamalpais in a protected "banana belt," the white-sand beach and the village enjoy a mild climate and are favorite destinations for San Franciscans escaping the fog.

A clutch of small cafes and shops, the village of Stinson Beach is ringed with eucalyptus and Monterey pines, where thousands of monarch butterflies spend the winter. Bolinas is even smaller and scruffier and is surrounded by spectacular wildlife preserves, beaches, and hiking trails.

A rustic village inhabited by rogue artists and craftspeople, Bolinas has some charming nineteenth-century buildings, particularly near the old downtown along Wharf Road. Part of Smiley's Bar dates from 1852 and St. Mary Magdalen Catholic Church from 1878. The Bolinas Lagoon is 1,200 acres of saltmarsh, mudflats, and calm sea waters harboring great blue herons and egrets, migrating geese, and ducks—as many as 35,000 birds have been spotted in a single day.

A mile of shallow tidepools are exposed at low tide on the Bolinas Bay shoreline. In the vast intertidal area live gooseneck barnacles, ochre and pink sea stars, purple and giant red anemones, chitons, and more exotic sea life. This is a marine reserve, and not a thing may be removed. At the north end of the reef, Agate Beach is a small county park. Keep an eye peeled for the swift incoming tide.

Stinson Beach Park (all ages)

Highway 1 and Panoramic Highway, Stinson Beach; (415) 868–0942.

A 3-mile-long sandy beach beloved by surfers and swimmers (many Marin beaches are not safe for swimming, due to undertows and currents; this one is an exception); great white sharks are occasionally sighted. Picnic tables, barbecues, restrooms, a snack bar, and, during summer, lifeguards. No pets.

Audubon Canyon Ranch (all ages)

Between Bolinas and Stinson Beach, 4900 Highway 1, Stinson Beach; (415) 868–9244; www.egret.org. Open to the public from March through July on weekends and holidays. **Free.**

This research center is located in a beautiful valley. In the tops of redwoods and pines standing in deep, wooded canyons, herons and egrets make their nests. A short trail leads to fixed telescopes for nest-watching, and you can walk on two 3-mile-long loop trails and a short nature trail. Watch for newts, frogs, foxes, deer, and quail. Adjacent to a circa-1870 house are exhibits, a bookshop, and picnic tables.

Slide Ranch (ages 4–12)

2025 Shoreline Highway, Muir Beach; (415) 381–6155. $$$.

A few miles south of Stinson Beach, on a hillside overlooking the sea, lies a ranch built in the early 1900s that is now an environmental education center where your children can milk a goat, harvest veggies, bake bread, and learn how to care for animals and nature. Special days are scheduled for ocean exploration and for children under five. Call ahead for a reservation.

Point Reyes Bird Observatory (all ages)

Four miles northwest from Bolinas, on Mesa Road; (415) 868–1221. **Free.**

A lovely, short, self-guided nature trail and a small museum. You are welcome to observe the activities here, which include banding rufous-sided towhees, song sparrows, and other birds. This is the Palomarin Trailhead, leading to four freshwater lakes that are waterfowl habitats and to Double Point Bay, where harbor seals breed and tidepools are inviting to look into (don't touch). Three miles from the trailhead, watch for Bass Lake, a secret swimming spot. There are portable potties near the trailhead.

Where to Eat

Bolinas Bay Bakery and Cafe. 20 Wharf Road, Bolinas; (415) 868–0211. Organic-ingredient pastries, breads, pies, pizza, soups—some of the best picnic goodies in the Western Hemisphere. Lunch, dinner, and a great place for breakfast on the back porch. $

Parkside Cafe. 43 Arenal, Stinson Beach; (415) 868–1272. Italian food, burgers, and pizza; breakfast, lunch, and dinner. $–$$

Stinson Beach Grill. 3465 Shoreline Highway, Stinson Beach; (415) 868–2002. Breakfast, lunch, or dinner, indoors or on the heated deck; fresh seafood, barbecued oysters, pasta, and Southwest cuisine. $–$$

Where to Stay

155 Pine. 155 Pine on Duxbury Reef, Bolinas; (415) 868–0263. A tiny B&B that welcomes families to stay in a cottage overlooking the ocean, within a short walk to the beach; fireplace, kitchen, decks. Sleeps up to six. $$–$$$

Golden Gate Hostel. Building 941, Fort Barry, in the Marin Headlands; (415) 331–2777. On the National Register of Historic Places, a spacious, homey place, with three kitchens, common rooms, a recreation room, a fireplace, and a piano. Family rooms with bunks. Walk right out the door onto a hiking trail. $

Ocean Court. 18 Arenal, Stinson Beach; (415) 868–0212. Large, simple motel units with kitchens, near the beach. $–$$

Seadrift Company. 2 Dipsea Road, P.O. Box 177, Stinson Beach 94970; (415) 868–1791; www.seadriftrealty.com. Vacation home rentals. $–$$$

Steep Ravine Cabins. 801 Panoramic Highway, 1 mile south of Stinson Beach; (800) 444–7275. Simple, rustic cabins from the 1930s, each sleeping up to five people, with woodburning stoves, bunks, water, no electricity. These are rented through the state park. $

For More Information

Marin County Visitors Bureau. 1013 Larkspur Landing Circle, Larkspur; (415) 925–2060; www.visitmarin.org.

North Coast

To a child California's northern coastline means flying kites on the beach, camping in the redwoods, and watching a whale spouting offshore. Parents love the fishing villages and Victorian loggers' towns, the art galleries and cozy seaside cafes.

The main coastal route, Highway 1, twists and turns atop marine terraces and clifftops, some as high as 900 feet above the shore. Views of mountains and sea are legendary, but young backseat passengers will demand frequent stops. Several forays to the North Coast will create sweeter vacation memories than trying to see all the sights in just a few days.

Set up your headquarters in Mendocino, Fort Bragg, or Bodega Bay, and make day-trip expeditions to nearby beaches and forest parks. Take time to investigate the historic towns. In Mendocino, for instance, the entire town is a Historical Preservation District of early Cape Cod and Victorian homes and steepled clapboard churches. Point Arena is prime whale-watching country. A chain of beaches stretches north from Bodega Bay, a small fishing village where seals, sailboats, and windsurfers share a harbor.

Fort Bragg

A lumbering and commercial fishing town since 1857, Fort Bragg today carefully preserves a cache of vintage wood-frame houses. Families find that restaurants and accommodations are more reasonably priced here than in Mendocino, 8 miles to the south. There are several coastal and forest state parks nearby, a picturesque fishing port at the mouth of the Noyo River, and the departure depot for the famous Skunk Train.

The annual Whale Festival in March is a two-weekend event with chowder, beer, and wine tasting; a doll show and classic car show; a run; banquet dinners; and a big arts and crafts fair with musical entertainment.

NORTH COAST

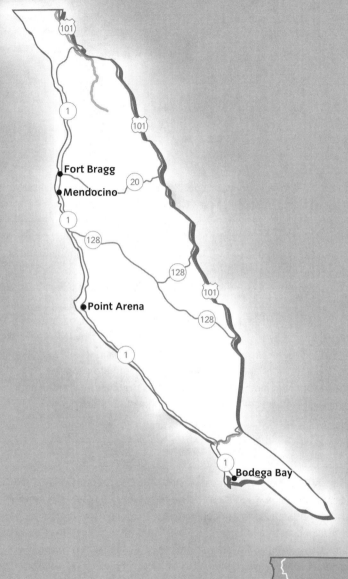

Skunk Train (all ages)

Laurel Street Depot at Main Street, Fort Bragg; (707) 964–6371 or (800) 77–SKUNK; www .skunktrain.com. Adults $$$$; ages 5 to 11 $$$; free for children under 5.

Hauling logs to sawmills in the 1880s, the Skunk Train—actually several historic diesel and steam trains—now takes tourists on half- or full-day trips to Willits and back. The route runs along Pudding Creek through redwood forests, crossing thirty bridges and trestles; it's a beautiful train ride—perfect for the grandparents and younger grandchildren. In the Fort Bragg train depot are two dozen retail shops and places to eat, scattered among railroad and logging artifacts. Snacks and lunch are available to buy along the way, or you can bring a picnic. Special events, such as barbecue-dinner rides and "Tour de Skunk," a skunk ride one way and bike ride the other, are held annually.

MacKerricher State Park (all ages)

Three miles north of Fort Bragg off Highway 1; (707) 964–9112.

A 1,598-acre park, 8 miles of beach and dunes, with a popular beach play area and tidepools at Pudding Creek, at the southern end of the park. Two freshwater lakes are stocked with trout. Horseback-riding, mountain-biking, and hiking trails are found throughout bluffs, headlands, dunes, forests, and wetlands. The headlands at Laguna Point are a prime spot for whale watching, and a permanent population of harbor seals reside here. The boardwalk affords wheelchair and stroller access, from the southwest corner of the parking lot. There are 140 developed campsites and RV sites for up to 35-foot vehicles, plus fire rings and toilets. Stretching the entire 8-mile length of the park, the paved Haul Road, a former logging road, is a fabulous jogging, biking, and walking route with ocean views, crossing beautiful sand dunes.

Karen's Favorite Beaches
Near Fort Bragg

- **Glass Beach,** at the foot of Elm Street. The sand is sprinkled with pebbles of glass and china that have been tumbled and smoothed in the sea.

- **Pudding Creek,** north of town, past the first bridge. Beach play area and tidepools.

- **Ten Mile River Beach,** 8 miles north of Fort Bragg. Acres and acres of salt marsh and wetlands at the mouth of the Noyo River, inhabited by nesting birds and ducks; a 4.5-mile, duney stretch of sand extends south from the river.

Mendocino Coast Botanical Gardens (all ages)

18220 Highway 1, 1.5 miles south of Fort Bragg; (707) 964–4352; www.gardenbythesea.org. Adults $$; kids ages 6 to 17 $; free for kids under 6. Year-round birding tours at 8:00 A.M. on the third Tuesday each month are free.

Wander 2 miles of path in lush gardens through acres of plantings, forest, and fern canyons. Something is blooming every season, and in the spring the color is lyrical. Rhododendrons and roses, heathers, succulents, camellias, and literally thousands of other plants crowd the gardens. From the bluff overlooking crashing waves, you can see gray whales during their winter migrating season. A picnic site perches on a scenic overlook. More than one hundred bird species visit the gardens. Smack in the middle of the Gardens, the Country Garden Restaurant and Grill serves lunch, dinner, and brunch at umbrella tables overlooking glorious blooming flowers and trees. Try the grilled fresh fish, grilled eggplant salad, mushroom crepe torte, or the apple-wood, rotisseried game hen.

Noyo Harbor (all ages)

Located 1.8 miles south of Fort Bragg, at the mouth of the Noyo River.

Headquarters for a large fleet of fishing trollers and canneries. Barking and posing, sea lions lounge on the wooden piers, waiting for the return of the boats at day's end. You can rent a fishing rod here and fish off the piers or the rocks. One of a handful of seafood restaurants on the harbor, The Wharf is a casual, family-friendly place to enjoy some fresh fish and watch the sun sink slowly behind gangs of wheeling gulls (707–964–4283). Come on the 4th of July for the giant salmon barbecue.

You can watch migrating whales from Todd's Point, just south of Noyo Bridge on Ocean View Drive. For small children and for people who get seasick easily, Noyo Harbor is the best place from which to take a whale-watching cruise, as whales are usually sighted within fifteen or twenty minutes.

For the Shell of It

344 North Main Street, Fort Bragg; (707) 961–0461.

Shell jewelry, seashells, posters, rocks, minerals, folk art—and everything about shells.

Lost Coast Adventures (ages 5 and up)

19275 South Harbor Drive, Fort Bragg; (707) 961–1143.

Kayak tours; mountain-bike, skin-diving, and scuba-diving rentals; boat charters for fishing, diving, and whale watching.

Guest House Museum (all ages)

343 North Main Street, Fort Bragg; (707) 961–2823. $; kids under 13 free.

A beautiful home from before the turn of the nineteenth century, this three-story house was built entirely of redwood and is filled with photos and artifacts of local history and antique logging equipment. There is also a lovely garden.

Papa Birds 🔒
131 East Laurel Street, Fort Bragg; (707) 964–5604; www.papabirds.com.

Looking for Papa Birds in Mendocino? It moved here and is still the same fabulous emporium of bird paraphernalia, from feeders and birdhouses to bird kites, books and toys, windsocks, tapes, and CDs.

Mendocino Chocolate Company 🔒
542 North Main Street, Fort Bragg; (707) 964–8800, www.mendocino-chocolate.com.

Here you'll find handmade truffles and chocolates and edible sea shells. Or try these specialties: a dark Rambo of a truffle, Mendocino Macho; Mendocino Breakers, dark-dipped caramels rolled in almonds; and old-fashioned Convent Fudge. Free samples; shipping worldwide.

Where to Eat

Cafe One. 753 North Main Street, Fort Bragg; (707) 964–3309. Healthy, organic, vegetarian food, plus seafood and poultry. Breakfast and lunch, with dinner on weekends. $–$$

Egghead Omelettes of Oz. 326 North Main Street, Fort Bragg; (707) 964–5055. Sit in a comfy booth in a Wizard of Oz environment, complete with yellow brick road, and enjoy big, big omelets, burgers, salads, and sandwiches; breakfast and lunch. $–$$

Mendocino Cookie Company. In the Company Store at 301 North Main Street, Fort Bragg; (707) 964–0282. Fresh double-chocolate-chip cookies, homemade muffins, scones, pastries, ice-cream cones, and shakes. $

North Coast Brewing Company. 444 North Main Street, Fort Bragg; (707) 964–BREW. In a casual brewpub indoors or on a sunny (sometimes) patio, a hearty menu of local fresh fish, Cajun black beans and rice, ribs, Mendocino Mud Cake, burgers, nachos, and Route 66 chili. Voted Mendocino County Restaurant of the Year. Tons of fun. $$

Purple Rose. 24300 North Highway 1, Fort Bragg; (707) 964–6507. Join the locals in this casual cafe for homemade tortillas filled with wonderful taco fillings and other great Mexican dishes. $

Where to Stay

Grey Whale Inn. 615 North Main Street, Fort Bragg; (707) 964–0640 or (800) 382–7244; www.greywhaleinn.com. This 1915 three-story landmark has spacious rooms and public areas, with high windows looking out to the sea or inward through the trees to town. The inn welcomes children and offers plenty of room for them to roam. You can walk right out the back door of the inn to take a long walk along the waterfront on the Old Coast Road. Rooms have sitting areas with armchairs, deep tubs, some fireplaces, and lots of books; some have extra beds. Breakfast is a big buffet. Owner Colette Bailey wins prizes at the county fair for her coffee cakes and fruit breads. $$–$$$

Hi Seas Beach Motel. 1201 North Main Street, Fort Bragg; (707) 964–5929. Simple rooms, all with ocean view, adjacent to Haul Road walking/biking route. $–$$

Pomo RV Park and Campground. 17999 Tregoning Lane, 1 mile south of Highway 20, Fort Bragg; (707) 964–3373. Secluded, spacious sites in a parklike setting. $

For More Information

Fort Bragg/Mendocino Coast Chamber of Commerce. 332 North Main Street, Fort Bragg; (707) 961–6300 or (800) 726–2780; www.mendocinocoast.com.

Mendocino

So closely does the town of Mendocino and this stretch of coastline resemble New England that much of the television show *Murder She Wrote* was filmed here.

Settled by Maine loggers in the middle nineteenth century, the town remained rough-and-tumble until the 1930s. The town languished for decades, only to be reborn as first an art colony and eventually a tourist destination. Couples come here for the galleries, the restaurants, and the romantic B&Bs. Families come to explore the beaches, to fish and whale-watch, to canoe up the rivers, and to hike in the forest parks.

The streets of Mendocino are crowded with country gardens that overflow picket fences, plus small shops, art galleries in historic buildings, and a few restaurants and inns. (Most of these are B&Bs that are inappropriate for children; plenty of family-oriented lodgings are found within a few miles north and south of town.)

Hundreds of California gray whales parade off the Mendocino coast on their 12,000-mile round-trip from the Arctic Circle to Baja, California. You can see them up close from whale-watching boats and from the bluffs around town—binoculars help—from late November through January and then again in March. Other good whale-watching sites are at Jug Handle State Reserve and Russian Gulch State Park.

Mendocino Headlands State Park (all ages)
Heeser Drive and Main Street, Mendocino; (707) 937–5804.

Wrapped around three sides of town, magnificent grassy headlands float high above swaying kelp beds in the sea, which boils through rocky arches and dark grottoes. With small children firmly in hand—there are no fences or railings—walk along clifftops and through meadows that in spring are abloom with wildflowers. Looking back at white storefronts, Victorian homes, and the distinctive water towers of town, you can easily imagine the days when horse-drawn carriages parked in front of the Mendocino Hotel and ladies with parasols swept along the boardwalks in their long gowns. Restrooms and a picnic area are on the north end of the park, along Heeser Drive.

Big River Beach and State Park (all ages)
Off Highway 1 on the south side of Mendocino; (707) 937–5804.

California's newest state park combines a gorgeous beach and a river lined with pristine forest and wildlife habitat and now connects by old logging roads the two adjacent state parks and a state forest. Where the deep Big River Valley meets the sea, a sandy, drift-woody beach and tidepools lie below the south cliff of Mendocino. You may see harbor seals, river otters, and great blue herons. Access the beach by a steep stairway from the headlands trail or from a small parking area off the highway, just south of town.

Kayaking and canoeing are popular on the river (see Catch a Canoe, below). And you can hike on forest trails—the old logging roads—into Jackson Demonstration State Forest and Mendocino Woodlands State Park on the north and to Van Damme State Park to the south. Flowers, blackberries, and legions of birds are among the glories to be found.

Ford House (all ages)
735 Main Street, Mendocino; (707) 937–5397. Open 11:00 A.M. to 4:00 P.M. year-round.
Free.

A visitor center for Mendocino Headlands State Park, a museum, and a good place to get a perspective on how the town is laid out. A scale model of Mendocino in the 1890s shows the dozens of tall wooden water towers that existed then. More than thirty of the towers, some double- and triple-deckers, remain in the skyline today. Here you can purchase guidebooks and history books, tide tables, and maps. The picnic tables in the meadow out back are delightful perches from which to watch the whales, which cruise by in the wintertime, close to the shoreline.

A Whale Festival is held here in March, with special exhibits, guided whale walks and cruises, whale-size hot dogs an art and crafts fair, and a concert. Children's activities are scheduled at Point Cabrillo Lighthouse.

Kelley House Museum (all ages)
Across the street from Ford House on Main Street, Mendocino; (707) 927–5791. Free.

Set back from the street next to a huge water tower and a duck pond surrounded by an old garden. Among the historical photos in the house are those of burly loggers hand-sawing ancient redwoods. Lumber for shipbuilding and for construction of the Gold Rush city of San Francisco brought easterners here in the mid-1800s. It took them six months by ship to reach this wilderness of mighty river valley and seacoast, inhabited only by Indians and fur trappers.

Van Damme State Park (all ages)
Three miles south of Mendocino, on Highway 1; (707) 937–5804. $ day use; $–$$$ camping.

Accessible right off the highway, a popular beach and campground, plus hiking trails. The weird and wonderful Pygmy Forest, a Registered National Landmark, is seen on a 0.3-mile easy trail through a lush fern canyon and spooky woods of dwarf cypress, rhododendron, and other bonsailike plants and trees. A fifty-year-old cypress may be only 8 inches tall and have a trunk less than 1 inch in diameter. There are developed campsites and a paved bike trail.

Catch a Canoe and Bicycles, Too! (ages 5 and up)

Stanford Inn by the Sea, P.O. Box 487, Mendocino 95460; (707) 937–0273; www.stanford inn.com/canoes.html. Rentals $$–$$$$ per hour; day rates available.

Paddle canoes or kayaks from the mouth of the Big River, 7 or 8 miles upstream on an estuary—the longest unchanged and undeveloped estuary in Northern California—stopping for a picnic at a tiny beach or a meadow. The river is lined with fir and redwood groves, wildflowers, and wild rhododendrons. You will undoubtedly see ospreys, wood ducks, and blue herons; probably deer; and maybe even a small black bear. Time your canoeing expedition to paddle up the river when the tide is coming in, and be on the return trip as the tide goes out. The rental company can advise you on this, and they also rent mountain bikes, outriggers and other types of boats, and auto racks.

Stanford Inn by the Sea

Highway 1 and Comptche-Ukiah Road, P.O. Box 487, Mendocino 95460; (800) 331–8884; www.stanfordinn.com. $$$–$$$$.

On a hillside above the river near Mendocino lies a luxurious twenty-six-room country inn surrounded by fabulous gardens. Llamas and horses graze in the meadows. Each spacious room and suite has a fireplace or woodburning stove, sitting area, down comforters, and a private deck from which to watch the sun set over the sea. Wine and a bountiful breakfast are included. There is spa, a sauna, and an Olympic-size swimming pool enclosed in a greenhouse crowded with tropical plants. Big River Nurseries are also located on the grounds of the inn, and it's fun to browse the rows of organic plants, veggies, and herbs; you can buy herbal wreaths, sprays and braids, and herbs and spices and have them shipped home. There is also a terrific vegetarian restaurant on-site.

Russian Gulch State Park (all ages)

Two miles north of Mendocino, on Highway 1; (707) 937–5804.

Sea caves, a waterfall, and a beach popular for rock fishing, scuba diving, and swimming in the chilly waters. From the headlands in the park, you can see the Devil's Punch Bowl, a 200-foot-long tunnel with a blowhole. Inland the park includes 3 miles of Russian Gulch Creek Canyon and 12 miles of paved and unpaved mountain biking, hiking, and horseback riding trails in dense forest and stream canyons. A small campground here is quite lovely, and a special equestrian campground offers riding trails into Jackson State Forest.

Jug Handle State Reserve (all ages)

Three miles north of Mendocino, on Highway 1; (707) 937–5804.

A 700-acre oceanside park notable for an "ecological staircase" of marine terraces rising from sea level to 500 feet. Each terrace is 100,000 years older than the one below, affording a unique opportunity to see geologic evolution. The plants and trees change from terrace to terrace too, from wildflowers and grasses to wind-strafed spruce, second-growth redwoods, and pygmy forests of cypress and pine.

Shops for Kids **in Mendocino**

- **Bookwinkle's Children's Books,** Gallery Bookshop, Main and Kasten Streets; (707) 937–BOOK; www.gallerybooks.com. Kids get lost in their big corner of the bookstore, while parents browse in a huge selection of books about the coast and choose bestsellers for a day at the beach. You will find wonderful cards, music, and magazines too.

- **Mendocino Chocolate Company,** 10483 Lansing Street; (707) 937–1107; www.mendocino-chocolate.com. Try a dark Rambo of a truffle, Mendocino Macho, or Mendocino Breakers, dark-dipped caramel rolled in almonds. Kids love the old-fashioned Convent Fudge and the chocolate seashells. If you love it, they will ship.

- **Out of This World,** 45100 Main Street; (707) 937–3335. A zillion science and nature-oriented toys and kits, binoculars, telescopes, robots, and puzzles. From here, look at the crashing surf from a lineup of telescopes.

- **Village Toy Store,** 10450 Lansing Street; (707) 937–4633; www.mendotoy store.com. Owned by former school teachers, Bill and Susie Carr, the shop specializes in old-fashioned toys like blocks, Lincoln Logs, Tinker Toys, Brio, dolls, puppets, classic books, trains, and puzzles, plus lots of things-to-do kits and a huge inventory of kites.

- **Wind and Weather,** 45080 Albion Street in the water tower; (707) 937–0323. Weather vanes, thermometers, sun dials, weather radios, and more fascinating contraptions.

Point Arena Pier (all ages)
Highway 1 between Gualala and Elk, go west on Port Road.

A nice stop on the way up the coast, the fishing pier juts 330 feet out into the sea from the edge of a cove, where fishing, crabbing, and whale watching are the main activities. In the rocks at the base of the cliffs, you can explore tidepools. A cliff-top trail leads to Schooner Gulch State Beach.

The original wooden fishing pier at Point Arena was dramatically smashed to pieces in a storm in 1983, along with all the buildings in the cove. In a cafe on the pier—the Galley at Point Arena—are photos of the rip-roarin' storm. The cafe serves chowder, snapper sandwiches, homemade pies, and crab in season. Adjacent to the pier are a few shops and other cafes.

Point Arena Lighthouse (all ages)
Lighthouse Road off Highway 1, 2 miles north of Point Arena; (707) 882–2777. Free; suggested donation $–$$.

Erected in 1870, then reerected after the 1906 San Francisco earthquake, the 115-foot lighthouse is one of the best locations for gray whale watching. Scramble around in the lighthouse and visit the museum of maritime artifacts below; tours are conducted from 10:00 A.M. to 3:30 P.M. daily. Black oystercatchers and cormorants wheel over the offshore rocks, and sea lions and harbor seals are often seen in the waters just south of the point. The four three-bedroom Point Arena Coast Guard Houses here are available to rent. Neat and clean, with kitchens, TV, and fireplaces, they're perfect for a family (877–725–4448).

Where to Eat

Bay View Cafe. 45040 Main Street, Mendocino; (707) 937–4197. Breakfast, lunch, and dinner, indoors or on the deck with a zowie sea view, upstairs in a water tower. Good, simple fare, such as burgers, salads, pasta, and steak. $–$$

Mendo Burgers. Lansing Street, Mendocino; (707) 937–1111. Beef, turkey, chicken, fish, and veggie burgers; cool 1950s decor; indoors or out. $

Mendocino Bakery and Cafe. 10483 Lansing Street, Mendocino; (707) 937–0836. Breakfast and lunch are fun on the small deck. Kids like the pizza, bagels, and muffins; parents like the espresso drinks. You can get an early, simple dinner here, too, with traditional Italian dishes on the menu. $–$$

Mousse Cafe. Corner of Kasten and Ukiah Streets, Mendocino; (707) 937–4323. In a cottage garden, a sophisticated cafe menu with things that children like to eat. People sit here all afternoon, having tea and munching chunks of Blackout Cake and bread pudding. Lunch and dinner daily; Sunday brunch. $$

The Ravens. At the Stanford Inn, Comptche–Ukiah Road at Highway 1, just south of Mendocino; (707) 937–5615. The only fine restaurant on the Mendocino coast serving only vegetarian food: soups, pizza, pasta, grilled veggies; breakfast and dinner. $$

Tote Fete. 10450 Lansing, Mendocino; (707) 937–3383. California cuisine to go: apricot chicken salad, homemade meat loaf, calzone, focaccia sandwiches, dynamite desserts. Go around the corner to the Tote Fete Bakery for cake by the slice, doughnuts, and more pastries. $$

Where to Stay

Inn at Schoolhouse Creek. 7051 North Highway 1, Little River; (800) 731–5525; www.schoolhousecreek.com. Lodge rooms, suites, and quaint cottages with kitchens, fireplaces, ocean-view decks, spa tubs, feather beds, all including a sumptuous buffet breakfast and evening snacks. This is a family-friendly place with access to the beach at Buckhorn Cove, lovely gardens, and forest glens. You can sit a spell by the fireplace in the parlor; browse the library of videos, books, games, and puzzles; hike in a fern canyon; or swing in a hammock. Kids get juice and cookies and special attention, pails for beach combing, and matchbook cars. $$$

Little River Inn. 7751 Highway 1, Little River; (707) 937–5942. A white wedding cake of a circa-1850 house anchors a beautiful country resort overlooking the sea, with an excellent restaurant, a fun 9-hole golf course, and tennis. Some of the spacious and comfortable rooms, each with ocean view and a deck, have two queens or doubles. You can walk from here to the beach and the Pygmy Forest at Van Damme State Park; Mendocino is ten minutes away. The golf course is short, relatively easy, and inexpensive—perfect for beginners. $$$

Mendocino Coast Reservations. P.O. Box 1143, Mendocino 95460; (800) 262–7801; www.mcmca.com. Vacation home rentals, most with fireplaces, ocean views, spas. $–$$$

Seafoam Lodge. 6751 North Highway 1, Little River, ten minutes south of Mendo-

cino; (707) 937–1827 or (800) 606–1827; www.seafoam.com. Families and pets are welcome at this inn, located on a private cove. Ocean-view units, continental breakfast in your room, some kitchens, decks, refrigerators. $$

Sea Rock Bed and Breakfast Inn. 11101 Lansing Street, 0.5 mile south of Mendocino; (707) 937–0926; www.searock.com. One- and two-bedroom garden cottages with ocean views, Franklin stoves, feather beds, hearty continental breakfast served in an ocean-view dining room, some kitchens. Children are welcome with supervision. No pets. $$

For More Information

Fort Bragg/Mendocino Coast Chamber of Commerce. 332 North Main Street, Fort Bragg; (707) 961–6300 or (800) 726–2780; www.mendocinocoast.com.

Mendocino Area State Parks. (707) 937–5804; www.mcn.org/1/mendoparks/ mendo. Information about camping, day use, and interpretive programs. For campsite reservations, call (800) 444–PARK.

Bodega Bay

The warmest and some of the most beautiful Northern California beaches are found near the fishing village of Bodega Bay. The climate is mild, even in winter. Dense fog occurs only about twenty days annually.

Weathered clapboard houses, a handful of seafood restaurants, and a few shops and motels are scattered around the edges of a large, protected harbor where pleasure boats from all over the world come to anchor away from the open sea. Although the town was founded in the 1870s, most of the buildings of architectural interest are circa-1910 California Craftsman–style bungalows.

Clamming in the tidal mudflats and windsurfing in the harbor waters are two popular activities. The combination of freshwater wetlands and salt marshes attracts a great variety of shorebirds and waterfowl, plus pond turtles, harbor seals, and sea lions.

Almost a dozen Sonoma Coast beaches run from Bodega Bay 16 miles north to Jenner, and each has its own treasures to discover. This stretch of coastline is dramatic with sea stacks, sheer cliffs, rugged rocky coves, and vast wildflowery meadows—a spectacular drive. In April at Westside Park on the edge of the bay, the Bodega Bay Fishermen's Festival attracts crowds for the blessing of the fishing fleet, a decorated boat parade, a big outdoor fair with food and entertainment, a lamb and oyster barbecue, and arts and crafts.

Bodega Head (all ages)

On the west side of the harbor entrance; parking at the end of Westside Road; (707) 875–3483.

A vast promontory overlooking the open sea. Rangers and docent volunteers are on hand during whale-watching months to lead walks on the 1.4-mile bluff trail and answer questions. This is a bracing and beautiful walk at any time of the year, a trek accompanied by pelicans, oystercatchers, and sometimes even deer.

Candy and Kites

1425 Highway 1, Bodega Bay; (707) 875–3777. Kite festivals in Bodega Bay take place in April and July.

A must-stop before you hit the sand, featuring a huge and colorful variety of kites and games for the beach, plus toys, books, saltwater taffy, and chocolates.

Bodega Bay Gifts

Ocean Corner, 2001 Highway 1, Bodega Bay; (707) 875–2449.

A big store, stuffed with seashells, games, T-shirts, and stuff.

UC Davis Marine Laboratory (all ages)

2099 Westside Road, Bodega Bay; (707) 875–2211. Free drop-in tours Fridays, 2:00 to 4:00 P.M. Call ahead to tour other days.

Half a mile of coastline and surrounding marine habitat is protected and studied by the university. Exhibits and working research projects such as aqua-farming are fascinating, and the student guides are great with kids.

Bodega Bay **Beaches**

- **Doran Beach Regional Park,** south end of the bay off Highway 1 on Doran Park Road; (707) 875–3540; www.sonoma-county.org/parks. A popular day-use beach for swimming, surfing, kite flying, clamming, and kayaking, with breezy RV and tent campsites, restrooms, showers. Get information and maps for county parks at the office here. The Bodega Bay Sandcastle Building Festival is held at Doran Beach in September.

- **Bodega Dunes,** on the north end of town off Westside Road, accessed on Bay Flat Road; (707) 875–3483. More than 900 acres of huge sand dunes, some as high as 150 feet. There is a 5-mile riding and hiking loop through the dunes and a hiking-only trail to Bodega Head. In a spectacular show of color, thousands of monarch butterflies flock to a grove of cypress and eucalyptus trees adjacent to the dunes every October through February. Restrooms; RV and tent campsites.

- **Salmon Creek Beach,** off Highway 1, 2 miles north of Bodega Bay. Two miles of wide, sandy beach edged with grassy dunes. The creek and lagoon are inhabited by throngs of seabirds. Restrooms. Ranger headquarters is located here (707–875–3540).

- **Portuguese Beach,** between Salmon Creek and Wright's Beach on Highway 1. Best beach for rock fishing and surf fishing.

- **Wright's Beach,** 6 miles north of Bodega Bay; (707) 875–3483. With a large parking area at beach level, the easiest access for all ages and abilities; thirty campsites.

- **Shell Beach,** between Wright's Beach and Goat Rock, on Highway 1. A small, pretty beach with great tidepools; the best of the Sonoma beaches for shelling. Restrooms.

- **Goat Rock,** 2 miles south of Jenner on Highway 1; (707) 875–3483. Although a dangerous place to swim, this beach is popular for beach-combing, shore fishing, and freshwater fishing at the mouth of the Russian River. Seals like it too; a large herd is often seen sunbathing and surfing where the river joins the sea. In spring they give birth to their pups here. This is protected territory for the seals, and visitors are advised to stay at a safe distance. More than 200 species of seabirds and shorebirds can be seen—great blue herons, white and brown pelicans, gulls, ospreys, even peregrine falcons.

Bodega Bay Surf Shack

Pelican Plaza, Bodega Bay; (707) 875–3944; www.bodegabaysurf.com.

Headquarters for rentals, maps, and advice on biking, beachcombing, kayaking, surfing, and windsurfing. Lessons and guided tours are available; beachwear is for sale. Visit the Web site for fascinating satellite reports, maps, and forecasts about waves and weather.

Chanslor Guest Ranch (ages 4 and up)

2660 Highway 1, on the north end of Bodega Bay; (707) 875–3333. Horseback rides $$$–$$$$; pony rides $$$.

Guided horseback rides on the beaches, along the bluffs, and through wetlands, plus hay-wagon and barbecue rides. Special rides for kids ages four and up on gentle horses, ponies, or donkeys.

Pomo/Miwok Trail (ages 6 and up)

Across Highway 1 from Shell Beach; (707) 875–3540.

Up and over the hills to a small redwood forest, a moderately strenuous walk that takes about an hour and passes through meadows, over creeks, and under shade trees, with coastal views all the way. At the top hikers are rewarded with a redwood grove and creek, a perfect picnic spot. The path goes on from here to the Russian River and the Pomo/Miwok Campground.

Vista Trail (ages 2 and up)

Located 4.8 miles north of Jenner, off Highway 1; (707) 875–3483.

A wheelchair-accessible, 1-mile loop in a meadow on a bluff, offering wide ocean views and picnic tables.

Fort Ross State Historic Park (all ages)

19005 Highway 1, 11 miles north of Jenner; (707) 847–3286.

The Russians arrived here in 1812 to harvest otter and seal pelts and to grow produce for their northern outposts. Their small settlement of hand-hewn log barracks, blockhouses, and homes, together with a jewel of a Russian Orthodox church, was protected with high bastions and a bristling line of cannons, just in case the Spanish decided to pay a call. Several of the buildings and the church remain in a magical greensward above the sea. Inside the restored buildings are perfectly preserved rifles, pistols, tools, furniture, and old photos. At the excellent visitor center are exhibits, films, and guidebooks. A delightful protected beach hides below the fort. Twenty coastal canyon campsites are open March through November; picnic areas, hiking trails, restrooms.

Salt Point State Park (all ages)

Located 15 miles north of Jenner, on both sides of Highway 1; (707) 847–3221 or (707) 865–2391. Day-use fee $$.

Six thousand acres and 7 miles of coastline, with long, sandy beaches, rich tidepools, rugged cliffs, sunny meadows, and hiking and biking trails. The dense forestlands of Salt Point are inhabited by gnarly pygmy pines and cypress, their ghostly gray, mossy trunks tickled by maidenhair ferns. For tidepooling take the Gerstle Cove Campground turnoff and follow the road to Gerstle Cove parking. No collecting is allowed.

Sea Ranch Lodge

60 Sea Walk Drive, off Highway 1, 20 miles north of Jenner in Sea Ranch; (707) 785–2371 or (800) 732–7662; www.searanchlodge.com. $$$–$$$$.

Nestled in grassy meadows on headlands above the ocean, a small lodge, a restaurant, and nearby rentable homes are headquarters for a coastal getaway. Whether or not you stay at the lodge, you can access several beaches (Shell Beach, Pebble Beach, and Black Point Beach are the best) and walk easy paths on the bluffs. Walk or bike on quiet, paved country roads on the east side of the Highway 1. An 18-hole, links-style golf course is laid on the bluffs, in meadows and forests.

From the Sea Ranch restaurant, you can easily see whales in the wintertime. The food is good—sandwiches, salads, homemade soups, fresh fish, for lunch and dinner. The lounge bar has a big fireplace. Twenty upscale rooms have ocean views; one room has a fireplace and a hot tub and no view.

The Children's Bell Tower (all ages)

West side of Highway 1, about a mile north of Bodega Bay, turn into the driveway just after the gift shop; (707) 875–2263; www.nicholasgreen.org.

A magical bell tower is a memorial for a young boy from the town, Nicholas Green, who was killed by highway robbers while vacationing in Italy with his family. His parents donated his organs to seven Italians waiting for transplants and people from all over Italy responded by sending 140 bells—school bells, church bells, ships' bells, mining bells, and cow bells, which all chime when the wind blows.

Where to Eat

Bodega Bay Grill. 2001 Highway 1, Bodega Bay; (707) 875–9190. In a small, clean cafe on the north edge of the bay, good fresh fish and chowder and Mexican food. $

Breakers Cafe. 1400 Highway 1, across from the kite shop on the north end of Bodega Bay, in the Pelican Plaza; (707) 875–2513. Great sea views from a sunny deck, killer breakfasts, fresh seafood and pasta, homemade pies. Breakfast, lunch, and dinner. $–$$

Dinucci's. Downtown Valley Ford on Highway 1, near Bodega Bay; (707) 876–3260. For decades a destination in itself. Huge home-style Italian dinners, seafood and steaks, a friendly long bar. $–$$

Mom's Apple Pie. 4550 Gravenstein Highway North, Sebastopol; (707) 823–8330. On the way to Bodega Bay, don't fail to stop at the small, take-out pie shop by the apple orchard. Betty Carr is famous for her luscious pies: apricot, blackberry, rhubarb, wild blueberry, chocolate cream, and more. You can also get Screamin' MiMi's Ice Cream here and coffee. Next door, Stella's Cafe is a farmhouse kind of place with a wood stove and an open kitchen where locals flock for American comfort food. $

Sandpiper Dockside Cafe. 1410 Bay Flat Road, Bodega Bay; (707) 875–2278. Best kept secret, a little place hidden below the main road, featuring homemade everything, including crab cioppino. $–$$

The Tides Wharf and Restaurant. 835 Highway 1, Bodega Bay; (707) 875–3652. On the wharf, with views of the bay and the boat action; a sunny deck for snacks and drinks, a tiny cafe, a souvenir shop, a gourmet food emporium and oyster bar, and a large, attractive restaurant serving great seasonal fresh seafood, from cracked Dungeness crab to cioppino, a huge variety of fish, and seafood salads. Every table has a view, and the seals have a view of you. Open for three meals a day. $–$$

Union Hotel. 3731 Main Street, Occidental; (707) 874–3444. Famous for decades for supercolossal, multicourse, family-style Italian dinners; very popular on Sunday afternoons and holidays. Choices include homemade ravioli, fried chicken, veal, antipasto, minestrone, salads, and more—much more. Occidental makes a nice stop on the way to or from Bodega. Take the Bohemian Highway through Freestone for about twenty minutes on a winding mountain road to this tiny village and enjoy its restaurants, galleries, and shops. Dinner guests are welcome to park RVs here overnight. $–$$

Where to Stay

Bodega Bay Lodge. 103 Coast Highway 1, on the south side of Bodega Bay; (707) 875–3525 or (800) 368– 2468; www.wood sidehotels.com. Perched above the bay and bird-filled marshes, all rooms and luxury suites with sea views, terraces or decks, cozy comforters, Jacuzzi tubs, robes; some fireplaces. In the lobby are a giant stone fireplace and two 500-gallon aquariums filled with tropical fish. Fresh, contemporary decor, swimming pool, spa, sauna, fitness center, complimentary bikes, golf packages. $$$–$$$$

Bodega Coast Inn. 521 Highway 1, Bodega Bay; (707) 875–2217. Each motel room has an ocean view, balcony, and refrigerator; some have fireplaces and spas; one is a two-bedroom with kitchenette. $$–$$$

Fort Ross Lodge. 20705 Coast Highway 1, Jenner; (707) 847–3333. Comfortable ocean-view rooms and suites, some with fireplaces and spas, microwaves, refrigerators, TV/VCR. Barbecues on your private patio; a convenience store across the road. $$$–$$$$

Inn at the Tides. 800 Highway 1, Bodega Bay; (800) 541–7788; www.innatthetides .com. On a grassy, landscaped hillside overlooking the town, a large complex of spacious, two-story units with fireplaces, sitting areas, a protected indoor/outdoor pool, and a spa. Continental breakfast is complimentary, and a top-notch restaurant serves California cuisine. $$$–$$$$

Pomo/Miwok Campground. Where the river meets the sea at Bridgehaven, ten minutes off Highway 1; (800) 444–7275. Forty walk-in tent sites in a dense redwood forest at the end of a paved road (a beautiful road for biking and walking). A few sites are near the parking lot; it's a five- to fifteen-minute walk to the others. If you arrive with no reservation, check the bulletin board to find available sites. Fire rings, picnic tables, and portable potties. $

Vacation Homes. (707) 875–4000, (707) 875–3942, or (707) 875–3000. From cabins to spacious vacation home rentals, from Bodega Bay to Timber Cove and beyond. $–$$$$

For More Information

Bodega Bay Chamber of Commerce and Sonoma Coast Visitors Center. 850 Highway 1, next to Texaco, Bodega Bay; (707) 875–3866; www.bodegabay.com.

Department of Parks and Recreation, Russian River District. P.O. Box 123, Duncans Mills 95430; (707) 865–2391. Information on private campgrounds.

Wine Country

D ue north across the Golden Gate, rugged mountain ranges and rich agricultural valleys shelter lakes, rivers, and a scattering of small, historic towns. Country pleasures are what families seek in Sonoma, Lake, and Napa Counties—everything from boating and fishing to biking and hiking, camping, and vestiges of California's early days.

The 1700s come alive in the small mission town of Sonoma, which contains the largest remaining Spanish plaza in the state. A few minutes away, in the Valley of the Moon, is a state park with riding trails and a delightfully spooky ruin in a redwood forest.

Kids like watching hot air balloons and glider planes in the Napa Valley, and parents are surprised to find that there's a lot to do and see besides wineries. The waters of Lake Berryessa attract vacationers for summer waterskiing and swimming and for year-round trout and bass fishing.

Primary destinations are the oceanarium and wildlife theme park Six Flags Marine World in Vallejo and Safari West near Calistoga, a preserve for African plains animals.

Flowing from the valleys to the sea in western Sonoma County, the Russian River offers fishing holes and campgrounds, redwood groves and sandy beaches.

Families that love to fish and water-ski head north to Clear Lake. The smooth green flanks of 4,200-foot Mount Konocti, a dormant volcano, loom dramatically above the placid blue waters, which hold more fish per acre than any other lake in the country.

Lakeport

The largest town on the shores of Clear Lake, Lakeport features a few historic buildings and an old-fashioned band shell and playground in a grassy lakefront park. Several smaller towns and small resorts are scattered around the lake. When school's out, families begin arriving with their boats, camping gear, fishing rods, and water sports equipment. The largest natural lake in the state and rated the number one bass lake in the western United States, Clear Lake is ringed with family-oriented resorts, marinas, and campgrounds.

WINE COUNTRY

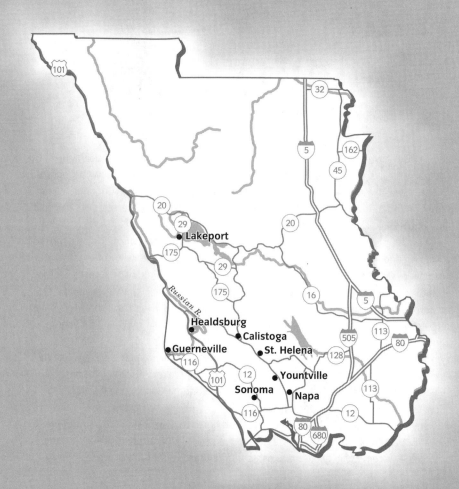

Pomo Indian tribal heritage is prominent throughout the county at the museum, at Anderson Marsh State Park, in the crafts and art found in retail shops, and at annual Native American events.

Winters are mild here, a good time for fishing expeditions, rockhounding, and bird-watching. You are likely to see bald eagles, and you can't miss the tremendous number of waterfowl and other migrating birds from Alaska and Canada that come to spend the season.

Lake County Museum (all ages) 🏛 🛍
255 North Main, Lakeport; (707) 263–4555. Free.

In a beautiful 1877 building that served as a school for more than fifty years, a big collection of stone tools, arrowheads, pioneer costumes and exhibits, and antique firearms, as well as a shop selling jewelry made by local Native Americans. The highlights of the collection are the superb Pomo Indian baskets.

Clear Lake State Park (all ages) Ⓐ 🌊 🎣 🛝
5300 Soda Bay Road, Kelseyville; (707) 279–4293; (campground reservations: 800–444–7275). $.

Here you can camp beside the lake; fish for bass, catfish, crappie, and perch; swim; and bird-watch. Interpretive displays on local history and the natural environment and wildlife are at the visitor center. Behind the center look for great blue herons on the banks of Kelsey Creek; the large nests in the treetops are heron rookeries. A 700-gallon aquarium shows Clear Lake fish and aquatic life. On Cole Creek are shady picnic sites, barbecues, and a swimming beach with lifeguards. Among miles of hiking trails, the short Indian Nature Trail showcases flora related to local tribes.

Anderson Marsh State Historic Park (all ages) 🦬 🎒 🏛 ⛺
Highway 53, between the towns of Lower Lake and Clearlake; (707) 994–0688.

Herons, pelicans, ducks, grebes, coots, cormorants, bald eagles, and other species of waterfowl are seen regularly here. The sight of a bald eagle fishing for its dinner is a moment to remember. Birdwatching is best in early spring and early in the morning when the birds are feeding. Numerous ancient Native American sites date from 8000 b.c., when the shores and swamps surrounding Clear Lake were almost exactly as they are today. In the historic Anderson Ranch House are a small museum and visitor center. To get very close to the wetlands wildlife, hike through the Redbud Audubon Society's McVicar Preserve within the state park, or rent a boat or canoe at Garner's Resort (707–994–6267) or Shaw's Shady Acres (707–994–2236), nearby.

Lake County **Pathways**

The rolling countryside around Clear Lake is as green as Ireland in spring and winter; wildflowery, dry, and warm in the summer and fall. Eleven routes for biking and walking—county roads, city streets, state highways, and dirt roads—are mapped and described in detail, from strenuous to easy, in a booklet available at the visitor center or by mail; you will also find the routes on the Web site (875 Lakeport Boulevard, Clearlake; 707–263–9644; www.lakecounty.com).

Konocti Harbor Resort and Spa (all ages)
8727 Soda Bay Road, Kelseyville; (800) 660–LAKE; www.konoctiharbor.com. $$–$$$$.

In the shadow of Mount Konocti, this sprawling lakeside resort and marina has two large swimming pools with lifeguards, lighted tennis courts, minigolf, play-grounds, a video games arcade, volleyball, and a lot more. The staffed Kids' Club provides child care and activities all summer and during concert evenings. If your family wants to stay put and enjoy the lake, this is the place. Older children particularly enjoy it, as there are kids to meet, beach volleyball, pool tables, and video games, plus Jet Skis, pedal boats, kayaks, and fishing poles to rent. Also here is a complete health spa, with exercise classes, a lap pool, and body and beauty treatments. Live, top-name entertainment occurs year-round in 1,000- and 5,000-seat venues—mostly country western, with some rock stars. The facility offers a wide variety of accommodations, including motel rooms, beach cottages, condo units, and family rate packages. The atmosphere is family-oriented and casual. Restaurants serve hearty American fare ($$).

On the Waterfront (all ages)
60 Third Street, Lakeport; (707) 263–6789.

Parasailing, plus rentals for Jet Skis, pedal boats, ski boats, and fishing and "patio boats"—an easy-to-handle sort of a barge, just the thing for families. Purchase beachwear and water-ski accessories here too.

Outrageous Waters (ages 4 and up)
Highway 53 at Highway/Dam Road, Clearlake; (707) 995–4817; www.outrageouswaters.com. $$$; over 55 $; kids 3 and under free.

Four scary water slides are thrilling and cooling on a summer's day. Little kids will like the "Lazy River" and a huge kids' pool with waterfalls. A mini–Grand Prix racetrack, batting cages, and, of course, video games are available.

Real Goods (all ages)
13371 Highway 101, Hopland; (707) 744–2100; www.realgoods.com.

A destination in itself, Real Goods is an unusual retail showplace of renewable energy products—solar, recycled, biodegradable, nontoxic, energy-efficient items for sustainable living, including toys, clothing, and books. Even the building itself demonstrates "green" concepts; the north and east walls of the main building were constructed of straw bales. Just exploring the surrounding landscaping is an educational experience. Outdoors are water features in which kids can play, and you can walk around and rest on the banks of a shady little lake.

Fetzer Vineyards Visitor Center (all ages)
Valley Oaks, 13601 Eastside Road, Hopland; (800) 846–863, (707) 744–7600; www.fetzer.com. Free.

On the way to Mendocino or on a day trip to Hopland, this makes a great stop for a picnic and an educational garden tour. The organic fruit, flower, and vegetable gardens here are glorious and laid out in themes such as wine education; food for the kitchen; attracting beneficial insects, hummingbirds, or monarch butterflies; vegetables, and more. Each area has sensory plants to smell, taste, and touch—fifty varieties of apples and pears, old-fashioned roses, aromatic herbs, berries, veggies. In the spring and summer, when everything is ripe and blooming, the place is heady with fragrance.

Adjoining the tasting room is a deli offering sandwiches, salads, and makings for a gourmet picnic, which you can enjoy at tables under the oaks or vine-covered arbors. Upscale rooms at the Fetzer Inn, here, include suites with queen beds and sofa beds, equipped kitchens, and private patios ($$$–$$$$).

Fetzer also has a tasting room and gourmet deli at 45070 Main Street in Mendocino, next to the Mendocino Hotel (707–937–6190).

Vichy Hot Springs (all ages)
2605 Vichy Springs Road, Ukiah; (707) 462–9515; www.vichysprings.com. $$$–$$$$.

Since 1854, a family-oriented country resort famous for natural, warm, carbonated water springs that fill a large swimming pool and several tubs. Simple, spacious rooms and cottages are nicely decorated with Waverly floral prints; some have full kitchens, one or two bedrooms, and verandas overlooking sweeping lawns, meadows, and gardens. You can explore the ranch, mountain bike, and hike to 40-foot Chemisal Falls. There is a year-round stream and lovely wildflowers. Buffet breakfast is included. Ask about day use. You can hike on 700 acres of countryside.

Grace Hudson Sun House (all ages)
431 South Main Street, Ukiah; (707) 462–3370; www.gracehudsonmuseum.org. Free.

An impressive complex housing American Indian baskets, artifacts, and paintings, this is a light, colorful place that children enjoy. The late Grace Hudson painted the faces and the domestic life of native Pomo Indians, while her ethnologist husband assembled the extraordinary collection, one of the most important in the Northern Hemisphere. Open to inspection, their home is a wonderful redwood Craftsman-style bungalow. A tree-shaded park with picnic tables surrounds the museum buildings. My granddaughters have found Native American–oriented toys, books, and games in the gift shop.

Montgomery Woods State Reserve (all ages)
Fourteen miles west of Ukiah on Orr Springs Road; (707) 937–5804; www.parks.ca.gov.
Free.

One of the least-visited state parks, this one shelters a miraculous virgin forest of redwood trees including the Mendocino Tree, which, at 367.5 feet, now holds the title of the world's tallest living thing. An easy loop trail of about 3 miles follows Montgomery Creek past 6-foot-tall woodwardia ferns, wild iris, columbine, and more gorgeous greenery to five redwood groves that have never been logged. The Mendocino Tree stands, without a marker to distinguish it, among two dozen or so redwoods that tower 350 feet and higher. The steep, winding road to the reserve is not at all appropriate for RVs.

Where to Eat

Boneyard BBQ. 13441 Highway 101, Brutocao Schoolhouse Plaza, Hopland; (707) 744–2020. Barbecued ribs and chicken, baked beans, burgers, sandwiches, hot wings, fish and chips—something for everyone, for lunch and dinner. $–$$

Main Street Cafe. 14084 Lakeshore Drive, Clearlake; (707) 995–6450. Indoors or outdoors, the locals' favorite for down-home cooking. Children like the burgers and sandwiches. $

Park Place. 50 Third Street, Lakeport; (707) 263–0444. In a comfy booth, or on the deck with lake views, everyone goes for the homemade pasta, Nancy's amazing vegetable soup, fresh fish, and steak. Veggies come from a local patch, and the blackberries in the sorbet are picked in the owner's backyard. You can motor here in your boat, and take a snooze in the park across the street. Open all day for breakfast, lunch, and dinner. $–$$

Where to Stay

Bellhaven Resort. 3415 White Oak Way, Kelseyville; (707) 279–4329; www.bellhaven.com. On Clear Lake's Soda Bay, a nice beach, a fishing and swimming pier, and cabins with kitchens, kayaks, and private dock. $–$$

B. J. Wall's Lakeside RV and Campground. 2570 Lakeshore Boulevard, Nice; (707) 274–3315. On Clear Lake, full hookups, campsites, shade trees, private beach, boat dock, showers, laundry. Walk to nearby restaurant and boat rentals. $

El Grande Inn. 15135 Lakeshore Drive, Clearlake; (707) 994–2000. On the lake, forty-five very nice rooms and suites, plus a pool, sauna, garden courtyard, and restaurant. $–$$

Featherbed Railroad Company. 2870 Lakeshore Boulevard, Nice; (800) 966–6322; www.featherbedrailroad.com. Irresistible, nine-car trains with cabooses are a sweet surprise overlooking the lake. The

Rosebud Caboose has bunkbeds for two kids, and there is a small swimming pool. A hearty breakfast is served in the ranch house or on the front porch. In a parklike setting, the resort also has a private beach and pier, boat dock, and boat ramp. $$

For More Information

Lake County Visitor Center. 875 Lakeport Boulevard, Lakeport; (800) 525–3743; www.lakecounty.com.

California State Park Campground Reservations. (800) 444–7275.

Calistoga

More than a century ago, people came to this little tree-shaded Victorian spa town in horse-drawn carriages to "take the waters." Steam rises from 200-degree mineral springs at a dozen or so health resorts—this is the place for rest and rejuvenation, for massages and mud baths. Children are not likely to go for a massage or for wine tasting at the many wineries in the area. They will love the town's museum, the Calistoga Gliderport, a unique wildlife preserve, and biking down Mount St. Helena. Except for the busy few blocks of the main street, Lincoln Avenue, this is the quiet side of Napa Valley, making biking and hiking particularly serene. This is a walking town, a compact grid of streets that look suspended in time. Stroll up and down the streets perpendicular to Lincoln, on the west side, and look for the sweet gazebo and playground in creekside Pioneer Park on Cedar Street.

Sharpsteen Museum (all ages)

1311 Washington Street, Calistoga; (707) 942–5911; www.sharpsteenmuseum.org. Free.

Kids love the unstuffy atmosphere of this place, which was built and donated by a thirty-year veteran of the Disney studios. His Disney memorabilia are on display, along with an elaborate diorama re-creating the 1800s resort town, plus a big collection of old photos; a stagecoach; a Victorian dollhouse; a barn and farming equipment; a cottage of the original hot springs resort; a general store; and a blacksmith shop.

Indian Springs Hot Springs Spa and Resort

1712 Lincoln Avenue, Calistoga; (707) 942–4913; www.indianspringscalistoga.com. $$–$$$.

Founded in 1865, Indian Springs is one of the oldest spa resorts in town, and it still has an old-fashioned air about it. Filled with mineral water from three natural geysers, the Olympic-size pool is heated to 92 degrees in summer and 101 degrees in winter. Horseshoes and a clay (!) tennis court, bicycles and bike surreys, croquet, hammocks, and Weber grills are available here. From a studio cottage to a large house, accommodations are simple and comfortable, including fireplaces, robes, and air-conditioning.

Giuseppe's **Truck**

865 Silverado Trail North, near Calistoga; (707) 942–6295. At the turn of the century, health addicts drove their horse-drawn carriages from San Francisco all the way to Calistoga to drink the waters. Bubbling up out of the ground with intense carbonation and more than sixty-five minerals essential for good health, Calistoga water has been bottled since the early 1900s. To commemorate the founding of the Calistoga Mineral Water company, and to have some fun, a larger-than-life sculpture was erected on the roadside at the mineral water facility—and it makes a great photo. Six tons, 14 feet tall, and 35 feet long, it's a huge sculpture of the 1926 truck that founder Giuseppe Musante and his dog Frankie drove over the narrow, winding dirt roads to the California State Fair in Sacramento, where his water won gold medals year after year.

Old Faithful Geyser (all ages)

A mile north of Calistoga, on Tubbs Lane; (707) 942–6463. Adults $$; kids 6 to 12 $; under 6 free.

One of only three regularly erupting geysers in the world. Every forty minutes or so, a column of 350-degree water and steam roars more than 60 feet into the air. That's it.

Safari West (all ages)

3115 Porter Creek Road, Santa Rosa, ten minutes east of Calistoga; (707) 579–2551; www.safariwest.com. Call for reservations and schedule. $$$$; kids 2 and under free.

Giraffes in Wine Country? Yes, at the far northern end of the valley, on open grasslands and rolling hills, sits a wildlife preserve with more than 400 exotic animals and birds, as well as African plains animals, including zebras, elands, giraffes, impalas, Watusi cattle, and rare endangered antelopes. Private half-day, narrated tours are conducted in safari vehicles. You can stay overnight here in a nice tent cabin outfitted with two double beds; breakfast is included, and African food is available for dinner.

It's hot and dry here in summer and early fall, so be prepared with hats and sunscreen. I don't recommend bringing toddlers along unless you know they can handle a two-hour, sometimes bumpy ride. The last time we went to Safari West, we saw a new-born zebra, and we loved it when the herd of Watusi cattle came pounding down the road and crowded up against the truck. What shoulders!

Robert Louis Stevenson State Park (all ages)
Seven miles north of Calistoga, on Highway 29; (707) 942–4575.

On the wooded slopes of Mount St. Helena, take forest trails for easy walks or embark on the steep, 5-mile scramble to the 4,343-foot summit. Mountain bikers use the fire road, which starts about 0.25 mile north of the parking lot. Spyglass Hill in Robert Louis Stevenson's Treasure Island is based on the landscape of Mount St. Helena; see a museum devoted to Stevenson's life and works at the library in St. Helena (707–963–3757). No dogs are allowed in the park, and there is no water.

Petrified Forest (all ages)
4100 Petrified Forest Road, 5 miles west of Calistoga; (707) 942–6667; www.petrified forest.com. Adults $$; kids 4 to 17 $; younger kids free.

For an unusual one-hour side trip, walk on an easy, 0.25-mile path through a redwood forest turned to stone six million years ago by a volcanic eruption, a site you're not likely to see elsewhere. One-hundred-foot tree trunks are swirled in opalescent purple and pink. The gift shop sells colorful polished stones, semiprecious gems, and fossils. Wheelchair access is marginal but doable; pets are okay.

Where to Eat

All Season's Cafe. 1400 Lincoln Avenue, Calistoga; (707) 942–9111. A classically trained chef invents American versions of Mediterranean foods with locally grown and produced ingredients. Home-smoked salmon and chicken, grilled Petaluma duck breast, pizzettas, pasta, fresh fish, and killer pies are featured. Salads, such as warm spinach with smoked chicken and lemon dressing, are tops here. The greens come from fields just a few blocks away. $$–$$$

Cafe Pacifico. 1237 Lincoln Avenue, Calistoga; (707) 942–4400. A Mexican motif is the backdrop for incredible breakfasts, lunches, and dinners. Try the blue-corn buttermilk pancakes, fresh enchiladas, and chiles rellenos. $–$$

Calistoga Inn. 1250 Lincoln Avenue, Calistoga; (707) 942–4101. In a charming, circa-1880 building with a splendid outdoor dining terrace on the Napa River, the inn serves inventive sandwiches, meal-size salads, lots of appetizers to share, and grilled meats, as well as microbrews from the on-site brewery. $–$$

Palisades Market. 1506 Lincoln Avenue, Calistoga; (707) 942–9549. Looks like an old grocery store on the outside, gourmet surprises await within. Market and deli with miraculous sandwich and salad combinations, wonderful fresh produce, and a myriad of locally made, packaged foodstuffs. $–$$

Where to Stay

Calistoga Club RV and Camping Resort.
580 Lommel Road, off upper Silverado Trail
in Calistoga; (707) 942–6565. Popular, rustic camping resort in an oak forest, with a
creek, meadows, an Olympic-size pool,
indoor/outdoor games, short hiking trails,
and a small fishing lake. Tent and RV sites;
basic cabins. Fewer people and greener
surroundings can be found here in winter
and spring. $

Carlin Country Cottages. 1623 Lake
Street, Calistoga; (707) 942–9102 or (800)
734–4624. Nice, simple cottages in a wide
courtyard, with Shaker-style furnishings.
Some cottages have Jacuzzi tubs; some
have one or two separate bedrooms with
kitchens. Spring-fed swimming pool.
$$–$$$

Comfort Inn. 1865 Lincoln Avenue, Calistoga; (707) 942–9400. Reasonably priced,
simple, modern rooms; pool and sauna;
continental breakfast. $–$$

Scott Courtyard. 1443 Second Street (2
blocks from downtown), Calistoga; (707)
942–0948. Roomy, circa-1940 bungalows
with kitchens, surrounded by lush gardens.
Small swimming pool, hot tub, library with
fireplace, fully equipped art studio for
guest use. I like this place for the separate
video/TV/exercise room and the art studio,
where children would enjoy hanging out—
unusual at a B&B. Full breakfasts, evening
wine-and-cheese. $$–$$$

For More Information

Calistoga Chamber of Commerce. 1458
Lincoln Avenue, Calistoga; (707) 942–6333;
www.calistogafun.com.

St. Helena

Families like the little town of St. Helena for its tree-shaded old-fashioned neighborhoods,
for postcard-perfect Main Street lined with nineteenth-century stone buildings—each with
a quaint shop or cafe inside—and for the biking and walking trails in the surrounding
countryside and the nearby state park. Kids who like to cook will enjoy visiting the Culinary Institute of America at Greystone and the West Coast annex of a famous gourmet
store, Dean and DeLuca. It's best to park your car and walk around.

Dean and DeLuca 🍴

601 Highway 29, just south of St. Helena; (707) 967–9980.

Huge gourmet market, wine shop, produce mart, and deli—a welcome offshoot of the
famous New York store. You'll find here an incredible variety of cheeses and meats, rotisserie chicken, and wonderful salads and entrees to go, plus packaged gourmet foodstuffs
of all kinds. I like the big glass jars of exotic dried mushrooms and marinating olives and
the amazing array of vinegars and oils to taste, from fig balsamic vinegar to olive oil
pressed in the most isolated, obscure orchard in Tuscany. You can enjoy your sandwiches,
fresh fruit smoothies, and espresso drinks in the back on the sunny patio.

Shops Kids Like in St. Helena

- **Tapioca Tiger,** 1224 Adams Street; (707) 967–0608. Unique clothing, hand-crafted furniture and toys. Sand table with objects moved by magnets.

- **Fideaux,** 1400 Oak Street; (707) 967–9935. Don't forget Muffie and Spot. Pick up a lavish cat bed, a handmade dog collar, chew toys, gourmet biscuits, a rubber frog, or a doggie futon.

- **Nature, Etc.,** 1327 Main Street; (707) 963–1706. Puzzles, games, books, toys, music, T-shirts, and more, all with an environmental or nature theme.

- **Hurd Beeswax Candle Factory,** on Highway 29 just north of town at the Freemark Abbey sign; (707) 963–7211. Watch fanciful and weird candles of every description being hand made. The large shop flickers with hundreds of unusual candles, including storybook characters, gnomes, and seasonal figures.

- **Freckles Children's Boutique,** 1309 Main Street; (707) 963–1201. For babies and children up to six, pricey, fanciful clothing, gifts, and toys.

Bothé-Napa Valley State Park (all ages)

3801 Highway 29 at Larkmead Lane, St. Helena; (707) 942–4575 (campground reservations: 800–444–7275).

Wilderness trails in a pine and redwood forest, plus a sycamore-shaded campground in Ritchie Creek Canyon. Surprising in a state park is the small swimming pool here, with a lifeguard; open June through Labor Day. Day-trippers picnic on the grass along the creek. It's a short walk from here into Bale Grist Mill State Park, a wooded glade with a 36-foot grinding wheel powered by a rushing creek. Costumed docents grind grain on the millstones and make bread during Old Mill Days in October and frequently on summer weekends. The fifty-site campground has hot showers and laundry tubs.

Napa Valley Trail Rides offers one- and two-hour, easy, slow, guided horseback rides in the park along Ritchie Creek and up on the ridges overlooking the valley (707–996–8566).

Culinary Institute of America at Greystone (CIA) (all ages)

🍴 🎨 🏛 🔒 🌿

2555 Main Street, just past Beringer Winery on Highway 29, St. Helena; (707) 967–1010; www.ciachef.edu. Museum and grounds are free. **Kitchen tours and demonstrations are a few dollars a person; call ahead for tours and for lunch and dinner reservations.**

A massive landmark guarded by towering palms, Greystone was built in 1889 with 22-inch-thick, hand-cut volcanic stone blocks. Today it's one of the nation's most prestigious culinary colleges, the Culinary Institute of America at Greystone (CIA). Plan at least an hour to wander around, see the food and wine museum, and browse the school store—a blockbuster of a gourmet emporium, where CIA logo attire and 1,500 cookbook titles are just part of an unbelievable inventory of tools and gifts in an environment reminiscent of southern Europe.

The attractive, noisy restaurant and outdoor terrace, which overlook an ancient oak forest and rolling vineyards, are pricey for families, and the food often fails to measure up to top valley restaurants. Graduate chefs are on view, preparing Spanish tapas and Mediterranean cuisine. A drink and snack on the terrace is a pleasant experience.

Kids enjoy the medieval castle look of the interior. Restless youngsters, accompanied, of course, can run around on the beautiful grounds; paths wind through aromatic herb gardens. Take budding chefs on the teaching kitchen tour in the upper reaches of the building.

Where to Eat

Gillwoods. 1313 Main Street, St. Helena; (707) 963–1788. Home-style American food: tuna sandwiches, grilled cheese, homemade soup, burgers, fried chicken, chili, ribs, meat loaf, apple pie. Breakfast, lunch, and dinner. $–$$

Green Valley Cafe and Trattoria. 1310 Main Street, St. Helena; (707) 963–7088; www.greenvalleycafe.com. Hearty minestrone, North Beach burgers, and homemade pasta entice at lunch; the dinner menu features more pasta plus grilled meats, chicken, and Italian specialties. Call ahead. $$–$$$

Model Bakery. 1357 Main Street, St. Helena; (707) 963–8192. A circa-1920 brick oven turns out sourdough and rustic breads, pizzettas, fruit tarts, and amazing desserts. The simple cafe serves wonderful soups, salads, and sandwiches for here or to take out. $

The Spot. Next to Dean and DeLuca, just south of St. Helena on Highway 29; (707) 963–2844. Grease is the word for the era but not the food. Superneat 1950s decor, a real family joint with a soda fountain and cool booths. Burgers, shakes, and sandwiches. $–$$

Taylor's Refresher. 933 Main Street on the south end of St. Helena; (707) 963–3486. For more than five decades, a roadside stop with picnic tables, serving burgers and dogs, fish and chips, garlic fries, Mexican food, plus Double Rainbow ice cream in fabulous shakes, floats, and malts. $

Tra Vigne Pizzeria. 1016 Main Street, St. Helena; (707) 967–9999. A new offshoot of the ultra-gorgeous main restaurant, this charming pizza house has booths, plasma TVs, and a billiard table to keep families happy while they wait for luscious, brick-oven baked, Cal-Ital pizzas. Besides traditional favorites, you can order the Benito (fennel sausage, hot coppa salami, smoked pork), the Ducati (roasted onions, broccoli rabe, smoked mozzarella, and chicken and apple sausage), and the Clam Pie (garlic paste and fresh-chopped clams) or just create your own. $–$$$

V. Sattui Winery. 111 White Lane, 11.2 miles south of St. Helena on Highway 29; (707) 963–7774. A pretty, shady picnic grove on two acres of lawn around a stone-walled 1885 winery. The gourmet deli sells literally hundreds of varieties of cheeses and meats, fresh breads, juices, and drinks. One disadvantage is the sight of the busy highway. Don't be concerned if you miss the wine tasting here; there are better choices for wine. $

Where to Stay

El Bonita. 195 Main Street, just south of St. Helena on Highway 29; (800) 541–3284 or (707) 963–3216. Hidden behind the original 1930s art deco motel are newer two-story motel units with private balconies looking into the trees and over the gardens. Large, two-room suites have microkitchens. Small pool, sauna, continental breakfast. $$–$$$

Harvest Inn. One Main Street, just south of St. Helena on Highway 29; (707) 963–9463. Somewhat pricey, but with great advantages: lush, rambling English gardens; a labyrinth of shady pathways, lawns, and bowers; and two nice pool terraces. If I had babies or toddlers, I would definitely choose this place and spend time walking, playing on the lawns, and lolling in the pools. Some suites have antiques, four-posters, fireplaces, and eclectic collections of elaborate furnishings; other rooms are simpler and more appropriate for a child or two. An expanded continental breakfast is served in a beautiful "great room." $$–$$$

For More Information

St. Helena Chamber of Commerce. 1010 Main Street, St. Helena; (707) 963–4456.

Wine Country Reservations. (707) 257–7757.

Yountville

Yountville is a tiny Wine Country burg whose few streets are lined with vintage cottages in overgrown country gardens. Washington Street, the main drag, holds a blizzard of shops, restaurants, and inns. A nice half-day excursion here will include a little shop and gallery browsing, a walk on an idyllic country road, a picnic and playtime at a great playground, and exploration of a fascinating old cemetery. There are several family-oriented restaurants within walking distance of the main attraction, Vintage 1870.

Wine Country **Biking**

Biking is big in Napa Valley. The advantages here are gorgeous scenery; miles of easy, flat routes; and easy access to rest stops, food and restaurants, and sightseeing attractions along the way. You can bike your brains out and still be within a few minutes of civilization. The mostly flat Silverado Trail, running 35 miles along the east side of the valley, is a main biker's route. Crisscrossing the valley between Highway 29 and the Silverado Trail are a myriad of leafy country roads. Bike shops will give you maps. Some bike shops will deliver rental bikes to your hotel and pick you up at the end of your ride in the valley.

Vintage 1870 🔒 🏛 🍴

6525 Washington Street, midtown Yountville; (707) 944–2451; www.vintage1870.com.

The landmark building in Yountville, a warren of shops, galleries, and cafes in a huge former winery. A good place to rest or run around, a nice lawn in back is bordered by trees and benches. If you're wending your way from Napa up the valley and someone needs a bathroom, Vintage 1870 is quickly accessible from the highway; restrooms are around back. Don't miss the Toy Cellar, a big store crowded with toys, dolls, and games, with a model train zipping around the ceiling.

Pacific Blues Cafe 🍴

In front of Vintage 1870, Yountville; (707) 944–4455.

Indoors or on the deck, a cafe serving breakfast burritos, biscuits and gravy, and hearty traditional breakfasts; for lunch and dinner, it's gourmet burgers and sandwiches, veggie specialties, fresh seafood, lots of appetizers, homemade soups, big salads, and microbrews on tap. A thoughtful kids' menu features grilled cheese, pizza, plain pasta, and more. $–$$$

Yountville Park and Pioneer Cemetery (all ages) 🏕 🏛 🏛

At the north end of town, on Washington Street.

An oak-shaded grassy commons, with a great children's playground and picnic tables. Next to the park is a wonderful cemetery with fascinating tombstones from the 1800s, including the graves of George Yount, founder of the town, and early pioneers from around the world. While living temporarily in New England in 1997, I became fond of cemeteries whose stones tell haunting stories, from shipwrecks to fires and storms. My granddaughter and I strolled around the Yountville graveyard, a pretty, tree-studded place, discussing burials and cremations. Now she is the family expert on what happens to people when they die.

Yount Mill Road Walk (all ages)
East of the playground on the north end of Yountville (park where the houses end).

An easy, 3-mile round-trip walk or bike ride, north to Highway 29 and back. Running along a tributary of the Napa River, the road is quiet, shady, and bedecked with lovely views of the mountains and vineyards. Watch for a plaque about George Calvert Yount, the first white settler in the valley. Yount wangled from Mexico the huge land grant of Rancho Caymus in the 1850s—composing much of the heart of the valley, including Yountville—and built grist- and sawmills on the river. You will see the remains of one of his large wooden barns.

The Napa Valley Museum (all ages)
55 Presidents Circle, Yountville; (707) 944–0500; www.napavalleymuseum.org. $; younger than 7 free.

Among old oaks and a redwood grove by a creek, an architectural surprise: a museum of contemporary art and the history of the valley, with indoor and outdoor exhibits and garden terraces to roam.

The museum is on the beautiful grounds of the Veterans Home of California, where you can take a walk under magnificent, century-old trees and lounge on the sweeping lawns. Adjacent is the **Yountville Golf Club,** a pretty 9-holer with a spectacular driving range and a casual indoor-outdoor cafe; this is a good place for beginning golfers (707–944–1992).

Napa River Ecological Reserve (all ages)
Yountville Cross Road at the Napa River; (707) 944–0500. Free.

A short walk beside the river, under oaks and sycamores, with oceans of wildflowers in the spring, and butterflies; watch out for poison oak. You can wade and fish here and play on the sandy riverbank.

Where to Eat

Compadre's. 6539 Washington Street, Yountville, adjacent to Vintage 1870; (707) 944–2406. Mexican food and a lively atmosphere, on delightful, palm- and oak-shaded patios. $$

Gordon's Cafe and Wine Bar. 6770 Washington Street, at the north end of Yountville near the park; (707) 944–8246.

In a former stagecoach stop, the best place in town for California cuisine picnic fare to go and casual, quick meals served at individual tables or the communal table. A small, noisy, popular and fun cafe and deli. Breakfast (cinnamon buns, yes!) and lunch every day; prix fixe dinner on Friday. $$

Rutherford Grill. 1880 Rutherford Road, Rutherford, on Highway 29 (watch for the two huge palms); (707) 962–1782. No reservations. Go for the smoky baby back ribs, for mountains of feathery onion rings, inventive pastas, grilled and spit-roasted poultry and meats, garlic mashed potatoes, jalapeño corn bread. Big booths inside; umbrella tables and a wine bar outside. This is a popular, fun place, and you may have to wait on week-ends. It has the advantage of being pleasantly noisy inside, so kids go unnoticed. $$–$$$

For More Information

Yountville Chamber of Commerce. 6516 Yount Street, Yountville; (707) 944–0904.

Napa

For 35 miles, from Napa north to Calistoga, the Napa Valley is crisscrossed by quiet country roads where families discover places to bike and hike, play on the riverbanks, and do a little shopping and sightseeing.

Some of the popular family attractions are state and regional parks, a geyser and a petrified forest, a gliderport, and two wildlife parks; some of these are near the town of Napa.

Old Town Napa (all ages)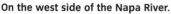
On the west side of the Napa River.

Here charming Victorian neighborhoods are bounded by Franklin, Division, Elm, and Riverside Streets. Extensive new development has transformed the downtown waterfront with upscale shopping, restaurants, and a small luxury hotel. You can rent kayaks and paddle the Napa River below downtown and south toward San Francisco Bay. Riverbank scenery is scant, the river is anything but pristine, and it's windy the farther south you go.

Napa has one of the best gourmet farmers' markets in Northern California, May through October, Tuesday mornings, in the parking lot at Copia (see below). Every Friday night the Napa Town Center mall is packed with families enjoying the live music, food, wine tasting, and fresh produce.

Six Flags Marine World (all ages)
At Highways 80 and 37, 2001 Marine World Parkway Way, Vallejo; (707) 643–6722; www.sixflags.com/parks/marineworld.com. $$$$; kids 2 years and under free; ask about family pricing.

What I like best about this oceanarium, wildlife, and amusement park is the chance to get close to animals and marine life, an enriching and educational experience for a child. My granddaughter Melati knows what a giraffe's blue tongue looks and feels like, because she fed one leaves and apples. She played tug-of-war with an elephant and hugged a chimpanzee.

With roller coasters, thirty-five rides, nine shows, and thirty-five animal habitats, it is a challenge to get everything into one day. Among the highlights are the live shows: the Batman Waterthrill show, the dolphin show (waves of cold water are splashed out of the pool by the animals onto people in the front rows—be ready!), Tiger Splash Attack, and the sea lion, elephant, and tropical bird shows. The most outrageous rides are the Boomerang and the Kong roller coasters, and the DinoSphere TurboRide, the world's first motion simulator adventure ride with 3-D. Rides for younger children are the ferris wheel, Monkey Business teacups, and the Shoreline Express railway.

There are cafes and food booths with some healthy choices. To avoid lines, arrive early and have lunch early. You can also enjoy your own picnic at tree-shaded tables on the grass by the lake. Rent a dolphin stroller for kids four and younger, as you will be walking your feet off! A carefree way to reach the park from the Bay Area is by ferry from San Francisco (707–643–3779). Ask about ferry packages and special event days.

Skyline Wilderness Park (all ages)

2201 Imola Avenue, on the east side of Napa; (707) 252–0481. $ parking fee.

A regional park with hilly woodlands and meadows for hiking, horseback riding, picnicking, and RV and tent camping. Find the waterfalls for a summer splash. Picnic and fish on the shores of Lake Marie, a 2.5-mile walk from the parking lot.

Lake Berryessa (all ages)

Seventeen miles east of Napa, at Highways 128 and 21; (707) 966–2111.

One of the state's most popular recreation lakes, with 165 miles of hilly, oak-covered shoreline. On the west shore, Knoxville Road gives access to marinas, park headquarters, a resort, beaches, and campgrounds. Oak Shores Park day-use area has the best beach and picnic sites, with lifeguards on weekends. Spring is ideal for bass fishing; fall, for trout. Marinas rent fishing, patio, and ski boats and other watercraft. This is a mild environment in which to learn windsurfing.

Napa Valley Wine Train (ages 3 and up)

1275 McKinstry Street off Soscol, Napa; (800) 427–4124 or (707) 253–2111; www.wine train.com. $$$$.

Elegant, restored Pullman railroad dining and observation cars take passengers on a relaxing ride up the valley, a three-hour chug from Napa to St. Helena and back, with a gourmet lunch or dinner included—a pricey and rather confining experience for youngsters, although a la carte snacks and meals are offered in a separate deli car, and there are Family Fun Nights when children three to twelve ride **free;** a supervisory staff keeps the kids happy with games, movies, and food.

Copia: the American Center for Wine, Food & the Arts (all ages)

500 First Street, Napa; (707) 259–1600; www.copia.org. Adults and teens ages 13 to 17 $$$; children $.

Budding chefs will enjoy the variety of food-related experiences at this new cultural center dedicated to wine, food, and the arts, from demonstration kitchen presentations to three-

and-a-half acres of organic gardens. Kids like the Fork in the Road exhibit of fun food facts about potato chips, peanut butter, soft drinks, and the like. In Kitchens of the Future watch hilarious 1950s videos. You can buy picnic fare at the American Market Cafe and sit outdoors overlooking the river on the terrace where summer concerts are held. Have a meal at Julia's Kitchen, browse the gift shop and the changing exhibits. Check the Web site for a lively schedule of classes, films, and events, including fun things like Christmas ornament making, special children's garden tours, Snack Attack cooking classes, and Family Flicks matinees.

Napa Fire Fighters Museum (all ages)
1201 Main Street, Napa; (707) 259–0609. Free.

Small but mighty, this museum is crowded with fire trucks and hose carts from the 1800s and early twentieth century; as well as toy fire trucks, hats, uniforms, a model firehouse, and two huge stuffed dalmatian dogs.

Where to Eat

Alexis Baking Company. 1517 Third Street, Napa; (707) 258–1827. Where the locals go for breakfast and coffee breaks, Sunday brunch, and lunch. Homemade pastries and desserts are remarkable. $$

Downtown Joe's Restaurant and Brewery. 902 Main Street, Napa; (707) 258–2337. Breakfast, lunch, or dinner on the patio overlooking the Napa River, adjacent to a small, grassy park where little ones can run while waiting for their dinners. Salads, sandwiches, pastas, and a microbrewery. $$

Gillwood's Bakery and Cafe. 1320 Town Center, Napa; (707) 253–0409. Luscious pastries and desserts, great old-fashioned breakfast, lunch and dinner. $–$$

Pasta Prego. 3206 Jefferson Street in the Grapeyard Center, Napa; (707) 224–9011. A friendly trattoria frequented by winery families. Served here are northern Italian food, seafood, pasta, and grilled fresh fish. For the most fun sit at the counter and watch the cooks. Lunch and dinner; indoors or on the tiny patio. $$–$$$

Soda Canyon Store. 4006 Silverado Trail, Napa; (707) 252–0285. At Soda Canyon Road just north of Napa, a great place to stop for a quick picnic or to pick up yummy provisions for lunch or snacks on the road. Locals start the day with breakfast burritos, smoothies, pastries, and espresso drinks. Gourmet deli sandwiches, cheeses, homemade salads, a nice selection of local wines, and packaged condiments that make nice gifts. $

Where to Stay

The Carneros Inn. 4048 Sonoma Highway, Napa; (707) 299–4900; www.the carnerosinn.com. A new, upscale resort lies on an idyllic site above rolling hills and dales surrounded by meadows where horses and cows graze. Clustered around small courtyards, one- and two-bedroom guest cottages have between 975 and 1,800 square feet of indoor and outdoor space; wood-burning fireplaces; flat-screen

TVs; private, heated patios; and gorgeous bathrooms, some with indoor/outdoor showers and soaking tubs. Ideal for a family are the double units that surround a private, fenced patio.

The large swimming pool and spa are open to the glorious view, and there is a full-service spa, a lobby "living room" with fireplace and games, and a fitness center. The sleek dining room serves sophisticated, French-inspired lunches and dinners with a view; you can order room service. Just down the hill, the casual Boon Fly Cafe serves breakfast and lunch, and there are boccie ball and croquet courts. The concierge will arrange guided walks for children and child care. $$$$

Embassy Suites Napa Valley. 1075 California Boulevard, adjacent to Highway 29, Napa; (707) 253–9540; www.embassysuites .com. Upscale Mediterranean-look hotel, with spacious suites, separate living room and sofa bed, small kitchens; conveniently located at the highway. Complimentary full breakfast and two hours of cocktails and snacks in the pleasant cafe by the lovely gardens. Indoor and outdoor pools, sauna, complimentary passes to nearby health club. Guest laundry. $$$–$$$$

For More Information

Napa Valley Conference and Visitors Bureau. 1310 Napa Town Center, Napa; (707) 226–3610; www.napavalley.com.

Napa Valley Reservations. 1819 Tanen Street, Napa, on the north end of town just off the highway; (707) 252–1985 or (800) 251–6272; www.napavalleyreservations .com.

Sonoma

On the west side of the Mayacamas Mountains, Sonoma Valley comprises a patchwork of vineyards and farmlands, with a fascinating early California history, best displayed in the town of Sonoma, which was laid out by a Mexican general in 1834. The site of many annual fiestas, parades, and art, wine, and food events, Sonoma Plaza is surrounded by the past, including a small California mission, a military compound from the days of the Mexican conquest, thick-walled adobe and Victorian homes, and a blizzard of upscale shops and restaurants. The plaza is popular for picnicking under the trees and for the two playgrounds. You can feed the ducks and, sometimes, pet the two-humped camel who comes to visit. April through October, the Tuesday night farmers' market is a big family event, usually with live entertainment.

Sonoma Mission and Sonoma Barracks (all ages)

First and Spain Streets, Sonoma; (707) 938–1519. Adults $; free for kids under 16.

The commandant who held sway in the Sonoma area when Mexico owned California, General Mariano Vallejo built a barracks compound for his soldiers, and it is now a state park and a museum on the plaza. The museum is an easy walk-through for children, offering re-created rooms and costumes of the early days. The museum shop is a great place to find educational and entertaining items for children, from paper dolls in period dress to small toys. In May a special Children's Day is held at the mission. The last of the California missions built, this one has a beautiful small chapel and museum.

Sonoma Walking/Biking Path (all ages)

Fifty yards north of East Spain Street, Sonoma. From Fourth Street East, west to Sonoma Highway 12; (707) 996–1090.

A paved path for walking, biking, and Rollerblading winds 1.5 miles from one end of Sonoma to the other, passing through parks and playing fields and ending on the west side at a big park with a playground. A block from Sonoma Plaza on the walking path, Depot Park has a playground, barbecues, and picnic tables under the trees: a good choice when the plaza is crowded. My granddaughter Laurel learned to Rollerblade on the trail, and her little sister, Melati, pedaled shakily along on her first "big girl's" bike ride.

Depot Park Museum (all ages)

270 First Street West, on the Sonoma Walking/Biking Path, Sonoma; (707) 938–1762. Open afternoons (hours vary) Wednesday through Sunday; gift shop. Free.

If you get hooked on local history, make a stop here to see a restored stationmaster's office, re-creations of Victorian households, and photos of early Sonomans.

General M. G. Vallejo Home (all ages)

About 0.5 mile northwest of the plaza off Spain Street, Sonoma; (707) 938–1519. The home is part of the state park property, so one admission ticket ($) is good at the mission, the barracks compound, and the Vallejo home.

Accessible by the walking path and by car, this beautiful yellow-and-white, "Yankee-style" Gothic Revival house was shipped around the Horn and erected in 1851 by the Mexican General Vallejo. Called *Lachryma Montis*, meaning "Tears of the Mountain," the house is shaded by huge magnolias and twined with rambling yellow roses.

My granddaughters love to wander through, looking at the original and period furnishings, and daydream about the days when Vallejo and his several daughters lived here before the turn of the twentieth century. There are tintypes of the daughters, their hair below their waists, wearing long, elaborate dresses, black stockings, and high-button shoes. Their bedrooms are as they were, with a tiny dollhouse, a miniature stove, tin bathtubs, lace coverlets, and cut velvet couches. The general's son had his own private pad, where his rifle, a narrow bed, and keepsakes are carefully preserved.

Zimbabwe Sculpture Gallery (ages 4 and up)
452 First Street on the plaza, Sonoma; (707) 935–6254.

Kids in an art gallery? Yes, this is something different. Dramatic African Shona stone sculpture, interesting oversize photographs of Africa, and a video to watch.

Half Pint (ages 1–8)
450 First Street East on the plaza, Sonoma; (707) 938–1722.

Kids' clothes of your dreams, beautiful European imports, trendy hats and shoes, a few toys.

Sonoma Traintown (ages 2–8)
20264 Broadway, 1 mile south of the plaza, Sonoma; (707) 938–3912. Open daily in summer and weekends during the rest of the year. Adults and children $; the carousel ride is $1.75.

Younger children love this: an open-air steam train ride through a redwood forest to a tiny farm that has a petting zoo; also, a Ferris wheel, a vintage carousel, Dragon Coaster, and Chattanooga Choo Choo Chairs, plus a snack shop. For lunch or dinner, go next door to Pizza Capri.

Sebastiani Trolley Ride and a Secret Picnic Site (all ages)
Sonoma Plaza, Sonoma; (707) 938–5532. Free.

On a replica of a San Francisco cable car, ride from Sonoma Plaza around town to and from Sebastiani Cellars, a few blocks away. Pick up picnic provisions, hop on the trolley, hop off at the winery, and walk 1 block to behind the winery to shaded picnic tables next to a vineyard with dazzling vineyard and hillside views. For an easy, twenty-minute stroll, walk north from the picnic area a few hundred yards and take the first left turn (Gehricke Road) past vineyards; take the first left, turn left again, turn left yet again, and you're back where you started.

Jack London State Park (all ages)
2400 London Ranch Road off Arnold Drive, Glen Ellen; (707) 938–5216. Day-use fee per auto $.

This area is called the Valley of the Moon, named for famous (some say infamous) resident, Jack London, author of the classic adventure tales *Call of the Wild* and *The Sea Wolf*. London's globe-trotting life early in the twentieth century is portrayed in photos and haunting artifacts in a wonderful Craftsman-style lodge, the "House of Happy Walls." Once London's ranch, the park comprises 800 acres of trails, crisscrossed by creeks winding through magnificent groves of oaks, madrones, fir, redwoods, and fern grottoes. You can picnic here in a wildflowery meadow and see the ruins of Wolf House, London's eccentric

stone mansion, found at the end of a 0.5-mile path through the trees (handicapped accessible by golf cart). Only walls and chimneys remain of the elaborate home that burned to the ground a few days before London and his wife, Charmian, could move in. Intrepid hikers will enjoy the steeper trails on the hillsides on the west side of the parking lot and will be rewarded with wide-open views of the valley. The easy 2-mile round-trip Lake Trail goes through the forest to a lake, where you can picnic under the trees. You can ride your horses in the park; for guided horseback riding, call (707) 996–8566.

Benziger Family Winery (all ages)
1883 London Ranch Road, Glen Ellen; (707) 935–3000 or (800) 989–8890; www.benziger.com.

Located here are beautiful valley oaks and gardens, an art gallery and picnic grounds, and a tasting room. This is the only winery in the valley to offer a motorized tram tour of the vineyards, and children are welcome. Call ahead for reservations.

Sugarloaf Ridge State Park (all ages)
Adobe Canyon Road off Highway 12, just north of Kenwood; (707) 833–5712 (campground reservations: 800–444–7275). Day-use fee $.

A 3,000-acre green and golden jewel of hillsides, redwood groves, creeks, wildflower-strewn meadows, and views. Take a short walk or a strenuous hike, picnic in the pines, park your RV overnight, or camp out in your tent.

Sonoma Valley Regional Park (all ages)
Across the road from the Garden Court Cafe, Highway 12 between Arnold Drive and Madrone Road, near Glen Ellen; (707) 539–8092. Parking fee $.

A mostly flat, paved path winding about 1 mile one-way through an oak forest, with a pretty creek along the way. You can bike and picnic; dogs must be leashed. My little granddaughter and her buddies like to pick up sticks and branches, drag them along on the walk, and build a fort on a fallen tree trunk.

Family Wineries of Sonoma Valley
9200 Sonoma Highway, Kenwood; (707) 833–5504.

Car full of kids, and parents want to taste wine? Right on the highway, this is an easy place to stop, taste wines, and let the kids and the designated driver play in the picnic area. Seven of the valley's finest small wineries offer wines unavailable for tasting elsewhere.

Winery Fun For Kids

A winery tour may last an hour or more, and youngsters can get restless. Choose your wineries well!

- **Niebaum Coppola Estate Winery,** 1991 St. Helena Highway, Rutherford; (707) 968–1100. My choice for "if you have time for only one winery," this winery has unique interest for young people because of the Hollywood movie connection. Renowned moviemaker Francis Ford Coppola restored to its former glory one of the oldest winery estates in the valley (Inglenook) and had his Hollywood designers create an extravaganza of a winery, gift store, museum, and park complete with bubbling fountains, promenades, and lawns.

  Ever see real Oscars up close? Here they are, Coppola's golden beauties, along with photos and other cool stuff from his movies, including the Tucker auto, the boat from Apocalypse Now, and costumes from Bram Stoker's Dracula.

- **Chateau Montelena,** 1429 Tubbs Lane, Calistoga; (707) 942–5105. Exotic ducks and swans glide around two red-lacquered gazebos in a small lake. Young children love to stand on the bridges and toss feed to attract the ducks and the koi fish. On the winery grounds a few picnic tables beneath weeping willows are within sight of the mossy, crenellated castle of French limestone where the wine is made.

- **St. Supéry Winery and Wine Discovery Center,** 8440 St. Helena Highway at Rutherford; (707) 963–4507. Besides lawns and picnic sites here, there is a lot to see that may be interesting to school-age children: A Victorian farmhouse, a wine-growing demonstration area, and relief maps of the valley are here too. You can easily leave the winery tour at any time; it's fun to walk on catwalks above the giant storage tanks.

- **Rutherford Hill Winery,** 200 Rutherford Hill Road, off the Silverado Trail, Rutherford; (707) 963–7194. Cool, delightfully spooky underground caves are fun to see on a thirty-five-minute tour. You can buy juices and picnic goodies here to enjoy at tables under the oaks or in the olive grove with wide valley views.

- **Sterling Vineyards,** 1100 Dunaweal Lane, Calistoga; (707) 942–3359. Tram tickets: all ages over ten $$; kids under ten **free.** Take a thrilling, four-minute gondola ride to a sky-high terrace for bird's-eye views. The winery tour is self-guided, and there are outdoor tables up here for picnicking—with your own provisions or you can buy simple deli items on-site. Children are given an activity bag with juice, raisins, crayons, cards to color, and stickers!

Annadel State Park (all ages)

Just east of Santa Rosa off Highway 12, end of Channel Drive; (707) 539–3911. Day-use fee $.

My children grew up hiking the trails of Annadel, a 5,000-acre paradise of streams, meadows, rolling foothills and canyons, and woodlands thick with oak, fir, and redwood. Biologists say this is the best example of northern oak woodland in existence. You can hike, horseback ride, bike; fish for bass and bluegill in Lake Ilsanjo—a 2.5-mile hike from the parking lot—and eat at picnic tables at the lake. Wildflowers explode from March through early summer; it can be hot and dry in late summer and early fall. Bring your own water.

Where to Eat

Basque Boulangerie Cafe. 60 First Street on the plaza, Sonoma; (707) 935–7687. French and Basque-style salads, pastries, muffins, cakes, and tarts; home-baked breads and rolls; espresso drinks. Sit at the counter or at a sidewalk table. Open from breakfast through late afternoon. $

Breakaway Cafe. 19101 Highway 12 in the Albertson's shopping plaza, Sonoma; (707) 996–5949. The best family place in town, with big booths, a toy corner, and all-American food, such as pork chops and mashed potatoes, roast chicken, burgers, salads, comforting soups, huge omelets, veggie specials, smoothies, and a kids' menu. They know kids here, and they like them. Ask about the Breakaway Kids Club card. Breakfast, lunch, and dinner. $–$$

Deuce. 691 Broadway, Sonoma; (707) 933–3823. Some of the best California cuisine in the Wine Country on a shady patio, just a couple of blocks from the plaza. The owners have twin young girls and are happy to see babies and families. $$–$$$

Juanita Juanita. 19114 Arnold Drive on the west side of town, Sonoma; (707) 935–3981. Absolutely the best Mexican food in the valley, in a tiny, friendly place

frequented by local families; sit on the patio in the summertime. Kids have decorated the walls. $

Mary's Pizza Shack. 452 West Spain Street, Sonoma; (707) 938–8300. Sit outdoors near the town plaza and have really good pizza. Grown-ups like the roasted garlic and chicken pizza with garlic-shallot butter. Ask for pizza sticks while you wait. $

Pizzeria Capri. 1286 Broadway, Sonoma; (707) 935–6805; www.pizzacapri.com. Fantastic pizza and pasta—a family place with live weekend entertainment and sports on TV. $

Rin's. 139 East Napa Street, Sonoma; (707) 938–1462. Indoors or on the patio, excellent Thai food. If your kids are not familiar with Asian food, start with chicken satay (they love the peanut sauce) and fried or plain rice. Kids are warmly welcomed in this casual place. Big advantage: The restaurant is open all day long. $–$$

Sonoma Cheese Factory and Deli. 2 West Spain Street, Sonoma; (707) 996–1931. Cheeses and deli foods to go, or eat here at picnic tables. The disadvantage is that this is the place where the tour buses stop, and it thus is often impossibly crowded. $

Where to Stay

El Pueblo Inn. 896 West Napa Street, Sonoma; (707) 996–3651; www.elpuebloinn.com. In a super-convenient location on Highway 12, a newly renovated motel with heated pool, courtyard garden, and rooftop Jacuzzi; some rooms have fireplaces, minirefrigerators, and two queen beds. Complimentary continental breakfast; rental bicycles available. $$–$$$$

Sonoma Valley Inn. 550 Second Street West, Sonoma; (707) 938–9200; www.sonomavalleyinn.com. Nice rooms around a courtyard with pool; some rooms with fireplace and microwave. Guest laundry. Across the street from a shopping center. $$–$$$

For More Information

Sonoma Valley Visitor's Bureau. In the plaza, 4532 First Street East, Sonoma; (707) 996–1090; www.sonomavalley.com.

Sonoma Reservations. (800) 576–6662. Motels, inns, spas, condos, homes.

Sonoma County Tourism Program. 520 Mendocino Avenue, Santa Rosa; (800) 576–6662; www.sonomacounty.com.

Healdsburg

The small town of Healdsburg sleeps peacefully under a canopy of trees. On most summer weekends, band and jazz concerts and outdoor festivals are held in the classic Spanish-style town plaza, which is ringed with cafes and shops. On the west side of town, the Dry Creek Valley is prime biking and wine-tasting territory. For an easy, scenic 20-mile loop on gently rolling hills, start at the town plaza, head south to Mill Street, cross under the highway and join Dry Creek Road heading north. Endless vineyards and rows of low, forested mountains remain in view throughout the ride.

Dry Creek General Store
3495 Dry Creek Road, Healdsburg; (707) 433–4171.

Buy sandwiches and picnic goodies to eat here, or bring them along in your bike baskets for a picnic by the side of the road.

Healdsburg Veterans Memorial Beach
Just on the edge of town, Old Redwood Highway on the Russian River; (707) 433–1625.

A very popular swimming spot, with a sandy beach, picnic areas, and lifeguards.

Healdsburg Museum (all ages)
221 Matheson Street, Healdsburg; (707) 431–3325. Free.

In the beautiful Carnegie Library building, circa 1910, displays of Pomo Indian basketry, artifacts from the Mexican rancho and pioneer eras, great old photos, and a fun shop with educational toys and books for kids.

California River Paddle Sports (ages 4 and up)
10070 Old Redwood Highway, Windsor; (707) 838–8919.

Kayak and canoe rentals, guided or self-guided paddles on the Russian River, and transport to the river.

Jimtown Store (all ages)
7606 Highway 126, Healdsburg; (707) 453–1212; www.jimtown.com.

Just out of town on a lovely country road, a charming, circa-1860 country store like no other. On the patio out back, dig into chili, grilled cheese and deli sandwiches, and chocolate cake; try the homemade scones and pastries on weekend mornings. You can order picnic lunches ahead too. Give the kids a few dollars and let them browse the shelves of old-fashioned toys and penny candy, while you look at antiques and collectibles.

Mrs. Grossman's (ages 3–12)
3810 Cypress Drive, Petaluma; (800) 429–4549; www.mrsgrossmans.com. **Free** tours Monday through Friday, four times a day; call for reservations and directions.

The largest sticker company in the country, Mrs. Grossman's makes absolutely wonderful stickers, hundreds and hundreds of different designs for every season, every holiday, every sport, and subject that kids like. An hour in length, tours include a fun, twenty-minute video, a thirty-minute walking tour of the factory in action, free stickers, and a mini-seminar on sticker projects. On-site are a sticker museum and a great big sticker and accessories store, with a workshop where you can make your own creations. Bring snacks or a picnic if you wish to eat indoors or on the patio.

Charles M. Schulz Museum (all ages)
2301 Hardies Lane, Santa Rosa; (707) 579–4452; www.schulzmuseum.org. Ages 4 and up, including adults, $$; under 4 **free.**

Snoopy, Woodstock, Charlie Brown, Lucy, and their buddies live here now, since their creator, Sparkie Schulz, passed away a few years ago. The beautiful new museum showcases original Peanuts cartoons and those of other famous artists; Schulz's studio and his tools and memorabilia are on display; and there is much to see, indoors and on the patio. My grandkids, Wyatt and Rachel, spent an hour or so in the Education Room using the cartooning instruction books, activity sheets, and art supplies provided. They loved the free movies. Check the Web site for the daily schedules of all the Peanuts movies and special TV programs.

You can get snacks and light meals next door at Snoopy's Redwood Empire Ice Arena, while watching the action on the rink.

Where to Eat

Bear Republic. 345 Healdsburg Avenue, Healdsburg; (707) 433–2337; www.bear republic.com. A hearty brewpub menu featuring burgers (including veggie) lots of appetizers, garlic cheese fries, salads, chili, soup, and homemade breads. Although a brewpub, this noisy, fun, casual place with an outdoor patio is very popular with families; try the homemade sodas. Just a few steps from the town fountain, where toddlers romp. $–$$

Costeaux French Bakery and Cafe. A block from the plaza, 417 Healdsburg Avenue, Healdsburg; (707) 433–1913. Award-winning breads and pastries, scrumptious sandwiches, and picnic items to stay or go; breakfast and lunch. $

El Farolito. 128 Plaza Street, Healdsburg; (707) 433–2807. In a town with a large Mexican population, really good Mexican food. $

Flying Goat Coffee Roastery Cafe. 324 Center Street, Healdsburg; (707) 433–9081. Hang out with the locals and read the paper; have a Goat Bar (chocolate, oats, nuts) or some coffee cake. Simple bistro food. $

Hamburger Ranch & Pasta Farm. 31195 North Redwood Highway, Cloverdale; (707) 894–5616. Harleys may be lined up in the parking lot on weekends at a rustic roadhouse that has satisfied local ranchers, loggers, and travelers for more than fifty years. The outdoor barbecue pit produces luscious beef burgers, turkey burgers, chicken, and pasta too. Don't fail to stop here on your way north. $–$$

Oakville Grocery. 124 Matheson Street on the square, Healdsburg; (707) 433–3200. An outdoor fireplace makes the terrace a cozy spot for pizza from the brick oven, rotisserie chicken, sandwiches, and wonderful pastries. The pricey, gourmet grocery sells top-quality seasonal local produce and local cheeses, charcuterie, and wines. $

Where to Stay

Alexander Valley Campground. Alexander Valley Road near the Healdsburg Bridge, Healdsburg; (707) 431–1453. A large tent and RV campground on the banks of the river, with swimming beaches and canoe rentals.

Vineyard Valley Inn. 178 Dry Creek Road, Healdsburg; (800) 499–0103. Simple hotel with sauna and whirlpool, coffee shop, free continental breakfast. $

For More Information

Healdsburg Chamber of Commerce. 217 Healdsburg Avenue, Healdsburg; (707) 433–6935; www.hbg.sonoma.net. Ask for the free tree booklet for a self-guided tour of fabulous big old trees on the plaza and side streets, including a dawn redwood, palms, oaks, magnolias, and more.

Russian River/Guerneville

Anchored by the town of Guerneville, the Russian River Valley cradles the river as it flows through forest canyons and past sandy beaches and vineyards. The river is generally slow-moving and calm, with quiet coves and sandy beaches along the way. Canoeing, kayaking, and tubing are popular activities; try them on the scenic, 10-mile stretch from Forestville to Guerneville, where there are nice beaches and stopping points for fishing and picnicking. Osprey, blue herons, deer, turtles, and more wildlife will accompany your trek.

A laid-back summer vacation town since the mid-1800s, Guerneville is draped lazily along the bank of the Russian River. The town is primarily souvenir shops, a few galleries and casual cafes, and a supermarket or two where you can stock up on provisions for camping and day trips on the coast, on the beaches, and in the redwood park. Sandy riverside beaches are easily accessible around Guerneville. Johnson's Beach is a good choice because of the lifeguards and roped-off children's swimming and wading area; rentals of canoes, kayaks, paddleboats, tubes, umbrellas, and beach chairs; and the snack bar. You can also launch your own watercraft here. Steelhead Beach at 9000 River Road in Forestville has shaded picnic tables and portapotties; no lifeguard.

When you stop in Guerneville for meals and at the beaches, do not be surprised to see quite a few gay men and lesbians. The town has been a gay weekend and vacation destination for years.

On the way out to the coast from Guerneville, stop at Duncans Mills, a charming village on the river with an old-fashioned general store, cafes, and boutique shops. Children can run around and take a short walk on the quiet country road that runs alongside the village. You can rent canoes and kayaks here and paddle around in the river nearby or head right out to the coast (707–865–9080).

Armstrong Grove Redwoods State Reserve (all ages)

In Guerneville, go north off Main Street on Armstrong Woods Road; 2.2 miles to the park entrance; (707) 869–2015. Day-use fee $.

Easy forest trails wind through magnificent stands of old-growth redwoods, some more than 300 feet tall. Picnic sites are cool and shady on the warmest summer days. Available are wheelchair access, a Braille trail, restrooms, a visitor center, no-reservation campsites, and mountain-biking and equestrian trails.

Austin Creek State Recreation Area (all ages)

Accessed through the Armstrong Redwood Reserve entrance; (707) 865–2391.

Located here are 5,000 relatively undeveloped acres of grasslands and hills, river glens and canyons, open forests, a hike-in campground, and a horse camp (carry your own water). You'll find wildflowers in the spring, good birding, and bluegill and black bass fishing in Redwood Lake. Hot and dry in the summer, glorious green in the winter and spring, the preserve is abundant with wildlife, from great blue herons, woodpeckers, and ravens to deer, foxes, and, occasionally, bobcats.

Running the **Russian**

Canoeing or kayaking the Russian River is a must-do for many visitors—May through October are the best months. Most rental companies will supply all equipment and shuttle you back to the starting point. Bring plenty of water and a change of clothes for the return ride, secure your car keys with a safety pin in your pocket, wear hats and rubber-soled shoes (to protect against sharp rocks), and beware of sunburn on the tops of your legs. If you bring an ice chest, also bring bungee cords to secure it to the canoe. No pets or glass containers.

- **Burke's Canoe Trips,** Mirabel Road at 8600 River Road, Forestville; (707) 887–1222; www.burkescanoetrips.com. Shuttle service and canoe rentals for 10-mile trips to a private beach. Campground with hot showers. $45 per canoe.

- **Gold Coast Coffee and Kayaks,** 23515 Steelhead Boulevard next to the Blue Heron, Duncans Mills; (707) 865–1441. Sit-on-top kayaks and all equipment for self-guided paddles. Coffee drinks and snacks too. From $10 per hour.

- **Russian River Adventures,** 20 Healdsburg Avenue, Healdsburg; (707) 433–5599; www.soar1.com/rradventures/welcome.htm. Guided tours of a secluded section of the river in an inflated SOAR canoe or catamaran, with gourmet picnic lunch on the riverside and cooler for drinks. Begins at the Memorial Beach Dam in Healdsburg. Full day is $99 per person; ages five to twelve are $49.

- **Trowbridge Canoe Trips,** 20 Healdsbug Avenue, Healdsburg; (800) 640–1386; www.trowbridgecanoe.com. Longest established operator in the area; canoe and kayak rentals, shuttle service to several put-in spots. $100 per full day with shuttle.

- **West Coast Kayaks,** Guerneville; (707) 869–9716; wckayaks@hotmail.com. Guided trips, focus on wildlife and natural surroundings. From $50 per half-day.

Bullfrog Campground here is accessed by a steep, narrow road that cannot be negotiated by RVs more than 20 feet long. Reservations by phone are advised, but you can also drop in and check the bulletin board at the campground for open sites (707–869–2015).

Armstrong Woods Pack Station (ages 10 and up)
Armstrong Grove; (707) 887–2939; www.redwoodhorses.com. $$$$.

Even beginning riders will enjoy the lunch ride, which meanders gently out of the redwood forest through a variety of wildlife habitats to ridgetops overlooking the Russian River Valley. On top of the world with a 360-degree view of five counties, a gourmet lunch is laid out on white tablecloths in a wildflower-strewn meadow. You can also ride your own horses on the guided pack trips and bring your own food. Children under ten require guide's permission; riders must be in good physical condition and able to mount without assistance.

Johnson's Beach & Resort (all ages)
16241 First Street, Guerneville; (707) 869–2022; www.johnsonsbeach.com. Open daily from mid-May to early October, 10:00 A.M. to 6:00 P.M. Free.

Families flock to this wide, sandy beach below town to swim in the Russian River (lifeguards on duty). There is a roped-off pool area for small kids, and visitors can rent canoes, kayaks, paddleboats, umbrellas, inner tubes, and beach chairs. This beach is the venue for Guerneville's annual blues and jazz festivals. Restrooms and snack bar on property.

Where to Eat

Coffee Bazaar. 14045 Armstrong Woods Road, Guerneville; (707) 869–9706. Snacks, lunches, and great ice cream, near the entrance to the state park. Sit outside in the summertime. Browse the used bookstore next door, log on at the MAC. $

Main Street Station. 16280 Main Street, Guerneville; (707) 869–0501. Good for a lunch stop while driving to the coast; hearty Italian meatball sandwiches and sausage sandwiches, country-style pizza, salads, smoothies, and great desserts. $–$$

Sweet's Cafe and Bakery. 16251 Main Street, Guerneville; (707) 859–3383. The best place for Belgian waffles, omelets, homemade croissants, espresso, lunches. $

Topolos at Russian River Vineyards. 5700 Gravenstein Highway 116, Forestville; (707) 887–1562. A perfect stop for lunch or dinner on the way to or from the Russian River or the Sonoma Coast, built in an interesting hop-kiln-style reminiscent of a century ago. Greek and California cuisine is served in a circa-1870 rustic estate home, in the dining room by the woodburning stove or outside on the garden patio (there is space outside for toddlers to cruise around while waiting for lunch): local seafood, duckling in black currant Madeira sauce, souvlaki, spanakopita, pork in raspberry Riesling sauce, seasonal specialties. The winery owners are the restaurant owners, and the bottle of wine you order may be opened by one of the winemakers, Jerry or Michael Topolos. Wheelchair access. $$–$$$

Where to Stay

Casini Ranch Family Campground.
22855 Moscow Road, Duncans Mills; (707)
451–8400. On the Russian River, adjacent
to a small village of shops and restaurants,
twenty minutes from the Sonoma Coast.
More than 200 RV and tent camping sites,
some on the river. It's just a few steps to
good fishing. Grocery, laundromat, showers, boat rental; pets okay. $

Fern Grove Cottages. 16650 Highway
116, Guerneville; (707) 869–8105; www
.ferngrove.com. A short stroll from town,
classic 1920s cottages are scattered
beneath the redwoods; kids like the Cowboy Cottage best. Choose from one- or
two-bedroom units with wood-burning fireplaces. Free continental breakfast and a
nice swimming pool. $$–$$$

For More Information

Russian River Chamber of Commerce.
16200 First Street, Guerneville; (707)
859–9000; www.russianriver.com.

**Redwood Empire Association and
North Coast Visitor Center.** 2802 Leav-
enworth, San Francisco; (415) 394–5991;
www.redwoodempire.com. Comprehensive brochures and other materials cover-
ing all of the Wine Country, the North
Coast, and Redwood Country.

Sonoma County Tourism Program. 520
Mendocino Avenue, Santa Rosa; (800)
576–6662; www.sonomacounty.com.

High Sierra North

A sapphire gem sparkling across the California and Nevada borders, Lake Tahoe lies above 6,000 feet in the icy embrace of the Sierra Nevada Range. In a dreamlike setting of snow-frosted peaks and evergreen forests, the lake is "clear enough to see the scales on a cutthroat trout at 80 feet," as Mark Twain put it. Families return year after year to the summer vacation towns, campgrounds, and ski resorts of the Tahoe region.

The choice of summer sightseeing and recreation is phenomenal: hiking and mountain biking on forest trails; fishing, swimming, and boating; exploring old logging towns. Some families head for state park campgrounds in the woods or on the lakeshore. Others rent a cabin at the beach, or they stay at a big resort with a pool and lots of organized activities.

Get an overview of the dazzling mountain landscape by taking the family on a slow cruise on one of the big paddlewheeler tour boats, across the lake to Emerald Bay. You'll see row after row of jagged granite peaks reflected in the deep blue water: 1,600 feet deep, and cold, very cold. Legends tell of Indian chiefs in full regalia and women in Victorian garb floating motionless and frozen at the bottom of the lake. Children love to hear the old Tahoe stories, especially tales of Tahoe Tessie, the Loch Ness–style monster whose spiny back is occasionally seen rippling above the surface. Watch for Tessie!

The sun shines an average of 274 days a year. Soft spring days are clear and wildflowery; fall is brisk, with aspen colors glittering through the pines. Winter days are lively at sixteen alpine ski resorts and as many cross-country ski areas. More ski resorts are concentrated here than anywhere else in North America.

The 72-mile-long Tahoe lakeshore is roughly divided into the South Shore, the West Shore, and the North Shore, each with unique attractions. Anchored by Tahoe City, the West Shore has an "Old Tahoe" feel, with log cabins from the 1920s and 1930s and old-fashioned cottage-style resorts. The Truckee River is a good reason to headquarter on the West Shore. You can spend a day rafting—it's exciting but not at all dangerous—and hike and bike on a paved trail that runs along the river and the lakeshore.

The North Shore is primarily the Incline Village area, the least developed and quietest part of the lake. On the South Shore, the only real city on the lake, South Lake Tahoe is famous for casinos, although families head for the historical sights and a chain of beautiful

HIGH SIERRA NORTH

beaches. Outdoor fun is nearby in the Tahoe and El Dorado National Forests and in Desolation Wilderness.

Taking Care

It's wise to remember that Lake Tahoe is at high elevation—6,227 feet at the lakeshore. For the first day or two of your visit, everyone in the family, and particularly the children, may feel more tired than usual. If someone feels nauseated for no apparent reason, it is likely to be altitude sickness; extra rest and limited physical activities are the cures. If you are not experienced skiers or hikers, you will do well to plan an easy first day. If someone in the family continues to feel sick, sleepy, and disoriented, discuss it with a doctor; the only way to get over persistent altitude sickness is to descend to a lower altitude.

High altitude also means greater risk of sunburn, especially in winter. Use sunscreen every day, no matter how cold it feels outdoors.

During the summer and on winter weekends, avoid driving to Tahoe on Friday afternoons or returning on Sunday afternoons, to elude heavy traffic. A snowstorm can transform Highways 50 and 80 into parking lots for hours. Every month of the year, check the weather and road conditions, and keep a bag of jackets, blankets, and dry provisions in the car, year-round.

South Lake Tahoe

Between Lake Tahoe and a magnificent wall of Sierra Nevada peaks, the city of South Lake Tahoe appears at first glance to be a canyon of neon and casinos, honky-tonk bars and flashy motels. Get off the main highway that bisects town, however, and you will see why families spend their vacations here. Beautiful beaches and family-oriented resorts are located all along the lakeshore. From here it's a short drive to a tremendous variety of outdoor recreation and sightseeing destinations in the Tahoe Basin.

Three public beaches in town—El Dorado, Regan, and Connelly—have extensive facilities, including playing fields and swimming pools. At Nevada Beach and Zephyr Cove, you can rent every imaginable type of watersports equipment and take lessons; take a boat tour of the lake, try parasailing, go fishing, or just lie in the sun.

A major new development in the heart of town along Highway 50 and the lakefront, Heavenly Village has two massive Marriott hotels, an ice-skating rink, a movieplex, shopping, and restaurants. Also new is the Stateline Transit Center, a hub for shuttles, buses, and trolleys that access the entire lake (www.laketahoetransit.com). Paralleling the highway and bordered by tall pines, Linear Park, a paved walking and biking trail, is a welcome addition.

Highlights of your visit to South Lake Tahoe might be a sleigh ride behind a team of beautiful blond Belgium horses or a summer sail across the lake on a huge catamaran. Watch for road signs announcing snow-play areas (usually $3.00 per car), public beaches, and trailheads.

Heavenly Valley Gondola and Aerial Tram (all ages)

Off Highway 50 on the east end of Ski Run boulevard, South Lake Tahoe; (775) 586–7700; www.skiheavenly.com. Tram or gondola $$.

An eight-passenger gondola whisks you 2.4 miles up the mountain to an observation deck at 9,123 feet, with views of the Carson Valley to the east, Desolation Wilderness to the west, and the entire lake.

Take the Heavenly Aerial Tram to the 10,000-foot summit where an easy 2-mile trail loops the mountaintop and a restaurant serves good, although pricey, meals. From the sundeck, take a guided nature, sunset, early evening birding, full moon, or stargazing hike.

Heavenly Valley Ski Resort (all ages)

4004 Ski Run Boulevard, South Lake Tahoe; (775) 586–7000 or (877) 243–0003; www.ski heavenly.com. Lift tickets: $$$$. Kids 5 and under ski and snowboard free.

One of the largest ski resorts in the western states, Heavenly Valley has an average of 360 inches of snow, covering more than eighty ski runs. On the summit you have the phenomenal experience of feeling like you are skiing right into the lake. If your legs can take it, start from the top of Sky Express and ski 5 miles nonstop downhill.

Ski Explorers is the program for children ages four to twelve, from new little skiers in the Enchanted Forest to hotdoggers taking "Shred-Ready" snowboard lessons. Besides all-day care and lessons, there are special presentations for kids by the ski patrol, demos by grooming vehicles, appearances by the avalanche dogs, and even cooking lessons. Heavenly offers Tahoe's only on-mountain, licensed child care for children six months to six years old.

Sugar Bowl Ski Area (all ages)

750 Mule Ears Court, Norden; (530) 426–9000 (snow phone: 530– 426–3847); www.sugar bowl.com. Kids 12 and under ski free.

On the slopes of 8,383-foot Mt. Judah, Sugar Bowl's express lifts and multimillion dollar expansion of trails and facilities make this one of the best medium-size ski resorts at the lake. Among recent additions is the huge learning center; a Flying Carpet lift to expanded terrain for beginning skiers and boarders; and the SnowBomb Terrain Park. With little kids, take the gondola from the village parking lot to the lifts, day care, and lessons areas. Kids' learning programs are Base Camp for ages four to five, Summit Adventure Camp for ages six to twelve, and Sugar Bears for ages three to six. You can stay right here at the Inn at Sugar Bowl in family units; ask about winter and summer packages.

Upper Truckee River Marsh (all ages)

(530) 542–5580.

Take an idyllic, 4-mile, self-guided kayak paddle on the Upper Truckee River, starting at the Highway 50 Bridge to the lake and down to Ski Run Beach. The river meanders quietly

Cruises

- **MS *Dixie II* Paddlewheeler,** 5 miles north of South Lake Tahoe on Highway 50, Zephyr Cove; (775) 588–3508. Several Emerald Bay cruises a day. $$; under 2 are **free.** In the wintertime, the Dixie becomes a ski shuttle, taking skiers from South Lake Tahoe to ski resorts on the West Shore. The paddlewheeler was a cotton barge on the Mississippi in 1927, then a floating casino at Tahoe, when it sank and was raised and converted into a tour boat.

- **_Tahoe Gal_ Paddlewheeler,** 850 North Lake Boulevard, Lighthouse Mall, Tahoe City; (800) 218–2464 or (530) 583–0141; www.tahoegal.com. Adults $$$; children $$. Breakfast, lunch, shoreline, and evening cruises.

- **_Tahoe Queen_ Paddlewheeler,** 9090 Ski Run Boulevard, South Lake Tahoe; (530) 541–3364; www.hornblower.com/laketahoe. Adults $$$$; children $$$; kids under 2 are **free.** Off-season family discounts. Huge, beautiful paddlewheeler makes day and evening trips to Emerald Bay. Besides summertime cruises, you can ride the Queen in the winter to Tahoe City and meet shuttle buses for major ski resorts; there is a big breakfast buffet in the morning and live music and food on the afternoon return cruise.

- **_Woodwind II_ Sailing Cruises,** Zephyr Cove Marina, South Lake Tahoe; (888) 867–6394 or (775) 588–3000. $$$; under 2 are **free.** This fifty-passenger, 41-foot trimaran with a glass bottom and indoor/outdoor seating is a comfortable boat, but a breezier experience without the indoor space of the paddlewheelers, so it's probably not a good choice if you have toddlers.

- **_Lake Link Meteor,_** (800) 238–2463; www.hornblower.com. A high-speed, ninety-passenger ski ferry travels from the South Shore to the North Shore in both directions in the mornings, with transfer by bus to either Squaw Valley or Heavenly Valley for a day of skiing. Return trips are on the *Tahoe Queen* sternwheeler, with dinner available. The package is about $90, including lift ticket and après ski party.

through meadows and forest, and you will likely see waterfowl and beautiful marshlands with water lilies and other aquatic plants. Rent kayaks and canoes at SunSports at the Ski Run Marina.

Emerald Bay

West from South Lake Tahoe on Highway 89, also called Emerald Bay Road, around the south end of the lake are a number of sightseeing, cultural, and recreation destinations. Emerald Bay is the most photographed place at Tahoe, a scintillating piece of water surrounded by dense pine forests and decorated with an island that is topped by a teahouse.

Built in 1928, Vikingsholm, the treasure of Emerald Bay, is a cross between an eleventh-century castle and an ancient church. Reached by a steep, downhill, 1-mile paved trail (or by tour boat), the thirty-eight-room mansion is considered the finest example of Scandinavian architecture in North America. The free ranger's tour of the fancifully furnished estate is well worth an hour of your time. This is a beautiful spot to have a picnic, swim and sunbathe, take a short hike, then take your time climbing back up to Highway 89.

From the highway it's an easy 2-mile loop hike to Eagle Falls and Eagle Lake, which are surrounded by the sheer walls of Desolation Wilderness, a glorious outback of rugged, alpine territory crisscrossed by trails and dotted with hundreds of lakes. Desolation Wilderness is best in the off-season, as easy accessibility makes it extremely popular for hiking and backpacking in high season. For an 11.4-mile loop day trip, take the Glen Alpine trailhead at the end of Fallen Leaf Lake Road and hike to Lake Aloha.

Near Emerald Bay, Baldwin, Pope, and Kiva Beaches are accessible by bus from South Lake Tahoe. The popular Emerald Bay State Park Campground has one hundred tent and RV sites and boat-in campsites (closed from mid-September until mid-June).

U.S. Forest Service Lake Tahoe Visitor Center (all ages)
🏕️ 🐾 👫 🌾

Emerald Bay Road, Baldwin Beach; (530) 573–2600. Open 8:30 A.M. to 8:30 P.M. during summer.

Here are exhibits of geology, animal habitats, and history. You can get maps and advice as to trail conditions and campground availability and sign up for a ranger-led interpretive walk. A children's program called Woodsy Rangers is presented each day.

A four-hour, 5-mile, rather strenuous loop hike from here to the summit of Mount Tallac rewards trekkers with magnificent views at 9,700 feet. For casual strollers and for the handicapped, the Rainbow Trail is a paved path wandering past signs that explain the natural habitat; over one hundred species of wildflowers bloom alongside the trail. The Stream Profile Chamber is a cross section of a real stream habitat filled with rushing water, fish, rocks, plants, and other wildlife. Children can get a peek at the underwater world of a mountain stream through floor-to-ceiling

Snow-Play Areas

You can rent sleds, tubes, saucers, and, in some cases, mini-snowmobiles and other snow toys at these snow-play areas. Some have lifts and refreshment stands; some disallow kids under four; and some disallow bringing your own equipment.

- **Boreal Ski Area,** Highway 80 at Castle Peak exit on Donner Summit; (530) 426–3666. Groomed sledding lanes at Playland Park, mini-snowmobiles. $12–$15 includes sled.

- **Granlibakken Ski Area,** 667 Lakeshore Drive, just south of Tahoe City; (530) 581–7333. Groomed sledding hill for saucers. $4.00 day use; $3.00 for saucer or bring your own; no sleds or tubes.

- **Donner Memorial State Park,** Donner Lake exit off Highway 80; (530) 587–3841. Bring your own saucers for free play on a tame slope.

- **Diamond Peak Ski Area,** on Ski Way off Highway 28 at the south end of Incline Village; (702) 832–1177. Supervised, groomed hill for ages three to six. $15 per hour.

- **Kirkwood Slide Mountain Tube Park,** 601 Kirkwood Road, Highway 88 at Carson Pass; (800) 967–7500. Handle tow, two hours $10, all day $20 including tube.

- **Northstar-at-Tahoe,** Highway 267 between Truckee and Lake Tahoe; (800) 466–6784. Tubing hill with lift. $16.00 first hour; $8.00 additional hours, includes tube. Lighted for night play, with entertainment. Three-hour rental of snow toys, $20.00; bungee trampoline, $9.00.

- **Sierra-at-Tahoe,** from South Lake Tahoe, 12 miles up Highway 50 west over Echo Summit; (530) 659–7453. Groomed hill with lifts. $15 for two hours; $30 all day, includes tube and tubing lift access. Older kids can rent snowscoots and snow bikes.

- **Soda Springs,** 1 mile east of Highway 80 at Soda Springs exit; (530) 426–3901. Elaborate tubing runs with lifts and groomed play areas for sledding. $10 for two hours, $16 all day. Mini-snowmobile rentals for kids ages six to twelve.

- **Squaw Valley,** 5 miles north of Tahoe City off Highway 89; (530) 583–6955. At the top of the cable car at High Camp, a tubing venue with lift. $9.00 an hour.

- **Tahoe Donner at Trout Creek,** off Highway 80 at Truckee-Donner exit; (530) 587–9400. Wide, groomed, supervised sledding hill. $4.00 includes sleds and disks; free for ages three and under. Deli nearby.

viewing windows and in 12-foot-high murals. In the fall, thousands of visitors come to watch brilliant red spawning salmon wiggle their way from Lake Tahoe up Taylor Creek.

Camp Richardson Resort

Five miles south of the "Y," Emerald Bay Road, South Lake Tahoe; (530) 541–1801. Camping $; other accommodations $–$$$$.

A favorite family summer vacation resort for decades, with small, simple rooms in a cavernous main lodge and cottages to rent. Summer and winter activity camps are offered for kids five to thirteen. There is a marina, a sandy beach, riding stables, restaurants, a 300-unit campground, a "trading post," and general store. The camp makes a convenient headquarters from which to set off on horseback or on foot into Desolation Wilderness. Paddleboats, Jet Skis, and other water toys are rented at the marina. Cross-country ski and snowshoe trails are open in the winter, with rentals, lessons, and tours.

Morning or afternoon guided horseback rides from Camp Richardson to Fallen Leaf Lake are a thrill for youngsters and the whole family. They take about three hours, include either breakfast or dinner, and are very popular, so reserve ahead. Children must be six years old; guided rides for children only are also available.

Fallen Leaf Lake is accessible by road off Highway 89 and makes a wonderful day trip from Camp Richardson. You can hike around the lake, swim, picnic or barbecue, and launch a boat.

Tallac Historic Site (all ages)

Five miles south of the "Y" at Camp Richardson, Highway 89; (530) 542–4166.

The rich and famous kicked up their heels in the 1920s at this beautiful lakeside compound of formerly private estates, an old casino, the Valhalla Boathouse, and a hotel. The buildings are restored and open for tours, and many musical and art events are held here in the summer.

Kayak Tahoe (ages 4 and up)

Camp Richardson, P.O. Box 11129, Tahoe Paradise 96155; (530) 544–2011. Day tours, camping trips, lessons, rentals.

Rent kayaks here or take a guided kayak tour. Today's new kayaks are lighter and easier to use than those you may remember from years past. Smaller children can ride with parents on most boats, and children from about seven years old can manage easily by themselves.

Sorensen's Resort (all ages)

14255 Highway 88, Hope Valley; (800) 423–9949 or (530) 694– 2203; www.sorensensresort.com. Lodging $$–$$$$; restaurant $$–$$$.

In a pine and aspen grove on the West Fork of the Carson River, Sorensen's Resort was a rest stop for emigrants in the 1800s. Rustic log cabins here have a homespun country decor, brass beds, wood stoves, and some kitchens. At night, lights twinkle around the cabin doors and wood smoke is in the air. This is a popular place for families, and reservations need to be made weeks or even months in advance.

You can sit in a rocker on your cabin porch while the kids fish in the small stocked pond for trout. An old logging road adjacent to the resort leads right into the Toiyabe National Forest. Ask about the guided hike on the Emigrant Trail. Worn smooth by pioneers on their way west, it's a fascinating route, with evidence of how wagons and animals were hauled up and down steep grades and cliffsides.

The fishing is great on the Carson, which winds through the valley beyond the resort. You can buy guidebooks and fishing licenses here and get advice on where to catch the big ones. Fishing and cross-country ski instruction and rentals are available. The resort offers a wide variety of special events and classes during the year, from llama treks to fly fishing, star watches, birding, hikes, and more. At the nearby Hope Valley Outdoor Center, you can rent winter and summer sports equipment of all kinds and sign up for hikes, kayak trips, and ski tours (530–694–2266; www.hopevalleyoutdoors.com).

Cozy with a woodburning stove, Sorensen's Country Cafe serves hearty breakfasts, lunches, and dinners, indoors and outside under the trees. Your family can sit with others at a big wooden table and tuck into beef stew, fresh fish, homemade bread, and fruit cobbler. Breakfast is all-you-can-eat waffles or bacon and eggs. A drive to Sorensen's just for a meal makes a nice getaway from South Lake Tahoe.

Kirkwood Resort

601 Kirkwood Road, Highway 88, at Carson Pass; (209) 258–6000 or (800) 967–7500; www.kirkwood.com. Lift tickets: adults and ages 13 to 18 $$$$; 6 to 12 $$$; 5 and under $$.

A year-round destination at 7,800 feet in elevation, Kirkwood is headquarters for fly fishing, cross-country and downhill skiing, and high-altitude hiking and backpacking. On hundreds of acres of alpine meadows, Nordic skiing is perfection. Come summer, meadows turn to waves of wildflowers. Biking, hiking, and lake and stream fishing are popular here and at nearby Caples Lake.

You can stay in a lodge room, or rent a condo or a house. In a Tyrolean-style village atmosphere, laid-back Kirkwood is less commercial and more like ski mountains used to be. Recent developments are a beautiful outdoor ice skating rink, a fitness and swim complex, snazzy boutique shops, a freestyle terrain park and half-pipe, an expanded tubing hill with a lift, and Bub's Sports Bar & Grill, with TVs and electronic games for kids.

Among a wide variety of accommodations, Mountain Club is a deluxe condo hotel with one- and two-bedrooms units with lofts.

The Mighty Mountain Ski Center offers child care, lessons, and a kids-only lift. Kamp Kirkwood entertains nonskiing kids, and there is an evening program for six to twelve year olds. A Children's Center is located at the Timber Creek Lodge, near a terrain garden and a beginner and intermediate chair. Children have their own cross-country trail—Kiddie Kilometer—with life-size cutouts of forest animals.

Where to Eat

Bandanas Whole Earth Pizza. 4076 Lake Tahoe Boulevard, South Lake Tahoe; (530) 541–8646. Great pizza, burgers, soup, sandwiches, pasta, salads in a fun atmosphere. Breakfast until noon; lunch, dinner until 10:00 P.M. $–$$

Beacon Bar and Grill. Highway 89 at Camp Richardson, South Lake Tahoe; (530) 541–0630; www.camprich.com. At the beach for lunch or dinner, try the signature clam chowder, gourmet burgers, sandwiches, salads, pasta, fish, and steaks. Light breakfast at the Camp General Store; treats at the ice-cream parlor. $–$$

The Cantina. 765 Emerald Bay Road, South Lake Tahoe; (530) 544–1233. Voted best Mexican food at Southshore, with outdoor dining, good Mexican food, lively atmosphere. Try Blue Corn Salmon, Texas Crab Cakes, or the Smoked Chicken Polenta. $–$$

Ernie's. Near the "Y," 1146 Emerald Bay Road, South Lake Tahoe; (530) 541–2161. Casual atmosphere; American breakfasts and lunches. $

Hot Pepper Grill. 3490 Lake Tahoe Boulevard, South Lake Tahoe; (530) 542–1015. Wonderful tacos and fresh Mexican food, for here or to go. $

The Red Hut. 2749 Highway 50, 3.5 miles south of Stateline, South Lake Tahoe; (530) 541–9024. Decked out in retro red-vinyl stools and booths, the Hut has been famous since 1959 for huge waffles (try the coconut waffle sandwich), biscuits and gravy, omelets, homemade soup, grilled cheese, and more comfort food. A second Red Hut is at 227 Kingsbury Grade (775–588–7588). $–$$

Sprouts Natural Food Cafe. 3123 Harrison Avenue at Highway 50, South Lake Tahoe; (530) 541–6969. Breakfast through dinner, healthy, homemade, all-organic food like real fruit smoothies; rice bowls chock-full with brown rice, beans, and veggies; Tahoe Turkey sandwiches; yummy soups. $–$$

Strawberry Lodge. Highway 50, Kyburz; (530) 659–7200. Good, simple American food and soda fountain specialties in a restored 1940s lodge. Stop here on the way in and out of South Lake Tahoe. $–$$

Womack's Texas Bar BQ. 4041 Highway 50, South Lake Tahoe; (530) 544–2268. A cozy little spot for nearly three decades serving what could be the best barbecue outside of Texas: baby back ribs, Louisiana gumbo, red beans and rice, peach cobbler, and sweet potato pie; kids' portions. $–$$$

Where to Stay

Embassy Suites Resort. 4130 Lake Tahoe Boulevard, South Lake Tahoe; (800) 362–2779. A contemporary mountain lodge, with two-room luxury suites that are a bargain for families: two double beds, a sofa bed, two TVs, and a microwave. Indoor pool and spa, sundeck, workout room; seasonal packages; free shuttle to the airport and the Heavenly Valley ski area and to casinos. Room rate includes full breakfast and a two-hour, early-evening party of snacks, drinks, and alcoholic beverages. $$$

Fireside Lodge. 515 Emerald Bay Road, South Lake Tahoe; (800) 692–2246 or (530) 544–5515; www.tahoefiresidelodge.com. The last lodge on the way to Emerald Bay, with National Forest trails and public access beaches nearby; old-Tahoe-style, log-cabin suites with gas fireplaces and kitchenettes. Complimentary bicycles; float tubes and kayaks; complimentary, expanded continental breakfast; picnic and barbecue areas; log swings; two queen-size bed suites. $$$

Forest Inn Suites Resort. 1 Lake Parkway, South Lake Tahoe; (800) 822–5950; www.forestsuites.com. Completely renovated throughout, one- and two-bedroom suites with kitchens and living rooms, in five acres of forest at the base of the high-speed gondola at Heavenly Ski Resort, adjacent to Harrah's Casino. Two swimming pools, health club, game room, complimentary breakfast, and transportation to ski areas and casinos. $$$

Lake Tahoe Accommodations. 2048 Dunlap Drive, South Lake Tahoe; (800) 544–3234 or (530) 544–3234. Condo and home rentals. $–$$$

Lakeland Village. 3535 Lake Tahoe Boulevard, South Lake Tahoe; (800) 822–5969 or (702) 785–2424; www.lakelandvillage.com. Spread out along the lake in nineteen acres of pines, with a private, sandy beach, two heated swimming pools, a wading pool, and tennis courts. Condo or lodge units, some with fireplaces and kitchens. Convenient shuttle buses connect the resort with nearby ski areas and downtown. $$–$$$

Rustic Cottages. 7449 North Lake Boulevard, Tahoe Vista; (888) 778–7842; www.rusticcottages.com. Vintage but not so rustic cottages across the street from a public beach, with fireplaces, kitchenettes, microwaves, refrigerators, and decks. You can use the huge video library, bikes, croquet and horseshoe equipment, sleds, snow saucers, snowshoes, and barbecues. Continental breakfast and chocolate chip cookies are complimentary; dogs are okay. For this location and amenities, these small, fresh and clean cottages are a steal. $$–$$$

Tahoe Keys Resort. 999 Tahoe Keys Boulevard, South Lake Tahoe; (530) 544–5397. Homes and condos for rent; indoor and outdoor swimming pools, health club, bicycles, outdoor games, playground, private beach, ski shuttles, powerboat rentals, parasailing, Jet Skis, boat launching—in other words, vacation central. $$–$$$

For More Information

California State Campgrounds Reservations. P.O. Box 942896, Sacramento 94296–0001; (800) 777–0369 or (916) 653–6995; www.cal-parks.ca.gov.

Ski Lake Tahoe. P.O. Box 10797, South Lake Tahoe 96158; (530) 541–2462 or

(800) 588–SNOW; www.skilaketahoe.com. Represents six major ski resorts; ask about packages and family discounts.

Road Conditions and Ski Reports. California (800) 427–7623 or (916) 445–1534; Nevada (877) 687–6237.

Lake Tahoe Visitor's Authority. 1156 Ski Run Boulevard, South Lake Tahoe; (800) AT–TAHOE; www.bluelaketahoe.com. Use this number to book reservations, get tickets to events, obtain airline tickets, and hear about weather and road conditions.

Tahoe City/West Shore

Summers have that "vacation in the mountains" feeling on the West Shore of Lake Tahoe, when families return to their cabins at the beach and to favorite campgrounds and cottage resorts in the pines. The small town of Tahoe City, whose main street is right on the lakeshore, is headquarters for restaurants and shopping. Two of the largest ski resorts are nearby, Squaw Valley USA—site of the 1960 Winter Olympics—and Alpine Meadows. Both resorts have condos and houses to rent.

On the south end of town at the junction of Highways 89 and 28, you can't miss Fanny Bridge. Here where the Truckee joins the lake, people are always lined up, leaning over to watch and feed the fish in the trout ladder—a line of fannies—hence the name Fanny Bridge. Bring bread or fish food for a fun half-hour.

The largest winter carnival in the western states, Snowfest, takes place in March and is based in Tahoe City, Truckee, and at ski resorts. Fireworks and a torchlight parade at Squaw Valley start off a weekend of parades, ice carving, ice-cream eating, and live comedy and musical performances. More than one hundred events include the Great Ski Race—a 30K Nordic event between Tahoe City and Truckee—a Snow Dog contest, celebrity races, and the Snowboard Spectacular. It's wall-to-wall people and lots of fun. Many children's events are scheduled, such as the dress-up-your-dog contest and snow sculpture.

Truckee River (all ages)

One of the loveliest places to walk, Rollerblade, and bike a good distance is the paved Truckee River Bike Path, which winds 4.5 miles, one-way, along the river into Tahoe City, then heads south along the lakeshore for 9 more miles through forested neighborhoods and parks. Much of the path is flat enough for baby strollers and wheelchairs. This is a beautiful path in fall, when the days are crisp and aspens turn gold. In the low-water days of late summer and fall, the river slides quietly along; in winter and spring it boils and crashes past ice-decorated trees and snowy islands.

Rafting the Truckee is a "must" on at least one of your Tahoe trips. It's a Class 1 river, meaning it's quite safe most of the year. Even if you've never rafted before, after a short lesson you can easily manage. If you have children under five, be sure to call ahead to ask if the rafting company allows younger kids.

You rent six-person rafts and life jackets and paddle merrily along downriver about 5 miles, stopping along the way to play and swim if you wish and maybe to picnic on a sand spit. Some people bring their fishing rods along. Paddling without stopping, it takes about two hours to reach your destination, which is River Ranch, where a shuttle bus takes you back to your car. Rentals are $30 per person, $20 for ages six to twelve, at the Truckee River Rafting Center (530–583–RAFT) and Fanny Bridge Raft Rentals (530–583–3021), both on the southern end of Tahoe City.

River Ranch Lodge ⓘ ⊖

Highway 89 at Alpine Meadows Road, Tahoe City; (530) 583–4264; www.riverranchlodge .com. Lodging $–$$$.

A small, charming hotel with a very popular indoor/outdoor restaurant and bar, River Ranch is on the south end of the Truckee Bike Path. The river-rafting trips end here, and rafters invariably hang out for a while in the sun, eating burgers and salads and watching other rafters and bikers arrive.

The Old West in Carson City

Carson City makes a great day trip, particularly during one of the annual festivals and celebrations. It is about forty-five minutes from South Lake Tahoe, by way of Highway 50. The town is rooted in the Old West, with ties to Kit Carson and pioneer times. The 2.5-mile **Kit Carson Trail** is a walk past Victorian homes, the Governor's Mansion, the Nevada State Museum, and the Krebs Peterson House, where John Wayne's last movie, *The Shootist*, was filmed. On your portable tape player or your car radio, you can tune in to recorded descriptive anecdotes.

The **Nevada State Railroad Museum** here displays more than two dozen restored railroad cars and locomotives. On "steam-up" weekend, visitors can hop aboard one of the historic trains and take a twenty-minute, 1-mile ride with a conductor who spins tales of early railroading days. The facility, at 400 Carson Road in Carson City (702–333–4550), is open daily; adults $, children under eighteen admitted free.

For kids ages three through twelve, the **Children's Museum of Northern Nevada** offers 8,000 square feet of interactive fun, such as a giant kaleidoscope to walk through, the giant piano from the movie Big, and more neato stuff (783 Carson Road in Carson City; 702–887–5436).

For information about events, museums, and attractions in Carson City, call 800–NEVADA.

Blackwood Canyon (all ages)

Off Highway 89, 9.5 miles south of Tahoe City, just north of Tahoe Pines; (530) 573–2600 or (916) 573–2600.

A few minutes south of Tahoe City, just north of Tahoe Pines, this is one of the most accessible yet least known wilderness areas at Tahoe. The road into the canyon is perfect for easy walks, Rollerblading, and biking. The paved road is the only development and has almost no traffic, making a good add-on to the shoreline bike path. On the leafy banks of Blackwood Creek and in the forests and meadows here are idyllic picnic spots. You can hike on the flat valley floor or drive up the road to the steep trails of 8,000-foot Barker Pass, hooking up with the Pacific Crest Trail.

Sunnyside Restaurant and Lodge

1850 West Lake Boulevard, 2 miles south of Tahoe City; (530) 583–7200; www.sunnyside resort.com. $–$$$.

With one of the most breathtaking blue-water and high-mountain views on the lake, the deck at Sunnyside is the place to be on a summer afternoon. Boats of every description come and go in the marina, French-fried zucchini and onion rings are tops, and once you and the kids get settled outside on the deck, you'll find it hard to move from the spot. Kids can run around a bit, staying away from the boats.

Here you can rent Jet Skis, sailboats, and power boats and take a sailing lesson. Winter evenings are warm and friendly in the lounge in front of a giant river rock fireplace. Sunnyside's lodge rooms are small and very nice, though rather pricey and not set up for families.

Homewood Mountain Resort (ages 3 and up)

5145 West Lake Boulevard, 5 miles south of Tahoe City, Homewood; (530) 525–2992 (snow phone: 530–525–2900); www.skihomewood.com. Lift tickets: adults and ages 11 to 18 $$$$; 10 and under ski free; and there are multiday and ski school packages.

One of the most accessible and most reasonably priced ski areas for children and beginning skiers, Ski Homewood offers nine lifts on a small mountain with big views of Lake Tahoe. Parking is easy, and licensed day care and a Ski and Play program are available. On Wild Wednesdays after January 1, adult lift tickets are sold on a two-for-one basis. Call ahead to book the Homewood shuttle from sites on the West Shore.

Chambers Landing (all ages)

One mile south of Homewood, on Highway 89; (530) 525–7672. Day-use fee $. Restrooms; no lifeguard.

A good place to plunk down on the beach for the day is at Chambers Landing, which has a short pier with a bar at the end where locals hang out. On one side of the pier is a private beach for people staying in the Chambers Landing condos and on the other side is a public beach, one of the nicest on the West Shore. It's a good beach for small children, because there are enough boating and water sports activities to keep them interested in the passing scene but not so many people that you feel overwhelmed. The upscale restaurant here has a glass-enclosed, heated terrace.

Sugar Pine Point State Park (all ages)

Five miles south of Tahoe City on Highway 89; (530) 525–7982. The facility has 175 camp-ground sites (reservations: 800–444–7275). Parking fee $$.

This is a place to spend a whole day, tour a vintage mansion, walk in the woods, swim and sunbathe, and picnic and play at the lakeside.

One of the grandes dames of Tahoe, a spectacular three-story, 12,000-square-foot Queen Anne–style summer home, the Ehrman Mansion, once a privately owned estate, is now owned by the National Park Service. The mansion is surrounded by sweeping lawns shaded by tall pines. Rangers give daily free tours of the house and the charming boat-house, while they impart stories of halcyon old days on the lake. Even little kids enjoy the tour because the house is full of interesting stuff and you clamber up wooden staircases, looking into family bedrooms. After the tour wander around the grounds, spread a blanket on the beach, or take a walk on flat, easy trails along the lakeshore. A longer hike is acces-sible from the large campground across the road.

In the wintertime, rangers lead free ski skating, winter survival skills, avalanche aware-ness, and Animals in Winter seminars. From here, you can cross-country ski or snowshoe on 14 kilometers of marked and skier-tamped trails.

Meeks Bay Resort and Marina (all ages)

Ten miles south of Tahoe City, Highway 89; (530) 525–7242 or (530) 573–2600. $.

Owned by the U.S. Forest Service, Meeks Bay is a popular Jet Ski and water-ski beach, with an unparalleled view of the lake. This is a good place for beachy activities such as rowing, canoeing, paddleboating (all rentable), and hanging out in the sun, though all the motors create plenty of noise during summer. My granddaughters and I have canoed from here around the coves and shorelines on either side of the bay. In just a few minutes, you are away from the fracas on the beach. Just watch the boat traffic when you are paddling in and out of the bay. A little cafe here serves snacks and burgers, and there is a 150-unit campground and a few cottages.

Squaw Valley USA (all ages)

Between Tahoe City and Truckee on Highway 89, Olympic Valley; (888) 766–9321 (snow phone: 530–583–6955); www.squaw.com. Lift tickets: adults and ages 13 to 15 $$$$; ages 12 and under $.

A huge summer and winter recreation area, Squaw Valley is spectacular in every season. Waves of wildflowers—or snowfields—roll across open meadows below a jagged circle of snowcapped peaks. Lodges, hotels, rental condos, and homes are scattered in forested areas.

To get an overall view of the valley, take the 150-passenger aerial cable car to the High Camp complex, a thrilling, 2,000-foot ascent to an 8,250-foot summit. Up here on the top of the world, you can ice-skate, hike, mountain bike, swim, picnic, play volleyball and ten-nis, bungee jump, or just blink in amazement at the surrounding mountains. Look for the indoor climbing wall at the bottom of the cable car.

The Village at Squaw Valley is a brand-new complex of multistory condos, shops, and restaurants clustered around plazas, right at the foot of the mountains (www.thevillage atsquaw.com; 888–805–5022). Wandering around, you will find Starbucks, which has indoor/outdoor fireplaces; a candle-making shop; a chocolate factory; outdoor trampolines; a fun cat and dog store; smoothies and great bagels at Mountain Nectar; and live entertainment and special events every summer weekend. You can park your car and get to nearby Truckee and to destinations around the lake by free shuttle bus. Tip: Look for the games arcade and a coffee counter with yummy treats in Olympic House in the older part of the village. For the sports-oriented family, Squaw Valley offers facilities unmatched in the western states.

A nice 4-mile hike from the floor of Squaw Valley is the Shirley Lakes trail, starting behind the Olympic Village Inn. Younger children like it, because they can stop to wade or swim in the creek, roll around in grassy meadows, or take naps under the pines.

One of the world's largest and best ski mountains—actually five peaks—Squaw Valley USA Ski Resort, where the 1960 Winter Olympics were held, has thirty lifts accessing more than 4,000 acres of skiable terrain. A new high-speed six-person chair operates even during storm conditions.

For two- to twelve-year-olds, Children's World is a separate venue offering special amenities, from ski rentals and lessons to meals. The staff is so friendly and caring that kids want to stay all day. Beginners have their own mostly flat learning area with a neato "people-mover" that they step onto and a little ski lift. A bright, spacious licensed day-care facility cares for toddlers with meals, music, games, snow play, and quiet time.

Save money on lift tickets and lessons by asking about the various deals that Squaw offers: frequent skier programs, multiday tickets, college days, and lodging packages. Kids thirteen and under ski every day for $5.00. There are snowboard clinics, women's clinics, Snow Sliders for ages four to twelve, and Mountain Buddies, a supervised camp-style program.

The Squaw Valley Nordic Center consists of 18 kilometers of groomed track and wilderness trails, plus a telemark downhill area accessed by lifts.

Squaw Valley USA Mountain Bike Park (ages 7 and up)

Tram ride and trail pass $$$; rentals $$$–$$$$; helmets $$. Tracks and roads are open from 10:00 A.M. to 5:00 P.M., and you can rent new bikes. Packages are available.

As soon as the snow melts, the High Camp tram starts transporting mountain bikers and their bikes to the Squaw Valley USA Mountain Bike Park. Because of the phenomenal access to alpine-level trails, mountain biking is wildly popular at Tahoe. Annual biking events at Squaw include the Fat Tire Fest in August and the Downhill Mania and American MB Championship, both in September.

Alpine Meadows Ski Area (all ages)
Six miles northwest of Tahoe City on Highway 89, P.O. Box 5279, Tahoe City 96145; (800) 441–4423; snow phone: (530) 581–8374; www.skialpine.com. Lift tickets: adults and ages 13 to 18 $$$$; ages 7 to 12 $$$; 6 and under $$. Stay and Ski packages at nearby condos save families money (800–949–3296). Free shuttle buses connect skiers with lodgings on the West and North Shores.

Priding itself on the longest ski season, Alpine is known for its laid-back, casual atmosphere. Intermediate and advanced ski runs have scary names like Chute That Seldom Slides, Promised Land, and Our Father.

Kids are VIPs at Kid's School and Ski Camp. On the Sun Kid beginner surface lift, children just step onto a slow conveyor belt with their equipment on, avoiding the sometimes intimidating chair lift until they are ready for it. Programs for all ages are offered for racing, snowboarding, telemark, freestyle, and just plain skiing; and there is ski instruction for people with mental and physical disabilities. Sled dog tours from here are an exciting way to get out into the beautiful forest and snow-covered meadows.

Where to Eat

Fireside Pizza Company. Village at Squaw Valley; (530) 584–6150; www.firesidepizza.com. Sit outside by firelight or inside at a place voted Best New Restaurant and Family Dining. Parents like the spicy appetizers and gourmet pizzas (try the pear and gorgonzola or portobello with goat cheese). On the Campfire Kids Menu are plain, kid-size pizzas with just cheese or pepperoni and even PB and J; or pasta with just cheese. $–$$

Fire Sign Cafe. 1785 West Lake Boulevard, Tahoe City; (530) 583–0871. Home-style cooking, cozy country atmosphere, breakfast and lunch. $–$$

Mamasake. Village at Squaw Valley, (530) 584–0110; www.mamasake.com. Snowboarders go nuts over the wall-size screen showing eye-popping movies of extreme boarders. The sushi is expensive and really good, and there are some non-sushi menu choices like New York bagel roll, salad roll, Heads Will Roll, and more fun food. $–$$$

Rosie's Cafe. 571 North Lake Boulevard, Tahoe City; (530) 583–8504. Reasonable and relaxed, serving breakfast, lunch, and dinner. By a roaring fire beneath the moose head and vintage Tahoe antiques, try the Cajun eggs, smoked salmon omelet, jambalaya, pot roast, prime rib, and some plainer family fare. $–$$

Where to Stay

Chinquapin Resort. 3600 North Lake Boulevard, 3 miles north of Tahoe City; (800) 732–6721. Spacious, one- to four-bedroom townhouses and condos with wonderful lake views. Fireplaces, fully equipped kitchens, pool, and tennis courts. $$$

Cottage Inn. 1690 West Lake Boulevard, 2 miles south of Tahoe City; (530) 581–4073. Fifteen mountain-style cottages with Scandinavian decor, fireplaces, hearty breakfasts, sauna, private beach. Ask for a unit away from the road. This is a popular place. $$$–$$$$

Granlibakken Resort. P.O. Box 6329, just north of Tahoe City 96145; (800) 543–3221; www.granlibakken.com. A perfect headquarters for families in summer or winter, a 160-room condominium resort with a beginners ski and snowboard hill, Nordic skiing, developed snow-play area, and a big swimming pool. Some units have fireplaces, kitchens, lofts, and decks or patios. The complimentary hot breakfast is huge! $–$$

Norfolk Woods Inn. 6941 West Lake Boulevard, Tahoma; (530) 525–5000. Across the road from the bike trail and the lake, small rooms in the lodge, plus rustic, remodeled cottages with two bedrooms and kitchens. Pool and hot tub. Rates include big breakfasts. $$–$$$$

Sierra Club Huts and Lodges. Clair Tappaan Lodge, P.O. Box 36, Norden 95724; (530) 426–3632; www.sierraclub.org/outings/lodges. Four rustic huts located a day's ski apart in the Tahoe backcountry, each sleeping about a dozen people and equipped with firewood; you supply food and sleeping bags. Summer and winter, the Claire Tappaan Lodge sleeps 140 people in dormitories and family rooms of five to twelve bunks; a cook is on hand and family-style meals are included. Groomed Nordic trails and hiking and biking trails are right outside the door. $

Squaw Valley Lodge. 201 Squaw Peak Road, Olympic Valley; (800) 922–9970 or (530) 583–5500; www.squawvalleylodge.com. A sprawling, all-suite lodge with one or two bedrooms and lofts, equipped kitchens, and luxurious amenities such as down comforters. Enjoy the tennis courts and big pool, and use of a nearby health club. Ski right out the door to the lifts! $$–$$$

Tahoe Taverns. 300 West Lake Boulevard, near Fanny Bridge in Tahoe City; (530) 583–3704. Large complex of nice condos in a pine grove, on the waterfront; pool, lawns, quiet, ultra-convenient location. $$$–$$$$

The Village at Squaw Valley. Between Tahoe City and Truckee off Highway 89, Olympic Valley; (866) 818–6963; www.thevillageatsquaw.com. A complex of new, one-, two-, and three-bedroom condos in multistory buildings that are upscale and loaded with amenities for families, from a little kids' playroom and a big-screen media room (both in the South building) to outdoor hot tubs, five fitness centers, and laundry rooms. Most units have mountain views; all have simple contemporary decor, daily maid service, fireplaces, sofa beds in the living rooms, two or more TVs and DVDs (movies are free), ski lockers, underground parking, and private balconies. They are compact or spacious, depending on the number of bedrooms. Kitchens are completely outfitted. Ask about ski and summer packages. $$$$

For More Information

North Lake Tahoe Resort Association. P.O. Box 1757, Tahoe City 96145; (888) 434–1262 or (530) 583–3494; www.my tahoevacation.com.

Truckee Donner Chamber of Commerce. 10065 Donner Pass Road, Truckee; (530) 584–2757.

Shuttle Service. (530) 583–6985; www.squaw.com. Take the shuttle buses to and from Squaw Valley, Truckee, South and North Lake Tahoe, and Reno lodgings. Truckee is free; other pick-up points are $10 round-trip.

Incline Village/North Shore

A small community on steep, forested hillsides above the North Shore of Lake Tahoe, Incline Village has three private beaches with breathtaking views. Lots of outdoor recreation is within a few minutes' drive. If you have small children, you'll like the quiet, family residential atmosphere here. With the kids in tow, you can get in beach time and take walks around town, visit a western theme park nearby, and plan a few half-day outings to easily accessible mountain meadows, lakes, and streams.

Incline's private beaches and a beautiful recreation center with a pool, playground, and tennis courts are available only to those who rent, own, or stay at selected hotel and motel accommodations in Incline. Renting a condo or house is the way to come here, and it can be as cost-effective as a resort or a motel. When you make your arrangements for accommodations, be sure to ask about getting an IVGID card, which will admit you and the family to the beaches and the rec center.

A paved sidewalk on Lakeshore Drive runs along the lake for several miles, past the beaches and lovely homes—perfect for jogging, baby carriage–pushing, walking, and biking. Giant sugar-pine cones are scattered liberally about, free for the taking. The gardens and the architecture are interesting sights in themselves.

Tahoe Tessie's Lake Tahoe Monster Museum (all ages)
8608 North Lake Boulevard, Kings Beach; (530) 546–8774. $; ages 2 and under **free.**

What's that swimming in the lake? It's a USO, an Unidentified Swimming Object! It's green, it's scaly, it's bumping into boat docks and terrorizing water-skiers. Part of the folklore of Lake Tahoe, a notorious sea creature has been seen and feared for centuries. Some say it's a huge sturgeon planted in the lake by accident. There's also the Mackinaw theory, the giant trout theory, the boa constrictor theory, and the brontosaurus theory. The little museum showcasing Tessie is touristy but fun—you see a life-size Tessie, read eyewitness accounts of Tessie sightings, see "real" photos of her, and buy Tessie T-shirts, souvenirs, and toys. Open July through mid-September.

Ponderosa Ranch (ages 4 and up)
100 Ponderosa Road, on the east side of Incline Village off Highway 28, Incline Village; (775) 831–0691; www.ponderosaranch.com. Open May through October, with limited winter operations, from 9:30 A.M. to 5:00 P.M. daily. Adults $$; ages 5 to 11 $; **free** for kids under 5.

Your kids don't remember the TV show *Bonanza*, but if they are about twelve or younger, they will love Ponderosa Ranch, a re-created western town and theme park based on the original set used to film *Bonanza*. Start with a haywagon breakfast, explore a mine, pan for gold, eat Hossburgers, and have sundaes in an old-fashioned ice-cream parlor. Kids can pet farm animals, have a free pony ride, pretend to be cowboys and cowgirls in a shooting gallery, and more.

North Tahoe **Beaches**

- **Burnt Cedar Beach,** 300 Lakeshore Drive, Incline Village; (702) 831–1310. A big heated pool with a lifeguard makes this a unique Tahoe beach, plus a playground, lawns shaded by tall sugar pines, and a small, sandy beach with shallow water for wading, deeper water for swimming, and a killer view! Kids use coat hangers and small nets to fish for crawdads in the rocks. You can buy lunch at the snack bar or bring a picnic; nice picnic tables and barbecues.

- **Ski Beach and Incline Beach,** 500 Lakeshore Drive, Incline Village; (702) 831–1310. Ski Beach, in front of the Hyatt Regency Lake Tahoe, and adjacent Incline Beach, are busier than Burnt Cedar—and noisier with Jet Skis and boats—but they have the advantage of being more fun for older children and long enough for a half-hour stroll. Lifeguards are here in the summer; boat and water toy rentals.

- **Sand Harbor State Park,** Highway 28, ten minutes south of Incline Village; (702) 831–0494. One of the most beautiful beach parks at the lake, with giant boulders, boat launching sites, pine groves, and white-sand beaches with lifeguards. Families return every year in July and August to the Music and Shakespeare Festival in the outdoor amphitheater overlooking the lake (530-583-9048.) Bring the kids, a picnic, and blankets, and lie stargazing while you listen to one of the bard's comedies or a reggae, Dixieland, or country western concert. Between Incline and Sand Harbor on the lakeshore highway, you may notice clusters of parked cars. There are a number of small beaches and fishing spots along this shoreline, including a nude beach, so don't say I didn't warn you!

- **Kings Beach State Recreation Area,** 12 miles northeast of Tahoe City, Highway 28; (530) 546–7248. Day-use fee $. Wildly popular, a long, sandy beach buzzing with summertime activity: volleyball, boat rentals, Jet Skis, paddleboats, playground, basketball court, picnic tables and barbecues, restrooms.

Spooner Lake (all ages)

Highway 28, 12 miles south of Incline Village; (888) 858–8844; www.spoonerlake.com.

Spooner Lake nestles among pine and aspen forests crisscrossed by easy hiking trails. You can have a picnic in a meadow and can fish for trout in the small lake. In winter, Spooner Lake becomes a small cross-country ski and snowshoe area; rent equipment here and cruise the groomed trails, or bring snow saucers and slide around ($16 trail pass).

Here is the trailhead for a moderately strenuous, uphill, 10-mile hiking and mountain-biking trail to Marlette Lake (you can rent bikes here, 775–749–5349). Spectacular views of the lake and surrounding mountains are the reward at the top, especially in fall when the aspens are blazing yellow. You can see vestiges of a huge system of wooden flumes that were built in the mid-1800s to move water from the lake to the booming silver-mining towns of Virginia City and Carson City, on the eastern side of the mountains.

Mount Rose (all ages)

Seven miles northeast of Incline Village on Highway 431. Hiking trails and undeveloped cross-country ski trails and sledding hills. No restrooms. Roadside parking.

Above Incline Village at 10,800 feet, Mount Rose is the highest peak in the area. From the scenic overlook on Highway 431, almost the entire 22-mile-long lake gleams below, rimmed by the Sierras on the west and the Carson Range on the east. Seven miles beyond the lookout point, on the east side of the road, is Tahoe Meadows, a scattering of glorious alpine meadows where you can enjoy cross-country skiing and summertime hiking, easy or strenuous. Tahoe Meadows Whole Access Trail is a wide, 1.3-mile loop designed for those in wheelchairs and baby strollers.

The 12-mile loop hike to the summit of Mount Rose starts on an old jeep road, near the cinder-block building close to the highway on the west side. Even if you can't make it to the top for the view that awaits, you might want to start up this trail; there is a pond with a frog chorus in residence and wildflowers galore. At the top you'll see the whole lake basin and the Carson Valley sweeping away into the distance—and even Lassen Peak, in Lassen National Park, on a clear day. Just beyond Tahoe Meadows, Mount Rose Camp-ground is nice and cool in midsummer and often has tent and RV sites available when campgrounds near the lake are full (775–882–2766). Stop here for fresh water and rest-rooms. You can walk from the campground to the top of the mountain and the Tahoe Meadows trail system.

Truckee (all ages)

Highway 80 at Highway 267; (530) 587–2757; www.truckee.com.

A popular stop on the way to the West Shore, the tiny town of Truckee was a rollicking rail-roading, logging, and ice-harvesting headquarters in the 1800s. The picturesque main street, Donner Pass Road, is lined with western wear and outdoor equipment stores, restaurants and saloons in brick and stone false-front buildings facing the railroad tracks, and the 1869 depot where Amtrak trains blast into town daily.

Kids like the Variety Company, an old-fashioned general store selling zillions of little cars and trucks, penny candy, and toys; give the kids $5 each and let them loose! A model train chugs around Truckee Train and Toy, ground zero for all kinds of toy trains and specialty dolls and toys. At Bud's Sporting Goods and Fountain, you can sit on a stool at the mirrored soda fountain and have a Cherry Coke or an ice-cream soda, while Dad shops for fishing gear.

The historic Union Pacific/Amtrak Depot houses the visitor center, where you can browse a huge array of brochures and maps and get sightseeing and outdoor recreation advice for the North Tahoe area; look at great photos of early days; check your e-mail; and ask about annual events. In May the town steps back in time with gunslingers trodding the boardwalks, gold panning, strolling musicians, and storytelling. Truckee Railroad Days features antique trains, handcar rides, a parade, exhibitors, and vendors, and the Railroad Regulators reenact scenes from the Wild West.

A half mile south of Truckee on Highway 267, stop in at the Truckee River Regional Park for ice skating in the wintertime (rentals, snack bar, lessons, evening bonfire, and overhead lights); in the summer for the picnic grounds, disc golf, skate park, nature trails, basketball and volleyball courts, and more (530–583–7720).

Tahoe Rim Trail (all ages)
(775) 588–0686; www.tahoerimtrail.org.

From eight trailheads around the lake, you can connect with the 165-mile hiking, equestrian, and mountain biking path that follows the ridgetops of the Lake Tahoe Basin, at elevations between 6,000 and 10,000 feet, passing through six counties and incorporating about 50 miles of the Pacific Crest Trail. Panoramic views of the Tahoe Basin, gorgeous forests, stunning lakes, and wildflowery meadows are among the rewards. One relatively easy segment starts at the west end of the Truckee River access parking lot on Highway 89, 0.25 mile south of the intersection of Highway 28 in Tahoe City. The first 2.5 miles meander through fir and pines to Paige Meadows. Farther on in Ward Canyon are a waterfall and big views.

Northstar-at-Tahoe (all ages)
Highway 267 between Truckee and Lake Tahoe; (800) 466–6784 or (530) 562–1010; www.northstarattahoe.com. Lodging $$$–$$$$; special packages available.

One of the largest resorts at the lake, Northstar is a self-contained family-oriented complex laid out in a spectacular mountain and forest setting. It includes a golf course; equestrian trails and stables; mountain biking and hiking trails; shops, a deli, and a grocery; several bars and restaurants; and a plethora of nice condos, lodge rooms, and beautiful homes to rent.

You can park your car and get around entirely on foot and on the resort shuttles. In the summer, chairlifts take hikers and bikers up to beautiful mountaintop trails, and there is a busy schedule of activities and events all year. Guided nature hikes include a lift ride and a chat with a naturalist about the plants, trees, animals, and the geology of the Sierras.

Older kids head for the teen center and the workout rooms. Parents love the lap pool. Little kids can play in the wading pool and the shallow end of the main pool, under the watchful eye of a lifeguard.

The Northstar ski resort is great for families, with a large number of intermediate- and beginning-level downhill and snowboarding runs. Minor's Camp cares for kids two to six, with ski lessons optional. Ski-and-learn packages are offered to separate age groups. Ask about the Mommy, Daddy, and Me program, the Parent Predicament sharing ticket, and the gondola ticket that gets you to the tubing area and the Nordic and snowshoe center. Check out the Web site for extensive advice and information about how to pack and plan for winter sports.

At the Action Zone, the excellent tubing area has a lift; no sleds or saucers. Try the bungee trampolines and the various snow toys.

Donner Lake (all ages)
Between Soda Springs and Truckee off Highway 80; (530) 582–7892.

Families who want a quiet, old-fashioned vacation in the mountains love Donner. On the 7.5 mile shoreline, you can camp, launch a boat, rent a cabin, fish, hike, ski, and enjoy the crystal-clear, blue waters. There are nearly thirty public piers on the north side for fishing and boating. Shoreline Park offers bank fishing and a pier, boat launching, picnic sites, and swimming. On the west end, a swimming area is supervised by lifeguards.

Above the lake on Highway 80, the Emigrant Gap viewpoint on Donner Summit, at 7,135 feet, is a must stop. Your family will get a dramatic geology lesson when you look out over hundreds of miles of high country to see the tremendous tilted block of the Sierras sloping toward the west. Glacial canyons are gouged out of the granite, and the Yuba and Bear Rivers have cut their own valleys.

On the west end of the lake is a trailhead for the Pacific Crest Trail. From here you can take a 15-mile strenuous hike along the ridge of the Sierra crest, descending down into Squaw Valley's Shirley Canyon.

Donner Memorial State Park (all ages)
Three miles west of Truckee, off Highway 80; (530) 544–3053.

Spend a half day here on the way to Tahoe, and get a history lesson too. Beneath towering evergreens at 5,950 feet, walking paths and picnic groves are cool and shady. The Emigrant Trail Museum depicts stories of the Donner Party, a group of pioneer families who were trapped here during the violent winter of 1846–47. A monument rests on a stone base 22 feet high—the snow level of that fateful winter. In the museum are artifacts and displays on the building of the railroad through the Sierras in the 1800s. In the distance, you can see train tracks, mostly covered with snow buildings, running along the rugged mountainsides above Donner Lake; the tracks are still in use by Amtrak today.

Rangers guide interpretive walks throughout the summer,

explaining local flora and fauna and the history of the Donner Party. In the wintertime, rangers lead free snowshoe history hikes and introductions to cross-country skiing. It's free to cross-country ski on a 3-mile loop.

Inexpensive Ski Areas

Low prices for lift tickets, lessons, and other expenses make these long-established ski resorts family favorites. Expert skiers and boarders will likely be bored; new skiers and children and adults looking to take it easy will love these shorter, less intimidating ski slopes. Kids' learn-to-ski programs are top notch.

- **Tahoe Donner,** Donner State Park exit off Highway 80, (530) 587–9444; www.skitahoedonner.com. Downhill skiing on fourteen runs; 110 kilometers of cross-country trails with warming huts. Tahoe Kids under six ski free. Nearby snow-play area.

- **Soda Springs,** 1 mile east of Highway 80 at Soda Springs exit; (530) 426–3901; www.skisodasprings.com. Oriented toward young children, with the tubing runs alongside the ski runs; mini-snowmobiles too.

- **Donner Ski Ranch,** 19320 Donner Pass Road on Old Highway 40, Norden; (530) 426–3635; www.donnerskiranch.com. Dozens of uncrowded runs; kids five and under are free; ages six to twelve are $10. Ask about value days.

- **Sierra-at-Tahoe,** From South Lake Tahoe,12 miles up Highway 50 west over Echo Summit; (530) 659–7453; www.sierra tahoe.com. Wild Mountain Ski and Snowboard camp for ages four to twelve; day care; kids four and under ski free. Good snow between 6,600- and 8,800-foot elevation; snow play on-site. At the new Telemark and Backcountry Center, ask about the guided snowshoe tours, easy enough for kids ages seven and up.

Diamond Peak Ski Area (all ages)

1210 Ski Way, on Highway 431 above Incline Village; (775) 832–1177; e-mail: ivgid@sierra.net; www.diamondpeak.com. Full-service ski resort, restaurants, ski school, equipment rental, child care. Lift tickets: $$$$; kids 6 to 12 $$$; kids 5 and under and adults over 80 free.

Diamond Peak Ski Area at Mount Rose is a medium-size ski resort with spectacular lake and mountain views and downhill and cross-country skiing. Intermediates and beginners are happy here; expert skiers will head for larger resorts. Snow conditions are less dependable than at higher-elevation resorts, but when the snow is primo, Diamond Peak is a good choice for families who prefer uncrowded ski runs and a casual, family-oriented atmosphere. Ask about discounts for the beginner lifts, twilight tickets, and family rates. There is an extensive shuttle network from area lodgings.

Boreal Ski Area (all ages)

Highway 80 at Donner Summit; (530) 426–3666. Lift tickets: adults $$$$; ages 5 to 12 $$; 4 and under are free.

A reasonably priced, nonintimidating choice for new skiers. With adult lift tickets starting at $36, Boreal focuses on families, with a variety of terrain features for kids, a family terrain zone, parent-shared passes, and packages and discounts. The Kids Club package for ages four to ten includes all-day pass, equipment rental, lesson, and supervision from 10:00 A.M. to 3:00 P.M., lunch and snack, for $75. Night skiing is popular at Boreal, especially with teenagers, who like the illuminated terrain park with its huge half-pipe, tabletop jumps, and rolls. The view from the top of the Sunset Boulevard run is dazzling. Admission is free at Boreal's Western American Ski Sport Museum, where ski history from the 1850s to the present is depicted in photos, displays, and vintage movies.

Royal Gorge USA (ages 7 and up)

Off Highway 80, Soda Springs; (530) 426–3871 or (800) 500–3871; www.royalgorge.com. Trail passes: adults $$$$; children $$$; under 12 are free.

Royal Gorge is the largest Nordic ski resort in the nation and has been voted the best in North America by ski magazines. The network of groomed trails is so vast and so varied that you definitely need to carry the trail map—all the better to locate the ten cozy warming huts and the four cafes, which make comforting destinations during a day of skiing or snowshoeing. You can rent everything here, including pulk sleds for small children, so you can pull them behind you. Accommodations in the Wilderness Lodge include meals and trail passes; you can also stay at Sugar Bowl or at Rainbow Lodge and connect directly to Royal Gorge trails; free shuttle bus to and from Sugar Bowl.

This is an especially good place to introduce children to the sport, as they offer a Pee Wee Snow School, group and private lessons for all ages, and four surface lifts to make it easy for beginners.

Where to Eat

Austin's. 120 Country Club Drive, Incline Village; (775) 832–7728. Voted Best Family Restaurant by the locals, a casual, friendly place serving hearty, Texas-style food, three meals a day. Bring your appetite for Mountain Man Omelet, pork chops and steak sandwiches, buttermilk fries, chicken-fried steak. Don't miss the homemade pie. $$

Azzara's. 930 Tahoe Boulevard in the Raley's Center, Incline Village; (702) 831–0346. Everything Italian, such as Sicilian artichokes, turkey with mozzarella and tomatoes, and pizza and pasta. Reservations are definitely required for dinner. $$–$$$

Gar Woods Grill and Pier. 5000 North Lake Boulevard, Carnelian Bay; (530) 546–3366. Indoors or on the glassed-in deck, year-round, a wonderful spot to have a long lunch or sunset dinner with the children while watching boating activity on the lake. Restless kids can play around on the small pier and the pathways along the water below the deck; those about five and under will need supervision. Sunday brunch at Gar Woods on a sunny day—it doesn't get any better. Reservations recommended. $$–$$$

Hacienda de la Sierra. 931 Tahoe Boulevard, across from Raley's, Incline Village; (702) 831–8300. Voted the best Mexican restaurant by locals, with a warm, colorful atmosphere, booths indoors or tables on the deck. Fajitas, huge burritos, combo platters. $–$$

O.B's. 10046 Donner Pass Road, Truckee; (530) 587–4164; www.obstruckee.com. For over three decades, good, hearty food in a historic, museumlike building adorned with old photos, barnboard walls, antique farm implements, and other artifacts of old Truckee. Get into a cozy booth and order chili, burgers, wraps, steak sandwiches, and more stick-to-your-ribs lunches and dinners; do not miss the mud pie and the old-fashioned apple pie. $–$$

Original Old Post Office. 5245 North Lake Boulevard, Carnelian Bay; (530) 546–3205. You may see people waiting on the porch for their turn at monster-size, all-American breakfasts. No reservations. $–$$

Steamer's Beachside Bar and Oven. 8290 North Lake Boulevard, Kings Beach; (530) 546–2218. One of the most popular pizza restaurants on the North Shore, with a great outdoor patio on the lakeside and indoor seating by the windows for when the weather turns cool. If your family likes calzones and pizza, they'll love Steamer's. The kids can run around on the beach while they wait for lunch or dinner. $

Where to Stay

BRAT Resort Properties. 120 Country Club Drive, Incline Village; (888) 266–3612; www.bratresort.com. Rental condos and houses, with ski and vacation packages.

Donner Lake Village Resort. 15695 Donner Pass Road, Truckee; (530) 587–6081; www.donnerlakevillage.com. Moderately priced, comfortable accommodations, from lodgettes sleeping four to town houses sleeping six. Right on the lake with great views, a private marina, and boat rentals. $$–$$$

Hyatt Regency Lake Tahoe. Lakeshore and Country Club Drive, Incline Village; (702) 832–1234. High-rise hotel and lakeside units, vacation packages. Camp Hyatt day and evening child care. $$$–$$$$

Inn at Incline. 1003 Tahoe Boulevard, Incline Village; (702) 444–6758. Motel units in a forest setting; indoor pool, sauna, spa. Continental breakfast, some kitchens. $$

Lodge at Ice Lakes. 1111 Soda Springs Road, Soda Springs; (530) 426–7660; www.icelakeslodge.com. A few minutes from Sugar Bowl and Royal Gorge, at Donner Summit right on a beautiful lake, a very nice, rustic lodge open year-round. Ground floor rooms have small patios, upstairs some have decks; some rooms have two queen beds. Hearty American food in the casual restaurant, with views of Serene Lakes and Castle Peak. Box lunches are available. Linger on the sofa in front of the massive stone fireplace. Hiking, biking, fishing, and canoeing in the summer. Cross-country skiing and snow play in the wintertime. $$–$$$

Truckee Tahoe Inn. 11331 Highway 267 between Truckee and Northstar; (530) 587–4525; www.bestwesterntahoe.com. Reasonably priced, newish motel with simple, fresh rooms and suites with sofa beds and complimentary continental breakfast, sauna, and spa. Ask about ski packages and off-season rates. $–$$

Vacation Station Lake Tahoe. 110 Country Club Drive, P.O. Box 7180, Incline Village, NV 89451; (800) 841–7443. Agency for rental of homes and condos. $–$$$

For More Information

Incline Village Crystal Bay Visitors Bureau and Convention Bureau. 969 Tahoe Boulevard, Incline Village; (800) GO–TAHOE or (775) 832–1606; e-mail: gotahoe@sierra.net; www.gotahoe.com.

Shasta Cascade

Where the Sierra Nevada Range ends and the Cascade Range begins, two colossal glaciated volcanoes are visible for hundreds of miles. Dormant 14,162-foot Mount Shasta and still active 10,457-foot Lassen Peak loom like misty ice gods above the forested recreation lands of northernmost California.

Families who crave recreation in the great outdoors, high-country scenery, and sightseeing in historic towns can spend a lifetime of vacations in the Shasta Cascade area. Roughly the size of Ohio, the region contains seven national forests, eight national and state parks, five mighty rivers, and hundreds of lakes.

Fishing is legendary on the McCloud, Sacramento, Klamath, Salmon, and Scott Rivers. Lush woodlands along the riverbanks are precious ribbons of wilderness that shelter birds, waterfowl, and other wildlife in great numbers.

One of the largest recreational lakes in the country, Lake Shasta is encircled by 370 miles of wooded shoreline that spreads out into four main arms fed by three rivers and a creek. Houseboating is one of the most popular ways for families to vacation on the lake.

On the fringes of the wild, dark forests of the Trinity Alps are sprinkled a handful of tiny towns favored by antiques hunters and trout fishers. The forty-niners, pioneers, and Chinese immigrants in the area left a rich cultural heritage that can be seen in the charming old buildings and museums of Weaverville.

A unique geophysical crossroads, mountainous Lassen Volcanic National Park boils and bubbles with mudpots and sulfury hot springs. On the slopes of both Lassen Peak and Mount Shasta are developed areas for downhill and Nordic skiing, as well as snow play.

Anchoring Highway 5, the main route to the Northwest, the city of Redding is the jumping-off point for adventures in the Shasta Cascade. A wide variety of motels, restaurants, recreation opportunities, and fishing outfitters, plus easy access to the Sacramento River, make this an important stop.

Mount Shasta City

At the foot of Mount Shasta, the laid-back small town of Mount Shasta City is where many families headquarter, heading out every day to explore the national forests in the summertime and to ski when the snow falls.

SHASTA CASCADE

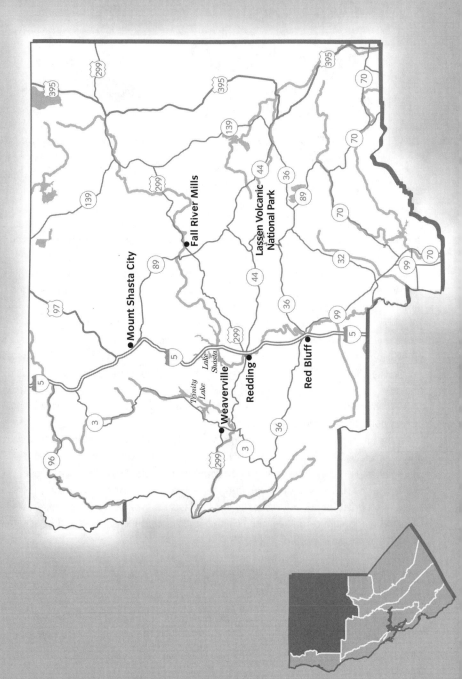

Thar She **Blows**

At 14,162 feet, Mount Shasta is the fourth-highest peak in the continental United States and the largest volcano by volume—80 cubic miles.

Shasta is near the southern end of the Cascade Range, which begins with the active volcano Lassen Peak and runs north to British Columbia, with volcanoes about every 50 miles—quite a sight from a plane. The Cascades are part of the notorious "Ring of Fire" that surrounds the Pacific Ocean.

The last recorded eruption of Mount Shasta was in 1786.

Mount Shasta Bike, Board, and Ski Park

(all ages)

Located 10 miles east of Mount Shasta City, at 104 Siskiyou Avenue; (530) 926–8600 (snow phone: 530–926–8686); www.skipark.com. Lift tickets: adults $$$$; ages 8 to 12 $$$; 7 and under $$. In the summer lift fees are $$ for adults and free for kids under 12.

A good-size winter resort, with mostly intermediate and beginner downhill runs at 5,000 feet, a ski school, Nordic and night skiing, and a nice day lodge with a restaurant. Powder Pups is the supervised ski program for kids ages four to seven; across the road from the ski park, Snowman's Hill is a snow-play area. At the Nordic skiing center are 16 miles of groomed trails and skating lanes, with a lodge, a warming hut, and shuttle service. The advantage of family skiing here is the reasonable cost, child-oriented staff, the lack of lift lines and crowds, and a carefree drive on Highway 5, which is seldom encumbered with enough snow to require chains.

In summer take the twenty-minute round-trip up the chairlift for the view of a lifetime. Hike around up here, picnic, and take the lift back down. Or bring your mountain bikes up (or rent them here) and pedal the excellent trails, ending up back at the lodge. In the summer and fall, the wildflowers in the meadows on top and at the base of the mountain are truly spectacular. There are frequent concerts and festivals in the beautiful outdoor amphitheater, and you can buy hot food to eat on the sunny deck or cold picnic fare to carry back to blanket. In response to the climbing craze, a 24-foot tower has climbing routes for ages four and up. There is also a free multimedia exhibit about the formation of Mount Shasta.

More Cross-Country Skiing (all ages)

Off Highway 89 beyond Mount Shasta Ski Park in the Shasta-Trinity National Forest; (530) 926–4511. Free.

Watch for signs to Bunny Flat and Sand Flat, marked cross-country trails for beginners and intermediates and maintained by the U.S. Forest Service. Restrooms and parking are available only at Bunny Flat, which is also a snow-play area.

Mount Shasta Resort

1000 Siskiyou Lake Boulevard, Mount Shasta City; (800) 958–3363 or (530) 926–3030; www.mountshastaresort.com. $$–$$$.

In a pretty wooded setting near walking trails and lakes, families settle into beautiful one- and two-bedroom chalets with fireplaces, sofa beds, fully equipped kitchens, spacious living rooms, and decks. The golf course here is spectacular and challenging; spend an hour on the practice range with budding golfers. There is an outdoor dining deck and a comfortable restaurant with views of the mountains, plus a snack bar with outdoor tables. Ask about ski and golf packages.

Backpacking in Shasta-Trinity National Forest (all ages)

Wilderness permits and maps are available at Mount Shasta Ranger District office, 204 West Alma, Mount Shasta City; (530) 926–4511.

The Shasta-Trinity National Forest offers exceptional backpacking. The Pacific Crest Trail can be accessed west of Mount Shasta City at Parks Creek, South Fork Road and Whalen Road, and at Castle Crags State Park.

Castle Crags State Park (all ages)

Forty-five miles north of Redding, off Highway 5; (530) 235–2684 (campground reservations: 800–447–7275 or 916–235–2684). $$ day-use fee.

A fortress of 6,000-foot granite pillars and monster boulders, with 2 miles of the Sacramento River gleaming below and good trout fishing in the streams. At this spectacular park you can swim, hike, rock climb, and camp in one of seventy-six developed sites. Get maps at the park office and amble up the sun-dappled Indian Creek Nature Trail, a 1-mile loop. The Crags Trail to Castle Dome is 5.5 strenuous miles up and into the Castle Crags Wilderness, connecting with the Pacific Crest Trail. People often stop at the park just to fill up jugs with natural soda water. The road is plowed all winter for ice fishing on Castle Lake.

Lake Siskiyou Camp Resort (all ages)

Three miles from Mount Shasta City, take Hatchery Road to a left onto Old Stage Road, then turn right at W. A. Barr Road; (530) 926–2618; www.lakesis.com. $ day-use fee.

One of the prettiest multiuse camping and RV facilities in the state, the resort is located at a large reservoir in a fresh, clean, pine-scented setting at the headwaters of the Sacramento River. You can rent a fully equipped trailer on-site or bring your own tent or RV. Day-trippers are welcome: Walk around the lake, lounge on the 1,000-foot-long sandy beach, swim, or launch a fishing boat. Available to rent are water toys, kayaks, canoes, paddleboats, sailboats, and fishing equipment. Also here are a store, a snack bar, outdoor movies, and a playground.

At the end of W. A. Barr Road, Gumboot Lake is a tiny, shallow bit of icy water stocked with trout, surrounded by meadows, mountains, and forests. Bring a picnic, an inflatable raft, or a canoe.

Castle Lake (all ages)

Passing the Lake Siskiyou Camp Resort entrance on W. A. Barr Road, go left on Castle Lake Road, 7 miles to the parking area; (530) 926–4511.

This is one of the most easily accessible alpine lakes in Northern California. The parking lot is a few yards from the lakeshore, and within a short easy stroll, you can be in an idyllic, seemingly isolated wilderness setting. Walk in either direction along the lakeshore through beautiful forest, putter around in the creek, fish in the lake, launch your skiff or kayaks, or have a picnic. The water here is wonderfully pure and clear, and the fishing and (chilly) swimming are great. For a 3-mile-round-trip, moderately strenuous hike, take the trail to the left of the lake near the stream, along the lakeside, and up above the lake to 5,900 feet. Bear to the right up 100 feet more to Heart Lake, a small lake that warms up in summer and is popular for swimming. One of the best photo ops of Mount Shasta is on Castle Lake Road, about 0.5 mile before the parking lot.

Where to Eat

Lily's. 1013 South Mount Shasta Boulevard, Mount Shasta City; (530) 926–3372; www.lilyrestaurant.com. Hearty breakfast, lunch, dinner, and weekend brunch on the deck surrounded by a lovely garden, from Mexican food to steaks, pasta, and veggies. This is a very popular place. $–$$

Michael's. 313 North Mount Shasta Boulevard, Mount Shasta City; (530) 926–5288. Italian specialties and continental dishes, homemade pasta, soups, sandwiches, burgers. Lunch and dinner. $–$$

Where to Stay

Mount Shasta KOA Campground. 900 North Mount Shasta Boulevard, Mount Shasta City; (530) 926–4029. A grassy, gardeny place with RV and tent sites, animal corrals, camping cabins, a store, a swimming pool, and a playground. $

Mount Shasta Ranch. 1008 W. A. Barr Road, five minutes from Lake Siskiyou, Mount Shasta City; (530) 926–3870; www.stayinshasta.com. In a beautiful country setting, a B&B with spacious rooms, suites, and a carriage house; a gigantic common living room and game room; and a full breakfast. Children are quite welcome in the carriage house. There are games, Ping-Pong, and pool tables. $$

Railroad Park Resort. 100 Railroad Park Road, Dunsmuir; (530) 235–4440; www.rrpark.com. One of the best places in the region for families to stay. Stop here for a meal and take a look at the collection of old railcars and railroading paraphernalia. Accommodations include an RV park, a campground, cabins, and motel rooms in railcars, plus a swimming pool. $$

Strawberry Valley Inn. 1142 South Mount Shasta Boulevard, Mount Shasta; (916) 926–2052. Lovely landscaped grounds and shade trees make this reasonably priced motel a winner; some rooms have two beds, and there are two-room suites. A huge breakfast buffet is served on a sunny patio or by the fireplace. $–$$

Tree House Best Western. 111 Morgan Way at Highway 5 and Lake Street, Mount Shasta City; (530) 926–3101. Large, nicely landscaped motel, with some two-bedroom units and refrigerators; large heated indoor pool; casual dining room with fireplace. $$

For More Information

Shasta Cascade Wonderland Association. 1619 Highway 273, Anderson; (530) 365–7500 or (800) 474–2782; www .shastacascade.org.

Mount Shasta Visitor Pavilion. 300 Pine Street, Mount Shasta City; (800) 926–4865; www.visitsiskiyou.com. Two blocks east of the Highway 5 central exit at Lake and Pine Streets.

U.S. Forest Service. 204 West Alma, Mount Shasta City; (530) 926–4511.

Lake Shasta

They call it California's Water Wonderland, a huge warm-water lake at the confluence of several major rivers. The surface waters reach eighty degrees in summer, perfect for swimming and waterskiing. Attracting avid anglers are sixteen species of fish, from bass to trout, sturgeon, salmon, and channel catfish.

With a filigreed shoreline of 370 miles, Shasta is very popular for all kinds of water sports and houseboating. Houseboats range from 15 to more than 50 feet long and sleep from four to twelve people. These boats are easy to navigate, even for first-timers. You can get air-conditioning, TV, and washers and dryers, among other amenities. Rentals at the dozen or so houseboat marinas on Lake Shasta cost $1,000 per week and up. The houseboats come completely equipped except for linens and food. You motor slowly along, exploring hidden inlets, fishing, and stopping at beaches and marinas. (See "Houseboating Tips for Families" in The Big Valley chapter)

The U.S. Forest Service operates developed and boat-in campgrounds at Shasta. More than two dozen private campgrounds and marinas are scattered along the river arms of the lake, primarily on the Sacramento near Lakehead and on the McCloud. You can sleep overnight in a boat anywhere on the lake. There are even floating restrooms!

Hike Lake Shasta (all ages)

Hiking around the lake can be a hot, dry experience in summer, but trails are green and gorgeous all other times of year. From Packer's Bay Road take Waters Gulch Trail through an oak forest (about 3 miles) up to great views of the Sacramento arm of the lake. Eastside Trail, also at Packer's Bay, is a 0.5-mile, easy walk to swimming and fishing spots. From the Bailey Cove parking lot, a trail runs for almost 3 miles through a pretty, wooded area with lake views, and you can swim at several places along the way.

Lake Shasta Caverns (ages 7 and up)

Fifteen miles north of Redding off Highway 5, take the O'Brien/Caverns exit; (530) 238–2341.

One of the most dramatic natural wonders in the western states, the caverns constitute a fantasy of multicolored columns, 20-foot-high stone draperies, stalactites and stalagmites, brilliant crystals, and unusual limestone and marble formations, all subtly lit for maximum effect. A fifteen-minute boat ride ferries you across the lake to a wooded island, where you go by bus 800 feet up a steep road through aromatic bay, oak, and manzanita. Groups of about twenty people are guided up and down hundreds of stone steps through a series of giant chambers. The atmosphere is damp and drippy and a constant fifty-eight degrees, which is refreshing in the summer, when outside temperatures can reach more than one hundred.

Shasta Dam (all ages)

Off Highway 5, just north of Redding, on Shasta Dam Boulevard; (530) 275–4463.

Walk out on the rim of the second-tallest concrete dam in the United States. Take a look at historic photos and watch a short film in the visitor center. The guided tour into the dam involves an elevator ride that kids under age eight may find scary.

Bridge Bay Resort

Twelve miles north of Redding, Bridge Bay exit off Highway 5, 10300 Bridge Bay Road, Redding; (530) 275–3021 or (800) 752–9669; www.sevencrown.com.

Under a big bridge over the lake, this full service marina has houseboat rentals, cabins, ski boats, patio boats, personal watercraft, and a clean, simple motel with a swimming pool and some kitchens—a great headquarters for plying the lake or trying out a houseboat. The houseboat rental company Seven Crown Resorts (800–752–9669) is one of the largest and oldest of its kind. They also have rental operations at Digger Bay on Shasta and in the California Delta and other states.

Blue Goose Excursion Train (all ages)

Yreka Depot, Yreka; (530) 842–4146. $$, kids under 3 are free.

Take a three-hour trip on the historic short-line Yreka Western Railroad from Yreka to Montague. A 1915 Baldwin engine pulls cars over the river through beautiful ranchlands of the Shasta Valley with views of Mount Shasta. You get time in the quaint burg of Montague to have lunch, shop, and take a horse-drawn wagon ride, then return to the Yreka Depot, where model trains and railroad memorabilia are on display.

Where to Eat

Tail of the Whale. Twelve miles north of Redding, at the Bridge Bay exit off Highway 5; (530) 275–3021. Dependable American food in a setting overlooking an arm of the lake and Bridge Bay Resort; seafood, prime rib, Cajun shrimp, a hearty, all-American menu. $

Where to Stay

Antlers Resort and Marina. P.O. Box 140, Lakehead 96051; (530) 238–2553; www.lakeshastavacations.com. Another source for houseboat rentals, cabins, water sports equipment, campground, grocery. $

Holiday Harbor. Eighteen miles north of Redding, on Shasta Caverns Road; (800) 776–BOAT; www.lakeshasta.com. Complete resort facilities, RV hookups, and waterskiing lessons; houseboat, water-sports, and equipment rentals; picnic grounds, playground, grocery. $

Lakeshore Villa RV Park. 20672 Lakeshore Drive, Lakehead; (530) 238–8688. Rent a cabin, a houseboat, a ski boat, or a fishing boat. Enjoy the pool, or just have lunch and watch the action. $

For More Information

Shasta Cascade Wonderland Association. 1619 Highway 273, Anderson; (530) 365–7500 or (800) 474–2782; www.shasta cascade.com.

Upper Sacramento River Exchange Center. 5819 Sacramento Avenue, Dunsmuir; (530) 235–2012; www.snowcrest .net/riverex. Information about location and condition of access and activities on the river, from fly-fishing to rafting outfitters.

Lassen Volcanic National Park

The largest plug dome volcano in the world, Lassen Peak last blew its top in 1921. Hot springs, boiling mudpots, and sulfury steam vents remind us that sometime in the next few hundred years, a drive through Lassen Volcanic National Park may not be a good idea. For now it's one of the wonders of the world.

You can drive through the park in half a day, including stops along the 35-mile route up and over the 8,000-foot summit, viewing the snow-covered peaks and crystalline lakes from a distance. Better yet, settle into a campground for a week of fishing on a few of the fifty lakes and hiking on some of the 150 miles of interconnecting wilderness trails. Several lakes allow nonpowered boating. Seventeen miles of the Pacific Crest Trail twist through aromatic conifer forests, magnificent stands of aspens and cottonwoods, and wildflower-washed meadows.

In the fall, the entire mountain and lake region seems to burst into flame—the aspen, birch, and oaks are spun gold; eastern maples, chokecherry, and dogwood (and poison oak!) turn red along the highways and hiking trails, and are reflected in the many mountain lakes. In winter cross-country skiers, snowshoers, and snow campers take off into the spectacular backcountry. The snow may fly as early as September and as late as May (be advised to carry chains). Campgrounds are all located above 5,650 feet and are open from Memorial Day to the end of September, depending on road and snow conditions.

Anglers from all over the world come to the Lassen area for wild trout fishing in the cold, clear waters of Hat Creek and the Fall and McCloud Rivers on the north side of the park. Nonfishing members of the family will enjoy wildlife viewing in the Hat Creek area, where osprey, bald eagles, elk, and a variety of waterfowl are commonly seen.

Visit Center

The main park headquarters is at 38050 Highway 36, just east of Mineral, near the park; (530) 595–4444; www.nps.gov/lavo. $$$ per car.

At one of the three park entrances, stop at the visitor center for the Lassen Park road guide and the current schedule of naturalist-led tours and kids' story hours. More than sixty points of interest and trails are indicated in the guide and are numbered to correspond to road signs. The park road winds around three sides of the park, past woodlands, meadows, streams, and lakes. Among the spectacular sights are Bumpass Hell near the southwest park entrance, where you walk on boardwalks over hot springs, steam vents, mudpots, and other eerie manifestations of Earth's hot insides. The Devastated Area Interpretive Trail, one of several that are wheelchair accessible, is a quarter-mile path through a lush forest of lodgepole pines and aspens, breathtaking in the fall. To get to the beautiful 30-foot cascade of Kings Creek Falls, meander 1.5 miles, one-way, through meadows and forests.

Lava Beds **National Monument**

Get started on exploring the spectacular, unusual geological and historic sites at Lava Beds by spending time at the new visitor center, where exhibits and videos explain what you will see. You can borrow lanterns and helmets here for self-guided and ranger-led tours of the lava tubes—there are more than 400 of them (I recommend only guided tours, for safety's sake). A popular lighted cave, Mushpot has a mile of fascinating catacombs, and Skull Cave is a 750-foot-tall chamber with ice floors. Although most of the sights are underground, you can also see a lot on walking trails. The Schonchin Butte 0.75-mile trail leads to a panoramic view from the fire lookout, which is staffed from June to September; ask the rangers about the Junior Fire Lookout badge. There are Modoc Indian War battlefields, spatter cones, craters, lava flows, petroglyphs, and more wild and crazy landscape. The monument is 8 miles from Tulelake off Highway 139; (530) 667–2282; www.nps.gov/labe.

Manzanita Lake (all ages)

In the national park, near the north entrance; (530) 335–7557.

A postcard-perfect, evergreen-surrounded lake at 5,890 feet in elevation with dazzling views of the mountain. Take the easy, 1.5-mile hike around the lake by yourselves or on a ranger's tour. Nonmotorized boating, camping, and trout fishing are the main activities here. Campsites are pretty and private. In fall Canada geese and wood ducks arrive in great numbers. Open in summer, the Camper Store sells food and supplies.

Lassen Park Ski Area (all ages)

Located 3 miles southwest of Chester on Highway 36, just inside the southwest park entrance; (530) 595–3376.

The entire main road through the park is available for cross-country skiing, with unending views of snowbound mountains, valleys, and lakes. Equipment can be rented for sledding, snowshoeing, snowboarding, and downhill and cross-country skiing. The small downhill skiing hill has four runs, all beginning and intermediate, with a warming hut. Ski lessons are free on Saturday, and a free two-hour, guided snowshoe hike is offered at 1:30 P.M. on Saturday, too, for ages eight and up; snowshoes are free. There are 7 miles of groomed ski trails near Manzanita Lake, with no attendant facilities.

Butte Lake (all ages)

From Old Station go 10.5 miles east on Highway 44, go south on Butte Lake Road, and drive 7 miles on a rough dirt road; (530) 595–4444.

A beautiful campground sits at lakeside at 6,049 feet in elevation, surrounded by ponderosa pines and rugged volcanic outcroppings. Motorized boats are not allowed, and the fishing is phenomenal. Interesting cinder cones and other volcanic formations, plus two more lakes nearby and backcountry trails, make this a great destination. Always call ahead about accessibility of the campground.

Lake Almanor (all ages)

Some 40 miles southeast of Lassen Peak, off Highway 89 near Chester; (530) 274–4739.

At this pine-fringed, 13-mile-long lake at 4,500 feet, the snowy peak of Lassen and surrounding mountains are mirrored in clear, calm waters. Families who like to swim, boat, fish, and water-ski enjoy the sandy beaches, small lodges, and campgrounds on the western shore; summer lake surface temperatures reach seventy-five degrees. The Lake Almanor Recreation Trail, an easy, flat, paved route for biking, walking, and cross-country skiing, follows the west shore of the lake.

The small town of Chester caters to vacationers with simple lakeside resorts, motels, and campgrounds.

Wild Horse Sanctuary (ages 14 and up)
Thirty miles east of Red Bluff at Highways 44 and A6, Shingletown; (530) 474–5770; www.wildhorsesanctuary.org. $$$$.

On this perfectly beautiful 5,000-acre ranch, your family will have the experience of a lifetime tracking wild mustangs on a two- or three-day horseback ride in the tree-studded foothills of Lassen Peak. Vibrating with spirit, muscle, and shiny coats, the horses are a spectacular sight. Nervous when they see riders, they hang around for a few minutes, watching, sometimes as close as 40 or 50 feet—while riders snap photos like mad—then they gallop off. Wild turkeys, deer, bald eagles, coyotes, foxes, owls, burros, and bobcats are also commonly sighted.

Some riding experience makes this more enjoyable, although it is not required. For children under fourteen, get approval in advance. The pace is leisurely as the group proceeds slowly through brush, over creeks and gullies, and across meadows. You stay overnight at a rustic camp by a small vernal lake, in basic frontier-style cabins. Hearty meals are prepared while guests rest, swim, help groom and feed the horses, and explore.

Snowmobiling in Lassen National Forest

In the national forest are six designated trail areas for snowmobiling, each with parking and **free** admission; for information call (530) 335–7575.

- **Ashpan:** Nine miles southwest of the junction of Highways 44 and 89; 39 miles of trails; warming hut.

- **Swain Mountain:** Nine miles north of the junction of Highways A21 and 36; 47 miles of trails.

- **Jonesville:** Two miles east of Cherry Hill Campground on Butte Meadows; 43 miles of trails.

- **Fredonyer:** Ten miles west of Susanville; 80 miles of trails.

- **Morgan Summit:** Five miles east of Mineral on Highway 36; 77 miles of trails; warming hut.

- **Bogard Rest Stop:** Thirty miles west of Susanville on Highway 44; 75 miles of trails.

Where to Eat

Creekside Grill. 278 Main Street, Chester; (530) 258–1966. In a charming country setting by a creek, with a fireplace and an outdoor dining deck, a fine chef produces sophisticated California cuisine and comfort food, too. $–$$

Peninsula Station Bar and Grill. 401 Peninsula Drive, Lake Almanor; (530) 596–3538. Fresh trout and reasonably priced, excellent meals with good selections for children. $–$$

Stover's St. Bernard Lodge. Mill Creek, 10 miles west of Chester; (530) 258–3382. Knotty pine walls, stained glass, and antiques in a casual dining room; hearty American food, such as huge hamburgers, fresh fish, steak, and fried chicken. Take a walk around the trout pond. $–$$

Where to Stay

Bailey Creek Cottages. 433 Durkin Drive, Lake Almanor; (530) 259–7829; www .baileycreek.com. Right on a highly rated, new public golf course, nice, new, one- and two-room suites with stone fireplaces, private decks, kitchens or kitchenettes, king beds or two twins, sofa beds, and roll-aways. $$$–$$$$

Childs Meadow Resort. 41500 Highway 36E, Mill Creek; (530) 595–3383 or (888) 595–3383; www.childsmeadow resort.com. Between Susanville and Red Bluff, a quiet resort in a picturesque meadow at the foot of the Cascades, 9 miles from the southwest entrance to Lassen National Park, open year-round. Nothing fancy, a fresh, clean motel with cabins, a store and cafe, and nearby hiking, fishing, biking, Nordic skiing, and snowmobiling; RV sites too. $–$$$

Drakesbad Guest Ranch. End of Warner Valley Road, Lassen Volcanic National Park; mailing address: Drawer K, Chester 96020; phone: Drakesbad #2 via Susanville operator (if no answer, 530– 529–9820); e-mail: calguest@mci.com. Secluded within the southeastern corner of the national park, a century-old hot springs resort in spectacular scenic surroundings at 5,700 feet. The old-fashioned western ranch experience brings families back year after year—it's the kind of place where you can just let the kids go to participate in the many activities: trail rides, a little kids' program, hikes, crafts, swimming, badminton, horseshoes, Ping-Pong, volleyball, and fishing. Rustic, comfortable lodge rooms, cabins, and bungalows, with kerosene lamps for light (cabins and bungalows have no electricity). Make reservations months in advance; for high-season weekends and holidays, a year ahead. $$–$$$

Lake Almanor Resort. 2706 Big Springs Road, Lake Almanor; (530) 596–3337; www.homestead.com/lakealmanorresort. A multifaceted, lively, nice lakefront resort on the north shore, with boat dock and fully equipped cabins and lodge units, and tent and RV sites. A three-bedroom, one-bath lakeside house has a sleeping porch, boat slip, and washer and dryer. The marina and playground areas are busy in summertime, and you can rent boats and kayaks, and lounge and swim at the lawn/beach area. $–$$

Spanish Springs Guest Ranch. P.O. Box 70, Ravendale 96123; (530) 234–2050. Family ranch vacations, cattle drives, buckaroo camp, horseback riding on a big working cattle ranch. Accommodations vary, from a log cabin to a vintage ranch house. The fishing for trout is easy in stocked ponds. Family-style, hearty meals are served in the ranch house. $$–$$$

For More Information

Plumas County Visitors Bureau. P.O. Box 4120, Quincy 95971; (800) 326–2247 or (530) 283–6345; www. plumas.ca.us. Call for booklets: *Family Bike Tours, Mountain* *Bike Trail Guide,* and *Hiking Guide,* with trail descriptions and maps.

Fall River Valley Chamber of Commerce. P.O. Box 475, Fall River Mills 96056; (530) 336–5840.

Redding

A regional hub at the junction of Highways 5, 299, and 44, Redding has attractive motels, as well as fishing and camping outfitters. A refuge for the last mature riparian woodland left in the state, the Sacramento River runs along the edge of town, bordered by a great walking path. Most of the attractions of the Shasta Cascade are within a short drive of Redding.

East of Redding, in the southeastern corner of the Klamath National Forest, McArthur-Burney Falls Memorial State Park in the McCloud River Valley offers waterfalls, swimming holes, great fishing, and campgrounds. Within the park Lake Britton is one of several lakes in the area, a trout-fishing mecca for trophy-size brown, rainbow, and eastern brook trout.

Turtle Bay Exploration Park (all ages)
800 Auditorium Drive near the intersection of Highways 299 and 273, Redding; (530) 243–8850, www.turtlebay.org. $$; under 4 are admitted free.

On a bend of the Sacramento River, indoor and outdoor activities and exhibits focus on the Sacramento River watershed, its natural sciences and resources, art, culture, and human history. Follow Paul Bunyan's huge footprints to hands-on interpretive sites like the Giant Tree Maze, a fish ladder, and a miniature Shasta Dam. Climb the fire lookout tower and play on child-size earth-moving equipment, and on the Spar Swings and the Log Slide. Wander in the butterfly house. Explore the Redding Museum of Art and History; take a look at owls, hawks, bees, turtles, and beetles at the Carter House Natural Science Museum. Stroll on 220 acres of paved walking trails through oak savanna and wetlands, to see otter ponds, a raptor exhibit, and botanic gardens in the Redding Arboretum by the River. There is so much to see here: a fabulous collection of Ansel Adams photographs; an elaborate, leafless replica of an oak tree, its roots extending beneath a see-through glass floor; a Wintu Indian bark house; a river seen from beneath the surface; and touchable pelts of native animals. A teenage staff of docents makes science and history fun.

Linking the park with a 16-mile-long bike trail and a 200-acre arboretumon the other side of the river is a spectacular new pedestrian bridge with a glass deck suspended from a white tower. At the end of the bridge is a glass-walled cafe.

Sacramento River Trail (all ages)

In Redding, drive north on Market Street to Riverside Drive on the south side of the Sacramento River, go west to the parking lot where the trail begins; (800) 874–7562.

A tree-shaded, 7.7-mile path along the riverbanks, through a residential area, and crossing over the river on a unique pedestrian bridge, then continuing to Caldwell Park. Interpretive signs and benches are found along the way.

Sacramento River Discovery Center (all ages)

From Highway 5 take the second Red Bluff exit onto Antelope Boulevard and turn right onto Sale Lane, Red Bluff; (530) 527–1196.

Interpretive trails wind through native riparian habitats, grasslands, wetlands, and woodlands.

The Fly Shop

Off Highway 5, on the south end of Redding, 4140 Churn Creek Road; (530) 222–3555; www.theflyshop.com.

Look for a weathered gray building with a big fish visible from the highway. Available here are equipment, tours, and advice on which fish are biting, where to catch 'em, and what the water conditions are.

Waterworks Park (ages 4 and up)

151 North Boulder Drive, Redding; (530) 246–9550. $$–$$$.

Ride a giant water slide and tube the 400-foot Raging River. Little kids like the watery playground designed just for them while teens head straight for the beach volleyball.

Park Marina Raft Rental (ages 4 and up)

2515 Park Marina Drive, Redding; (530) 246–8388.

Everything you need to raft the Sacramento River, including life jackets. In three or four hours, rafters and canoers float south down the Sacramento River from Redding to Anderson River Park. Beneath overhanging sycamores, cottonwoods, oaks, and willows, you can slide quietly along or stop to fish the salmon-spawning riffles. Raft-rental companies pick you up at the park and shuttle you back to Redding.

McArthur-Burney Falls Memorial State Park (all ages)

Eleven miles northeast of Burney, off Highway 89; (530) 335–2777. $$.

In the Shasta-Trinity National Forest, the big attraction here is two million gallons of water a day tumbling over a misty, fern-draped, 129-foot cliff. Take a short hike down into the forest gorge to the base of the falls, where wild tiger lilies, maples, dogwoods, black oaks, and pines decorate the streamside. The walk is about a half-hour for the fit and fast, an hour for amblers and photographers, and two hours for walkers who take side trails. Good trout fishing can be had in the deep pool at the base of the falls and in the 2-mile stream above and below. Pleasant hikes in and near the park in evergreen forests include a 1.5-mile flat route to Lake Britton Dam, then 3 miles farther to Rock Creek.

Lake Britton (all ages)

In McArthur-Burney Falls Memorial State Park, off Highway 89; (530) 335–2777 (camp-ground reservations: 800–444–7275).

Located here are 18 miles of shoreline amid evergreen forests near the Pit River. Camping and RV sites are not too private but are nice in the off-season. Accessible by boat (rentals here), with a terrific swimming hole at its foot, Clark Creek Falls is a jet of frigid water crashing into the lake. Crappie, bass, and catfish bite all season.

Ide Adobe State Historic Park (all ages)

Two miles south of Red Buff, 21659 Adobe Road; (530) 529–8599. $ per car.

On the way to the Shasta region, a lovely rest stop on the river. The park is cool and shady, with giant oaks, lawns, picnic tables, historical displays, an old adobe home, and a small visitor center. You can fish here, but swimming in the fast current is not advisable. Crafts demonstrations are presented most summer weekends.

Where to Eat

Jack's Grill. 1743 California Street, Redding; (530) 241–9705. In a casual, noisy, hometown atmosphere, sixteen-ounce steaks, deep-fried prawns, big plates of good old American food. Dinner only. $

Westside Deli French Bakery. 1600 California Street, Redding; (530) 222–0787. Sandwiches and pastry treats. $

Wild Bill's Rib-Steakhouse and Saloon. 500 Riverside Way, Red Bluff; (530) 529–9453. A casual place with a deck on the river; steaks, pasta, and fish. $

Where to Stay

Hilltop Inn. 2300 Hilltop Drive, Redding; (530) 221–6100. A large, very nice motel with simple, spacious rooms, swimming pools, a wading pool, and complimentary continental breakfast. Two reasonably priced restaurants. $

Lava Creek Lodge. 1 Island Road, 12 miles north of Highway 299, east of Redding in Fall River Mills; (530) 336–6288. A small, rustic fishing lodge with cabins in a wooded setting on a lovely piece of the Fall River, adjacent to Ahjumawi Lava Springs State Park. The rustic main lodge has a huge stone fireplace and a deck that overlooks the lakeside lawn. You can take fly-fishing lessons here, and rent boats to fish on your own. Hearty American fare is served in the dining room. $

Red Lion Motor Inn. 1830 Hilltop Drive, Redding; (530) 221–8700. A big garden court with a swimming pool, a wading pool, a putting green, and lots of trees. Rooms are large and very nice. One coffee shop, one upscale restaurant. Pets allowed with advance notice. $$

River Inn. 1835 Park Marina Drive, Redding; (530) 241–9500. Located at the edge of town on a small lake, with mountain views, nice motel rooms, a pool, barbecue, and a boat launch into the Sacramento River. $–$$

For More Information

Redding Convention and Visitors Bureau. 7777 Auditorium Drive, Redding; (800) 874–7562; www.visitredding.org.

Fall River Valley Chamber of Commerce. P.O. Box 475, Fall River Mills 96056; (530) 336–5840.

Weaverville/Trinity

Glaciers chiseled the jagged peaks of the Trinity Alps aeons ago, then melted away, leaving more than fifty sparkling alpine lakes among the brooding conifers of the Trinity Alps Wilderness, part of the Shasta-Trinity National Forest. Black bears, mountain lions, Roosevelt elk, mink, river otters, eagles, and spotted owls inhabit the upper reaches of one of the wildest and least visited national forests in the country.

Thousands of feet below snowy peaks, Trinity Lake snakes several miles through a rugged valley, where a few small summer resorts and villages attract families who like the quiet side of the Shasta Cascade region. More than two dozen U.S. Forest Service campgrounds are scattered on the west side of the lake. Call (530) 623–2121 for information.

Sometimes a stretch of calm water, sometimes rapids raging in a gorge, the Trinity River leaps with salmon and steelhead, yielding fish of ten pounds or more. Wildflowers run riot in the spring, and fall foliage is brilliant all along the river.

Surrounded by a dramatic mountain backdrop, Weaverville's original structures were destroyed by fire and replaced in the mid-1800s by brick buildings with wooden overhangs and exterior spiral staircases. A circa-1900 bandstand and the second-oldest courthouse in California contribute to an Old West atmosphere.

A gorgeous driving tour is the 130-mile-long Trinity Scenic Byway from Redding to Arcata along the river canyon and through the national forests on the southern border of the Trinity Alps. Pick up a self-guiding brochure at the chamber of commerce in Weaverville so as not to miss the nice places to stop and swim, fish, camp, and take it easy; this is a curvy, curvy road, not recommended in the wintertime—spring is best, when the redbud are in bloom. Look for the foot-long cones of the gray pine on the roadside.

Joss House State Historic Park (all ages)

Oregon and Main Streets, Weaverville; (530) 623–5284. $.

Remnants of the Gold Rush remain at the colorful Joss House, the "Temple Amongst the Forest Beneath the Clouds," built in forty-niner days for the Taoist worship of those Chinese who built the California railroads and sought gold on the river. Carved altars, tapestries, and elaborate artifacts are restored to their former glory. Shady picnic sites lie beside a creek in the park.

Jake Jackson Museum and Trinity County Historical Park (all ages)

508 Main Street, Weaverville; (530) 623–5211. Free.

Gold Rush and pioneer days are re-created in a stamp mill, a miner's cabin, a blacksmith shop, and other displays.

Trinity Lake (all ages)

Accessed off Highway 3 between Weaverville and Coffee Creek; main campground and resort area is 10 to 15 miles north of Weaverville; (530) 623–2131 or (530) 623–6101.

More than 1,507 miles of rugged shoreline and hundreds of coves seem to absorb and hide houseboats, water-skiers, Jet Skis, and fishing boats. The west side is dotted with campgrounds, resorts, and boat launch ramps, while the east side, with somewhat restricted auto access, is largely undeveloped. Try your luck at fishing for trophy-size largemouth bass, trout, kokanee salmon, and catfish.

South Fork Trinity River National Recreation Trail (all ages)

Maps and information: Shasta-Trinity National Forest, 2400 Washington Avenue, Redding; (530) 244–2978; www.fs.fed.us/r5/shastatrinity.

The beautiful trail follows the South Fork Trinity River for 21 miles, from Scott Flat Campground near Forest Glen to Wildwood Road, and for 4 miles from a trailhead near Hyampom to Forest Glen.

Wilderness and Fishing **Expeditions**

- **W.O.A. Float Tours,** Horse Creek; (530) 496–3652. Scenic float trips on 6 miles of the Klamath River; oar-powered drift boat; quiet, dry, and safe for all ages, even babies. Streamside picnic, gold panning, bird-watching.

- **Turtle River Rafting Company,** P.O. Box 313, Mt. Shasta 96067; (530) 926–3223; www.turtleriver.com. Guided raft trips on the Klamath, Rogue, Trinity, and Sacramento Rivers.

- **Trinity River Rafting,** P.O. Box 572, Big Bar 96010; (530) 623–3033; www.trinityriverrafting.com. Whitewater rafting on the Trinity River, guided and self-guided. Raft and kayak rentals.

- **Bigfoot Rafting Company,** Highway 299W, Big Flat; (800) 722–2223; www.bigfootrafting.com. One- to three-day white-water trips on the Trinity; also scenic floats for beginners.

- **Trinity Trail Rides,** HC2 Box 4940, Trinity Center 96091; (530) 266–3343. Horseback pack trips into the Trinity Alps.

Lewiston ⓜ ⓣ ⓨ

Twenty-nine miles west of Redding off Highway 299; (530) 623–2131 or (530) 623–6101.

A half-hour from Weaverville, and so tiny that you can see all of it in a glance, the country village of Lewiston is strung out prettily along the rushing Trinity River. A 1903 landmark is the Old Lewiston Bridge, one of the last one-lane bridges still in use. Buildings from the 1860s are on the National Register of Historic Places. Several antiques shops have literally thousands of square feet of collectibles of all descriptions.

Cold, constantly moving water flows into Lewiston Lake from Trinity Lake, an ideal situation for large rainbow, brook, and brown trout. Salmon and steelhead show up below the Lewiston Dam, below the bridge, and in the smaller streams.

Coffee Creek Guest Ranch ⓨ ⓣ △ ⓧ

Coffee Creek Road, HC2 Box 4940, Trinity Center 96091; (530) 266–3343 or (800) 624–4480; www.coffeecreekranch.com. Lodging (including meals, sports, and activities) $$$–$$$$; packages available.

Not much changed since the 1920s, this is a great place for families. Offered are rustic housekeeping cabins and weekly activities such as square dancing, trail rides, bonfires, movies, tennis, tubing, badminton, and more. Situated on 127 acres, with Coffee Creek rushing through, the resort is within 2 miles of trailheads into the Trinity Alps Wilderness

Area. You can have three hearty, family-style meals a day here. There is a heated swimming pool, a rifle range and trapshoot, flyfishing in Coffee Creek for rainbow and German brown trout, guided hikes, and archery. Also available are babysitting for ages three and under, supervised play and organized games and activities for ages three to seventeen, and even overnight camping and riding lessons. This is summer camp for everyone in the family! Bring your cowboy hats and your fishing poles. Open in the wintertime too—dogsled and sleigh rides!

Scott Museum (all ages)
Airport Road, Trinity Center; (530) 266–3367. Free.

Indian artifacts, covered wagons, stagecoaches, and artifacts from old pioneer and Gold Rush days.

Where to Eat

Allan's Oak Pit Bar-B-Q. 1324 Nugget Lane off Main, at the edge of Weaverville; (530) 623–2182. Barbecued chicken, beef, and pork dinners, plus sandwiches. $–$$

Mustard Seed. 210 Main, Weaverville; (530) 623–4432. Home-style breakfast and lunch in a yellow Victorian house, featuring Belgian waffles, quiche, tacos and burritos, and homemade apple pie under the elm. $–$$

Pacific Brewery. Across from the Joss House, 401 Main Street, Weaverville; (530) 623–3000. Hearty American fare in a circa 1850 brick building. Breakfast, lunch, and dinner. $–$$

Sam's Eclectic Kitchen and Serendipity Bookstore. Turnpike and Deadwood Road off Trinity Dam Boulevard, Lewiston; (530) 778–3856. Pizza, sandwiches, light dinners, coffeehouse. $

Where to Stay

Lakeview Terrace Resort. Trinity Dam Boulevard off Highway 3, HC 01 Box 250, Lewiston 96052; (530) 778–3803; www.lakeviewterraceresort.com. On Lewiston Lake, one- to five-bedroom simple, clean cabins about 20 to 30 yards apart under the trees, completely equipped, and, thankfully, with no TVs or phones. There is also an RV site with lake views, hot showers, and laundry facilities. You can rent 14-foot fishing boats and patio boats holding up to eight people. Cabins rent for about $80–$100 per night for four to six people, and pets are okay.

Ripple Creek Cabins. Off Highway 3, north of Coffee Creek; (530) 266–3505. Old-fashioned housekeeping cabins on the Trinity River, with a nearby swimming hole and trails leading to alpine lakes. Borrow inner tubes and bikes here. No TV or phones, except at the office. Well-behaved, leashed pets okay. Open in the wintertime for cross-country skiing. $

Weaverville Victorian Inn. 1709 Main, Weaverville; (530) 623–4432. A nice place for families, offering spacious motel rooms, a swimming pool, a woodsy setting, and guest laundry facilities. $

Wyntoon Resort. Highway 3 just north of Trinity Center, P.O. Box 70, Trinity Center 96091; (530) 266–3337. RV, trailer, and tent campgrounds on ninety wooded acres; a marina; boat, water sports; and bike rentals. $

For More Information

Trinity County Chamber of Commerce. 317 Main Street, Weaverville; (800) 421–7259 or (530) 623–6101; www.trinity county.com.

Shasta Trinity National Forest. 2400 Washington Avenue, Redding; (530) 244–2978.

Redwood Country

The largest and oldest trees in the world live in a narrow band along the Northern California coastline and a few miles inland, with magnificent groves clustered in the "Redwood Empire" of Northern California. Walking beneath a 300-foot redwood forest canopy among these silent giants from the age of the dinosaurs will be an unforgettable experience for your family, ranking right up there with Yosemite and the Grand Canyon. The deepest, oldest groves have a truly prehistoric look: in fact, The Lost World, Jurassic Park was shot in Humboldt County redwood parks.

Beaches, birdwatching, camping, fishing, and country pleasures are more reasons to spend vacations in Humboldt County. Eureka, Ferndale, and Arcata are charming, walkable "all-American" towns, each chockablock with Victorian buildings. And, there is much new in the way of family-friendly restaurants, shops, museums, and outdoor recreation.

Eureka

The hub of Redwood Country, Eureka is home port to more than 500 fishing boats in Humboldt Bay. The town's founding coincided with the birth of Victorian architecture, and blocks and blocks of elaborate 1850–1904 houses remain. A stunning example is the William Carson Mansion at Second and M Streets, a mixture of several styles that took one hundred workers more than two years to build. The house is said to be the most photographed Victorian home in America. You don't need to drag the kids on a sightseeing tour of the Victorians, because these structures are everywhere you look.

Use Eureka as your base for exploring the redwood parks. If your family likes to fish, head for the Mad, the Van Duzen, the Eel, and other rivers. Recently named the Best Small Art Town in America, Eureka is a uniquely creative community, as demonstrated in many art-, music-, and culture-related events, festivals, and galleries. Take note of the flamboyant murals around town—ask for a mural walk map at the chamber of commerce.

REDWOOD COUNTRY

Redwood National Park

101

199

101

Trinidad

96

Redwood National Park

299

Arcata

Eureka

Ferndale

36

101

Avenue of the Giants

Garberville

Humboldt Bay Maritime Museum (all ages)

1410 Second Street, Eureka; (707) 444–9440. Free.

A favorite haunt for kids. In a replica of the oldest home in Eureka, the museum displays nautical relics, old navigation equipment, an early radar unit, a lighthouse lens, and fragments of wrecked ships.

Indian West Emporium

326 Second Street, Eureka; (707) 442–3042.

Native American art and artifacts; western memorabilia, and vintage clothing. Kids are not always happy to shop and browse in art galleries, but this shop and the Many Hands Gallery at Second and Seventh Streets are chock-full of cool things of interest to youngsters.

Clarke Memorial Museum (all ages)

Third and E Streets, Eureka; (707) 443–1947. Free.

This 1920s Italian Renaissance former bank with a glazed terra-cotta exterior houses an extraordinary collection of Indian basketry and ceremonial regalia, antique weapons, maritime artifacts, and photos of early Humboldt days.

Geppetto's

416 Second Street, Eureka; (707) 443–6255.

A toy store offering costumes, dolls, games, and hundreds of stuffed bears.

Moon's Play and Learn

3022 Broadway, Eureka; (707) 442–5761.

In the largest toy store north of the Bay Area, you'll find bright kites, windsocks and wind toys, puzzles, craft kits, science and nature items, books, and kinetic yard art kits.

Humboldt State University (HSU) Natural History Museum and Store
(all ages)
1315 G Street, Arcata; (707) 826–4479. Free.

Kids can touch a dinosaur tail, million-year-old fossils, and the inhabitants of a tidepool; see live native animals; identify sea shells; and learn about the natural history of the region. When you're in Trinidad, visit the Humboldt State University Marine Lab and Aquarium, where you'll find touch tanks and ocean exhibits.

Sequoia Park (all ages)

Glatt and W Streets, downtown Eureka.

Fifty-two delightfully green acres of virgin redwoods are home to a little zoo, a playground, formal gardens, walking paths, and a duck pond.

Easy **Wildlife Walks**

- **Eureka Waterfront,** park at the Carson Mansion on the north end of town. Enjoy glimpses of the mansion gardens, then walk 1 block south on Second Street and turn right into the Adorni Center parking lot. A paved waterfront path offers beautiful views of the bay and boats.

- **Sequoia Park,** park near the Duck Pond. Take a 1-mile loop trail in redwood and alder groves.

- **Woodley Island,** take Highway 255/R Street across the Samoa Bridge, and park at the Samoa Cookhouse or along the road. From here you can walk or bike along the edge of Humboldt Bay, 6 miles north to Arcata. The birdlife is extraordinary, from marbled godwits to curlews, dowitchers, falcons, and many more.

- **Humboldt Bay National Wildlife Refuge,** 1020 Ranch Road, Loleta, just south of Eureka; (707) 733–5406. Take Hookton Road exit from Highway 101 and follow it 1.2 miles to the Hookton Slough trailhead, a 1.5-mile path along the south edge of Humboldt Bay. Thousands of birds and ducks migrate through these beautiful grasslands, freshwater marshes, and mudflats, including 25,000 black brants, which fly from their nesting grounds in the Arctic to Baja. Look for herons, owls, ospreys, mallards, egrets, terns, and more. Restrooms.

- **Russ Park,** on the south end of Main in Ferndale: go left on Ocean Street. Three miles of pleasant, wildflowery trails and good birdwatching in a 110-acre, closed-canopy spruce and redwood forest. Restrooms.

- **Ferndale Bottoms,** on the east side of Ferndale. The bottoms are great for walking and biking; a network of country lanes between lovely meadows lead to the Eel River Estuary. You can launch a canoe or kayak at the end of Morgan Slough Road or take a guided boat tour of the estuary (Eel River Delta Tours; 707–786–4187). Loons, cormorants, harriers, egrets, and over 150 feathered species live in or pass through these wetlands. Where the Eel meets the sea, watch for sea lions, seals, and river otters.

- **Loleta Bottoms,** from Loleta drive (or bike) west on Cannibal Island Road to Crab Park, at the mouth of an arm of the Eel River. You can scramble around the edge of the estuary and walk back east on the quiet road, watching for plovers, tundra swans, and curlews. Go right on Cock Robin Island Road, where mudflats attract masses of shorebirds. Continue back to your car or on toward Loleta, where the Loleta Cheese Factory is a good place to stop for sandwiches, snacks, and cheese tasting (fabulous organic cheese).

Hum Boats (all ages)
At the foot of F Street, Eureka; (707) 443–5157.

Rent boats here or arrange to take a guided tour of Humboldt Bay: sea kayaks, sailboats, water-taxi rides.

Blue Ox Millworks Historical Park (all ages)
At the foot of X Street, Eureka; (800) 248–4259; www.blueoxmill.com. $$.

A museumlike sawmill and job shop that makes custom trim for Victorian buildings, using the same machines that created the originals. Take a self-guided tour on catwalks overlooking the artisans and watch them turn columns, carve rosettes, and form wooden gutters and gewgaws, or call ahead to ask about scheduled tours. Surrounded by an enchanting wetlands wildlife sanctuary, the Blue Ox has set up a re-creation of a loggers' camp, a school, a bird-viewing station, and other attractions.

Samoa Cookhouse (all ages)
Across the Samoa Bridge from downtown Eureka, on Samoa Boulevard; (707) 442–1659; www.humboldtdining.com/cookhouse.

Built on Woodley Island in 1885, this is the last surviving lumber camp cookhouse in the West. Giant American breakfasts are served from 6:00 A.M., including biscuits with sausage gravy, platters of pancakes, and scrambled eggs. Lunch and dinner are served family-style at long oilcloth-covered tables with charmingly mismatched chairs. Huge loaves of bread, cauldrons of soup, big bowls of salad and vegetables, baked ham, and roast beef are followed by wedges of homemade pie. Prices are quite reasonable and kids four and under eat **free.**

Even if you don't eat here, stop in to see the free museum of logging equipment, artifacts, and fantastic photos of early days. A short walk from the restaurant is a quiet bayside village and a nice playground.

M.V. Madaket (all ages)
At the foot of C Street, Eureka; (707) 444–9440. $$–$$$.

Cruise the bay on a fantastic wooden steam-driven ferry built in the 1920s, an exciting way to get a new perspective on the harbor and the shoreline. The historical and natural sights are explained as you pass oyster farms, fishing and pleasure craft, the third largest colony of harbor seals in the West, and zillions of fresh- and salt-water birds.

Avenue of the Giants (all ages)

Off both sides of Highway 101 just north of Garberville; (707) 946–2311.

The highlight of your visit is likely to be the sight of the 2,000-year-old coastal redwoods in the Eel River Valley. A 30-mile scenic drive called the Avenue of the Giants, within Humboldt Redwoods State Park, is well marked, with turnouts and parking areas accessing short loop trails into the forest. Begin your tour at the visitor center, 2 miles south of Weott, where a movie, exhibits, and trail maps will help get you oriented (restrooms here too). Ask for advice on the length and type of walks and drives you can take. At the south end of the avenue, accessed via the Phillipsville exit off the highway, you will find small grocery stores.

Humboldt Redwoods State Park (all ages)

Off Highway 101, visitor center 2 miles south of Weott on the Avenue of the Giants; (707) 946–2409; www.humboldtredwoods.org. Day-use fee $$ per car.

The largest and one of the least visited state parks, in part because it encompasses several small towns, the park is divided by the highway and has no main entrance. Most visitors do not realize that most of the park lies to the west and is reached by leaving the Avenue of the Giants and taking Mattole Road.

Not to be missed is the Rockefeller Forest in the Big Trees area, a 5-mile drive in on Mattole-Honeydew Road. Since the former champion sequoia Dyerville Giant, 362 inches in diameter, fell in rain-saturated ground in spring 1991, the new champ is a 363-inches-in-diameter behemoth in the Rockefeller Forest. Tiptoeing along boardwalks and spongy pathways in the damp, cool stillness at the foot of these magical giants, you'll hear only the bustle of chipmunks. A short trail leads to a sandy riverbank, for sunbathing, wading, picnicking, and fishing.

A hundred miles of trails in the park are frequented by hikers, backpackers, mountain bikers, and horseback riders. Meanderings will turn up old homesteaders' cabins and several campgrounds, some for RVs and others consisting of simple sites in the backcountry. Apple blossoms bloom in orchards planted by early settlers. In fall big-leaf maples, alders, and buckeyes turn red and gold. Sighted in the farthest reaches of the park are bobcats, black-tailed deer, foxes, ring-tailed cats, and even black bears.

Having survived aeons of ice ages and climate changes, only fragments of the original redwood forests now survive their greatest threat—logging companies. From the late nineteenth century to today, the virgin stands have been largely decimated, primarily by clear-cutting, which destroys not only the trees but many of the creeks, rivers, and hillsides as well as wildlife habitats. Established in 1918 for the purpose of rescuing the Eel River Valley from the lumbermen, the Save-the-Redwoods League is credited with the establishment of the California parks that shelter most of the old-growth redwoods remaining in the world.

At the visitor center are a museum and exhibits, a native plant garden, a slide show, and bookstore. Guided walks and talks are available.

About **Redwoods**

- A coastal redwood can live to be more than 2,000 years old.

- The tallest living things on Earth, some redwoods grow to exceed 300 feet in height.

- The world's tallest tree is a coastal redwood in Redwood National Park, at 367.8 feet.

- Redwoods' ecosystems contain up to ten times the living matter of tropical forest ecosystems.

- Humboldt Redwoods State Park shelters the largest remaining stand of ancient redwoods in the world.

- Winter rainfall in the northern redwoods can reach 100 inches a year.

King Range National Conservation Area

(all ages) 🚹 🎣 ⛺ 🚗
Maps and information at BLM headquarters, 1695 Heindon Road, off Janes Road in Arcata; (707) 825–2300.

Rugged and largely inaccessible, the "Lost Coast" between Mattole Point and Shelter Cove is 24 miles of shoreline, mountain streams, trails, and forests for camping, hiking, and fishing, with five campgrounds. Two-lane Mattole Road is a corkscrew called Wild Cat, which winds through spectacular mountainous countryside. It's scenic, but not fun for backseat passengers or little kids. The easiest route in is from Redway to Shelter Cove, where you can wander on a black-sand beach, have lunch in a cafe, camp in your RV or tent, and fish off the shore.

Where to Eat

Cafe Marina. Woodley Island, Eureka; (707) 443–2233. Overlooking the docks of Humboldt Bay on a deck with umbrella tables: fresh seafood and typical American fare. Breakfast, lunch, and dinner. $–$$

Cafe Waterfront Oyster Bar and Grill. Corner of First and Seventh Streets, Eureka; (707) 443–9190. Enjoy Eureka's famous seafood and sea views—fish burgers, clams, and oysters in a casual Victorian setting. Breakfast, lunch, and dinner. $–$$

O-H's Townhouse. 206 West Sixth Street, Eureka; (707) 443–4652. Family-owned for forty years, a casual place with oilcloth-covered tables, and a meat and seafood market. A big menu of fresh, fresh fish, a variety of great steaks, and Cajun-style prime rib. $$–$$$

Ramone's Bakery and Cafe. 209 E Street, Eureka; (707) 445–2923. Where the locals go for cappuccino, killer bagels, breakfast and lunch, homemade soups, salads, sandwiches. $–$$

Sea Grill. 316 E Street, Eureka; (707) 443–7187. Voted Best Seafood Restaurant in the county for several years, and a noisy, popular place. Come early to avoid the crowds and enjoy choosing from a huge seafood menu; reservations are usually necessary. Lunch and dinner. $$–$$$

Where to Stay

Campton House. 305 M Street, Eureka; (800) 772–1622 or (707) 443–1601. A charming Craftsman-style cottage with three spacious, comfortable bedrooms, two baths, a parlor, dining room, and kitchen—perfect for a big family or a family reunion. Across the street from the Carson Mansion, within walking distance of all the sights and restaurants in town. A simple continental breakfast and afternoon tea are included, and so is use of the pool and sauna at the adjacent motel. $$–$$$

Eureka Inn. 518 Seventh Street, Eureka; (707) 442–6441 or (800) 862–4906; www.eurekainn.com. A fabulous English Tudor–style, half-timbered hotel built in the 1920s, with a huge fireplace in the lobby, a comfy dinner house, a casual cafe, and a poolside dining area, all serving great American food and fresh seafood. Christmastime is festive; a towering, glittering tree is the backdrop for nightly live entertainment. The staff is particularly friendly, and families feel welcome here. Rooms vary in size and amenities. $$$

Giant Redwoods RV and Camp. 455 Boy Scout Camp Road, Myers Flat; (707) 943–3198. Twenty-three acres of riverfront on the Avenue of the Giants, a quiet family camp with full hookups and tent sites. $

Red Lion Inn. 1929 Fourth Street, Eureka; (800) 547–8010 or (707) 445–0844; www.redlion.com. A large, family-friendly motel, with a pool, a restaurant, and family suites. $$–$$$

Thunderbird Inn and Suites. 232 West Fifth Street, Eureka; (800) 521–6996. Featuring a heated pool, a recreation and games area, guest laundry facilities, some refrigerators, some two-bedroom units, barbecues, and restaurants. $$

For More Information

Eureka/Humboldt County Convention and Visitors Bureau. 1034 Second Street, Eureka; (707) 443–5097 or (800) 346–3482; www.redwoodvisitor.org. Call for a copy of *Destination Redwood Coast*.

Redwood Empire Association. 1925 13th Avenue, Oakland; (510) 536–8828; www.redwoodempire.com.

Arcata

Seven miles north of Eureka by way of scenic Highway 255 bordering Humboldt Bay, Arcata is an old loggers' town and the home of Humboldt State University. The town is headquarters for visitors to Redwood National Park, several miles to the north.

Just north, the coastal village of Trinidad on Trinidad Bay offers a pier, beaches, fishing access, a few shops, and a handful of terrific restaurants. Trinidad State Park and Patrick's Point State Park are nearby.

Arcata Marsh and Wildlife Sanctuary (all ages)

569 South G Street, Arcata; (707) 826–2359. Guided walks are scheduled on Saturday, rain or shine.

Spend a couple of hours here on 4.5 miles of quiet footpaths in a stunning bayside setting, with freshwater ponds, a salt marsh, tidal mudflats, and winding water channels alive with birds and ducks. This is also a good place to jog or have a picnic; leashed dogs are allowed. You would never guess this is a wastewater reclamation project, and, in fact, a model for the nation. Stop at the interpretive center here for maps and information about birding walks throughout the region, and ask about guided walks at the marsh. In March the annual spring migration bird festival, called Godwit Days, is a big event, bringing birders from across the country (800–908–WING). For daily bird sightings, call (707) 822–LOON.

Historic Logging Trail and Community Forest (all ages)

Fourteenth and Union Streets, Arcata; (707) 822–3619.

Logging sites and equipment from a century ago, a few old-growth sequoias, and many second-growth trees are here—as are easy, pleasant walking trails, picnic sites, restrooms, and a playground.

Humboldt Lagoons State Park (all ages)

Thirty miles north of Eureka on Highway 101, Orick; (707) 488–2171.

It's a 0.75-mile paddle or row to a six-site boat-in campground at Ryan's Cove, located on a mysterious 520-acre lagoon. There is much wildlife to see, including Roosevelt elk. On the edge is a 3-mile, very quiet beach, plus access to the Coastal Trail. For day-use and environmental campsites, enter the park (by car) at Milepost 114.5.

Patrick's Point State Park (all ages)

Five miles north of Trinidad, on Highway 101; (707) 677–3570.

Forest trails, picnic sites, a sandy beach, and world-class sea views from a vast headland. Developed campsites and showers; RV sites to 31 feet.

Fishing in Redwood Country

This is prime ocean- and river-fishing country. For first-timers and beginning fisherpersons, stick to the riverbanks and the piers or go on a guided expedition with a company that provides equipment, transportation, and advice.

- Surf and rock fishing, lingcod, salmon:
  - K Street and the F Street piers in Eureka
  - South jetty, 11 miles south of Eureka
  - North jetty, 6 miles from the west end of Samoa Bridge
- Clamming on beaches near Eureka and Arcata.
- King and silver salmon, as well as steelhead, on the Eel, the Mad, the Van Duzen, the Little River, and Redwood Creek, all near Eureka, and on the Klamath, farther north.
- Twenty lakes in Humboldt County are stocked with trout.
- Fishing conditions: North Coast Fishphone, (707) 444–8041.
- Eel River Headquarters, (707) 946–2311.
- **Celtic Charter Service.** Woodley Island Marina; (707) 442–7580. A 50-foot twin-diesel sport-fishing boat takes families on salmon- and rock-cod-fishing and whale-watching expeditions.
- **Time Flies.** Eighth and J Streets, Arcata; (707) 822–8331. Large selection of fresh- and saltwater-fishing gear.
- **Eureka Fly Shop.** 505 H Street, Eureka; (707) 444–2000. Everything for fly-fishing.

Redwood National Park (all ages)

Visitor center between the park entrance and the town of Orick; (707) 488–3461.

Twenty-two miles north of Arcata and stretching for more than 40 miles, Redwood National Park is a World Heritage Site encompassing three state parks: Prairie Creek, Del Norte, and Jedediah Smith. There are more than 300 developed campsites in the three state parks within the national park, as well as shoreline trails and beaches, swimming in the Smith River and Redwood Creek, and ranger-guided tours. You will need a free permit to drive the steep, 17-mile road to Tall Trees Grove, where a 3-mile-round-trip walking trail leads to some of the world's tallest trees.

The first mile or so of the easy, flat Redwood Creek Trail along the creek is okay for strollers. In late summer and fall, kids can wade in the streambed; with older kids, wear your tennis shoes and walk up the creek, looking for swimming holes and sandbars.

Redwood Trails Horseback Rides offers rides in the park. Kids must be five years and up for the regular horseback rides (half hour, one hour, three hours, or six hours); pony rides for kids two and up (707–488–3895).

Prairie Creek Redwoods State Park (all ages)

Six miles north of Orick, take the Elk Prairie Parkway exit off Highway 101. For park information call (707) 464–6101. Some trails are wheelchair accessible.

A World Heritage Site, featuring 12,000 acres of magnificent coastal redwoods, 70 miles of mountain-biking and hiking trails, herds of Roosevelt elk, a museum, Gold Bluff Beach, gorgeous campgrounds, and fabulous Fern Canyon, where lush ferns cover 50-foot rock walls. The visitor center is particularly interesting, with a museum, a natural history bookstore, displays of animals that live in the area—gray fox, great horned owl, elk, mountain beaver, raccoon, black bear—and a touch table and nature books.

For a drive-through, take the Newton B. Drury Parkway through the redwoods, past walls of ferns and magnificent trees. Many trails are accessed at the turnouts. Part of *The Lost World: Jurassic Park* was filmed here. If I were to camp and stay at only one redwood park, this would be the one, because of the almost surreal beauty and the variety of environments and wildlife.

Where to Eat

Bon Boniere Ice Cream. 215 F Street in the Jacoby Storehouse, Arcata; (707) 822–6388. Since 1898 this company has been famous for making ice cream, caramel popcorn, and other sweets. It also has soup, salad, and sandwiches. Another site is in Old Town Eureka on F Street. $–$$

Plaza Grill. 791 Eighth Street, Arcata; (707) 826–2345. On the third floor of historic Jacoby's Storehouse, on the town plaza, a casual cafe with a beautiful long bar, a fireplace, and town views. Families love the burgers, sandwiches, fish platters, and the kids' menu. $–$$

Wildflower Cafe and Bakery. 1604 G Street, Arcata; (707) 822–0360. Yummy muffins and pastries to go, and vegetarian cuisine for breakfast, lunch, and dinner. Homemade soup, Mexican and Chinese food, hearty daily specials like quiche and stroganoff. $

Where to Stay

Mad River Rapid RV Park. 3501 Janes Road, Arcata; (707) 822–7275. Beautifully landscaped sites with all amenities; game room, pool, tennis; part of the Mad River Quality Inn resort. $

For More Information

Trinidad Chamber of Commerce. Main Street and Patrick Point Drive, Trindad; (707) 441–9827.

Arcata Chamber of Commerce. 1062 G Street, Arcata; (707) 822–3619; www.arcata.com/chamber.

Ferndale

Five miles off Highway 101 through idyllic dairylands, the village of Ferndale is two long streets of more than 200 glorious Victorian buildings. The entire tiny town is a State Historic Landmark. Pick up a walking tour map at most businesses in town. It will take a couple of hours to stroll Main Street, take pictures of the old buildings, and browse in the shops. Save a roll of film for the Gingerbread Mansion on Berding Street, a masterpiece of Victorian architecture.

On the edge of the Eel River Delta, a resting point on the Pacific flyway, Ferndale is within minutes of great birdwatching and some nice walks. Running 5 miles west out of town, Centerville Road leads to the beach, where a wide variety of birdlife and animals can be seen on walks north and south—swans, geese, sandpipers, pelicans and cormorants, seals, and whales.

On the east side of town are country lanes leading to the Eel River Estuary, where there are great routes for walking and biking. You can launch canoes and kayaks here in quiet waters or take a guided boat tour of the estuary (Eel River Delta Tours; 707–786–4187). More than 150 feathered species live in or pass through these wetlands, including loons, cormorants, harriers, and egrets. Where the Eel meets the sea, watch for sea lions, seals, and river otters.

Ferndale Museum (all ages)
Corner Shaw and Third Street across from Main, Ferndale; (707) 786–4466. $.

A small but mighty exhibit of Ferndale history and the agriculture of the "Cream City," with period rooms, an operating seismograph, and a blacksmith shop.

Kinetic Sculpture Museum (all ages)
393 Main Street, Ferndale; (707) 786–9259. Free.

Here, in one of the strangest museums in the world, are some of the wild and weird, hand-made, people-powered machines that travel over land, mud, and water in the World Championship Great Arcata to Ferndale Cross-County Kinetic Sculpture Race held annually in May. Called the "triathlon of the art world," this three-day event is great fun to watch, as the fantastical contrivances are driven, dragged, and floated over roads, sand dunes, Humboldt Bay, and the Eel River! Among the machines in past races were "Nightmare of the Iguana" and "Tyrannosaurus Rust," which was powered by cavemen!

Fun Shops in Ferndale

- **Wild Things,** 444 Main Street; (707) 786–9331. Teddy bears, bird houses, Beanie Babies, and wildlife items.

- **Golden Gait Mercantile,** 421 Main Street; (707) 786–4891. Time is suspended in the 1850s with barrels of penny candy, big-wheeled coffee grinders, and glass cases lined with old-fashioned restoratives and hair pomades. Remember Burma Shave?

- **Dave's Saddlery,** 491 Main; (707) 786–4004. Cowboy boots, beaded hatbands, hand-tooled saddles and silver buckles, Ferndale T-shirts.

- **Ferndale Antique Mall,** 597 Fernbridge Drive; (707) 725–8820. On the way into town, watch for a large, light green building with striped awnings and a red door, a veritable bazaar of forty dealers selling everything from estate jewelry to Victorian furniture.

Where to Eat

Curley's Grill. 460 Main in the Victorian Inn, Ferndale; (707) 786–9696. California cuisine, homemade soup and foccacia, local fresh fish, grilled sandwiches, and more; served indoors in an old-fashioned dining room or on the patio. Lunch and dinner. $–$$

Diane's Cafe and Espresso. 553 Main Street, Ferndale; (707) 786–4950. Cafe au lait in huge cups, homemade sandwiches, salads, soups. $

Loleta Cheese Factory. 252 Loleta Drive, Loleta; (800) 995–0453. Between Ferndale and Eureka, yummy cheeses, deli items,

and sandwiches to take away or eat here on the patio. Surrounding are great country roads for biking. $

For More Information

Victorian Village of Ferndale. 248 Francis Street, Ferndale; (707) 786–4477; www.victorianferndale.org/chamber.

Index

About the Author

A native Northern Californian who lives in Sonoma in the heart of the Wine Country, Karen Misuraca is the author of *The 100 Best Golf Resorts of the World, Quick Escapes San Francisco, The California Coast, Insiders' Guide to Yosemite, Our San Francisco,* and *Backroads of the California Wine Country.*

She specializes in writing about golf, California, and international travel and contributes to magazines, including *Alaska Airlines Magazine* and *Distinction,* and to TravelClassics.com.

Misuraca and her partner, Michael Capp, explore Northern California's outdoors with her three daughters, five granddaughters, and a grandson.